Confronting Inequality

APA BRONFENBRENNER SERIES ON THE ECOLOGY OF HUMAN DEVELOPMENT

Confronting Inequality

How Policies and Practices Shape Children's Opportunities

Edited by

LAURA TACH, RACHEL DUNIFON, and DOUGLAS L. MILLER

 AMERICAN PSYCHOLOGICAL ASSOCIATION

The opinions and statements published are the responsibility of the authors, and such opinions and statements do not necessarily represent the policies of the American Psychological Association.

Published by
American Psychological Association
750 First Street, NE
Washington, DC 20002
https://www.apa.org

Order Department
https://www.apa.org/pubs/books
order@apa.org

In the U.K., Europe, Africa, and the Middle East, copies may be ordered from Eurospan
https://www.eurospanbookstore.com/apa
info@eurospangroup.com

Typeset in Meridien and Ortodoxa by Circle Graphics, Inc., Reisterstown, MD

Printer: Sheridan Books, Chelsea, MI
Cover Designer: Anne Likes Red, Inc., Silver Spring, MD

Library of Congress Cataloging-in-Publication Data

Names: Tach, Laura, editor. | Dunifon, Rachel E. (Rachel Elizabeth), editor. |
  Miller, Douglas Lee, 1973- editor.
Title: Confronting inequality : how policies and practices shape children's opportunities /
  edited by Laura Tach, Rachel Dunifon, and Douglas Miller.
Description: Washington, DC : American Psychological Association, [2020] |
  Series: APA Bronfenbrenner series on the ecology of human development |
  Includes bibliographical references and index.
Identifiers: LCCN 2019059338 (print) | LCCN 2019059339 (ebook) |
  ISBN 9781433832666 (paperback) | ISBN 9781433832925 (ebook)
Subjects: LCSH: Income distribution—United States. | Children—Health and hygiene—
  Economic aspects—United States. | Education—Economic aspects—United States.
Classification: LCC HC110.I5 C637 2020 (print) | LCC HC110.I5 (ebook) |
  DDC 362.70973—dc23
LC record available at https://lccn.loc.gov/2019059338
LC ebook record available at https://lccn.loc.gov/2019059339

http://dx.doi.org/10.1037/0000187-000

Printed in the United States of America

10 9 8 7 6 5 4 3 2 1

This series is dedicated to the personal memories and lasting theoretical insights of our friend, colleague, and mentor, Urie Bronfenbrenner. His thinking about human development has profoundly influenced so many students and colleagues in multiple areas of enquiry. We hope this series will provide another vehicle through which Urie's ideas on the bioecology of human development can continue to flourish.

CONTENTS

CONTRIBUTORS

Emma Adam, PhD, Edwina S. Tarry Professor of Education and Social Policy, Northwestern University, Evanston, IL

Rochelle Cassells, PhD, Psychology faculty, Sarah Lawrence College, Bronxville, NY

Janet Currie, PhD, Henry Putnam Professor of Economics and Public Affairs, Princeton University, Princeton, NJ

Stefanie DeLuca, PhD, James Coleman Professor of Sociology & Social Policy, Johns Hopkins University, Baltimore, MD

Rachel Dunifon, PhD, Professor of Policy Analysis and Management; Interim Dean of the College of Human Ecology, Cornell University, Ithaca, NY

Chloe N. East, PhD, Assistant Professor of Economics, University of Colorado–Denver

Kathryn Edin, PhD, Professor of Sociology and Public Affairs, Princeton University, Princeton, NJ

Gary Evans, PhD, Elizabeth Lee Vincent Professor of Human Ecology, Cornell University, Ithaca, NY

Emily Hittner, MS, PhD student in Human Development and Social Policy, Northwestern University, Evanston, IL

C. Kirabo Jackson, PhD, Abraham Harris Professor of Education and Social Policy, Northwestern University, Evanston, IL

Ariel Kalil, PhD, Professor, Harris School of Public Policy, University of Chicago, Chicago, IL

Nadav Klein, PhD, Postdoctoral Scholar, Harris School of Public Policy, University of Chicago, Chicago, IL

Jens Ludwig, PhD, Edwin A. and Betty L. Bergman Distinguished Service
Professor, Harris School of Public Policy, University of Chicago, Chicago, IL

Susan E. Mayer, PhD, Professor Emeritus, Harris School of Public Policy,
University of Chicago, Chicago, IL

Douglas L. Miller, PhD, Professor of Policy Analysis and Management,
Cornell University, Ithaca, NY

Timothy Nelson, PhD, Lecturer, Department of Sociology, Princeton
University, Princeton, NJ

Marianne E. Page, PhD, Professor of Economics, University of California,
Davis

C. Cybele Raver, PhD, Deputy Provost, Professor of Applied Psychology,
New York University, New York, NY

Sean F. Reardon, EdD, Professor of Poverty and Inequality in Education,
Graduate School of Education, Stanford University, Stanford, CA

Anna Rhodes, PhD, Assistant Professor of Sociology, Rice University,
Houston, TX

Maya Rossin-Slater, PhD, Assistant Professor, Stanford University School
of Medicine, Stanford, CA

Laura Tach, PhD, Associate Professor of Policy Analysis and Management,
Cornell University, Ithaca, NY

Sarah Collier Villaume, MA, PhD student in Human Development and
Social Policy, Northwestern University, Evanston, IL

Tyler W. Watts, PhD, Assistant Professor of Developmental Psychology,
Department of Human Development, Teachers College, Columbia
University, New York, NY

Allison Young, BA, PhD student, Department of Sociology, Johns Hopkins
University, Baltimore, MD

ACKNOWLEDGMENTS

We would like to thank the Bronfenbrenner Center for Translational Research for their support of this series. The chapters that appear in this volume were presented at a fall 2018 conference hosted by the Bronfenbrenner Center and cosponsored by the Center for the Study of Inequality and the Cornell Population Center. We thank Lori Biechle, Carrie Chalmers, Meg Cole, Elizabeth Day, Sam Dodini, John Eckendrode, Amanda Eng, Hope Harvey, Kimberly Kopko, Martha Johnson, Erin Mathios, Lisa McCabe, Karl Pillemer, Cassandra Robertson, Cindy Lu Thompson, Maureen Waller, and Christopher Wildeman for their assistance with the conference and this edited volume.

Confronting Inequality

Introduction

What Does It Take to Achieve Equality of Opportunity for Children?

Laura Tach, Rachel Dunifon, and Douglas L. Miller

Inequality is one of the defining social problems of the 21st century. As economic inequality has grown, so too has inequality in the social contexts central to healthy child development, including families, neighborhoods, education systems, and social programs. Parents' resources and investments in children are increasingly polarized along economic lines (Kalil, Ziol-Guest, Ryan, & Markowitz, 2016; Kornrich & Furstenberg, 2013; Ramey & Ramey, 2010; Schneider, Hastings, & LaBriola, 2018). Neighborhoods have become more economically segregated, particularly for children, generating greater inequity in children's exposure to educational and community resources (Owens, 2016; Reardon & Bischoff, 2011). These trends have had deleterious consequences for children's health and well-being in the short run, and they have undermined opportunities for upward social mobility in the long run. In fact, the fraction of children who can expect to attain at least the same standard of living as their parents—a hallmark of the American Dream—has fallen markedly, from 90% of children born in the 1940s to just 50% of children born in the 1980s who are entering adulthood in the 21st century (Chetty et al., 2017).

Although inequality can seem intractable, a long tradition of research examines policies and practices that aim to disrupt the intergenerational persistence of inequality and to promote equality of opportunity for children. Much of this work has occurred within the traditional silos of standard academic disciplines, such as economics, psychology, or sociology, but great innovations have also come at the interface of different disciplines, when researchers

http://dx.doi.org/10.1037/0000187-001
Confronting Inequality: How Policies and Practices Shape Children's Opportunities, edited by L. Tach, R. Dunifon, and D. L. Miller

use perspectives and methods from one field to inform, critique, or advance another. The late psychologist Urie Bronfenbrenner, to whom this series is dedicated, was an early pioneer on this front. In his foundational work on ecological systems theory, he argued that research endeavors that do not explicitly consider multiple disciplinary perspectives and levels of analyses are doomed to fail or, at the very least, stagnate (Bronfenbrenner, 2005). Bronfenbrenner was also a leader in what we might now call applied social science research, which informs, and is informed by, real-world settings beyond the academic ivory tower. Bronfenbrenner (1977) rejected the simplistic distinction between basic and applied research, however, claiming that the best way to understand a social issue is to try to change it. His work certainly lived up to this maxim, as he not only developed foundational theoretical models of human–environment interaction but also used them to inform the development of many influential social programs, most notably Head Start.

This volume was preceded by a conference at Cornell University in the fall of 2018. This gathering celebrated Bronfenbrenner's legacy and brought together cutting-edge research from psychology, economics, and sociology to illuminate what we know, and what we still need to know, about how to improve equality of opportunity for children. We asked leading scholars in these disciplines to assess the state of research about effective policies and practices for reducing inequality across a range of childhood developmental settings. We deliberately brought together different disciplinary and methodological traditions to forge new, and richer, insights about these issues. Finally, we asked the authors to consider promising new approaches and perspectives that can help chart a course for future research, policies, and interventions that support healthy development and upward social mobility among children and their families. The resulting papers generated a dialogue, captured in this volume, that provides tangible evidence of the benefits of working across disciplines and contexts.

In the chapters that follow, we consider several domains central to human development and equality of opportunity—health, family, and community—from multidisciplinary perspectives. Part I of the volume considers the state of knowledge about access to health-promoting environments and resources. In Chapter 1, developmental psychologists Emma Adam, Sarah Collier Villaume, and Emily Hittner present a "stress disparities" framework, arguing that stress exposure and its biological consequences are a key pathway by which adverse circumstances "get under the skin and into the mind" to affect health and developmental outcomes. They present evidence about promising interventions that have effectively reduced stress disparities, and they argue that interventions that reduce stress disparities may in turn reduce inequities in children's long-run opportunities and well-being. Chapter 2 reviews the state of knowledge about the largest U.S. safety net program targeting the nutrition and health of low-income mothers and young children—the Special Supplemental Nutrition Program for Women, Infants, and Children (WIC). Economists Janet Currie and Maya Rossin-Slater argue that there is overwhelming evidence that "WIC works" to promote infant health at birth and to reduce early-life health inequalities. However, the mechanisms for understanding why such benefits accrue, and why barriers to program take-up and retention persist, remain elusive and should be the focus of future research in order to understand which aspects of the intervention increase health equality among children. Chapter 3 zooms out even further, taking a multigenerational perspective on health-related policy interventions. Economists Chloe N. East and Marianne E. Page argue that early-life health experiences affect not only later-life outcomes, but also the well-being of the next generation; as a result, health inequalities in one generation persist into the next. The silver lining of this story, however, is that policies, programs, and societal changes that improve early-life health and reduce disparities—such as access to means-tested programs like Medicaid or Head Start—have even more positive benefit–cost ratios when we take multigenerational beneficial impacts into account.

In Part II, we turn our attention to the family system, which provides resources, interactions, and experiences that shape children's development. Although economic inequality in children's access to these parental resources has been growing, the contributors in this section provide novel approaches to redressing these inequities. In Chapter 4, the interdisciplinary team of Susan E. Mayer, Ariel Kalil, and Nadav Klein use insights from behavioral science to understand the origins of inequality in parental decision-making and to develop "behavioral nudge" interventions that can enhance parents' decisions in ways that have a payoff for their children's future well-being; they present early evidence of the effectiveness of such an approach. Next, in Chapter 5, sociologists Timothy Nelson and Kathryn Edin critique the child support system because, rather than promoting involvement with their children, it drives low-income, nonresident fathers away from their family responsibilities. Drawing on qualitative interviews with low-income men, Nelson and Edin propose an alternative to the current child support enforcement system— one that allows for in-kind forms of child support that are more aligned with the ways in which fathers want to invest in their children. This may ultimately promote father–child bonds outside of nuclear family arrangements in ways that have lasting benefits for children and the family system more broadly.

Part III investigates broader social settings consequential for healthy child development, with a focus on educational institutions and residential environments. In Chapter 6, psychologists Tyler W. Watts and C. Cybele Raver argue that poverty reduces children's chances of receiving high-quality, enriching care outside the home. Although classic randomized controlled trials of early childhood interventions showed substantial short- and long-run gains, many other early childhood programs, such as Head Start, demonstrate short-run gains that fade out over time. The authors draw from their own experiences implementing and evaluating a large-scale early childhood intervention to grapple with this "fade out" puzzle. They urge early childhood education interventions to be bolder in transforming the learning environments that children experience in order to improve children's life chances. Chapter 7 turns to the educational environments of school-age children and tackles the classic question of whether school spending matters, based on a large body of research that has arguably produced a mixed set of findings. Economist C. Kirabo Jackson argues that both classic and contemporary scholarship on this issue is clear, once units of analysis and methodological approaches are taken into account. He argues unequivocally that more school spending does indeed improve student achievement on average, laying the groundwork for a renewed focus on school spending as a key mechanism to promote opportunities for children. He also argues that we need more research to understand precisely which forms of school spending are the most effective. The final chapter in Part III, Chapter 8, puts a new spin on an age-old question—Do neighborhoods matter?—through the lens of housing mobility programs that relocate disadvantaged families to higher-opportunity neighborhoods. Sociologists Stefanie DeLuca, Anna Rhodes, and Allison Young argue that person–environment interactions are key when understanding whether and how neighborhoods matter for youth. Parent engagement with schools, parent–child interactions, youth developmental stage, and youth friendship networks are key proximal processes that help to explain why some youth benefit from neighborhood mobility and others do not. They conclude with a call for a more nuanced consideration of social ties as enabling features of so-called "moves to opportunity."

In Part IV of this volume, we provide commentary from leading disciplinary scholars: psychologists Rochelle Cassells and Gary Evans (Chapter 9), economist Jens Ludwig (Chapter 10), and sociologist Sean F. Reardon (Chapter 11). We asked each commentator to discuss key themes and insights from a multidisciplinary set of chapters in this volume and to chart a course for future research and practice, given their insights. We close this volume with the Conclusion, in which we describe a set of crosscutting themes drawing both from the individual contributions and from the insights gained by putting the chapters in dialog with one another. We see great value in the diversity of epistemological approaches and methodological tools brought to bear on a topic that is both timeless and timely. Collectively, the contributions to this volume show us that we know a lot about what works, but there is also room for improvement and still a lot left for us to learn. We conclude by charting a path forward for scholarship, focusing on opportunities for multidisciplinary insights and work that blurs the traditional divides between basic and applied social science.

REFERENCES

Bronfenbrenner, U. (1977). Toward an experimental ecology of human development. *American Psychologist, 32*, 513–531. http://dx.doi.org/10.1037/0003-066X.32.7.513

Bronfenbrenner, U. (Ed.). (2005). *Making human beings human: Bioecological perspectives on human development*. Thousand Oaks, CA: Sage.

Chetty, R., Grusky, D., Hell, M., Hendren, N., Manduca, R., & Narang, J. (2017). The fading American dream: Trends in absolute income mobility since 1940. *Science, 356*, 398–406. http://dx.doi.org/10.1126/science.aal4617

Kalil, A., Ziol-Guest, K., Ryan, R., & Markowitz, A. (2016). Changes in income-based gaps in parent activities with young children from 1988 to 2012. *AERA Open, 2*, 1–17. http://dx.doi.org/10.1177/2332858416653732

Kornrich, S., & Furstenberg, F. (2013). Investing in children: Changes in parental spending on children, 1972–2007. *Demography, 50,* 1–23. http://dx.doi.org/10.1007/s13524-012-0146-4

Owens, A. (2016). Inequality in children's contexts: The economic segregation of households with and without children. *American Sociological Review, 81,* 549–574. http://dx.doi.org/10.1177/0003122416642430

Ramey, G., & Ramey, V. A. (2010). The rug rat race. *Brookings Papers on Economic Activity, 2010,* 129–176. http://dx.doi.org/10.1353/eca.2010.0003

Reardon, S. F., & Bischoff, K. (2011). Income inequality and income segregation. *American Journal of Sociology, 116,* 1092–1153. http://dx.doi.org/10.1086/657114

Schneider, D., Hastings, O. P., & LaBriola, J. (2018). Income inequality and class divides in parental investments. *American Sociological Review, 83,* 475–507. http://dx.doi.org/10.1177/0003122418772034

HEALTH

1

Reducing Stress Disparities

Pathways to Equity Through the Study of Stress Biology

Emma Adam, Sarah Collier Villaume, and Emily Hittner

Research, intervention, and policy focused on identifying solutions for disparities in child health and developmental outcomes are gaining insight from a new source: the study of stress biology. Recent theoretical models have implicated disparities in stress exposure and the biological consequences of that exposure (Heissel, Levy, & Adam, 2017; Levy, Heissel, Richeson, & Adam, 2016; Miller & Chen, 2013; Miller, Chen, & Parker, 2011) as one pathway by which adverse circumstances for children and adolescents "get under the skin and into the mind," affecting the body and brain (Johnson, Riis, & Noble, 2016; McEwen, 2012). Differential exposure to stress, in turn, contributes to the emergence and maintenance of disparities in health, academic, and human capital outcomes.

Stress is not equally distributed in society; stress disparities exist along many dimensions and their intersections. Here, due to their pervasiveness, we focus on disparities by income (G. W. Evans & English, 2002) and by ethnic–racial group membership (Levy et al., 2016). Individuals of lower socioeconomic circumstances and historically disenfranchised ethnic and racial groups (e.g., Black, Hispanic, and Native American individuals in the United States) have been found to be exposed to higher levels of multiple sources of stress (G. W. Evans & English, 2002; Levy et al., 2016). Stress exposure activates a wide array of stress-sensitive biological systems that, in turn, have implications for health, cognition, and everyday functioning (Lupien, McEwen, Gunnar, & Heim, 2009; McEwen, 2012).

http://dx.doi.org/10.1037/0000187-002
Confronting Inequality: How Policies and Practices Shape Children's Opportunities, edited by
L. Tach, R. Dunifon, and D. L. Miller

Disparities in exposure to both everyday and traumatic stressors, by way of their impact on stress biology, contribute to the emergence of disparities in developmental trajectories of health and human capital (Halfon & Hochstein, 2002; Heissel, Levy, & Adam, 2017). Differences in stress biology can serve as a marker for the presence of disparities in stress exposure and a pathway by which they are instantiated into health and developmental outcomes. More recently, however, stress science is also beginning to provide insights for potential solutions (McEwen, 2012). Through offering insights on how stress exposure can be reduced, coping promoted, and stress biology reregulated through social policy and other intervention efforts, stress science is providing clues to how to reduce stress disparities and gaps in health and academic outcomes.

In this chapter, we provide (a) an overview of the concept of stress disparities and evidence that stressors are unequally distributed by economic class and ethnic–racial group; (b) a description of stress biology, with a focus on biological systems that are both affected by stress and have implications for daily functioning, cognition, and health, along with some evidence that these systems vary by socioeconomic status (SES) or ethnicity–race; and (c) a description of how stress biology has been used to inform policy and intervention research, including evidence from existing studies and clinical trials demonstrating that stress-sensitive biological systems respond to either policy or behavioral interventions with potential positive implications for health and behavioral outcomes. We also provide our suggestions for future directions of stress disparities research to improve the potential of this research to provide not only an equal but also an equitable start for all children and adolescents.

STRESS DISPARITIES

In this section, we define stress disparities and describe stress disparities occurring by SES and by ethnic–racial group membership, as evidenced by differences in multiple types of stress exposure and differences of stress biology.

Defining Stress Disparities

Many past researchers have noted that living in low socioeconomic contexts is associated with higher levels of exposure to stressors, with resulting implications for stress biology, health, and developmental outcomes (Brooks-Gunn, Klebanov, & Liaw, 1995; G. W. Evans & English, 2002). A separate literature has focused on the increased stress exposure associated with being a member of a disenfranchised ethnic or racial group and the implications of this race-based stress for health and developmental outcomes (Adam et al., 2015; Levy et al., 2016). We coined the general term *stress disparities* to capture both of these (Heissel, Levy, & Adam, 2017) and, indeed, any circumstance in which (a) social or demographic factors are related to systematically different levels of exposure to stressors, and (b) differential stress exposure has resulting implications for differences in stress biology.

We believe that these stress disparities serve as plausible explanatory pathways or mechanisms for the emergence of disparities in health or developmental outcomes.[1] For example, we believe that stress disparities play roles in both ethnic–racial and socioeconomic disparities in health and developmental outcomes. Additionally, we hypothesize that individuals in other social categories experiencing significant social disenfranchisement, stigma, or reduced access to resources (e.g., LGBTQ individuals, undocumented immigrant populations) are also likely to suffer increased levels of stress exposure and altered stress biology, with stress disparities playing a potential role in negative health or attainment outcomes in these groups.

Types of Stress Exposures

Stress disparities can emerge from a variety of types of stressors, including traumatic stress (i.e., extreme stressors, either short- or long-term, that pose a fundamental threat to physical or social safety), acute or chronic major life events, and accumulated minor events and daily hassles (Grant et al., 2003, 2014). It has been shown that, often, stress disparities emerge from a combination of these stressor types, with stress disparities most evident and effect sizes on outcomes larger when exposure to multiple stressors is considered (G. W. Evans & English, 2002). For example, individuals living in poverty are more likely to encounter traumatic stressors (e.g., exposure to violence, severe abuse or neglect, or loss of or long-term separation from a caregiver), as well as chronic stressors (e.g., food insecurity, crowding, noise, substandard housing). When compared with higher income individuals, they are also more likely to encounter three or more of these stressor types simultaneously (G. W. Evans & English, 2002).

Stress disparities according to ethnicity and/or race include increased exposure to ethnic and racial discrimination. This involves structural forms of racism (e.g., residential segregation; discrimination in education, employment, and housing) that limit life chances and thereby disproportionately expose persons of color to the stress of unfair treatment, as well as the stresses of poverty noted above (Pager, Bonikowski, & Western, 2009; Pager & Shepherd, 2008). In addition, regardless of level of income, it has been shown that people of color face frequent everyday forms of discrimination including tokenism, stereotypes creating differing school and workplace expectations, and negative social interactions, including microaggressions, in which they are treated with differing expectations, disrespect, fear, or suspicion (Adam et al., 2015; Brondolo et al., 2008; Broudy et al., 2007; Jackson & Stewart, 2003). These

---

[1]We acknowledge that many other factors also contribute to the creation and maintenance of disparities in health and human capital, such as disparities in the quality of schooling and differences in access and the quality of health care. Our argument here is that disparities in stress exposure play a plausible additional role that has not received sufficient attention in the literature or in the generation of and policy solutions for disparities in health and developmental outcomes.

situations create social signals of exclusion that can precipitate feelings of sad-
ness, shame, loneliness, or anger, which, in turn, precipitate changes in multiple aspects of stress biology (Adam et al., 2015; Brondolo, Rieppi, Kelly, &
Gerin, 2003; Doane & Adam, 2010). These changes in stress biology, in turn,
have been shown to impact the body and brain in ways that matter for health
and human capital, completing the cycle by which stress disparities become
instantiated as lifelong (and potentially intergenerational) disparities in health
and developmental outcomes (Heissel, Levy, & Adam, 2017; Kuzawa & Sweet,
2009; Levy et al., 2016; Thayer & Kuzawa, 2015).

Timing of Stress Exposures

Past theory and research have revealed that the developmental timing of stress
exposure matters greatly, modifying both the strength and nature of the effects
of stress on stress biology and health, as well as on developmental outcomes.
Stressors that occur during periods of rapid developmental change are thought
to have larger impacts on developmental outcomes than those occurring
during periods of slower developmental change; such periods are frequently
referred to as *sensitive periods*. Stress researchers have focused primarily on
two processes/timelines by which experience affects biology: (a) the biological
embedding of experiences occurring during sensitive periods of development
(especially early-life experiences, from the prenatal period through adolescence), and (b) the cumulative wear-and-tear effects of stressors impacting
already-developed biological systems (especially during adulthood and aging)
(McEwen, 2012). Some theorists have differentiated timing effects further,
either (a) specifying differential processes taking place in prenatal, postnatal,
adolescence, adulthood, and aging (Halfon & Hochstein, 2002; Lupien et al.,
2009) or (b) describing the multiple time-scales over which experiential effects
unfold and become evident in later functioning (Adam, 2012; Hertzman,
2012). The key distinction made in all theories, however, is between biological
embedding of early stress experiences and the cumulative effects of later stress
(Shonkoff, Boyce, & McEwen, 2009).

Biological Embedding of Early Experience

Past theory and research have suggested that early experiences of stress from
the prenatal period through adolescence may be particularly important for the
impact of traumatic experiences on stress biology. This research has highlighted
that stressful experiences occurring during this time not only transiently affect
stress biology but may permanently alter the structure and function of the biological stress systems still developing at each time point, thus becoming "built
into" the structure and functioning of emerging biological systems. These effects
of early experience on biology have been called *programming effects* (particularly
used for the lifelong impact of prenatal experiences; Lupien et al., 2009) and
biological embedding (Hertzman, 2012). Numerous reviews and empirical articles
have detailed the dramatic effects of early social experience on stress biology

and lifelong health and cognitive functioning (Felitti et al., 1998; Lupien et al., 2009; Shonkoff et al., 2012).

Cumulative Impact of Acute and Chronic Stressful Events

Other theory and research suggest that cumulative impacts of acute and chronic stress over time are important, with these processes occurring to some extent during childhood and adolescence (Desantis, Kuzawa, & Adam, 2015) and being the most common manner in which stress exposure influences stress biology during adulthood (McEwen, 2012). The notion here is that the frequent or chronic activation of stress biology over time creates wear and tear on the biological systems being used, leading to less effective functioning of biological stress systems. This, in turn, has downstream implications for the parts of the body and brain that are regulated by those systems, as well as for long-term health and daily functioning. This cumulative wear and tear on multiple biological stress systems has been termed *allostatic load* (McEwen, 1998), a concept on which we elaborate later in this chapter.

Interactions Between Early and Later Stress Experiences

Importantly, interactions between early stress and ongoing and later cumulative stress may be important in maintaining and accentuating disparities in developmental trajectories that began with early adverse exposures (Desantis et al., 2015; Halfon & Hochstein, 2002; Hertzman, 2012; Lupien et al., 2009). Other theory and literature suggest that, from a life-course health and development perspective, additional sensitive periods occur across the life span whenever rapid biological and/or social changes are occurring. Potential sensitive periods postchildhood include adolescence, the transition to parenting, menopause/andropause, and older adulthood during the aging process (Halfon & Hochstein, 2002). Very little research has traced how developmental trajectories of health and well-being unfold through the combination of stress exposures during early sensitive periods, later sensitive periods, and the accumulation of acute and chronic stress across the life span. Understanding life-span histories of stress exposures across multiple developmental periods is likely the key to more fully understanding long-term trajectories of health and development (Adam et al., 2015; Halfon & Hochstein, 2002).

OVERVIEW OF STRESS-SENSITIVE BIOLOGICAL SYSTEMS

Having covered some key background concepts regarding stress disparities and the impact of experience on stress biology in different developmental periods, we describe several relevant biological stress systems in more detail, noting some of their impacts on health and developmental outcomes and whether disparities in these systems have been observed by income and/or ethnicity–race. We focus on primary stress mediators (McEwen & Seeman, 1999)—systems that are the "first responders" of stress experiences, helping us to cope with the stressor at hand, primarily through mobilizing energy resources and helping to prevent or contain injury. For our purposes, these include the autonomic nervous system (ANS), the hypothalamic–pituitary–adrenal axis (HPA axis), the immune and inflammatory systems, and the alertness/sleep system.[2] These primary stress mediators regulate each other and have impacts on a variety of downstream neurological and biological systems that are important for long-term health and well-being. Although many nuanced indicators of these systems are available, we focus on measures of these systems that are most relevant for policy and intervention research, in that they can be noninvasively obtained in large scale studies in community settings.

Autonomic Nervous System

One of the fastest responding regulatory systems of the body is the ANS, which includes sympathetic and parasympathetic processes. The main function of the ANS is to mobilize energy to control internal bodily processes and deliver oxygenated blood to the body. Although many aspects of autonomic physiological activation can be examined (e.g., cardiac, vascular, respiratory), researchers and practitioners have highlighted blood pressure as one uncensored, prognostic, and mechanistic system that is an important index for physiological states of stress, threat, and effort (Blascovich, Vanman, Mendes, & Dickerson, 2011), with important health and developmental consequences.

Blood pressure measurement reflects the amount of pressure exerted against blood vessel walls during the phases of the cardiac cycle (Franklin & Mitchell, 2008). Such measurement is conducted either in clinical settings, typically by medical personnel, or by trained research staff in community or home-based settings, most often using automated blood pressure cuffs. For research purposes, multiple measures (at least three) are taken in a row, with the first measure usually discarded due to *white coat* effects (i.e., transient blood pressure increases in response to the novelty of anxiety associated with the blood pressure measurement process; see Den Hond, Celis, Vandenhoven, O'Brien, & Staessen, 2003), and the remaining measures are averaged.

Recent guidelines recommend measuring using ambulatory blood pressure monitoring (Flynn et al., 2017). Ambulatory blood pressure continuously monitors blood pressure throughout the day as individuals go about their daily activities and sleep, taking readings typically every 15 to 30 minutes (Pickering, Shimbo, & Haas, 2006). Ambulatory blood pressure not only gives an average blood pressure level but also provides information about the diurnal rhythm of blood pressure along with its variability without white coat effects

---

[2]Past definitions of primary stress mediators have focused on the ANS and the HPA axis, but recent evidence has revealed acute responding of the inflammatory system and alertness/sleep systems to stressors, with consequences for a wide range of downstream biological systems, which we believe meet the criteria for consideration as a primary stress mediator.

on the readings. Ambulatory blood pressure has well-documented normalized 24-hour values in children, adolescents, and adults (Wühl et al., 2002) that provide important naturalistic insights for large-scale policy research (Mancia et al., 1995).

Among others,[3] distinctions are typically made between systolic blood pressure (peak pressure in arteries during one heartbeat) and diastolic blood pressure (lowest pressure in arteries during one heartbeat) as, although correlated, these can index unique aspects of stress responses (Blascovich et al., 2011). For instance, increases in systolic blood pressure can be an adaptive response to acute stress (Brownley, Hurwitz, & Schneiderman, 2000), yet prolonged exposure to stress and persisting high levels of systolic blood pressure exert prolonged stress on the heart (Ayada, Toru, & Korkut, 2015; Vrijkotte, van Doornen, & de Geus, 2000).

The prevalence of hypertension (i.e., clinically diagnosed high levels of blood pressure) has increased among both children and adults since the 1990s, a concerning trend following several decades of decline (Elliott & Black, 2007; Falkner, Gidding, Portman, & Rosner, 2008; Muntner, He, Cutler, Wildman, & Whelton, 2004). In fact, the prevalence of high blood pressure in children and adolescents is estimated to be as high as to 19% in males and 13% in females (Rosner, Cook, Daniels, & Falkner, 2013). This is concerning given that elevated blood pressure during youth not only predicts adult hypertension (X. Chen & Wang, 2008) but also is associated with poor physical health (e.g., higher risk of stroke, heart attack, and chronic kidney failure; Chobanian et al., 2003), mental health (e.g., higher levels of anxiety, depression; Lande et al., 2009; Pickering, 2001), and cognition (e.g., decreased attention, concentration, and short-term memory; Lande, Kaczorowski, Auinger, Schwartz, & Weitzman, 2003). With worldwide estimates of high blood pressure at as much as 1.13 billion individuals (World Health Organization, 2019), understanding blood pressure as a key mechanism linking childhood stress and adult health is a public health priority (Chobanian et al., 2003; Falkner, Lurbe, & Schaefer, 2010).

Although a range of factors affect blood pressure, including genetic and lifestyle factors, it is also strongly affected by psychosocial stress (Spruill, 2010). Relevant to our arguments regarding stress disparities, blood pressure has been found to be higher in lower SES adults and adolescents (Conen, Glynn, Ridker, Buring, & Albert, 2009; Kaczmarek, Stawinska-Witoszynska, Krzyzaniak, Krzywinska-Wiewiorowska, & Siwinska, 2015; Leng, Jin, Li, Chen, & Jin, 2015), but there is little evidence as to whether BP differences exist by family SES in children (Colhoun, Hemingway, & Poulter, 1998). Higher blood pressure in low SES populations has been shown to be partly attributable to greater job strain (Landsbergis, Schnall, Pickering, Warren, &

---

[3]Other measures of blood pressure include pulse pressure (i.e., subtracting DBP from SBP), mean arterial pressure (i.e., weighted average of DBP and SBP), and total peripheral resistance (i.e., combination of mean arterial pressure and cardiac output). Each offer insights in the physiological bases of stress reactivity.

Schwartz, 2003; Schnall, Schwartz, Landsbergis, Warren, & Pickering, 1992). Differences in blood pressure also consistently have appeared by ethnicity–race, being higher in African American children and adults than in Whites (Bosworth et al., 2006; Levinson et al., 1985). Psychosocial stress related to ethnicity–race, such as the stress associated with negative stereotypes of one's ethnic–racial group, has predicted elevated blood pressure among African Americans (Blascovich, Spencer, Quinn, & Steele, 2001).

Immune System

When faced with stress, the body not only mobilizes the ANS but also triggers changes in the immune response. Evolutionary perspectives have suggested that threatening situations that stimulate ANS "fight or flight" behavior also carry risk of injury or infection (Maier, 2003; Segerstrom & Miller, 2004). As such, synchrony across the ANS and inflammatory system was not only considered evolutionarily adaptive but also continues to be relevant in understanding links between psychological stress and health. Indeed, there has been decades of accumulating evidence that link disparities in early-life stress and inflammation (Miller, Chen, & Cole, 2009; Segerstrom & Miller, 2004). Coupled with a lack of coping resources (e.g., lack of support in personal relationship, less self-efficacy; Kiecolt-Glaser, McGuire, Robles, & Glaser, 2002; Uchino, Cacioppo, & Kiecolt-Glaser, 1996), higher levels of perceived chronic stress have been linked with immune dysregulation; the immune system is less likely to adaptively engage in a successful response to viral challenges (Glaser et al., 1992; Glaser, Kiecolt-Glaser, Speicher, & Holliday, 1985; Keller, Shiflett, Schleifer, & Bartlett, 1994; Yang & Glaser, 2002). Stress-related changes in immune responsivity in turn have been shown to have downstream effects (Glaser & Kiecolt-Glaser, 2005) on mental health (e.g., depression, anxiety; Connor & Leonard, 1998; Kiecolt-Glaser, Page, Marucha, MacCallum, & Glaser, 1998; Maes, Ombelet, De Jongh, Kenis, & Bosmans, 2001; Reiche, Nunes, & Morimoto, 2004), physical health (e.g., infection, autoimmune disease, coronary artery disease; Cohen et al., 1998; Rozanski, Blumenthal, & Kaplan, 1999; Whitacre, Cummings, & Griffin, 1994), and cognition (e.g., memory consolidation and impairment; McKim et al., 2016; Rachal Pugh, Fleshner, Watkins, Maier, & Rudy, 2001).

In understanding mechanisms linking psychological stress, the immune response, and health, researchers have proposed that the endocrine system serves as one avenue through which psychological stress influences immunologic functioning (Kiecolt-Glaser et al., 2002; Rabin, 1999). In addition to sympathetic changes in the immune response, pituitary and adrenal hormones released in response to stress have been shown to mediate associations between stress and immune functioning (Cacioppo, Berntson, Sheridan, & McClintock, 2002; Miller, Cohen, & Ritchey, 2002), although more research elucidating these interactions is needed (Lovallo, 2016).

Inflammation has been found to vary systematically by SES in both adults and children, with lower SES typically linked with more heightened inflammatory responses (Gruenewald, Cohen, Matthews, Tracy, & Seeman, 2009;

Schmeer & Yoon, 2016). In addition, racial and ethnic differences in inflammation have been found, with Latinx and African American children at greater risk for low-grade inflammation than White children (Albert, 2007; Schmeer & Tarrence, 2018).

HPA Axis

Perceptions of psychosocial stress, particularly those that involve uncontrollable or social-evaluative experiences, have been shown to trigger changes in the HPA axis as evidenced by acute reactivity of cortisol, a key product of the HPA axis (Dickerson & Kemeny, 2004; Hankin, Badanes, Abela, & Watamura, 2010; Kirschbaum & Hellhammer, 1989). A larger and more extended HPA axis response to psychosocial stress has been associated with clinical depression (Burke, Davis, Otte, & Mohr, 2005; Lopez-Duran, Kovacs, & George, 2009).

In addition to acutely responding to stress, cortisol has been shown to follow a daily diurnal pattern that is characterized by high cortisol levels at waking, a sharp increase in cortisol (called the cortisol awakening response) reaching its highest point about 30 minutes after waking, and a decline across the rest of the day (Adam & Kumari, 2009; Linkowski et al., 1993; Schmidt-Reinwald et al., 1999). Extensive laboratory and naturalistic research have shown the responsivity of this diurnal cortisol rhythm to acute stressors (Adam, 2006; Doane & Adam, 2010) and the daily challenges (actual or anticipated) we face in the course of everyday life (Adam, Hawkley, Kudielka, & Cacioppo, 2006; Rohleder, Beulen, Chen, Wolf, & Kirschbaum, 2007; Stalder, Hucklebridge, Evans, & Clow, 2009). These acute changes typically have been shown to provide energy and attentional focus to help the individual cope with daily demands (Adam et al., 2006; P. D. Evans, Hucklebridge, Loveday, & Clow, 2012; Stalder, Evans, Hucklebridge, & Clow, 2010). However, repeated and sustained exposure to stress (i.e., chronic stress) has been shown to set into motion a cascade of physiological changes that disrupt the responsivity of cortisol and produce a flattened cortisol pattern (i.e., lower levels of cortisol at waking and higher evening levels of cortisol; Fries, Hesse, Hellhammer, & Hellhammer, 2005; Gunnar & Vazquez, 2001) that is associated with worse cognitive functioning and a wide range of mental and physical health outcomes (Adam et al., 2017; P. D. Evans et al., 2011).

Disparities in HPA-axis activity have been found by SES and by race, with lower income individuals and Black and Latinx individuals in the United States having altered basal cortisol levels (either notably higher or lower than typical) and flatter diurnal cortisol rhythms (Desantis et al., 2015; Lupien, King, Meaney, & McEwen, 2001). These forms of HPA axis dysregulation have been found to be typically indicative of stress exposure. Indeed, both the stress of poverty and experiences of racial discrimination have been found to predict these types of cortisol alterations (Adam et al., 2015; G. W. Evans & English, 2002; Zeiders, Doane, & Roosa, 2012; Zeiders, Hoyt, & Adam, 2014). Research on racial disparities in cortisol has, to our knowledge, not been conducted in young children, but disparities have been found to be present in adolescents, and differences in acute reactivity have even been found in infancy and are predicted by maternal reports of discrimination during pregnancy (Thayer & Kuzawa, 2015). Racial differences in cortisol in adulthood have been found to be substantially explained by cumulative developmental histories of exposure to discrimination, with discrimination experiences during adolescence playing a particularly important role (Adam et al., 2015).

Sleep

Sleep is another system that is sensitive to social stressors and that is inhibited by activation of the sympathetic nervous system. Although sleep is affected by individual biological rhythms, daily schedules, and activity choices (Adam, Snell, & Pendry, 2007), sleep is also a stress-sensitive system, which is inhibited by activation of the sympathetic nervous system (Åkerstedt, 2006; Chrousos, 2009). Perceived stressors contribute to changes in both sleep quantity and quality (M. D. Hanson & Chen, 2010; Hicken, Lee, Ailshire, Burgard, & Williams, 2013; Sadeh, 1996; Sadeh, Raviv, & Gruber, 2000). In children, separation from or death of loved ones, child abuse, natural disasters, acute violence, and family stress all have been associated with poorer sleep, such as fewer sleep hours, more night awakenings, and lower sleep efficiency (Sadeh, 1996; Sadeh et al., 2000).

There are several aspects of sleep that can be studied in relation to health, including sleep duration, quality, latency (the time between getting in bed and falling asleep), and efficiency (total time sleeping divided by total time in bed). In experimental settings, sleep deprivation has been associated with an increase in levels of evening cortisol, circulating levels of proinflammatory cytokines, catecholamines, C-reactive protein, and elevations in blood pressure (Chrousos, 2009; Lusardi et al., 1999; McEwen, 2006; Meier-Ewert et al., 2004). As such, sleep deprivation has been shown to be a stressor that can both pose acute risk and inflict chronic damage to the organs and cardiovascular functioning (Lusardi et al., 1999). Short sleep has been associated with health consequences in adulthood, including hypertension, diabetes, cardiovascular disease, and increased mortality (Cappuccio, Cooper, D'Elia, Strazzullo, & Miller, 2011; Gottlieb et al., 2006; Hale & Do, 2007; Lauderdale et al., 2006). In children and adolescents, shorter sleep duration has been associated with greater probability of being overweight (Lumeng et al., 2007; Snell, Adam, & Duncan, 2007), higher risk for depression and anxiety disorders (Dahl, 1996), behavioral disturbance, increased accidents, and impairments in attention, memory, and cognition, including executive functioning (Beebe, 2011; Sadeh, 2007; Sadeh, Gruber, & Raviv, 2003).

Socioeconomic and racial disparities in sleep have been found in children, adolescents, and adults—with low SES, Black, and Latinx children and adolescents showing shorter sleep than Whites (Buckhalt, 2011; Hale & Do, 2007). In nationally representative data, Blacks and Hispanics have been shown to have lower sleep hours (approximately 30 min; Adam et al., 2007), as well as lower sleep quality (Thomas, Bardwell, Ancoli-Israel, & Dimsdale, 2006) and lighter sleep (Tomfohr, Pung, Edwards, & Dimsdale, 2012) when compared with non-Hispanic Whites. Perceived racial discrimination and, in particular, vigilance regarding racism has been found to be a predictor of lesser levels of deep sleep for Blacks (Tomfohr et al., 2012).

Multiple Stress-System Dysregulation: Allostatic Load

Importantly, there is feedback and coregulation across these and other stress-sensitive biological systems. The combined dysregulation across these systems, known as *allostatic load* (McEwen, 1998), has been linked with disparities in health and cognition across the lifespan (Adler & Stewart, 2010; Everson-Rose & Lewis, 2005; McEwen, 2004; Szanton, Gill, & Allen, 2005). Allostatic load is typically measured by constructing a count index of the number of different biological stress indicators that are elevated (or suppressed, for some indices) beyond a certain cut point (McEwen & Seeman, 1999). Disparities in allostatic load have been shown to exist by both SES and race, with lower SES individuals and ethnic and racial minorities having higher allostatic load in both adolescence and adulthood (McEwen & Seeman, 1999; Rainisch & Upchurch, 2013). In Black adolescents, allostatic load is predicted by higher perceived racial discrimination (Brody et al., 2014). Although allostatic load is rarely measured in childhood, early dysregulation of the elements of an allostatic load index are apparent (G. W. Evans & English, 2002), and cascading effects impacting related biological systems, resulting in allostatic load, are expected to be observed over time.

INTERVENTIONS DEMONSTRATED TO ALTER STRESS BIOLOGY

Evidence that early and ongoing disparities in stress exposure affect the body and brain in lasting ways does not immediately provide a hopeful message for those exposed to early or cumulative stress. Importantly, however, evidence of plasticity in biological systems, even into adulthood, and of the reversibility of previous negative impacts on biology is increasing (Lupien et al., 2009; Lupien et al., 2013). Researchers are investigating how they can change environments for children and adolescents (and adults) in ways that reduce stress exposure or reduce the psychological, behavioral, and biological impacts of stress (Lupien et al., 2013). Here, we reflect on social policies and interventions that we believe show promise of reducing stress disparities (i.e., disparities in stress exposure and stress biology) and their impact on disparities in health and developmental outcomes. We review how stress biology has been utilized in the development and evaluation of social policy and intervention research, focusing on studies that have: (a) intervened on poverty, race-based stress, or the social processes by which these types of stress are thought to have their effects on child and adolescent outcomes; and (b) measured biological outcomes relevant for health and/or developmental outcomes, including academic functioning, and prioritizing studies that consider impacts on children and adolescents.

It is worth noting that it is possible to reduce negative impacts of stress disparities by (a) reducing stress exposure itself (i.e., reducing material hardship or race-based social stress) or (b) helping individuals respond to and function more effectively in the face of the stressors that they do experience. Ultimately, we believe that responsibility to reduce stress disparities does not lie with those who are subjected to unjust treatment. To that end, we first consider how policy can reduce stress exposure in ways meaningful for stress biology. We also recognize that systemic change requires considerable time and commitment (on the part of policymakers and citizens alike) to redress inequities. In the meantime, interventions that help young people respond to the stressors they do experience are essential for reducing the consequences of stress disparities.

In this section, we review evidence regarding (a) policy that has changed families' living circumstances or material resources to reduce exposure to neighborhood or family disadvantage; (b) family/parenting interventions that worked to increase warm and supportive parenting and a positive home environment in the context of adversity, past trauma, or economic disadvantage; and (c) school-based interventions that have aimed to help students cope with and function more effectively in the context of the stressful circumstances.

Policies Aimed at Reducing Exposure to Stress and Disadvantage

Changes in policy can increase resources and reduce exposure to stress in ways that are likely to affect stress biology in both parents and their children. Some policies have changed over time or varied across geographic boundaries in ways that allow for quasi-experimental estimates of their impacts. Other prospective new policies have been tested experimentally through demonstration projects or other studies. Here, we consider studies of policy changes in which investigators included measures of stress or stress biology as outcomes or as pathways by which the policy changes are thought to affect health or academic outcomes.

Although there are many ways in which income inequality can limit a person's opportunity, two key (and related) pathways are a person's physical environment (e.g., home, neighborhood) and material resources (including cash and near-cash resources). Many families are forced to make choices between spending on housing, neighborhood quality and safety, and spending on other goods (Edin & Lein, 1997)—tradeoffs that can have implications for the well-being of both parents and children, given the importance of each (Adam & Chase-Lansdale, 2002; Coley, Leventhal, Lynch, & Kull, 2013; Crowley, 2003; Heissel, Sharkey, Torrats-Espinosa, Grant, & Adam, 2018; McGrath, Matthews, & Brady, 2006). Here, we consider several policy-related experiments or quasi-experiments that have acted on families' housing and neighborhood quality (via voucher or relocation programs) or income (via cash or near-cash transfers) and measured their impacts on stress biology.

Housing Voucher/Relocation Programs

Several publicly funded programs were created during the 1980s and 1990s in response to concerns about the poor conditions experienced in public housing developments, including the Moving to Opportunity for Fair Housing Demonstration (MTO), the Yonkers Project, and HOPE VI. As a random assignment experiment that reached over 4,000 families across five large cities, MTO is one of the most well-studied, with its initial and long-term findings both receiving a great deal of attention (Chetty, Hendren, & Katz, 2016; DeLuca, Clampet-Lundquist, & Edin, 2016). It is also the only such project to directly measure health outcomes, and several relevant health impacts have been identified among female heads of household. Assignment to the experimental[4] condition was associated with a large, significant reduction in the prevalence of extreme obesity and in symptoms of psychological distress more than 10 years after random assignment (Kling, Liebman, & Katz, 2007). Blood-spot data also revealed lower levels of risk for diabetes (measured through hemoglobin A1c levels) and inflammatory risk for cardiovascular disease (measured through C-reactive protein levels) among adults in the experimental group (Sanbonmatsu et al., 2011).

These findings are consistent with improvements in health found in other relocation studies that asked respondents about their physical and mental health but did not collect biomarker data. Participants in the Yonkers relocation project reported fewer diagnosed health conditions two years after moving to lower poverty neighborhoods (Fauth, Leventhal, & Brooks-Gunn, 2004). At the 7-year follow-up, only movers who stayed in their relocation neighborhoods reported better physical health than those who left them during the follow-up period (Fauth, Leventhal, & Brooks-Gunn, 2008). The evaluation of these and other relocation projects, such as HOPE VI, suggest that vouchers supporting a move to a lower poverty neighborhood can be beneficial for the health of those who want to move (Keene & Geronimus, 2011) and are able to find stability in their new neighborhood (Fauth et al., 2008; Ludwig et al., 2011). From these data, it is difficult to identify the aspect(s) of lower-poverty neighborhoods that matter or the biological mechanisms through which they operate. It is also important to note that relocation projects have not resulted in universally positive impacts on health or academic attainment (Chetty et al., 2016; Sharkey & Faber, 2014). Further study is needed to understand how to reduce stress disparities experienced by those living in disadvantaged neighborhoods, including whether improvements to housing conditions or their material resources can improve stress biology.

Income Supplements

Evidence that increases in household cash (or near cash) resources improve stress biology comes from several sources, including the expansion of the

---

[4]For simplicity, the term *experimental* refers to those who received low-poverty vouchers.

Earned Income Tax Credit (EITC), the rollout of the Food Stamp Program, and evidence from several cash transfer experiments. The 1993 expansion of the EITC increased payments to families with two or more children. Considering changes in the health of women who received the increased payments, W. N. Evans and Garthwaite (2010) estimated that income supplementation led to a 23% reduction in the total number of risky biomarkers for metabolic or cardiovascular disease. In particular, recipients were significantly less likely to report elevated levels of diastolic blood pressure and markers of inflammation (measured through C-reactive protein and albumin). Additionally, recipient mothers were more likely to report being in good or excellent health and indicated fewer poor mental health days in the last month compared to non-recipient mothers (W. N. Evans & Garthwaite, 2010).

Another policy change that offers insight into the impact of increased income comes from county-level variation in when the federal Food Stamp Program was implemented. By considering the duration of food stamp availability from conception through early childhood, researchers estimated that having access to food stamps for the entirety of the period between conception and age 5 leads to a significant reduction in the number of markers for metabolic syndrome, with an effect of about 0.4 standard deviations (*SD*s; Hoynes, Schanzenbach, & Almond, 2012). Although food stamp access in utero had previously been associated with reduced incidence of low birth weight (Almond, Hoynes, & Schanzenbach, 2011), finding an association with health later in life suggests there are additional mechanisms through which food stamp receipt improves health. As food stamps are a *near-cash* source of aid (i.e., they augment families' total budget for consumption), it is possible that access to food stamps improves health in part by acting as an income supplement, which in turn reduces income-related stress for families.

Other research has also found that greater income during pregnancy and early childhood impacts child well-being in part through improvements to stress biology. One study that followed mothers across multiple pregnancies observed higher prenatal cortisol during pregnancies in which they reported less household income (Aizer, Stroud, & Buka, 2009). Children carried during these pregnancies completed, on average, a half year less of schooling than their siblings who experienced relatively lower prenatal cortisol (regardless of birth order; Aizer et al., 2009). Additionally, children whose parents had received cash transfers through the Oportunidades program in Mexico had lower average cortisol levels than children in comparison villages, with the largest difference in child cortisol found for those whose mothers had high depressive symptoms before receiving the income supplements (Fernald & Gunnar, 2009). In studies in Kenya, changes in income arising from a cash transfer experiment (Haushofer & Shapiro, 2016) and annual variation in rainfall that affected agricultural yields (Chemin, de Laat, & Haushofer, 2013) have also provided evidence that average cortisol levels are impacted by changes in household income. Future income supplementation experiments should continue to examine cortisol and examine a broader range of stress biomarkers and/or measures of allostatic load.

Family and Parenting Interventions

Beyond programs that attempt to reduce the impact of poverty by targeting income itself, a number of programs have targeted the family context with the aim of supporting positive parenting of individuals exposed to economic disadvantage (Brooks-Gunn et al., 1995). One theoretical rationale for targeting the home or family context of individuals living in poverty is provided by the family stress model, which argues that the stress associated with poverty or financial strain causes stress in parents, which in turn impacts their parenting in ways that are detrimental for child and adolescent development (K. J. Conger, Rueter, & Conger, 2000; R. D. Conger et al., 2002). Thus, when targeting income directly through policy or experimental income supplementation is not an option, intervention efforts to improve parent–child interactions are thought to be one way to improve the well-being of children and adolescents living in poverty and other stressful contexts. When an extreme breakdown in parenting is judged to have occurred, such as in the presence of child abuse or neglect, experimental interventions target the quality of the parent–child relationship in an attempt to improve the home environment or support placements outside the familial home. These interventions also attempt to ameliorate the effects of early traumatic stress on children. Similar interventions have targeted enhancing parenting in families of children adopted from early institutional (orphanage) care; such children may require enriched parenting to help counter the stress effects of early social deprivation and trauma encountered in institutional settings. We focus here on those interventions that included measures of stress biology as part of their outcome assessments.

Interventions Reducing or Reversing the Effects of Early Traumatic Stress

Some of the earliest insights into the malleability of stress biology in response to intervention in human populations came from studies of children exposed to the trauma of child abuse and neglect. As evidence has accumulated that child abuse and neglect can leave lasting marks on biological stress systems (Bernard, Butzin-Dozier, Rittenhouse, & Dozier, 2010; Gunnar & Vazquez, 2001), several interventions have been developed to reach children involved with the child welfare system, who disproportionately come from families facing the stresses of poverty or other hardship. Although each intervention has its own approach and theory of change, the interventions typically last from 6 to 12 weeks, with components that address the needs of both caregiver and child. For example, the Attachment and Biobehavioral Catch-up (ABC) intervention is an 8-week program for families of children aged 0 to 2 years that have experienced maltreatment, domestic violence, or placement instability that is focused on increasing parent–child synchrony, promoting nurturing parenting, and reducing parental behavior that would frighten or alarm the child (Bernard, Dozier, Bick, & Gordon, 2015). The Multidimensional Treatment Foster Care for Preschoolers (MTFC-P) program is a therapeutic intervention designed to promote attachment and behavior for children in foster care and increase placement stability. The intervention includes both individual and group support for foster parents, individualized treatment for children, and weekly playgroup sessions focused on social and emotional development and school readiness (P. A. Fisher, Stoolmiller, Gunnar, & Burraston, 2007).

Finally, the Kids in Transition to School program focuses on promoting school readiness among children in foster care as they transition to kindergarten, with child group sessions that focus on increasing school readiness (e.g., early literacy) and promoting prosocial and self-regulatory skills and parent group sessions that address behavioral management and school involvement (Graham, Pears, Kim, Bruce, & Fisher, 2018). Of the studies that have considered biological outcomes, most have measured cortisol, with some considering impacts on other outcomes. Overall, these interventions have shown that HPA-axis functioning can be improved, or further dysregulation prevented, in young children who have experienced neglect or maltreatment. After intervention, children in the treatment group have shown better-regulated diurnal cortisol than control participants, with higher waking levels (Bernard, Dozier, et al., 2015; D. B.-D. Fisher et al., 2007) and steeper slopes across the day (Bernard, Dozier, et al., 2015; P. A. Fisher et al., 2007; Graham et al., 2018). There is evidence that improved cortisol regulation can persist for several years after intervention (Bernard, Hostinar, & Dozier, 2015). Of note, not *every* intervention has found an impact on diurnal cortisol (Nelson & Spieker, 2013), and no impacts on afternoon/evening cortisol have emerged from these studies.

Participation in interventions that improved cortisol regulation was also associated with other promising outcomes for treatment group members, including greater incidence of secure attachment and impacts on cognitive flexibility and theory of mind (Bernard et al., 2012); lasting reductions in caregiving stress (P. A. Fisher & Stoolmiller, 2008); and more typical patterns of neural activation during response inhibition 5 years after intervention (Jankowski et al., 2017). In contrast, many of the control group children showed a blunted cortisol diurnal rhythm several years after intervention (Bernard, Dozier, et al., 2015; P. A. Fisher et al., 2007), consistent with studies that have found flattened cortisol slopes in children who stay with their birth parents rather than being placed in foster care following contact with the child welfare system (Bernard et al., 2010; Bernard, Dozier, et al., 2015). Together, these studies provide evidence that stress-sensitive systems influenced by early traumatic stress, such as child maltreatment, can be responsive to early intervention.

Community-Based Interventions for Families Under Stress
Although programs targeting children in the child welfare system primarily reach children and families during early childhood, programs that reach families experiencing stress disparities (e.g., high poverty, exposure to race-based discrimination) in their communities are far broader in the type of intervention, ages at time of intervention, and biological stress markers studied, including cortisol, inflammatory markers, and risk markers for metabolic syndrome.

Cortisol outcomes. Several interventions considered impacts on cortisol, including a home visiting program for mothers of infants from primarily low income families at medical risk (Bugental, Schwartz, & Lynch, 2010) and a preventive intervention offered following the death of one of an adolescent's parents (Luecken et al., 2010). Both interventions were associated with impacts on average cortisol levels relative to control group youth. In infants, the intervention was associated with reductions in midmorning cortisol at 1 year of age that predicted better verbal short-term memory 2 years later. The bereavement program also showed long-term impacts of the intervention, with treatment participants showing an increase in average cortisol level relative to control youth during a conflict discussion task that occurred 6 years after participation. Treatment youth also reported lower externalizing problems, suggesting lower incidence of the attenuated cortisol/elevated mental health symptoms profile that might otherwise follow from experiencing the death of a parent at a young age (Adam, 2006; Shirtcliff & Essex, 2008).

Immune/inflammatory and other biological outcomes. The Strong African American Families Program (SAAF) was a preventive intervention that randomly assigned over 600 rural Georgia families of 11-year-old children between a family-focused parenting intervention and a literature-only control condition (Brody et al., 2004). The program focused on the promotion of a regulated and communicative home environment, which was expected to operate by increasing (a) involved/vigilant parenting, racial socialization, and discussion of behaviors like sex and alcohol use; and (b) protective factors among youth, including self-regulation, future orientation, more negative attitudes about risk behaviors, and acceptance of parental influence. The seven-week intervention included separate skill-building for parents and youth as well as joint sessions in which families practiced applying the skills they learned.

Those who participated in SAAF were followed through early adulthood, with several studies measuring biological stress outcomes. Studies conducted when they were 19 and 25 years old identified several associations in the control group that were not present for those who received the intervention. In particular, among control youth: (a) higher adolescent-reported unsupportive parenting was associated with having more risk factors for metabolic syndrome (E. Chen, Miller, Yu, & Brody, 2018), and (b) having lived more adolescent years in poverty was associated with lower volume of several regions of the brain's limbic system (Brody et al., 2017). There is some evidence that improvements in parenting (i.e., a reduction in *un*supportive parenting) in the treatment group partially accounted for the reduced risk observed relative to the control condition (E. Chen et al., 2018; J. L. Hanson et al., 2019). Those who participated in the intervention also had lower levels of inflammatory cytokines measured in late adolescence, with the lowest levels of inflammation found among those who experienced more nurturant and less harsh parenting following the intervention (Miller, Brody, Yu, & Chen, 2014).

In two of the family-focused interventions, MTFC-P and SAAF, long-term follow-up has included brain scans of the young people who had experienced either the intervention or control conditions. Both studies found that control, but not intervention, youth showed reduced connectivity between subcortical and cortical regions of the brain involved in self-regulation, attention, and behavior (J. L. Hanson et al., 2018). These differences in connectivity have been associated with attention and behavior problems more common among control children in the MTFC-P study (Bruce et al., 2013; Pollak et al., 2010) and have been partially accounted for by improvements in self-regulation and parental support that developed via the SAAF intervention (Brody et al., 2017; Jankowski et al., 2017). Differences in connectivity and volume were identified in a region of the hippocampus that is sensitive to corticosteroid levels and influenced by both stress exposure and parental support (Fa et al., 2014; J. L. Hanson et al., 2019; Luby et al., 2012; Pagliaccio et al., 2014; Teicher, Anderson, & Polcari, 2012). Together, these results provide evidence that young people randomly assigned to the control condition went on to develop markers of chronic stress exposure that are less prevalent in the intervention group, some of which in turn predicted cognitive and behavioral functioning and longer term health outcomes.

School-Based Interventions

Disparities in stress exposure occur not only at home but also through social and academic stressors faced in school. Schools are also where young people spend a substantial proportion of their waking hours. Student choices (including whether to participate in physical activity, consume healthy food/drink, or engage in risky behaviors) and experiences (including experiences of social support or social exclusion from teachers or peers) during this time can affect their health and well-being in the short term and contribute to the formation of habits and health trajectories that will affect their health later in life (Kimm et al., 2005). The school context is, therefore, an optimal space in which to implement interventions that aim to reduce student stress, improve health behaviors, and improve young people's health, performance, and well-being.

Although there are multiple aspects of children's and adolescents' school experiences that could be targeted to reduce stress disparities through interventions, very few published studies have done so with attention to effects on stress biology. For example, numerous rigorous randomized control studies have attempted to manipulate aspects of children's school contexts, such as bullying reduction programs, class size experiments, teacher training programs, or manipulations of per-pupil budgets, but we are not aware of school context-based interventions that have measured impacts on stress biology.

Rather, most school-based interventions incorporating biological measures have focused on modifying student perceptions of and responses to a wide range of stressors (including poverty-related stressors and stressors associated with discrimination and social exclusion). The most commonly employed approaches involve training in meditation or mindfulness. We focus first on school-based meditation or mindfulness interventions as an example of a well-studied approach with promising links to stress biology; we then focus on a new study of our own designed to promote positive functioning and better regulation of stress biology, specifically in the face of exposure to race-based social stress.

Mindfulness and Meditation Interventions

With a rich history in Hindu and Buddhist traditions, meditation and mindfulness can be broadly understood as a practice of training attention to the present moment (Chambers, Gullone, & Allen, 2009; Kabat-Zinn, 2005). Although there are multiple traditions out of which many modern approaches have been developed, the main distinction has been drawn between *focused attention* practices, in which one concentrates on a single object (e.g., an image, body part, or the breath) and *open monitoring*, which promotes nonjudgmental awareness and observation. More recently, some scholars have argued for understanding these attributes as orthogonal, with beginners primarily engaged in learning to concentrate without letting the mind wander (Chambers et al., 2009; Chiesa, 2013). Interventions based on these principles have been implemented in schools, with wide variety in the approach and intensity of training and practice time that students experience (Esch, 2014). As such, our aim is not to draw inferences about the effects of specific practices or programs but rather to review relevant studies that have evaluated impacts on stress biology. We denote the type of practice where possible and otherwise use the general term *meditation* or *mindfulness* to refer to the broader category of included studies. Literature on connections between mindfulness, meditation, the stress response, and student biology and behavior suggests that school-based mindfulness or meditation practice may benefit young people through reductions in perceived stress and improved stress biology (Hölzel et al., 2011; Lane, Seskevich, & Pieper, 2007; Turakitwanakan, Mekseepralard, & Busarakumtragul, 2013).

Cortisol outcomes. Among adolescents, a school-based behavioral stress-education program was found to decrease cortisol levels and depressive symptomatology in adolescents making the transition to high school, with effect sizes on the order of 0.3 *SD*s for youth high in anger at baseline (Lupien et al., 2013). Completion of a mindfulness-based social emotional learning program was associated with steeper school-day cortisol slopes than peers in the control condition for fourth- and fifth-grade students (Schonert-Reichl et al., 2015). Studies outside the school context also found lower average cortisol after 2 to 4 months of meditation intervention, with effects ranging from 0.75 *SD* to 1.25 *SD* (MacLean et al., 1997). Others have found decreased acute cortisol levels following meditation sessions (Carlson, Speca, Faris, & Patel, 2007; Jevning, Wilson, & Davidson, 1978; Sudsuang, Chentanez, & Veluvan, 1991). A school-based yoga and mindfulness intervention for teachers led to lower waking cortisol levels after 16 weeks, compared with teachers at control schools (Harris, Jennings, Katz, Abenavoli, & Greenberg, 2016). Although these results are promising, findings have been inconsistent. Some studies have found no effects on cortisol outcomes (Sieverdes et al., 2014), and many have employed data collection or analysis methods that are not adequate for modeling diurnal cortisol rhythms, which is problematic given the important associations between daily cortisol slopes and a wide range of health outcomes (Adam et al., 2017).

Blood pressure outcomes. Meditation interventions have also improved blood pressure among adolescents and adults. Several school-based interventions have reached students at elevated risk for hypertension (i.e., in the upper third or half of the distribution for their age or school) and led to reductions of approximately 0.3 to 0.4 *SD*s in systolic and diastolic blood pressure (Barnes, Pendergrast, Harshfield, & Treiber, 2008; Barnes, Treiber, & Johnson, 2004; Gregoski, Barnes, Tingen, Harshfield, & Treiber, 2011). As few studies have enrolled students across the blood pressure distribution, there is limited evidence of the extent to which meditation can be expected to change blood pressure levels in young people with healthy baseline levels. A meta-analysis of meditation studies with mostly adult populations finds that those with healthy blood pressure see reductions comparable in magnitude with those with elevated blood pressure (Anderson, Liu, & Kryscio, 2008). In contrast, a study in college students found a reduction in systolic blood pressure of 0.4 *SD*s for those at elevated risk of hypertension, but a (nonsignificant) reduction of less than 0.2 *SD*s for the full sample (Nidich et al., 2009). Further study will be needed to better estimate how meditation affects stress biology in healthy children and adolescents.

Sleep outcomes. Although there is not much literature on meditation or mindfulness and sleep among adolescents, several studies with adults have found improvements in sleep quality (Hülsheger, Feinholdt, & Nübold, 2015) and duration (Carlson & Garland, 2005) following a brief mindfulness or meditation intervention. Results from a small pilot study suggest that a school-based mindfulness intervention can improve sleep quality among high school women who reported poor sleep (Bei et al., 2013). These studies are fairly preliminary, and additional evidence is needed to identify the mechanisms through which meditation improves sleep.

Inflammation outcomes. Very little work has considered impacts of mindfulness or meditation on inflammation in adolescents, but several studies in adults provide evidence of impacts on certain inflammatory markers. Specifically, randomized mindfulness interventions have found reductions in proinflammatory gene expression (measured through NF-κB levels; Black & Slavich, 2016; Creswell et al., 2012) and small reductions in levels of C-reactive protein (Creswell et al., 2012; Malarkey, Jarjoura, & Klatt, 2013). A meta-analysis concluded that there is insufficient evidence to determine whether mindfulness impacts other common inflammatory markers including antibodies and interleukins (Black & Slavich, 2016). There is a need for additional research that meets standards for rigorous causal research design including the use of an appropriate control condition. Thus, preliminary evidence suggests that meditation and mindfulness interventions can improve regulation of stress biology, particularly for populations under current stress, but much additional research is needed, especially studies on the long-term impacts of these interventions.

Racial and Ethnic Identity Promotion Interventions

In addition to these more general approaches designed to reduce the emotional and biological effects of stress exposure, our research group has been focused on testing interventions designed specifically to reduce the social, emotional, and biological effects of race-based stress and especially the stress of racial discrimination. Past theory and research have suggested that having a strong ethnic and racial identity, and in particular positive affect and pride in one's ethnic or racial heritage, tends to buffer or reduce the stress of discrimination and to be associated with positive outcomes, particularly for children and youth of color (Rivas-Drake et al., 2014). Correlational evidence has suggested that ethnic pride is also associated with better regulated stress biology in the form of steeper diurnal cortisol rhythms (Zeiders, Causadias, & White, 2018). In the Biology, Identity and Opportunity study, we are conducting a randomized controlled trial to test whether an 8-week ethnic and racial identity promotion intervention for high school freshman (see Umaña-Taylor & Douglass, 2017; Umaña-Taylor, Douglass, Updegraff, & Marsiglia, 2018; Umaña-Taylor, Kornienko, Douglass Bayless, & Updegraff, 2018) has positive effects on stress biology, as well as emotional, cognitive, physical, and academic outcomes. Ideally, we hope that such an intervention is positive for all youth but are hoping that it has particularly strong effects for youth of color, in that it could help to close ethnic and racial disparities in stress biology and developmental outcomes.

SUMMARY OF STUDIES OF POLICIES AND INTERVENTIONS AFFECTING STRESS BIOLOGY

Overall, we have provided evidence that the reduction of biological stress disparities need not rely only on increases in individual coping; indeed, the preliminary evidence reviewed here suggests that policies designed to reduce levels of economic and race-based stress in children in families can have positive effects on stress biology. Given the pervasiveness of stress disparities, a combination of policy interventions that reduce stress exposure and interventions designed to promote better coping with stress may hold the most promise. Future random assignment studies will preferably (a) measure and attempt to reduce disparities in stress exposure and/or increase coping with stress, (b) include a comprehensive battery of stress biology measures, and (c) follow children and adolescents longitudinally postintervention to observe not only short-term but also long-term effects on stress biology and developmental outcomes.

SUGGESTIONS FOR FUTURE RESEARCH AND CONCLUSION

In this chapter, we have argued that greater attention is needed to the disparities in stress exposure, biological responses to that stress exposure, and in understanding the origins of both economic and ethnic–racial disparities in health, developmental, and human-capital outcomes. Future research attempting to understand the origins of disparities should consider adding a "stress disparities" lens to their work, including both measures of various types of stress exposure and measures of stress biology. As the field advances, possible studies should move beyond examining single stress biomarkers to the inclusion of multiple aspects of the biological stress response and its downstream effects on related biological systems. Researchers should be aware that cumulative measures of stress exposure may have greater impact on stress biology and cumulative cross-system measures of stress biology may be better predictors of long-term outcomes. Studies should, if possible, gather multiple waves of stress biology data, in order to allow changes in stress biology can be observed in relation to changes in stress exposure, or in response to an intervening policy or program. In addition, studies would be advised to pay attention to the possibility of sensitive period effects, being particularly attentive to the possible embedding effects of early life stress, but not forget the possibility that ongoing, cumulative stress, and the interactions between early and ongoing stress may play an important role.

In choosing measures of stress, and of biology, researchers should engage in close conversation with community partners, who are aware both of the types of stressors typically encountered in their communities (which may be different than those expected a priori by researchers), and also are sensitive to the types of biological measures that will be perceived as acceptable for measurement within that community (which is in turn strongly based on the level of community trust the researcher has established through past interactions). Certain biological markers, such as DNA gathered to examine genetic polymorphisms, may be rightfully rejected or regarded with suspicion, as they can be perceived to locate the source of the stress-related negative outcomes as emerging from within the individual.

Overall, we believe that taking a stress disparities framing is an important new way to shed light on the origins and consequences of the vastly unequal distribution of resources, adversities, and stress within U.S. society and across the world. The addition of stress measures (including measures of stressor exposure and stress biomarkers) to intervention and policy studies designed to reduce disparities helps to shed light on the efficacy of social interventions and social policies and the pathways by which they have their effects on health and human capital outcomes. Additional policy research should add measures of stress exposure and stress biology as both potential outcomes of policy change and plausible mechanisms for the maintenance of inequality and consider the reduction in inequalities of perceived and biological stress as an important target and indicator by which we can measure progress toward reducing inequality and promoting equity.

REFERENCES

Adam, E. K. (2006). Transactions among adolescent trait and state emotion and diurnal and momentary cortisol activity in naturalistic settings. *Psychoneuroendocrinology, 31,* 664–679. http://dx.doi.org/10.1016/j.psyneuen.2006.01.010

Adam, E. K. (2012). Emotion–cortisol transactions occur over multiple time scales in development: Implications for research on emotion and the development of emotional disorders. *Monographs of the Society for Research in Child Development, 77,* 17–27. http://dx.doi.org/10.1111/j.1540-5834.2012.00657.x

Adam, E. K., & Chase-Lansdale, P. L. (2002). Home sweet home(s): Parental separations, residential moves, and adjustment problems in low-income adolescent girls. *Developmental Psychology, 38,* 792–805. http://dx.doi.org/10.1037/0012-1649.38.5.792

Adam, E. K., Hawkley, L. C., Kudielka, B. M., & Cacioppo, J. T. (2006). Day-to-day dynamics of experience–cortisol associations in a population-based sample of older adults. *Proceedings of the National Academy of Sciences, 103,* 17058–17063. http://dx.doi.org/10.1073/pnas.0605053103

Adam, E. K., Heissel, J. A., Zeiders, K. H., Richeson, J. A., Ross, E. C., Ehrlich, K. B., . . . Eccles, J. S. (2015). Developmental histories of perceived racial discrimination and diurnal cortisol profiles in adulthood: A 20-year prospective study. *Psychoneuroendocrinology, 62,* 279–291. http://dx.doi.org/10.1016/j.psyneuen.2015.08.018

Adam, E. K., & Kumari, M. (2009). Assessing salivary cortisol in large-scale, epidemiological research. *Psychoneuroendocrinology, 34,* 1423–1436. http://dx.doi.org/10.1016/j.psyneuen.2009.06.011

Adam, E. K., Quinn, M. E., Tavernier, R., McQuillan, M. T., Dahlke, K. A., & Gilbert, K. E. (2017). Diurnal cortisol slopes and mental and physical health outcomes: A systematic review and meta-analysis. *Psychoneuroendocrinology, 83,* 25–41. http://dx.doi.org/10.1016/j.psyneuen.2017.05.018

Adam, E. K., Snell, E. K., & Pendry, P. (2007). Sleep timing and quantity in ecological and family context: A nationally representative time-diary study. *Journal of Family Psychology, 21,* 4–19. http://dx.doi.org/10.1037/0893-3200.21.1.4

Adler, N. E., & Stewart, J. (2010). Health disparities across the lifespan: Meaning, methods, and mechanisms. *Annals of the New York Academy of Sciences, 1186,* 5–23. http://dx.doi.org/10.1111/j.1749-6632.2009.05337.x

Aizer, A., Stroud, L., & Buka, S. (2009). *Maternal stress and child well-being: Evidence from siblings.* Unpublished manuscript, Brown University, Providence, RI.

Åkerstedt, T. (2006). Psychosocial stress and impaired sleep. *Scandinavian Journal of Work, Environment & Health, 32,* 493–501. http://dx.doi.org/10.5271/sjweh.1054

Albert, M. A. (2007). Inflammatory biomarkers, race/ethnicity and cardiovascular disease. *Nutrition Reviews, 65*(12, Pt. 2), S234–S238. http://dx.doi.org/10.1111/j.1753-4887.2007.tb00369.x

Almond, D., Hoynes, H. W., & Schanzenbach, D. W. (2011). Inside the war on poverty: The impact of food stamps on birth outcomes. *The Review of Economics and Statistics, 93,* 387–403. http://dx.doi.org/10.1162/REST_a_00089

Anderson, J. W., Liu, C., & Kryscio, R. J. (2008). Blood pressure response to transcendental meditation: A meta-analysis. *American Journal of Hypertension, 21,* 310–316. http://dx.doi.org/10.1038/ajh.2007.65

Ayada, C., Toru, Ü., & Korkut, Y. (2015). The relationship of stress and blood pressure effectors. *Hippokratia, 19,* 99–108.

Barnes, V. A., Pendergrast, R. A., Harshfield, G. A., & Treiber, F. A. (2008). Impact of breathing awareness meditation on ambulatory blood pressure and sodium handling in prehypertensive African American adolescents. *Ethnicity & Disease, 18,* 1–5.

Barnes, V. A., Treiber, F. A., & Johnson, M. H. (2004). Impact of transcendental meditation on ambulatory blood pressure in African-American adolescents. *American Journal of Hypertension, 17,* 366–369. http://dx.doi.org/10.1016/j.amjhyper.2003.12.008

Beebe, D. W. (2011). Cognitive, behavioral, and functional consequences of inade-
quate sleep in children and adolescents. *Pediatric Clinics of North America, 58,* 649–665.
http://dx.doi.org/10.1016/j.pcl.2011.03.002

Bei, B., Byrne, M. L., Ivens, C., Waloszek, J., Woods, M. J., Dudgeon, P., . . . Allen,
N. B. (2013). Pilot study of a mindfulness-based, multi-component, in-school group
sleep intervention in adolescent girls. *Early Intervention in Psychiatry, 7,* 213–220.
http://dx.doi.org/10.1111/j.1751-7893.2012.00382.x

Bernard, K., Butzin-Dozier, Z., Rittenhouse, J., & Dozier, M. (2010). Cortisol production patterns in young children living with birth parents vs. children placed in foster
care following involvement of Child Protective Services. *Archives of Pediatrics &
Adolescent Medicine, 164,* 438–443. http://dx.doi.org/10.1001/archpediatrics.2010.54

Bernard, K., Dozier, M., Bick, J., & Gordon, M. K. (2015). Intervening to enhance
cortisol regulation among children at risk for neglect: Results of a randomized clinical trial. *Development and Psychopathology, 27,* 829–841. http://dx.doi.org/10.1017/
S095457941400073X

Bernard, K., Dozier, M., Bick, J., Lewis-Morrarty, E., Lindhiem, O., & Carlson, E.
(2012). Enhancing attachment organization among maltreated children: Results
of a randomized clinical trial. *Child Development, 83,* 623–636. http://dx.doi.org/
10.1111/j.1467-8624.2011.01712.x

Bernard, K., Hostinar, C. E., & Dozier, M. (2015). Intervention effects on diurnal cortisol
rhythms of Child Protective Services-referred infants in early childhood: Preschool
follow-up results of a randomized clinical trial. *JAMA Pediatrics, 169,* 112–119. http://
dx.doi.org/10.1001/jamapediatrics.2014.2369

Black, D. S., & Slavich, G. M. (2016). Mindfulness meditation and the immune system:
A systematic review of randomized controlled trials. *Annals of the New York Academy
of Sciences, 1373,* 13–24. http://dx.doi.org/10.1111/nyas.12998

Blascovich, J., Spencer, S. J., Quinn, D., & Steele, C. (2001). African Americans and
high blood pressure: The role of stereotype threat. *Psychological Science, 12,* 225–229.
http://dx.doi.org/10.1111/1467-9280.00340

Blascovich, J., Vanman, E. J., Mendes, W. B., & Dickerson, S. (2011). *Social psychophysiology for social and personality psychology.* Thousand Oaks, CA: Sage. http://
dx.doi.org/10.4135/9781446287842

Bosworth, H. B., Dudley, T., Olsen, M. K., Voils, C. I., Powers, B., Goldstein, M. K.,
& Oddone, E. Z. (2006). Racial differences in blood pressure control: Potential
explanatory factors. *The American Journal of Medicine, 119*(1), 70.e9–70.e15. http://
dx.doi.org/10.1016/j.amjmed.2005.08.019

Brody, G. H., Gray, J. C., Yu, T., Barton, A. W., Beach, S. R. H., Galván, A., . . . Sweet,
L. H. (2017). Protective prevention effects on the association of poverty with brain
development. *JAMA Pediatrics, 171,* 46–52. http://dx.doi.org/10.1001/jamapediatrics.
2016.2988

Brody, G. H., Lei, M.-K., Chae, D. H., Yu, T., Kogan, S. M., & Beach, S. R. H. (2014).
Perceived discrimination among African American adolescents and allostatic load:
A longitudinal analysis with buffering effects. *Child Development, 85,* 989–1002. http://
dx.doi.org/10.1111/cdev.12213

Brody, G. H., Murry, V. M., Gerrard, M., Gibbons, F. X., Molgaard, V., McNair, L., . . .
Neubaum-Carlan, E. (2004). The Strong African American Families Program:
Translating research into prevention programming. *Child Development, 75,* 900–917.
http://dx.doi.org/10.1111/j.1467-8624.2004.00713.x

Brondolo, E., Brady, N., Thompson, S., Tobin, J. N., Cassells, A., Sweeney, M., . . .
Contrada, R. J. (2008). Perceived racism and negative affect: Analyses of trait and
state measures of affect in a community sample. *Journal of Social and Clinical Psychology, 27,* 150–173. http://dx.doi.org/10.1521/jscp.2008.27.2.150

Brondolo, E., Rieppi, R., Kelly, K. P., & Gerin, W. (2003). Perceived racism and
blood pressure: A review of the literature and conceptual and methodological

critique. *Annals of Behavioral Medicine, 25*, 55–65. http://dx.doi.org/10.1207/ S15324796ABM2501_08

Brooks-Gunn, J., Klebanov, P. K., & Liaw, F.-R. (1995). The learning, physical, and emotional environment of the home in the context of poverty: The Infant Health and Development Program. *Children and Youth Services Review, 17*, 251–276. http://dx.doi.org/10.1016/0190-7409(95)00011-Z

Broudy, R., Brondolo, E., Coakley, V., Brady, N., Cassells, A., Tobin, J. N., & Sweeney, M. (2007). Perceived ethnic discrimination in relation to daily moods and negative social interactions. *Journal of Behavioral Medicine, 30*, 31–43. http://dx.doi.org/10.1007/ s10865-006-9081-4

Brownley, K. A., Hurwitz, B. E., & Schneiderman, N. (2000). Cardiovascular Psychophysiology. In J. T. Cacioppo, L. G. Tassinary, & G. G. Berntson (Eds.), *Handbook of psychophysiology* (2nd ed., pp. 224–263). New York, NY: Cambridge University Press.

Bruce, J., Fisher, P. A., Graham, A. M., Moore, W. E., III, Peake, S. J., & Mannering, A. M. (2013). Patterns of brain activation in foster children and nonmaltreated children during an inhibitory control task. *Development and Psychopathology, 25*, 931–941. http://dx.doi.org/10.1017/S095457941300028X

Buckhalt, J. A. (2011). Insufficient sleep and the socioeconomic status achievement gap. *Child Development Perspectives, 5*, 59–65. http://dx.doi.org/10.1111/j.1750-8606. 2010.00151.x

Bugental, D. B., Schwartz, A., & Lynch, C. (2010). Effects of an early family intervention on children's memory: The mediating effects of cortisol levels. *Mind, Brain and Education, 4*, 159–170. http://dx.doi.org/10.1111/j.1751-228X.2010.01095.x

Burke, H. M., Davis, M. C., Otte, C., & Mohr, D. C. (2005). Depression and cortisol responses to psychological stress: A meta-analysis. *Psychoneuroendocrinology, 30*, 846–856. http://dx.doi.org/10.1016/j.psyneuen.2005.02.010

Cacioppo, J. T., Berntson, G. G., Sheridan, J. F., & McClintock, M. K. (2002). Multilevel integrative analyses of human behavior: Social neuroscience and the complementing nature of social and biological approaches. In J. T. Cacioppo, G. G. Berntson, R. Adolphs, C. S. Carter, R. J. Davidson, M. McClintock, . . . S. E. Taylor (Eds.), *Foundations in social neuroscience* (pp. 21–46). Cambridge, MA: MIT Press.

Cappuccio, F. P., Cooper, D., D'Elia, L., Strazzullo, P., & Miller, M. A. (2011). Sleep duration predicts cardiovascular outcomes: A systematic review and meta-analysis of prospective studies. *European Heart Journal, 32*, 1484–1492. http://dx.doi.org/ 10.1093/eurheartj/ehr007

Carlson, L. E., & Garland, S. N. (2005). Impact of mindfulness-based stress reduction (MBSR) on sleep, mood, stress and fatigue symptoms in cancer outpatients. *International Journal of Behavioral Medicine, 12*, 278–285. http://dx.doi.org/10.1207/ s15327558ijbm1204_9

Carlson, L. E., Speca, M., Faris, P., & Patel, K. D. (2007). One year pre–post intervention follow-up of psychological, immune, endocrine and blood pressure outcomes of mindfulness-based stress reduction (MBSR) in breast and prostate cancer outpatients. *Brain, Behavior, and Immunity, 21*, 1038–1049. http://dx.doi.org/10.1016/ j.bbi.2007.04.002

Chambers, R., Gullone, E., & Allen, N. B. (2009). Mindful emotion regulation: An integrative review. *Clinical Psychology Review, 29*, 560–572. http://dx.doi.org/10.1016/ j.cpr.2009.06.005

Chemin, M., de Laat, J., & Haushofer, J. (2013, July). *Negative rainfall shocks increase levels of the stress hormone cortisol among poor farmers in Kenya* (Working paper). http:// dx.doi.org/10.2139/ssrn.2294171

Chen, E., Miller, G. E., Yu, T., & Brody, G. H. (2018). Unsupportive parenting moderates the effects of family psychosocial intervention on metabolic syndrome in African American youth. *International Journal of Obesity, 42*, 634–640. http://dx.doi.org/ 10.1038/ijo.2017.246

Chen, X., & Wang, Y. (2008). Tracking of blood pressure from childhood to adulthood: A systematic review and meta-regression analysis. *Circulation, 117*, 3171–3180. http://dx.doi.org/10.1161/CIRCULATIONAHA.107.730366

Chetty, R., Hendren, N., & Katz, L. F. (2016). The effects of exposure to better neighborhoods on children: New evidence from the Moving to Opportunity Experiment. *The American Economic Review, 106*, 855–902. http://dx.doi.org/10.1257/aer.20150572

Chiesa, A. (2013). The difficulty of defining mindfulness: Current thought and critical issues. *Mindfulness, 4*, 255–268. http://dx.doi.org/10.1007/s12671-012-0123-4

Chobanian, A. V., Bakris, G. L., Black, H. R., Cushman, W. C., Green, L. A., Izzo, J. L., Jr., . . . National High Blood Pressure Education Program Coordinating Committee. (2003). Seventh report of the Joint National Committee on Prevention, Detection, Evaluation, and Treatment of High Blood Pressure. *Hypertension, 42*, 1206–1252. http://dx.doi.org/10.1161/01.HYP.0000107251.49515.c2

Chrousos, G. P. (2009). Stress and disorders of the stress system. *Nature Reviews: Endocrinology, 5*, 374–381. http://dx.doi.org/10.1038/nrendo.2009.106

Cohen, S., Frank, E., Doyle, W. J., Skoner, D. P., Rabin, B. S., & Gwaltney, J. M., Jr. (1998). Types of stressors that increase susceptibility to the common cold in healthy adults. *Health Psychology, 17*, 214–223. http://dx.doi.org/10.1037/0278-6133.17.3.214

Coley, R. L., Leventhal, T., Lynch, A. D., & Kull, M. (2013). Relations between housing characteristics and the well-being of low-income children and adolescents. *Developmental Psychology, 49*, 1775–1789. http://dx.doi.org/10.1037/a0031033

Colhoun, H. M., Hemingway, H., & Poulter, N. R. (1998). Socio-economic status and blood pressure: An overview analysis. *Journal of Human Hypertension, 12*, 91–110. http://dx.doi.org/10.1038/sj.jhh.1000558

Conen, D., Glynn, R. J., Ridker, P. M., Buring, J. E., & Albert, M. A. (2009). Socio-economic status, blood pressure progression, and incident hypertension in a prospective cohort of female health professionals. *European Heart Journal, 30*, 1378–1384. http://dx.doi.org/10.1093/eurheartj/ehp072

Conger, K. J., Rueter, M. A., & Conger, R. D. (2000). The role of economic pressure in the lives of parents and their adolescents: The Family Stress Model. In L. J. Crockett & R. K. Silbereisen (Eds.), *Negotiating adolescence in times of social change* (pp. 201–223). Cambridge, England: Cambridge University Press.

Conger, R. D., Wallace, L. E., Sun, Y., Simons, R. L., McLoyd, V. C., & Brody, G. H. (2002). Economic pressure in African American families: A replication and extension of the family stress model. *Developmental Psychology, 38*, 179–193. http://dx.doi.org/10.1037/0012-1649.38.2.179

Connor, T. J., & Leonard, B. E. (1998). Depression, stress and immunological activation: The role of cytokines in depressive disorders. *Life Sciences, 62*, 583–606. http://dx.doi.org/10.1016/S0024-3205(97)00990-9

Creswell, J. D., Irwin, M. R., Burklund, L. J., Lieberman, M. D., Arevalo, J. M. G., Ma, J., . . . Cole, S. W. (2012). Mindfulness-based stress reduction training reduces loneliness and pro-inflammatory gene expression in older adults: A small randomized controlled trial. *Brain, Behavior, and Immunity, 26*, 1095–1101. http://dx.doi.org/10.1016/j.bbi.2012.07.006

Crowley, S. (2003). The affordable housing crisis: Residential mobility of poor families and school mobility of poor children. *The Journal of Negro Education, 72*, 22–38. http://dx.doi.org/10.2307/3211288

Dahl, R. E. (1996). The regulation of sleep and arousal: Development and psychopathology. *Development and Psychopathology, 8*, 3–27. http://dx.doi.org/10.1017/S0954579400006945

DeLuca, S., Clampet-Lundquist, S., & Edin, K. (2016). *Coming of age in the other America.* New York, NY: Russell Sage Foundation.

Den Hond, E., Celis, H., Vandenhoven, G., O'Brien, E., & Staessen, J. A. (2003). Determinants of white-coat syndrome assessed by ambulatory blood pressure or self-measured home blood pressure. *Blood Pressure Monitoring, 8*, 37–40. http://dx.doi.org/10.1097/00126097-200302000-00008

Desantis, A. S., Kuzawa, C. W., & Adam, E. K. (2015). Developmental origins of flatter cortisol rhythms: Socioeconomic status and adult cortisol activity. *American Journal of Human Biology, 27*, 458–467. http://dx.doi.org/10.1002/ajhb.22668

Dickerson, S. S., & Kemeny, M. E. (2004). Acute stressors and cortisol responses: A theoretical integration and synthesis of laboratory research. *Psychological Bulletin, 130*, 355–391. http://dx.doi.org/10.1037/0033-2909.130.3.355

Doane, L. D., & Adam, E. K. (2010). Loneliness and cortisol: Momentary, day-to-day, and trait associations. *Psychoneuroendocrinology, 35*, 430–441. http://dx.doi.org/10.1016/j.psyneuen.2009.08.005

Edin, K., & Lein, L. (1997). Work, welfare, and single mothers' economic survival strategies. *American Sociological Review, 62*, 253–266. http://dx.doi.org/10.2307/2657303

Elliott, W. J., & Black, H. R. (2007). Prehypertension. *Nature Reviews: Cardiology, 4*, 538–548. http://dx.doi.org/10.1038/ncpcardio0989

Esch, T. (2014). The neurobiology of meditation and mindfulness. In S. Schmidt & H. Walach (Eds.), *Meditation—Neuroscientific approaches and philosophical implications* (pp. 153–173). Heidelberg, Germany: Springer International. http://dx.doi.org/10.1007/978-3-319-01634-4_9

Evans, G. W., & English, K. (2002). The environment of poverty: Multiple stressor exposure, psychophysiological stress, and socioemotional adjustment. *Child Development, 73*, 1238–1248. http://dx.doi.org/10.1111/1467-8624.00469

Evans, P. D., Fredhoi, C., Loveday, C., Hucklebridge, F., Aitchison, E., Forte, D., & Clow, A. (2011). The diurnal cortisol cycle and cognitive performance in the healthy old. *International Journal of Psychophysiology, 79*, 371–377. http://dx.doi.org/10.1016/j.ijpsycho.2010.12.006

Evans, P. D., Hucklebridge, F., Loveday, C., & Clow, A. (2012). The cortisol awakening response is related to executive function in older age. *International Journal of Psychophysiology, 84*, 201–204. http://dx.doi.org/10.1016/j.ijpsycho.2012.02.008

Evans, W. N., & Garthwaite, C. L. (2010, August). *Giving mom a break: The impact of higher EITC payments on maternal health* (NBER Working Paper No. 16296). Cambridge, MA: NBER.

Everson-Rose, S. A., & Lewis, T. T. (2005). Psychosocial factors and cardiovascular diseases. *Annual Review of Public Health, 26*, 469–500. http://dx.doi.org/10.1146/annurev.publhealth.26.021304.144542

Fa, M., Xia, L., Anunu, R., Kehat, O., Kriebel, M., Volkmer, H., & Richter-Levin, G. (2014). Stress modulation of hippocampal activity—Spotlight on the dentate gyrus. *Neurobiology of Learning and Memory, 112*, 53–60. http://dx.doi.org/10.1016/j.nlm.2014.04.008

Falkner, B., Gidding, S. S., Portman, R., & Rosner, B. (2008). Blood pressure variability and classification of prehypertension and hypertension in adolescence. *Pediatrics, 122*, 238–242. http://dx.doi.org/10.1542/peds.2007-2776

Falkner, B., Lurbe, E., & Schaefer, F. (2010). High blood pressure in children: Clinical and health policy implications. *Journal of Clinical Hypertension, 12*, 261–276. http://dx.doi.org/10.1111/j.1751-7176.2009.00245.x

Fauth, R. C., Leventhal, T., & Brooks-Gunn, J. (2004). Short-term effects of moving from public housing in poor to middle-class neighborhoods on low-income, minority adults' outcomes. *Social Science & Medicine, 59*, 2271–2284. http://dx.doi.org/10.1016/j.socscimed.2004.03.020

Fauth, R. C., Leventhal, T., & Brooks-Gunn, J. (2008). Seven years later: Effects of a neighborhood mobility program on poor Black and Latino adults' well-being. *Journal of Health and Social Behavior, 49*, 119–130. http://dx.doi.org/10.1177/002214650804900201

Felitti, V. J., Anda, R. F., Nordenberg, D., Williamson, D. F., Spitz, A. M., Edwards, V., . . . Marks, J. S. (1998). Relationship of childhood abuse and household dysfunction to many of the leading causes of death in adults. *American Journal of Preventive Medicine, 14*, 245–258. http://dx.doi.org/10.1016/S0749-3797(98)00017-8

Fernald, L. C. H., & Gunnar, M. R. (2009). Poverty-alleviation program participation and salivary cortisol in very low-income children. *Social Science & Medicine, 68*, 2180–2189. http://dx.doi.org/10.1016/j.socscimed.2009.03.032

Fisher, D. B.-D., Serbin, L. A., Stack, D. M., Ruttle, P. L., Ledingham, J. E., & Schwartzman, A. E. (2007). Intergenerational predictors of diurnal cortisol secretion in early childhood. *Infant and Child Development, 16*, 151–170. http://dx.doi.org/10.1002/icd.474

Fisher, P. A., & Stoolmiller, M. (2008). Intervention effects on foster parent stress: Associations with child cortisol levels. *Development and Psychopathology, 20*, 1003–1021. http://dx.doi.org/10.1017/S0954579408000473

Fisher, P. A., Stoolmiller, M., Gunnar, M. R., & Burraston, B. O. (2007). Effects of a therapeutic intervention for foster preschoolers on diurnal cortisol activity. *Psychoneuroendocrinology, 32*, 892–905. http://dx.doi.org/10.1016/j.psyneuen.2007.06.008

Flynn, J. T., Kaelber, D. C., Baker-Smith, C. M., Blowey, D., Carroll, A. E., Daniels, S. R., . . . Subcommittee on Screening and Management of High Blood Pressure in Children. (2017). Clinical practice guideline for screening and management of high blood pressure in children and adolescents. *Pediatrics, 140*, e20171904. http://dx.doi.org/10.1542/peds.2017-1904

Franklin, S. S., & Mitchell, G. F. (2008). Aging, arterial function, and systolic hypertension. In J. L. Izzo, Jr., D. A. Sica, & H. R. Black (Eds.), *Hypertension primer* (4th ed., pp. 144–148). Philadelphia, PA: Lippincott, Williams, & Wilkins.

Fries, E., Hesse, J., Hellhammer, J., & Hellhammer, D. H. (2005). A new view on hypocortisolism. *Psychoneuroendocrinology, 30*, 1010–1016. http://dx.doi.org/10.1016/j.psyneuen.2005.04.006

Glaser, R., & Kiecolt-Glaser, J. K. (2005). Stress-induced immune dysfunction: Implications for health. *Nature Reviews: Immunology, 5*, 243–251. http://dx.doi.org/10.1038/nri1571

Glaser, R., Kiecolt-Glaser, J., Bonneau, R., Malarkey, W., Kennedy, S., & Hughes, J. (1992). Stress-induced modulation of the immune response to recombinant hepatitis B vaccine. *Psychosomatic Medicine, 54*, 22–29. http://dx.doi.org/10.1097/00006842-199201000-00005

Glaser, R., Kiecolt-Glaser, J. K., Speicher, C. E., & Holliday, J. E. (1985). Stress, loneliness, and changes in herpesvirus latency. *Journal of Behavioral Medicine, 8*, 249–260. http://dx.doi.org/10.1007/BF00870312

Gottlieb, D. J., Redline, S., Nieto, F. J., Baldwin, C. M., Newman, A. B., Resnick, H. E., & Punjabi, N. M. (2006). Association of usual sleep duration with hypertension: The Sleep Heart Health Study. *Sleep, 29*, 1009–1014. http://dx.doi.org/10.1093/sleep/29.8.1009

Graham, A. M., Pears, K. C., Kim, H. K., Bruce, J., & Fisher, P. A. (2018). Effects of a school readiness intervention on hypothalamus-pituitary-adrenal axis functioning and school adjustment for children in foster care. *Development and Psychopathology, 30*, 651–664. http://dx.doi.org/10.1017/S0954579417001171

Grant, K. E., Compas, B. E., Stuhlmacher, A. F., Thurm, A. E., McMahon, S. D., & Halpert, J. A. (2003). Stressors and child and adolescent psychopathology: Moving from markers to mechanisms of risk. *Psychological Bulletin, 129*, 447–466. http://dx.doi.org/10.1037/0033-2909.129.3.447

Grant, K. E., McMahon, S. D., Carter, J. S., Carleton, R. A., Adam, E. K., & Chen, E. (2014). The influence of stressors on the development of psychopathology. In M. Lewis & K. Randolph (Eds.), *Handbook of developmental psychopathology* (pp. 205–223). Boston, MA: Springer. http://dx.doi.org/10.1007/978-1-4614-9608-3_11

Gregoski, M. J., Barnes, V. A., Tingen, M. S., Harshfield, G. A., & Treiber, F. A. (2011). Breathing awareness meditation and LifeSkills Training programs influence upon ambulatory blood pressure and sodium excretion among African American adolescents. *Journal of Adolescent Health, 48,* 59–64. http://dx.doi.org/10.1016/j.jadohealth.2010.05.019

Gruenewald, T. L., Cohen, S., Matthews, K. A., Tracy, R., & Seeman, T. E. (2009). Association of socioeconomic status with inflammation markers in Black and White men and women in the Coronary Artery Risk Development in Young Adults (CARDIA) study. *Social Science & Medicine, 69,* 451–459. http://dx.doi.org/10.1016/j.socscimed.2009.05.018

Gunnar, M. R., & Vazquez, D. M. (2001). Low cortisol and a flattening of expected daytime rhythm: Potential indices of risk in human development. *Development and Psychopathology, 13,* 515–538. http://dx.doi.org/10.1017/S0954579401003066

Hale, L., & Do, D. P. (2007). Racial differences in self-reports of sleep duration in a population-based study. *Sleep, 30,* 1096–1103. http://dx.doi.org/10.1093/sleep/30.9.1096

Halfon, N., & Hochstein, M. (2002). Life Course Health Development: An integrated framework for developing health, policy, and research. *The Milbank Quarterly, 80,* 433–479, iii. http://dx.doi.org/10.1111/1468-0009.00019

Hankin, B. L., Badanes, L. S., Abela, J. R. Z., & Watamura, S. E. (2010). Hypothalamic–pituitary–adrenal axis dysregulation in dysphoric children and adolescents: Cortisol reactivity to psychosocial stress from preschool through middle adolescence. *Biological Psychiatry, 68,* 484–490. http://dx.doi.org/10.1016/j.biopsych.2010.04.004

Hanson, J. L., Gillmore, A. D., Yu, T., Holmes, C. J., Hallowell, E. S., Barton, A. W., . . . Brody, G. H. (2019). A family focused intervention influences hippocampal–prefrontal connectivity through gains in self-regulation. *Child Development, 90,* 1389–1401. http://dx.doi.org/10.1111/cdev.13154

Hanson, M. D., & Chen, E. (2010). Daily stress, cortisol, and sleep: The moderating role of childhood psychosocial environments. *Health Psychology, 29,* 394–402. http://dx.doi.org/10.1037/a0019879

Harris, A. R., Jennings, P. A., Katz, D. A., Abenavoli, R. M., & Greenberg, M. T. (2016). Promoting stress management and wellbeing in educators: Feasibility and efficacy of a school-based yoga and mindfulness intervention. *Mindfulness, 7,* 143–154. http://dx.doi.org/10.1007/s12671-015-0451-2

Haushofer, J., & Shapiro, J. (2016). The short-term impact of unconditional cash transfers to the poor: Experimental evidence from Kenya. *The Quarterly Journal of Economics, 131,* 1973–2042. http://dx.doi.org/10.1093/qje/qjw025

Heissel, J. A., Levy, D. J., & Adam, E. K. (2017). Stress, sleep, and performance on standardized tests: Understudied pathways to the achievement gap. *AERA Open.* http://dx.doi.org/10.1177/2332858417713488

Heissel, J. A., Sharkey, P. T., Torrats-Espinosa, G., Grant, K., & Adam, E. K. (2018). Violence and vigilance: The acute effects of community violent crime on sleep and cortisol. *Child Development, 89,* e323–e331. http://dx.doi.org/10.1111/cdev.12889

Hertzman, C. (2012). Putting the concept of biological embedding in historical perspective. *Proceedings of the National Academy of Sciences, 109,* 17160–17167. http://dx.doi.org/10.1073/pnas.1202203109

Hicken, M. T., Lee, H., Ailshire, J., Burgard, S. A., & Williams, D. R. (2013). "Every shut eye, ain't sleep": The role of racism-related vigilance in racial/ethnic disparities in sleep difficulty. *Race and Social Problems, 5,* 100–112. http://dx.doi.org/10.1007/s12552-013-9095-9

Hölzel, B. K., Carmody, J., Vangel, M., Congleton, C., Yerramsetti, S. M., Gard, T., & Lazar, S. W. (2011). Mindfulness practice leads to increases in regional brain gray matter density. *Psychiatry Research: Neuroimaging, 191*, 36–43. http://dx.doi.org/10.1016/j.pscychresns.2010.08.006

Hoynes, H. W., Schanzenbach, D. W., & Almond, D. (2012). Long run impacts of childhood access to the safety net. *American Economic Review, 106*, 903–934.

Hülsheger, U. R., Feinholdt, A., & Nübold, A. (2015). A low-dose mindfulness intervention and recovery from work: Effects on psychological detachment, sleep quality, and sleep duration. *Journal of Occupational and Organizational Psychology, 88*, 464–489. http://dx.doi.org/10.1111/joop.12115

Jackson, P. B., & Stewart, Q. T. (2003). A research agenda for the Black middle class: Work stress, survival strategies, and mental health. *Journal of Health and Social Behavior, 44*, 442–455. http://dx.doi.org/10.2307/1519789

Jankowski, K. F., Bruce, J., Beauchamp, K. G., Roos, L. E., Moore, W. E., III, & Fisher, P. A. (2017). Preliminary evidence of the impact of early childhood maltreatment and a preventive intervention on neural patterns of response inhibition in early adolescence. *Developmental Science, 20*, e12413. http://dx.doi.org/10.1111/desc.12413

Jevning, R., Wilson, A. F., & Davidson, J. M. (1978). Adrenocortical activity during meditation. *Hormones and Behavior, 10*, 54–60. http://dx.doi.org/10.1016/0018-506X(78)90024-7

Johnson, S. B., Riis, J. L., & Noble, K. G. (2016). State of the art review: Poverty and the developing brain. *Pediatrics, 137*, e20153075. http://dx.doi.org/10.1542/peds.2015-3075

Kabat-Zinn, J. (2005). *Wherever you go, there you are: Mindfulness meditation in everyday life.* New York, NY: Hachette Books.

Kaczmarek, M., Stawinska-Witoszynska, B., Krzyzaniak, A., Krzywinska-Wiewiorowska, M., & Siwinska, A. (2015). Who is at higher risk of hypertension? Socioeconomic status differences in blood pressure among Polish adolescents: A population-based ADOPOLNOR study. *European Journal of Pediatrics, 174*, 1461–1473. http://dx.doi.org/10.1007/s00431-015-2554-0

Keene, D. E., & Geronimus, A. T. (2011). "Weathering" HOPE VI: The importance of evaluating the population health impact of public housing demolition and displacement. *Journal of Urban Health, 88*, 417–435. http://dx.doi.org/10.1007/s11524-011-9582-5

Keller, S. E., Shiflett, S. C., Schleifer, S. J., & Bartlett, J. A. (1994). Stress, immunity, and health. In R. Glaser & J. K. Kiecolt-Glaser (Eds.), *Handbook of human stress and immunity* (pp. 217–244). San Diego, CA: Academic Press. http://dx.doi.org/10.1016/B978-0-12-285960-1.50013-7

Kiecolt-Glaser, J. K., McGuire, L., Robles, T. F., & Glaser, R. (2002). Psychoneuroimmunology: Psychological influences on immune function and health. *Journal of Consulting and Clinical Psychology, 70*, 537–547. http://dx.doi.org/10.1037/0022-006X.70.3.537

Kiecolt-Glaser, J. K., Page, G. G., Marucha, P. T., MacCallum, R. C., & Glaser, R. (1998). Psychological influences on surgical recovery. Perspectives from psychoneuroimmunology. *American Psychologist, 53*, 1209–1218. http://dx.doi.org/10.1037/0003-066X.53.11.1209

Kimm, S. Y., Glynn, N. W., Obarzanek, E., Kriska, A. M., Daniels, S. R., Barton, B. A., & Liu, K. (2005). Relation between the changes in physical activity and body-mass index during adolescence: A multicentre longitudinal study. *Lancet, 366*, 301–307. http://dx.doi.org/10.1016/S0140-6736(05)66837-7

Kirschbaum, C., & Hellhammer, D. H. (1989). Salivary cortisol in psychobiological research: An overview. *Neuropsychobiology, 22*, 150–169. http://dx.doi.org/10.1159/000118611

Kling, J. R., Liebman, J. B., & Katz, L. F. (2007). Experimental analysis of neighborhood effects. *Econometrica, 75*, 83–119. http://dx.doi.org/10.1111/j.1468-0262.2007.00733.x

Kuzawa, C. W., & Sweet, E. (2009). Epigenetics and the embodiment of race: Developmental origins of U.S. racial disparities in cardiovascular health. *American Journal of Human Biology, 21*, 2–15. http://dx.doi.org/10.1002/ajhb.20822

Lande, M. B., Adams, H., Falkner, B., Waldstein, S. R., Schwartz, G. J., Szilagyi, P. G., . . . Palumbo, D. (2009). Parental assessments of internalizing and externalizing behavior and executive function in children with primary hypertension. *The Journal of Pediatrics, 154*, 207–212.e1. http://dx.doi.org/10.1016/j.jpeds.2008.08.017

Lande, M. B., Kaczorowski, J. M., Auinger, P., Schwartz, G. J., & Weitzman, M. (2003). Elevated blood pressure and decreased cognitive function among school-age children and adolescents in the United States. *The Journal of Pediatrics, 143*, 720–724. http://dx.doi.org/10.1067/S0022-3476(03)00412-8

Landsbergis, P. A., Schnall, P. L., Pickering, T. G., Warren, K., & Schwartz, J. E. (2003). Lower socioeconomic status among men in relation to the association between job strain and blood pressure. *Scandinavian Journal of Work, Environment & Health, 29*, 206–215. http://dx.doi.org/10.5271/sjweh.723

Lane, J. D., Seskevich, J. E., & Pieper, C. F. (2007). Brief meditation training can improve perceived stress and negative mood. *Alternative Therapies in Health and Medicine, 13*, 38–44.

Lauderdale, D. S., Knutson, K. L., Yan, L. L., Rathouz, P. J., Hulley, S. B., Sidney, S., & Liu, K. (2006). Objectively measured sleep characteristics among early-middle-aged adults: The CARDIA study. *American Journal of Epidemiology, 164*, 5–16. http://dx.doi.org/10.1093/aje/kwj199

Leng, B., Jin, Y., Li, G., Chen, L., & Jin, N. (2015). Socioeconomic status and hypertension: A meta-analysis. *Journal of Hypertension, 33*, 221–229. http://dx.doi.org/10.1097/HJH.0000000000000428

Levinson, S., Liu, K., Stamler, J., Stamler, R., Whipple, I., Ausbrook, D., & Berkson, D. (1985). Ethnic differences in blood pressure and heart rate of Chicago school children. *American Journal of Epidemiology, 122*, 366–377. http://dx.doi.org/10.1093/oxfordjournals.aje.a114117

Levy, D. J., Heissel, J. A., Richeson, J. A., & Adam, E. K. (2016). Psychological and biological responses to race-based social stress as pathways to disparities in educational outcomes. *American Psychologist, 71*, 455–473. http://dx.doi.org/10.1037/a0040322

Linkowski, P., Van Onderbergen, A., Kerkhofs, M., Bosson, D., Mendlewicz, J., & Van Cauter, E. (1993). Twin study of the 24-h cortisol profile: Evidence for genetic control of the human circadian clock. *The American Journal of Physiology, Endocrinology and Metabolism, 264*, E173–E181. http://dx.doi.org/10.1152/ajpendo.1993.264.2.E173

Lopez-Duran, N. L., Kovacs, M., & George, C. J. (2009). Hypothalamic–pituitary–adrenal axis dysregulation in depressed children and adolescents: A meta-analysis. *Psychoneuroendocrinology, 34*, 1272–1283. http://dx.doi.org/10.1016/j.psyneuen.2009.03.016

Lovallo, W. R. (2016). *Stress and health: Biological and psychological interactions* (3rd ed.). Thousand Oaks, CA: Sage.

Luby, J. L., Barch, D. M., Belden, A., Gaffrey, M. S., Tillman, R., Babb, C., . . . Botteron, K. N. (2012). Maternal support in early childhood predicts larger hippocampal volumes at school age. *Proceedings of the National Academy of Sciences, 109*, 2854–2859. http://dx.doi.org/10.1073/pnas.1118003109

Ludwig, J., Sanbonmatsu, L., Gennetian, L., Adam, E., Duncan, G. J., Katz, L. F., . . . McDade, T. W. (2011). Neighborhoods, obesity, and diabetes—A randomized social experiment. *The New England Journal of Medicine, 365*, 1509–1519. http://dx.doi.org/10.1056/NEJMsa1103216

Luecken, L. J., Hagan, M. J., Sandler, I. N., Tein, J. Y., Ayers, T. S., & Wolchik, S. A. (2010). Cortisol levels six-years after participation in the Family Bereavement Program. *Psychoneuroendocrinology, 35,* 785–789. http://dx.doi.org/10.1016/j.psyneuen. 2009.11.002

Lumeng, J. C., Somashekar, D., Appugliese, D., Kaciroti, N., Corwyn, R. F., & Bradley, R. H. (2007). Shorter sleep duration is associated with increased risk for being overweight at ages 9 to 12 years. *Pediatrics, 120,* 1020–1029. http://dx.doi.org/ 10.1542/peds.2006-3295

Lupien, S. J., King, S., Meaney, M. J., & McEwen, B. S. (2001). Can poverty get under your skin? Basal cortisol levels and cognitive function in children from low and high socioeconomic status. *Development and Psychopathology, 13,* 653–676. http:// dx.doi.org/10.1017/S0954579401003133

Lupien, S. J., McEwen, B. S., Gunnar, M. R., & Heim, C. (2009). Effects of stress throughout the lifespan on the brain, behaviour and cognition. *Nature Reviews: Neuroscience, 10,* 434–445. http://dx.doi.org/10.1038/nrn2639

Lupien, S. J., Ouellet-Morin, I., Trépanier, L., Juster, R. P., Marin, M. F., Francois, N., . . . Plusquellec, P. (2013). The DeStress for Success Program: Effects of a stress education program on cortisol levels and depressive symptomatology in adolescents making the transition to high school. *Neuroscience, 249,* 74–87. http://dx.doi.org/ 10.1016/j.neuroscience.2013.01.057

Lusardi, P., Zoppi, A., Preti, P., Pesce, R. M., Piazza, E., & Fogari, R. (1999). Effects of insufficient sleep on blood pressure in hypertensive patients: A 24-h study. *American Journal of Hypertension, 12,* 63–68. http://dx.doi.org/10.1016/S0895-7061(98)00200-3

MacLean, C. R. K., Walton, K. G., Wenneberg, S. R., Levitsky, D. K., Mandarino, J. P., Waziri, R., . . . Schneider, R. H. (1997). Effects of the Transcendental Meditation program on adaptive mechanisms: Changes in hormone levels and responses to stress after 4 months of practice. *Psychoneuroendocrinology, 22,* 277–295. http:// dx.doi.org/10.1016/S0306-4530(97)00003-6

Maes, M., Ombelet, W., De Jongh, R., Kenis, G., & Bosmans, E. (2001). The inflammatory response following delivery is amplified in women who previously suffered from major depression, suggesting that major depression is accompanied by a sensitization of the inflammatory response system. *Journal of Affective Disorders, 63,* 85–92. http://dx.doi.org/10.1016/S0165-0327(00)00156-7

Maier, S. F. (2003). Bi-directional immune–brain communication: Implications for understanding stress, pain, and cognition. *Brain, Behavior, and Immunity, 17,* 69–85. http:// dx.doi.org/10.1016/S0889-1591(03)00032-1

Malarkey, W. B., Jarjoura, D., & Klatt, M. (2013). Workplace based mindfulness practice and inflammation: A randomized trial. *Brain, Behavior, and Immunity, 27,* 145–154. http://dx.doi.org/10.1016/j.bbi.2012.10.009

Mancia, G., Sega, R., Bravi, C., Vito, G., Valagussa, F., Cesana, G., & Zanchetti, A. (1995). Ambulatory blood pressure normality: Results from the PAMELA study. *Journal of Hypertension, 13,* 1377–1390. http://dx.doi.org/10.1097/00004872-199512000-00003

McEwen, B. S. (1998). Protective and damaging effects of stress mediators. *The New England Journal of Medicine, 338,* 171–179. http://dx.doi.org/10.1056/ NEJM199801153380307

McEwen, B. S. (2004). Protection and damage from acute and chronic stress: Allostasis and allostatic overload and relevance to the pathophysiology of psychiatric disorders. *Annals of the New York Academy of Sciences, 1032,* 1–7. http://dx.doi.org/ 10.1196/annals.1314.001

McEwen, B. S. (2006). Sleep deprivation as a neurobiologic and physiologic stressor: Allostasis and allostatic load. *Metabolism: Clinical and Experimental, 55*(10, Suppl. 2), S20–S23. http://dx.doi.org/10.1016/j.metabol.2006.07.008

McEwen, B. S. (2012). Brain on stress: How the social environment gets under the skin. *Proceedings of the National Academy of Sciences, 109*, 17180–17185. http://dx.doi.org/10.1073/pnas.1121254109

McEwen, B. S., & Seeman, T. (1999). Protective and damaging effects of mediators of stress. Elaborating and testing the concepts of allostasis and allostatic load. *Annals of the New York Academy of Sciences, 896*, 30–47. http://dx.doi.org/10.1111/j.1749-6632.1999.tb08103.x

McGrath, J. J., Matthews, K. A., & Brady, S. S. (2006). Individual versus neighborhood socioeconomic status and race as predictors of adolescent ambulatory blood pressure and heart rate. *Social Science & Medicine, 63*, 1442–1453. http://dx.doi.org/10.1016/j.socscimed.2006.03.019

McKim, D. B., Niraula, A., Tarr, A. J., Wohleb, E. S., Sheridan, J. F., & Godbout, J. P. (2016). Neuroinflammatory dynamics underlie memory impairments after repeated social defeat. *The Journal of Neuroscience, 36*, 2590–2604. http://dx.doi.org/10.1523/JNEUROSCI.2394-15.2016

Meier-Ewert, H. K., Ridker, P. M., Rifai, N., Regan, M. M., Price, N. J., Dinges, D. F., & Mullington, J. M. (2004). Effect of sleep loss on C-reactive protein, an inflammatory marker of cardiovascular risk. *Journal of the American College of Cardiology, 43*, 678–683. http://dx.doi.org/10.1016/j.jacc.2003.07.050

Miller, G., Chen, E., & Cole, S. W. (2009). Health psychology: Developing biologically plausible models linking the social world and physical health. *Annual Review of Psychology, 60*, 501–524. http://dx.doi.org/10.1146/annurev.psych.60.110707.163551

Miller, G. E., Brody, G. H., Yu, T., & Chen, E. (2014). A family-oriented psychosocial intervention reduces inflammation in low-SES African American youth. *Proceedings of the National Academy of Sciences, 111*, 11287–11292. http://dx.doi.org/10.1073/pnas.1406578111

Miller, G. E., & Chen, E. (2013). The biological residue of childhood poverty. *Child Development Perspectives, 7*, 67–73. http://dx.doi.org/10.1111/cdep.12021

Miller, G. E., Chen, E., & Parker, K. J. (2011). Psychological stress in childhood and susceptibility to the chronic diseases of aging: Moving toward a model of behavioral and biological mechanisms. *Psychological Bulletin, 137*, 959–997. http://dx.doi.org/10.1037/a0024768

Miller, G. E., Cohen, S., & Ritchey, A. K. (2002). Chronic psychological stress and the regulation of pro-inflammatory cytokines: A glucocorticoid-resistance model. *Health Psychology, 21*, 531–541. http://dx.doi.org/10.1037/0278-6133.21.6.531

Muntner, P., He, J., Cutler, J. A., Wildman, R. P., & Whelton, P. K. (2004). Trends in blood pressure among children and adolescents. *JAMA, 291*, 2107–2113. http://dx.doi.org/10.1001/jama.291.17.2107

Nelson, E. M., & Spieker, S. J. (2013). Intervention effects on morning and stimulated cortisol responses among toddlers in foster care. *Infant Mental Health Journal, 34*, 211–221. http://dx.doi.org/10.1002/imhj.21382

Nidich, S. I., Rainforth, M. V., Haaga, D. A., Hagelin, J., Salerno, J. W., Travis, F., . . . Schneider, R. H. (2009). A randomized controlled trial on effects of the Transcendental Meditation program on blood pressure, psychological distress, and coping in young adults. *American Journal of Hypertension, 22*, 1326–1331. http://dx.doi.org/10.1038/ajh.2009.184

Pager, D., Bonikowski, B., & Western, B. (2009). Discrimination in a low-wage labor market: A field experiment. *American Sociological Review, 74*, 777–799. http://dx.doi.org/10.1177/000312240907400505

Pager, D., & Shepherd, H. (2008). The sociology of discrimination: Racial discrimination in employment, housing, credit, and consumer markets. *Annual Review of Sociology, 34*, 181–209. http://dx.doi.org/10.1146/annurev.soc.33.040406.131740

Pagliaccio, D., Luby, J. L., Bogdan, R., Agrawal, A., Gaffrey, M. S., Belden, A. C., . . . Barch, D. M. (2014). Stress-system genes and life stress predict cortisol levels and amygdala and hippocampal volumes in children. *Neuropsychopharmacology, 39,* 1245–1253. http://dx.doi.org/10.1038/npp.2013.327

Pickering, T. G. (2001). Mental stress as a causal factor in the development of hypertension and cardiovascular disease. *Current Hypertension Reports, 3,* 249–254. http://dx.doi.org/10.1007/s11906-001-0047-1

Pickering, T. G., Shimbo, D., & Haas, D. (2006). Ambulatory blood-pressure monitoring. *The New England Journal of Medicine, 354,* 2368–2374. http://dx.doi.org/10.1056/NEJMra060433

Pollak, S. D., Nelson, C. A., Schlaak, M. F., Roeber, B. J., Wewerka, S. S., Wiik, K. L., . . . Gunnar, M. R. (2010). Neurodevelopmental effects of early deprivation in postinstitutionalized children. *Child Development, 81,* 224–236. http://dx.doi.org/10.1111/j.1467-8624.2009.01391.x

Rabin, B. S. (1999). *Stress, immune function, and health: The connection.* New York, NY: Wiley-Liss.

Rachal Pugh, C., Fleshner, M., Watkins, L. R., Maier, S. F., & Rudy, J. W. (2001). The immune system and memory consolidation: A role for the cytokine IL-1beta. *Neuroscience and Biobehavioral Reviews, 25,* 29–41. http://dx.doi.org/10.1016/S0149-7634(00)00048-8

Rainisch, B. K. W., & Upchurch, D. M. (2013). Sociodemographic correlates of allostatic load among a national sample of adolescents: Findings from the National Health and Nutrition Examination Survey, 1999–2008. *Journal of Adolescent Health, 53,* 506–511. http://dx.doi.org/10.1016/j.jadohealth.2013.04.020

Reiche, E. M. V., Nunes, S. O. V., & Morimoto, H. K. (2004). Stress, depression, the immune system, and cancer. *The Lancet: Oncology, 5,* 617–625. http://dx.doi.org/10.1016/S1470-2045(04)01597-9

Rivas-Drake, D., Syed, M., Umaña-Taylor, A., Markstrom, C., French, S., Schwartz, S. J., . . . Ethnic and Racial Identity in the 21st Century Study Group. (2014). Feeling good, happy, and proud: A meta-analysis of positive ethnic–racial affect and adjustment. *Child Development, 85,* 77–102. http://dx.doi.org/10.1111/cdev.12175

Rohleder, N., Beulen, S. E., Chen, E., Wolf, J. M., & Kirschbaum, C. (2007). Stress on the dance floor: The cortisol stress response to social-evaluative threat in competitive ballroom dancers. *Personality and Social Psychology Bulletin, 33,* 69–84. http://dx.doi.org/10.1177/0146167206293986

Rosner, B., Cook, N. R., Daniels, S., & Falkner, B. (2013). Childhood blood pressure trends and risk factors for high blood pressure: The NHANES Experience 1988–2008. *Hypertension, 62,* 247–254. http://dx.doi.org/10.1161/HYPERTENSIONAHA.111.00831

Rozanski, A., Blumenthal, J. A., & Kaplan, J. (1999). Impact of psychological factors on the pathogenesis of cardiovascular disease and implications for therapy. *Circulation, 99,* 2192–2217. http://dx.doi.org/10.1161/01.CIR.99.16.2192

Sadeh, A. (1996). Stress, trauma, and sleep in children. *Child and Adolescent Psychiatric Clinics of North America, 5,* 685–700. http://dx.doi.org/10.1016/S1056-4993(18)30356-0

Sadeh, A. (2007). Consequences of sleep loss or sleep disruption in children. *Sleep Medicine Clinics, 2,* 513–520. http://dx.doi.org/10.1016/j.jsmc.2007.05.012

Sadeh, A., Gruber, R., & Raviv, A. (2003). The effects of sleep restriction and extension on school-age children: What a difference an hour makes. *Child Development, 74,* 444–455. http://dx.doi.org/10.1111/1467-8624.7402008

Sadeh, A., Raviv, A., & Gruber, R. (2000). Sleep patterns and sleep disruptions in school-age children. *Developmental Psychology, 36,* 291–301. http://dx.doi.org/10.1037/0012-1649.36.3.291

Sanbonmatsu, L., Ludwig, J., Katz, L. F., Gennetian, L. A., Duncan, G. J., Kessler, R. C., . . . Lindau, S. T. (2011, November). *Moving to Opportunity for fair housing demonstration program: Final impacts evaluation.* Washington, DC: U.S. Department of Housing and Urban Development, Office of Policy Development and Research.

Schmeer, K. K., & Tarrence, J. (2018). Racial–ethnic disparities in inflammation: Evidence of weathering in childhood? *Journal of Health and Social Behavior, 59,* 411–428. http://dx.doi.org/10.1177/0022146518784592

Schmeer, K. K., & Yoon, A. (2016). Socioeconomic status inequalities in low-grade inflammation during childhood. *Archives of Disease in Childhood, 101,* 1043–1047. http://dx.doi.org/10.1136/archdischild-2016-310837

Schmidt-Reinwald, A., Pruessner, J. C., Hellhammer, D. H., Federenko, I., Rohleder, N., Schürmeyer, T. H., & Kirschbaum, C. (1999). The cortisol response to awakening in relation to different challenge tests and a 12-hour cortisol rhythm. *Life Sciences, 64,* 1653–1660. http://dx.doi.org/10.1016/S0024-3205(99)00103-4

Schnall, P. L., Schwartz, J. E., Landsbergis, P. A., Warren, K., & Pickering, T. G. (1992). Relation between job strain, alcohol, and ambulatory blood pressure. *Hypertension, 19,* 488–494. http://dx.doi.org/10.1161/01.HYP.19.5.488

Schonert-Reichl, K. A., Oberle, E., Lawlor, M. S., Abbott, D., Thomson, K., Oberlander, T. F., & Diamond, A. (2015). Enhancing cognitive and social-emotional development through a simple-to-administer mindfulness-based school program for elementary school children: A randomized controlled trial. *Developmental Psychology, 51,* 52–66. http://dx.doi.org/10.1037/a0038454

Segerstrom, S. C., & Miller, G. E. (2004). Psychological stress and the human immune system: A meta-analytic study of 30 years of inquiry. *Psychological Bulletin, 130,* 601–630. http://dx.doi.org/10.1037/0033-2909.130.4.601

Sharkey, P., & Faber, J. W. (2014). Where, when, why, and for whom do residential contexts matter? Moving away from the dichotomous understanding of neighborhood effects. *Annual Review of Sociology, 40,* 559–579. http://dx.doi.org/10.1146/annurev-soc-071913-043350

Shirtcliff, E. A., & Essex, M. J. (2008). Concurrent and longitudinal associations of basal and diurnal cortisol with mental health symptoms in early adolescence. *Developmental Psychobiology, 50,* 690–703. http://dx.doi.org/10.1002/dev.20336

Shonkoff, J. P., Boyce, W. T., & McEwen, B. S. (2009). Neuroscience, molecular biology, and the childhood roots of health disparities: Building a new framework for health promotion and disease prevention. *JAMA, 301,* 2252–2259. http://dx.doi.org/10.1001/jama.2009.754

Shonkoff, J. P., Garner, A. S., Siegel, B. S., Dobbins, M. I., Earls, M. F., McGuinn, L., . . . Wegner, L. M. (2012). The lifelong effects of early childhood adversity and toxic stress. *Pediatrics, 129,* e232–e246. http://dx.doi.org/10.1542/peds.2011-2663

Sieverdes, J. C., Mueller, M., Gregoski, M. J., Brunner-Jackson, B., McQuade, L., Matthews, C., & Treiber, F. A. (2014). Effects of Hatha yoga on blood pressure, salivary α-amylase, and cortisol function among normotensive and prehypertensive youth. *Journal of Alternative and Complementary Medicine, 20,* 241–250. http://dx.doi.org/10.1089/acm.2013.0139

Snell, E. K., Adam, E. K., & Duncan, G. J. (2007). Sleep and the body mass index and overweight status of children and adolescents. *Child Development, 78,* 309–323. http://dx.doi.org/10.1111/j.1467-8624.2007.00999.x

Spruill, T. M. (2010). Chronic psychosocial stress and hypertension. *Current Hypertension Reports, 12,* 10–16. http://dx.doi.org/10.1007/s11906-009-0084-8

Stalder, T., Evans, P., Hucklebridge, F., & Clow, A. (2010). Associations between psychosocial state variables and the cortisol awakening response in a single case study. *Psychoneuroendocrinology, 35,* 209–214. http://dx.doi.org/10.1016/j.psyneuen.2009.06.006

Stalder, T., Hucklebridge, F., Evans, P., & Clow, A. (2009). Use of a single case study design to examine state variation in the cortisol awakening response: Relationship with time of awakening. *Psychoneuroendocrinology, 34,* 607–614. http://dx.doi.org/10.1016/j.psyneuen.2008.10.023

Sudsuang, R., Chentanez, V., & Veluvan, K. (1991). Effect of Buddhist meditation on serum cortisol and total protein levels, blood pressure, pulse rate, lung volume and reaction time. *Physiology & Behavior, 50,* 543–548. http://dx.doi.org/10.1016/0031-9384(91)90543-W

Szanton, S. L., Gill, J. M., & Allen, J. K. (2005). Allostatic load: A mechanism of socioeconomic health disparities? *Biological Research for Nursing, 7,* 7–15. http://dx.doi.org/10.1177/1099800405278216

Teicher, M. H., Anderson, C. M., & Polcari, A. (2012). Childhood maltreatment is associated with reduced volume in the hippocampal subfields CA3, dentate gyrus, and subiculum. *Proceedings of the National Academy of Sciences, 109,* E563–E572. http://dx.doi.org/10.1073/pnas.1115396109

Thayer, Z. M., & Kuzawa, C. W. (2015). Ethnic discrimination predicts poor self-rated health and cortisol in pregnancy: Insights from New Zealand. *Social Science & Medicine, 128,* 36–42. http://dx.doi.org/10.1016/j.socscimed.2015.01.003

Thomas, K. S., Bardwell, W. A., Ancoli-Israel, S., & Dimsdale, J. E. (2006). The toll of ethnic discrimination on sleep architecture and fatigue. *Health Psychology, 25,* 635–642. http://dx.doi.org/10.1037/0278-6133.25.5.635

Tomfohr, L., Pung, M. A., Edwards, K. M., & Dimsdale, J. E. (2012). Racial differences in sleep architecture: The role of ethnic discrimination. *Biological Psychology, 89,* 34–38. http://dx.doi.org/10.1016/j.biopsycho.2011.09.002

Turakitwanakan, W., Mekseepralard, C., & Busarakumtragul, P. (2013). Effects of mindfulness meditation on serum cortisol of medical students. *Journal of the Medical Association of Thailand, 96,* S90–S95.

Uchino, B. N., Cacioppo, J. T., & Kiecolt-Glaser, J. K. (1996). The relationship between social support and physiological processes: A review with emphasis on underlying mechanisms and implications for health. *Psychological Bulletin, 119,* 488–531. http://dx.doi.org/10.1037/0033-2909.119.3.488

Umaña-Taylor, A. J., & Douglass, S. (2017). Developing an ethnic–racial identity intervention from a developmental perspective: Process, content, and implementation of the Identity Project. In N. J. Cabrera & B. Leyendecker (Eds.), *Handbook on positive development of minority children and youth* (pp. 437–453). Cham, Switzerland: Springer International. http://dx.doi.org/10.1007/978-3-319-43645-6_26

Umaña-Taylor, A. J., Douglass, S., Updegraff, K. A., & Marsiglia, F. F. (2018). A small-scale randomized efficacy trial of the Identity Project: Promoting adolescents' ethnic–racial identity exploration and resolution. *Child Development, 89,* 862–870. http://dx.doi.org/10.1111/cdev.12755

Umaña-Taylor, A. J., Kornienko, O., Douglass Bayless, S., & Updegraff, K. A. (2018). A universal intervention program increases ethnic–racial identity exploration and resolution to predict adolescent psychosocial functioning one year later. *Journal of Youth and Adolescence, 47,* 1–15. http://dx.doi.org/10.1007/s10964-017-0766-5

Vrijkotte, T. G. M., van Doornen, L. J. P., & de Geus, E. J. C. (2000). Effects of work stress on ambulatory blood pressure, heart rate, and heart rate variability. *Hypertension, 35,* 880–886. http://dx.doi.org/10.1161/01.HYP.35.4.880

Whitacre, C. C., Cummings, S. O., & Griffin, A. C. (1994). The effects of stress on autoimmune disease. In R. Glaser & J. K. Kliecolt-Glaser (Eds.), *Handbook of human stress and immunity* (pp. 77–100). San Diego, CA: Academic Press. http://dx.doi.org/10.1016/B978-0-12-285960-1.50008-3

World Health Organization. (2019, September). *Hypertension* (Fact sheet). Geneva, Switzerland: Author. Retrieved from https://www.who.int/news-room/fact-sheets/detail/hypertension

Wühl, E., Witte, K., Soergel, M., Mehls, O., & Schaefer, F. (2002). Distribution of 24-h ambulatory blood pressure in children: Normalized reference values and role of body dimensions. *Journal of Hypertension, 20,* 1995–2007. http://dx.doi.org/10.1097/00004872-200210000-00019

Yang, E. V., & Glaser, R. (2002). Stress-induced immunomodulation and the implications for health. *International Immunopharmacology, 2*, 315–324. http://dx.doi.org/10.1016/S1567-5769(01)00182-5

Zeiders, K. H., Causadias, J. M., & White, R. M. B. (2018). The health correlates of culture: Examining the association between ethnic–racial identity and diurnal cortisol slopes. *Journal of Adolescent Health, 62*, 349–351. http://dx.doi.org/10.1016/j.jadohealth.2017.09.020

Zeiders, K. H., Doane, L. D., & Roosa, M. W. (2012). Perceived discrimination and diurnal cortisol: Examining relations among Mexican American adolescents. *Hormones and Behavior, 61*, 541–548. http://dx.doi.org/10.1016/j.yhbeh.2012.01.018

Zeiders, K. H., Hoyt, L. T., & Adam, E. K. (2014). Associations between self-reported discrimination and diurnal cortisol rhythms among young adults: The moderating role of racial–ethnic minority status. *Psychoneuroendocrinology, 50*, 280–288. http://dx.doi.org/10.1016/j.psyneuen.2014.08.023

2

Does the WIC Program Promote Equality of Opportunity in Early Life?

Janet Currie and Maya Rossin-Slater

A growing body of evidence shows that early-life health has consequences for long-term health, human capital development, and economic outcomes (Almond & Currie, 2011; Almond, Currie, & Duque, 2018; Barker, 1990). Hence, public programs targeting fetal and early-childhood health can be important investments into population well-being, the value of which may not fully materialize for many years. Moreover, social safety-net programs that serve young children in disadvantaged households may be critical for reducing the persistence of inequality in health at birth over the life cycle and across generations (Aizer & Currie, 2014; Chen, Oster, & Williams, 2016; Chetty et al., 2016; Currie, 2011), fostering equality of opportunity. It is possible that social investments in young children are responsible for the facts that infant mortality has fallen from 9.2 deaths per 1,000 births in 1990 to 5.8 in 2017 and that African American rates of infant mortality, although still roughly twice as high as non–African American rates, have fallen even more rapidly. However, despite these investments, and despite the United States being one of the richest countries in the world, the United States is still in 56th place among the 225 countries with infant mortality data reported in the Central Intelligence Agency World Factbook (U.S. Central Intelligence Agency, 2017). America's health disadvantage remains particularly acute for minority and low socioeconomic status groups. For instance, the 2017 rate of low birth weight among singleton non-Hispanic Black infants in the

http://dx.doi.org/10.1037/0000187-003
Confronting Inequality: How Policies and Practices Shape Children's Opportunities, edited by L. Tach, R. Dunifon, and D. L. Miller

United States is 11.4%, which is higher than the rate reported for national averages in many developing countries in Africa, Asia, and South America.[1]

These sobering statistics beg the question of whether U.S. social programs are effectively addressing the needs of the most vulnerable pregnant women and children. The federal Special Supplemental Nutrition Program for Women, Infants, and Children (WIC) is the largest U.S. safety-net program that explicitly targets the nutrition and health of low-income pregnant and postpartum women and children below the age of 5 years. Originally implemented in the 1970s, WIC provides participants with monthly vouchers for nutritious food packages from local grocery stores, along with basic medical checkups, health education, and referrals to other social service agencies. Annual expenditure on WIC was $5.6 billion in 2017, and, in September 2017, it served approximately 1.7 million women, 1.8 million infants, and 3.9 million children (U.S. Department of Agriculture, Food and Nutrition Service, 2019).

Is WIC an effective investment into early-life health among poor children, and does it promote equality of opportunity? And if so, how could it be improved to do even more? To address these questions, we begin by providing background information about the WIC program. We then review the extensive literature on the impacts of WIC on infant health, focusing on more recent studies with research designs that can better distinguish causation from correlation (for other recent reviews of early childhood and nutrition policies in the United States that include summaries of research on WIC, see Currie & Rossin-Slater, 2015; Hoynes & Whitmore Schanzenbach, 2016; Rossin-Slater, 2015). We next discuss the structure of the program in more detail, identifying some issues that can limit WIC's cost-effectiveness and program access.

We conclude by describing current knowledge gaps in the evidence on WIC and pointing to directions for future research. Briefly, we find overwhelming evidence that prenatal "WIC works" to promote infant health at birth and close health gaps between the rich and poor. However, we still know little about why WIC works for infants. And there are virtually no studies with a rigorous research design that examine the impact of WIC for older children or for their mothers. Hence, there is a great deal left to learn about WIC, and the possibility exists that the program could be improved to do even more to promote maternal, infant, and child health in the United States.

---

[1]*Low birth weight* is defined as less than 2,500 g. For recent data on low birth-weight rates by race/ethnicity in the United States, see Womack, Rossen, and Martin (2018). For data on low birth-weight rates around the world, see UNICEF (2014). It is important to note that reporting is incomplete in many countries, and that there may be differences in the way that a live birth is defined, which could impact comparisons across countries.

BACKGROUND INFORMATION ABOUT THE WIC PROGRAM

WIC is a supplemental feeding program for pregnant and postpartum women, infants, and children up to the age of 5 years. In addition to belonging to one of these groups, a WIC participant must either have income less than 185% of the federal poverty line or must have Medicaid coverage (available to pregnant women with incomes less than 200%–300% of the federal poverty line, depending on the state). Because Medicaid has expanded to cover almost half of all births in the United States, the program has a potentially very large reach. For instance, in New York, the threshold for WIC eligibility was about $38,000 for a family of three in 2012, while the median household income in New York was $47,680 (Burnett, 2014). The income cutoff for WIC is the same as for the Supplemental Nutrition Assistance Program (SNAP; formerly known as Food Stamps), so that families can access both types of benefits at the same time. The income cutoff is also the same as for school meal programs, so that in principle, children could transition from WIC to school breakfast and lunch when they turn 5 years old.

In addition to the income requirements, women's nutritional status must be evaluated, and they must be deemed to be at nutritional risk, though in practice this requirement does not seem to be binding as few applicants meet all the requirements for a healthy diet (Bitler, Currie, & Scholz, 2003). To maintain their benefits, clients are required to attend nutritional counseling and breastfeeding education sessions in WIC program offices at regular intervals, and recipients may also receive smoking cessation services.

WIC clients receive vouchers or checks (or in some cases debit cards), which can be used to purchase only specifically selected nutritious food items.[2] In addition, food packages are tailored to the differing needs of pregnant and postpartum breastfeeding women, infants, and children. In September 2017, the average value of the food package provided per person was $39.75 (U.S. Department of Agriculture, Food and Nutrition Service, 2019). WIC-approved foods include iron-fortified infant formula and infant cereal, iron-fortified adult cereal, fruit and vegetable juice, milk, eggs, cheese, beans, peanut butter, and canned fish. WIC packages are periodically reevaluated and altered to conform to evolving standards for a healthy diet. For example, in 2014, new guidelines were issued that increased the dollar amount for children's fruit and vegetable purchases by more than 30% (U.S. Department of Agriculture, Food and Nutrition Service, 2014). On average, WIC programs also spend $8.00 to $10.00 per participant on nutrition counseling and other services for clients.

---

[2]As an example, the New York regulations state the following about infant cereal:

> This is the only brand of cereal allowed for infants up to 12 months old: Gerber Cereal for Baby; plain varieties only: barley, oatmeal, rice, whole wheat, or mixed; 8 and 16-ounce containers are allowed; NOT ALLOWED: Organic, extra ingredients such as DHA, fruit, formula, or added protein.

Given that the monetary value of the benefits (except for infant formula) is small relative to most participants' monthly food budgets, one of the open questions about WIC is *why* it works (if indeed it does). Possible answers are that the healthy WIC food packages and/or the nutritional counseling nudge people's diets in a healthier direction, or that the availability of WIC benefits helps to facilitate access to medical care. The latter factor is likely to be particularly important, as many WIC program offices are located within maternal and child health clinics. It is even possible that WIC may encourage some vendors to carry healthy foods that they would not otherwise offer, potentially affecting dietary quality more broadly. Identifying the mechanisms through which WIC works could help to make the program better and might shed light on what modifiable risk factors are most associated with poor infant health outcomes in the United States.

WIC program participants can redeem their benefits at authorized stores, purchasing anything from the list of WIC approved items. Stores then receive reimbursement from their state WIC office. There are currently approximately 48,000 WIC-authorized stores (Tiehen & Frazao, 2016). Stores that wish to participate in WIC apply to state agencies in order to become authorized. They agree to stock specific brands and sizes of WIC-authorized foods and to meet other criteria established by the state. For example, they must agree to make their records available to the state and to submit to inspections. States are not obligated to authorize all stores that apply; they are obligated to authorize enough stores so that WIC participants have access to WIC foods. Some states maintain a waiting list of stores that would like to become authorized. State agencies are also expected to ensure that authorized stores abide by program regulations. Perhaps because of these requirements, the majority of WIC outlets are large retail chains (Tiehen & Frazao, 2016).

Another important function of state WIC agencies is to negotiate contracts with infant formula manufacturers. Formula can cost families $150.00 per month and is the single most expensive item in WIC packages. Since 1989, the federal government has required states to use competitive bidding in an attempt to bring down the cost to the government of infant formula. The manufacturer who wins the contract gains exclusive access to the WIC market for a number of years and offers a rebate to the government for each unit of formula sold. These rebates are substantial: In 2016, the government spent $5.6 billion on food costs but received $1.7 billion in rebates on infant formula, for a net food cost of $3.9 billion (Center on Budget and Policy Priorities, 2017).

WIC ELIGIBILITY AND TAKE-UP

Figure 2.1 shows U.S. Department of Agriculture estimates of the number of people who are eligible for benefits and the percentage that take up benefits in each eligibility category. Keeping in mind that there are around 3.8 million births per year, the figure indicates that over half of infants are eligible for

FIGURE 2.1. National WIC Eligibility and Participation (2014)

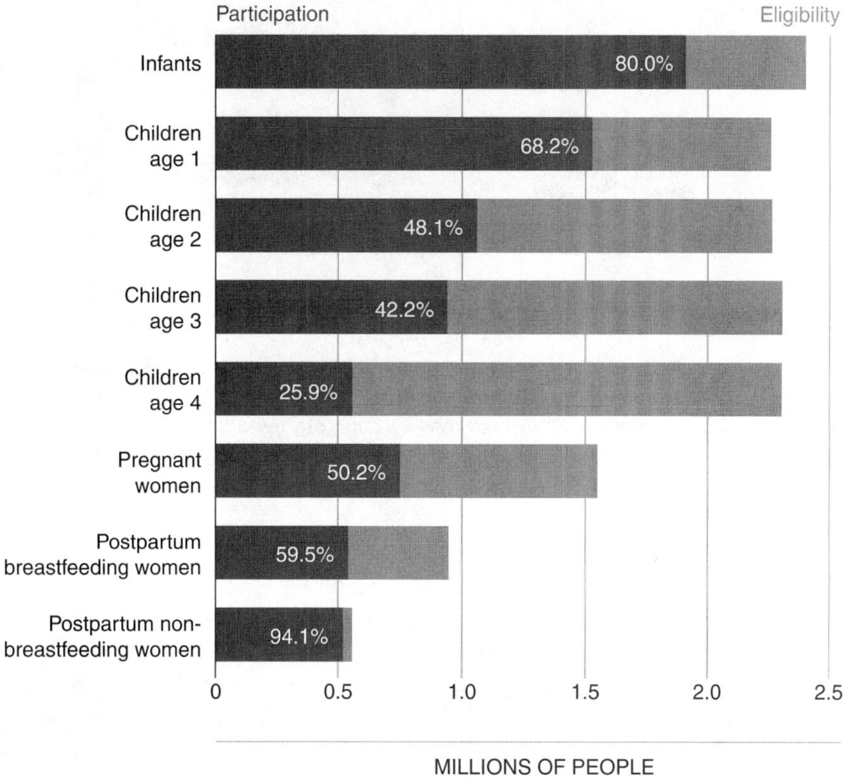

MILLIONS OF PEOPLE

Adapted from "National WIC 2015 Eligibility and Coverage Rates by Year and Participant Category," by U.S. Department of Agriculture, Food and Nutrition Service, 2018 (https://www.fns.usda.gov/wic/wic-2015-eligibility-and-coverage-rates). In the public domain.

WIC and that 80% of those eligible receive benefits. Coverage among postpartum nonbreastfeeding women is also high. However, coverage rates drop off substantially as children age, even though eligibility rates remain high. Coverage rates are also only 50.2% and 59.5% among pregnant and postpartum breastfeeding women, respectively. The high cost of infant formula may be one reason for the high take-up among infants and nonbreastfeeding postpartum women. Many children drop out at the year one mark when packages no longer include formula, and children must be recertified. The relatively low take-up for the other groups begs the questions of why more eligible women and children do not participate, and what impact increasing participation rates might have on health outcomes.

Figure 2.2 shows that participation rose somewhat during the Great Recession but has since fallen back to prerecession levels; this suggests that either eligibility or take-up is affected by economic downturns, but that overall, participation has remained roughly stable over time. Participation

FIGURE 2.2. WIC Participation Over Time, By Eligibility Category

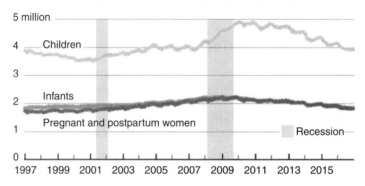

Infants = under age 1; Children = age 1 to under age 5. From "Policy Basics: Special Supplemental Nutrition Program for Women, Infants, and Children," by Center on Budget and Policy Priorities, 2017 (https://www.cbpp.org/research/food-assistance/policy-basics-special-supplemental-nutrition-program-for-women-infants-and). Adapted with permission.

also varies by state: in 2015, the highest overall participation among eligible individuals was in California and Vermont (65%) and the lowest in Utah (37%; U.S. Department of Agriculture, Food and Nutrition Service, 2018). These differences suggest that state-specific factors, such as administrative issues that impact the ease with which families can enroll, may influence take-up. Note that WIC is not an entitlement program, which means that when funding runs out, eligible families can be turned away. However, in recent years, these budget constraints have not been binding, so that lack of WIC funds has not been an important driver of participation rates.

The discussion of take-up highlights one of the persistent challenges for researchers studying WIC—those who participate may be systematically different than those who do not. If women who enroll in WIC are, for example, more concerned about their children's health or more motivated to change their behaviors than other women, then the measured positive effects of WIC could reflect these unobserved characteristics of mothers who enroll in the program. Conversely, if women with health problems or previous poor birth outcomes are referred to WIC, or if only the poorest and most disadvantaged families find it worthwhile to meet program requirements in order to obtain benefits, then studies comparing participants to nonparticipants may underestimate the true positive effects of WIC enrollment.

Moreover, there is very little quantitative research into the determinants of childhood WIC participation and the differences between eligible participants and nonparticipants. Jacknowitz and Tiehen (2009) examined data from the Early Childhood Longitudinal Birth Cohort Study and found that eligible individuals who exited the program cited scheduling and transportation problems, as well as the effort required to remain enrolled. A study of over 3,000 parents in New York State by Woelfel et al. (2004) suggested, in addition, that long waiting times and child care were problems for many people.

Chorniy, Currie, and Sonchak (2018a) used WIC data from South Carolina to examine determinants of WIC participation. Not surprisingly, poorer and less educated women are more likely to participate, other things being equal, and older children are also more likely to participate if they have younger covered siblings. Higher birth orders are less likely to participate than lower birth orders, although it is unclear whether this reflects the fact that women with large families tend to be from more disadvantaged backgrounds, or it is an independent causal effect of birth order. However, overall these demographic characteristics explain little of the variation in WIC participation, suggesting that institutional factors associated with the way that WIC is administered may be more important.

EFFECTS OF WIC ON EARLY-LIFE HEALTH

Research on how WIC impacts infant health dates back several decades (see Currie, 2003, for a review of many of the early studies on this topic). This research faces a substantial challenge due to a lack of experimental design. As discussed earlier, WIC participation is not randomly assigned, which means that a naive comparison of the outcomes of WIC recipients with those of children in other families cannot separate the causal effects of the program from the influences of other (often unobservable) differences between families. To the extent that WIC participants are more disadvantaged in unobserved respects than other observably similar people (which may, for example, be why they are choosing to participate in WIC), any positive effects of WIC will tend to be understated.

Nevertheless, many studies from the 1980s and 1990s report a favorable relationship between WIC food receipt during pregnancy and infant health. Among the studies discussed in Currie (2003)'s review, WIC participation is associated with a 10% to 43% reduction in the likelihood of a low-birth-weight birth. However, if WIC participants are positively selected (i.e., if they tend to have characteristics, such as healthier behaviors or more information, that are associated with better birth outcomes), then these benefits of WIC could be overstated.

To overcome this concern, more recent work has tried to use comparison groups that are more similar to WIC participants. Bitler and Currie (2005) compared children born to mothers who report receiving WIC during pregnancy with those born to other low-income women whose births were covered by Medicaid. Pregnant women on Medicaid are automatically eligible for WIC, so focusing on women covered by Medicaid isolates a group of women who are all eligible. Bitler and Currie's results show that infants of WIC participants have 64- to 78-g higher birth weights, are 30% less likely to be born low birth weight or preterm (< 37 weeks gestation), and are 10% less likely to be admitted to the neonatal intensive care unit than infants of mothers who did not get WIC benefits. They also found a 50% reduction in the incidence of very low birth weight (< 1,500 g). Importantly, this study found that WIC participants have average observable characteristics that are associated with worse and not better birth outcomes, implying that, if anything, some of the earlier studies on WIC could have underestimated the program's benefits.

Other studies have relied on sibling comparisons to deal with the issue of nonrandom selection into WIC. By comparing the outcomes of children in the same family, this type of research design controls for all time-invariant family background characteristics that could be correlated with WIC participation and child health. Kowaleski-Jones and Duncan (2002) used data from the Children of the National Longitudinal Survey of Youth and found a small, but statistically significant, effect on mean birth weight and a positive effect on temperament scores using sibling comparisons. Unfortunately, their sample size is quite small: They had only 104 sibling pairs and only 71 with discordant WIC participation necessary to identify the effect of WIC. Lee and Mackey-Bilaver (2007) used a sibling comparison design in large-scale administrative data from Illinois to show that children whose mothers received WIC benefits during pregnancy have a lower incidence of anemia, failure-to-thrive, and nutritional deficiencies and are less likely to have a subsequent child abuse or neglect report than their non-WIC-exposed siblings. Foster, Jiang, and Gibson-Davis (2010) used data from the Child Development Study of the Panel Study of Income Dynamics to analyze the effects of WIC participation on birth outcomes. Although a propensity score matching analysis reveals no statistically significant effects, a sibling comparison shows improvements in birth weight and reductions in preterm births. Similarly, Sonchak (2016) used birth records data from South Carolina to show that WIC-exposed infants have higher birth weights and lower preterm birth rates than their non-WIC siblings.

One concern with the sibling comparison methodology is that there may be unobservable time-varying factors that explain why a mother participates in WIC during one pregnancy or not another. For instance, a woman may not know about WIC during one pregnancy and learn about it during the other, despite being eligible for the program during both. It is unlikely that this difference in knowledge per se would lead to any bias in the estimated effect of WIC. However, if the mother was referred to WIC because she had a negative birth outcome previously, then the effect of WIC could be overestimated. Hence, it is important to understand why there is a difference in participation between siblings in studies that use sibling comparison designs.

Currie and Rajani (2015) addressed this issue using a large sample of women from New York City; they documented that women are more likely to participate in WIC when they are young, unmarried, unemployed, or have developed a chronic health condition, such as high blood pressure or diabetes. They further showed that WIC-exposed children have lower rates of low birth weight and that these improvements appear driven by a reduction in the likelihood that a mother gains too little weight during pregnancy (which is a credible mechanism for effects on birth weight). The fact that women appear to be *less* advantaged during the pregnancies when they take-up WIC again suggests that sibling comparisons could lead to an underestimate of the effects of WIC. Another issue in the research on WIC is *gestational-age bias*. The longer a pregnancy lasts, the more time a woman has to sign up for WIC, so that there may be a mechanical link between having any WIC participation during pregnancy, longer pregnancy durations, and higher birth weights. This problem is sometimes addressed by controlling for gestational age or limiting the sample to full-term births, although, of course, if WIC has a causal impact on gestation, then this approach will miss that margin. Another approach would involve controlling for WIC enrollment prior to the third trimester, but such data are not generally available. For example, birth certificates now record whether a mother ever received WIC benefits during pregnancy but not when she enrolled. In the absence of such data, best practice is to show estimates with and without controls for gestational age and/or treat small-for-dates and gestational age as additional outcome variables.

Joyce, Gibson, and Colman (2005) and Joyce, Racine, and Yunzal-Butler (2008) controlled for gestational length and found positive, but slightly smaller, impacts on birth weight when compared with the prior literature (e.g., a 7- to 40-gram increase in average birth weight depending on the subsample considered and about a 9% reduction in the low birth-weight rate). Currie and Rajani (2015) showed that even among full-term infants, WIC was associated with a reduction in the likelihood of being small-for-gestational-age. Fingar, Lob, Dove, Gradziel, and Curtis (2017) attempted to overcome gestational-age bias by using California births data for 2010 linked to census, hospital discharge, and WIC participant records. They used a survival analysis method in which outcomes are compared in each week of gestation. They showed that WIC enrollment is associated with a lower risk of preterm birth from weeks 29 to 36, a lower risk of low birth weight from weeks 26 to 40, and a lower risk of perinatal death from weeks 29 to 43.

Other recent studies employ natural experiment research designs to identify the causal impacts of WIC on infant health. Figlio, Hamersma, and Roth (2009) merged birth records and school records in Florida. In order to find a comparison group of infants who were similar to infants whose mothers used WIC during pregnancy, they made use of the fact that household income eligibility for a reduced-price lunch in elementary school is the same as for WIC. Household income can vary around this threshold. In the school data, they can identify births in households that were eligible for reduced-price school lunch in the past but are not eligible in the birth year. Treating this group as a comparison group, and the infants who got WIC as a treatment group, Figlio et al. found a substantial 160% reduction in the likelihood of low birth weight when the mother used WIC during pregnancy.

Hoynes, Page, and Stevens (2011) exploited county-by-year variation in the initial rollout of the WIC program in the 1970s. Some counties implemented the program earlier than others, and the study provides evidence that this timing pattern was not related to other observable determinants of infant health (e.g., local labor market conditions or population demographics). Their analysis shows that the availability of WIC in a given county was associated with a 2- to 7-g increase in average birth weight. Scaling by the estimate of the WIC participation rate during the time period of analysis, these results translate into 18- to 29-g increases in birth weight among WIC participants. It is likely that these estimates are less applicable to the modern WIC program, however. On the one hand, the current WIC program operates on a much larger scale and provides a wider range of services than when it was first introduced. On the other hand, participants could possibly be less needy on average today than those first served by the program.

To study the effects of WIC access during a more recent time period, Rossin-Slater (2013) used data on sibling births in Texas from the 2000s and leveraged within-ZIP-code variation in WIC clinic openings and closings. The idea behind this research design is to compare the outcomes of children whose mothers had a WIC clinic in their ZIP code of residence during one pregnancy and not during another. Unlike in the other studies of siblings, Rossin-Slater used only the variation in WIC participation between siblings that is driven by WIC clinic openings and closings rather than differences in participation between siblings that could be caused by other factors. The study also provided evidence that within-ZIP changes in WIC clinic availability are uncorrelated with changes in maternal demographic characteristics. Rossin-Slater found that WIC access is associated with increased likelihood of food benefit take-up, higher pregnancy weight gain, higher average birth weight, and greater likelihood of breastfeeding initiation at the time of hospital discharge. The effect magnitudes are larger than those in Hoynes et al. (2011), which suggests that the WIC program may serve as a more significant early-life health intervention today than it did at the time of its inception. For instance, among mothers with a high school education or less (who are most likely to be low income and eligible for WIC), WIC access is associated with a 32-g increase in average birth weight and a 14% reduction in the likelihood of low birth weight.

In sum, the literature on WIC suggests that WIC works in terms of improving infant health at birth. Although early studies may be subject to bias due to nonrandom selection into WIC, more recent approaches that use a variety of research designs to identify causal effects still point to statistically significant beneficial effects. Given that a large literature documents lasting positive impacts of health at birth on outcomes throughout the life cycle (Almond & Currie, 2011; Almond et al., 2018), the WIC program appears to be tremendously cost-effective.

As an example, we conduct a back-of-the-envelope calculation to assess the cost savings that result from WIC due to the program's effect on the rate of very-low birth-weight (VLBW) births. Table 2.1 considers documented immediate, medium-term, and long-term costs of VLBW that include elevated risk of infant death and medical care, costs related to childhood disability, medical costs and lost income due to adult disability, and loss in life expectancy. Drawing on the literature, we use estimates of the effects of VLBW

TABLE 2.1. Cost Savings Due to Reduction in Very Low Birth Weight (< 1,500 g) Associated With Prenatal WIC Participation (2018)

Type of outcome	Cost of outcome (1)	Δ in outcome per VLBW Birth (2)	Cost of VLBW due to outcome (3) = (1) × (2)	Cost per VLBW birth averted by WIC (4) = (3) × 0.007[a]
Infant death	5,184,000[b]	0.2062[c]	1,068,941	7,483
VLBW infant medical care	207,739[d]	1	207,739	1,454
Childhood neurosensory disability	549,000[e]	0.100[f]	54,900	384
Adult disability (% income loss)	520,753[g]	0.033[h]	17,185	120
Adult disability (medical costs)	698,220[i]	0.1006	69,822	489
Reduction in life expectancy	89,551 per year[j]	11.68	1,038,780	7,271
Total cost averted with WIC per birth				$17,201
Cost per birth × number of WIC-eligible births[k]				$33,936,497,938

Note. VLBW = very low birth weight. [a]We use the Bitler and Currie (2005) estimate that WIC reduces the probability of VLBW by 0.007. [b]Data from Cutler and Meara (2000). [c]Data from Matthews, MacDorman, and Thoma (2015). [d]Data from Rogowski (1998). [e]Data from Stabile and Allin (2012). [f]Data from Hack et al. (2002). [g]Authors' calculation of average lifetime income from the American Communities Survey using a 3% present discounted value. [h]Data from Bharadwaj, Lundborg, and Rooth (2018). [i]Data from Centers for Disease Control and Prevention, National Center on Birth Defects and Developmental Disabilities (2018). [j]Data from Lee, Chertow, and Zenios (2009). [k]The total number of live births in the United States in 2016 was 3,945,875, with approximately half eligible for WIC.

on these outcomes and of the average costs of these outcomes in order to compute a cost of VLBW. To obtain an estimate of the effect of WIC on the likelihood of a VLBW birth, we rely on Bitler and Currie (2005), who found that WIC reduced the incidence of VLBW from 0.014 to 0.007. Multiplying the cost of VLBW by 0.007 yields an estimated cost averted per WIC-affected pregnancy of $17,201 (in 2018). Multiplying this per-pregnancy cost averted by the number of mothers eligible for WIC yields a benefit close to $34 billion for each birth cohort. Note that this calculation is likely to be an underestimate, because it includes only some of the costs of VLBW, does not include other health benefits (e.g., improvements in birth weight above the 1,500 g threshold for VLBW) and does not take into account that most children who participated in WIC prenatally continue to participate for the first year of life (and possibly for some years after).

WIC STRUCTURE, COST-EFFECTIVENESS, AND ACCESS

As is the case with many U.S. safety-net programs, WIC is structured as a public–private partnership—the government contracts with private firms to deliver benefits to participants.[3] The effect of this structure on program cost-effectiveness is ambiguous and depends on whether private organizations are more or less efficient at providing benefits to WIC participants than public agencies. Moreover, if private firms have profit-maximization incentives that do not align with a goal of improving welfare among low-income pregnant women and young children in the most cost-effective way, then there could be program waste that drives up costs without producing value for program recipients. Because WIC is not an entitlement program (i.e., its budget is not always large enough to cover all eligible individuals), excess costs preclude the program from having the widest reach possible.

Further, because WIC is an in-kind transfer program, the recipients' benefits specify product quantities (e.g., one gallon of milk, two boxes of cereal) and not prices. As noted earlier, WIC participants take these benefits to WIC-authorized vendors, which consist of food retailers of varying sizes and formats. Supercenters (e.g., Wal-Mart), large grocery chains (e.g., Safeway), as well as small grocery, convenience, and even liquor stores can operate as WIC vendors. When WIC participants use their benefits, the vendors are reimbursed by the WIC program at a set rate (which varies across states). Because the participants are insensitive to prices, this program structure creates an incentive for vendors to charge the highest possible prices for WIC-approved goods that will be reimbursed by WIC, which drives up program costs. Moreover,

---

[3]Other examples of such partnerships include Medicaid, which now operates mainly by reimbursing private managed care plans rather than insuring beneficiaries directly; Head Start, which involves local entities that contract with the federal government; and the National School Lunch Program, which often contracts with private, food service-management companies to prepare and deliver lunches to schools.

there is an incentive to engage in price discrimination—to charge WIC customers higher prices than others. Although it is illegal to charge WIC customers more than others for the same good, it is not illegal to charge higher prices for WIC goods than for other goods, although rules established in 2006 required states to establish vendor peer groups for gauging prices in order to ensure that state WIC programs were not overpaying for food.[4]

In a recent study, Meckel (2017) examined the way that WIC retail vendors responded to a new technology that was introduced in order to eliminate fraud and shows that it had unintended consequences. She studied the implementation of an electronic payment system in the Texas WIC program, which improved the government's ability to determine if the vendor was either charging higher prices to WIC customers than other customers or substituting non-WIC products for WIC products, which are two forms of illegal fraud. She showed that the technology led to a substantial 10% to 26% decline in participation among single-outlet WIC vendors. She found that these vendors were previously the most likely to engage in fraudulent price discrimination practices, so some of the decline in participation may have been due to anticipated lower profits without fraud. However, since installing the equipment necessary to participate in the fraud reduction program was expensive, some of the decline in participation may also have been due to this expense. In turn, reducing the number of outlets reduced the probability that pregnant women would participate in WIC by 3% to 5%. Another unintended consequence was that prices rose for non-WIC shoppers, presumably because costs rose for vendors. Thus, although the technology was successful in reducing fraud (and program costs), the fraud reduction program reduced access to WIC for pregnant women in Texas and increased food prices.

Meckel's (2017) research suggests that although small private vendors can drive up program costs through the prices they charge (fraudulently or not), they may also play an important role in making WIC accessible. WIC rules on approved foods are complicated and often changing, which means that it could be difficult for a WIC participant to distinguish between allowed and prohibited goods in a large grocery store. There may also be less stigma associated with using benefits at a small local vendor rather than a generic store that also serves many non-WIC customers. Consistent with these ideas, Grodsky, Violante, Barrows, and Gosliner (2017) provided qualitative evidence from interviews with WIC participants in San Jose, California, on their challenges in navigating WIC benefits at large stores that also contain many ineligible items.[5]

---

[4]See Saitone, Sexton, and Volpe (2014). These regulations were implemented in response to the rapid rise of WIC-only stores between 2000 and 2006. These stores provided only WIC foods and served only WIC clients, and the evidence suggests that they charged higher prices than other retail stores. The new program rules eliminated many of these stores.

[5]Additionally, see Moffitt (1983) and Currie and Gahvari (2008) for discussions about stigma in welfare program participation and the role of in-kind benefits.

WIC KNOWLEDGE GAPS AND DIRECTIONS FOR FUTURE RESEARCH

Despite the large evidence base regarding the beneficial impacts of WIC on health at birth, several significant knowledge gaps limit our ability to value WIC's long-term investment into population health and well-being. First, there is limited research on how WIC affects child outcomes beyond birth and early childhood. The evidence is mixed on whether WIC is associated with higher breastfeeding rates (Chatterji & Brooks-Gunn, 2004; Gregory, Gross, Nguyen, Butz, & Johnson, 2016; Marshall et al., 2013; Metallinos-Katsaras, Brown, & Colchamiro, 2015), which may reflect the fact that although WIC promotes breastfeeding through its health education component, it also provides participants with free infant formula.

Jackson (2015) used propensity score matching and sibling comparison designs to study how prenatal and early-childhood exposure to WIC is associated with child cognitive development. She documented improvements in the Bayley Mental Development assessment at age two, as well as higher reading and math test scores at around age 11. Chorniy, Currie, and Sonchak (2018b) used a sibling comparison design to show that prenatal WIC participation leads to fewer diagnoses of attention-deficit/hyperactivity disorder and other common childhood mental health conditions, and reduces grade repetition in children observed at ages 6 to 11 years. To the best of our knowledge, there is no current evidence on any longer run effects of WIC.

A second gap in our knowledge is that nearly all of the existing WIC research focuses on the effects of prenatal exposure to the program. Yet pregnant women account for less than a quarter of all WIC participants; the rest of the caseload is made up of infants and children ages one to four (Hoynes & Whitmore Schanzenbach, 2016). We know very little about how postnatal access to and participation in WIC influences children's outcomes in the short and long term. As discussed earlier, it is difficult to isolate the effects of childhood WIC participation because, on the one hand, many child participants participated prenatally and, on the other, participation rates decline rapidly with age, and we do not know how the remaining children on the program differ from those who leave.

A third issue is that the research on WIC has focused on the question of "Does WIC work?" Given the evidence that WIC does improve health at birth, a natural next question is "Why does WIC work?" Previous studies have shown that WIC participants during pregnancy have higher weight gain and also use more health services, suggesting that these are both possible mechanisms, but we know little about the effectiveness of specific components of WIC, such as nutrition education, although this is an integral part of the program.[6]

---

[6]Many programs also offer smoking cessation or referral to smoking cessation services. Yunzal-Butler, Joyce, and Racine (2010) found that services offered in the context of WIC have a significant effect on smoking, although it is smaller than the effect of other antismoking intervention programs.

A fourth and related issue is whether there are changes that could be made to the WIC program that could enhance its efficiency and effectiveness. Critiques of the WIC program have often focused on things like the components of the food packages, but as the work by Meckel (2017) showed, it is also important to consider the incentives for providers to participate and clients' access to WIC retailers. Additionally, Rossin-Slater (2013) demonstrated that, for participants, ease of access to clinics is also important. Hence, there are many aspects of WIC that could potentially be tweaked to improve the program. Further research could help us to hone in on those that are most important.

REFERENCES

Aizer, A., & Currie, J. (2014). The intergenerational transmission of inequality: Maternal disadvantage and health at birth. *Science, 344*, 856–861. http://dx.doi.org/10.1126/science.1251872

Almond, D., & Currie, J. (2011). Human capital development before age five. In O. Ashenfelter & D. Card (Eds.), *Handbook of labor economics* (Vol. 4B, pp. 1315–1486). San Diego, CA: Elsevier.

Almond, D., Currie, J., & Duque, V. (2018). Childhood circumstances and adult outcomes: Act II. *Journal of Economic Literature, 56*, 1360–1446. http://dx.doi.org/10.1257/jel.20171164

Barker, D. J. P. (1990). The fetal and infant origins of adult disease. *British Medical Journal, 301*, 1111. http://dx.doi.org/10.1136/bmj.301.6761.1111

Bharadwaj, P., Lundborg, P., & Rooth, D.-O. (2018). Birth weight in the long run. *The Journal of Human Resources, 53*, 189–231. http://dx.doi.org/10.3368/jhr.53.1.0715-7235R

Bitler, M. P., & Currie, J. (2005). Does WIC work? The effects of WIC on pregnancy and birth outcomes. *Journal of Policy Analysis and Management, 24*, 73–91. http://dx.doi.org/10.1002/pam.20070

Bitler, M. P., Currie, J., & Scholz, J. K. (2003). WIC eligibility and participation. *The Journal of Human Resources, 38*, 1139–1179.

Burnett, J. (2014). *State median household income*. Retrieved from Council of State Governments website: http://knowledgecenter.csg.org/kc/content/state-median-household-income

Center on Budget and Policy Priorities. (2017). *Policy basics: Special supplemental nutrition program for women, infants, and children*. Retrieved from https://www.cbpp.org/research/food-assistance/policy-basics-special-supplemental-nutrition-program-for-women-infants-and

Centers for Disease Control and Prevention, National Center on Birth Defects and Developmental Disabilities. (2018). *Disability and health healthcare cost data*. Retrieved from https://www.cdc.gov/ncbddd/disabilityandhealth/data-highlights.html

Chatterji, P., & Brooks-Gunn, J. (2004). WIC participation, breastfeeding practices, and well-child care among unmarried, low-income mothers. *American Journal of Public Health, 94*, 1324–1327. http://dx.doi.org/10.2105/AJPH.94.8.1324

Chen, A., Oster, E., & Williams, H. (2016). Why is infant mortality higher in the United States than in Europe? *American Economic Journal: Economic Policy, 8*, 89–124. http://dx.doi.org/10.1257/pol.20140224

Chetty, R., Stepner, M., Abraham, S., Lin, S., Scuderi, B., Turner, N., . . . Cutler, D. (2016). The association between income and life expectancy in the United States, 2001–2014. *JAMA, 315*, 1750–1766. http://dx.doi.org/10.1001/jama.2016.4226

Chorniy, A. V., Currie, J., & Sonchak, L. (2018a). *Determinants of postnatal WIC take-up* (Working Paper). Princeton, NJ: Princeton University, Center for Health and Wellbeing.

Chorniy, A. V., Currie, J., & Sonchak, L. (2018b). *Does prenatal WIC participation improve child outcomes* (Working Paper 24691)? Cambridge, MA: National Bureau of Economic Research.

Currie, J. (2003). U.S. food and nutrition programs. In R. A. Moffitt (Ed.), *Means-tested transfer programs in the United States* (pp. 199–290). Chicago, IL: The University of Chicago Press. http://dx.doi.org/10.7208/chicago/9780226533575.003.0005

Currie, J. (2011). Inequality at birth: Some causes and consequences. *The American Economic Review, 101,* 1–22. http://dx.doi.org/10.1257/aer.101.3.1

Currie, J., & Gahvari, F. (2008). Transfers in cash and in-kind: Theory meets the data. *Journal of Economic Literature, 46,* 333–383. http://dx.doi.org/10.1257/jel.46.2.333

Currie, J., & Rajani, I. (2015). Within-mother estimates of the effects of WIC on birth outcomes in New York City. *Economic Inquiry, 53,* 1691–1701. http://dx.doi.org/10.1111/ecin.12219

Currie, J., & Rossin-Slater, M. (2015). Early-life origins of life-cycle well-being: Research and policy implications. *Journal of Policy Analysis and Management, 34,* 208–242. http://dx.doi.org/10.1002/pam.21805

Cutler, D. M., & Meara, E. (2000). The technology of birth: Is it worth it? In A. M. Garber (Ed.), *Frontiers in health policy research* (Vol. 3, pp. 33–68). Cambridge, MA: MIT Press.

Figlio, D., Hamersma, S., & Roth, J. (2009). Does prenatal WIC participation improve birth outcomes? New evidence from Florida. *Journal of Public Economics, 93,* 235–245. http://dx.doi.org/10.1016/j.jpubeco.2008.08.003

Fingar, K. R., Lob, S. H., Dove, M. S., Gradziel, P., & Curtis, M. P. (2017). Reassessing the association between WIC and birth outcomes using a fetuses-at-risk approach. *Maternal and Child Health Journal, 21,* 825–835. http://dx.doi.org/10.1007/s10995-016-2176-9

Foster, E. M., Jiang, M., & Gibson-Davis, C. M. (2010). The effect of the WIC program on the health of newborns. *Health Services Research, 45,* 1083–1104. http://dx.doi.org/10.1111/j.1475-6773.2010.01115.x

Gregory, E. F., Gross, S. M., Nguyen, T. Q., Butz, A. M., & Johnson, S. B. (2016). WIC participation and breastfeeding at 3 months postpartum. *Maternal and Child Health Journal, 20,* 1735–1744. http://dx.doi.org/10.1007/s10995-016-1977-1

Grodsky, D., Violante, A., Barrows, A., & Gosliner, W. (2017, May). *Using behavioral science to improve the WIC experience: Lessons from the field from San Jose, California* (Final Paper). Retrieved from http://www.ideas42.org/wp-content/uploads/2017/07/I42_WIC-Paper-Final.pdf

Hack, M., Flannery, D. J., Schluchter, M., Cartar, L., Borawski, E., & Klein, N. (2002). Outcomes in young adulthood for very-low-birth-weight infants. *The New England Journal of Medicine, 346,* 149–157. http://dx.doi.org/10.1056/NEJMoa010856

Hoynes, H., Page, M., & Stevens, A. H. (2011). Can targeted transfers improve birth outcomes? Evidence from the introduction of the WIC program. *Journal of Public Economics, 95,* 813–827. http://dx.doi.org/10.1016/j.jpubeco.2010.12.006

Hoynes, H. W., & Whitmore Schanzenbach, D. (2016). U.S. food and nutrition programs. In R. A. Moffitt (Ed.), *Economics of means-tested transfer programs in the United States* (Vol. 1, pp. 219–301). Chicago, IL: University of Chicago Press.

Jacknowitz, A., & Tiehen, L. (2009). Transitions into and out of the WIC program: A Cause for concern? *The Social Service Review, 83,* 151–183. http://dx.doi.org/10.1086/600111

Jackson, M. I. (2015). Early childhood WIC participation, cognitive development and academic achievement. *Social Science & Medicine, 126,* 145–153. http://dx.doi.org/10.1016/j.socscimed.2014.12.018

Joyce, T., Gibson, D., & Colman, S. (2005). The changing association between prenatal participation in WIC and birth outcomes in New York City. *Journal of Policy Analysis and Management, 24,* 661–685. http://dx.doi.org/10.1002/pam.20131

Joyce, T., Racine, A., & Yunzal-Butler, C. (2008). Reassessing the WIC effect: Evidence from the pregnancy nutrition surveillance system. *Journal of Policy Analysis and Management, 27,* 277–303. http://dx.doi.org/10.1002/pam.20325

Kowaleski-Jones, L., & Duncan, G. J. (2002). Effects of participation in the WIC program on birthweight: Evidence from the National Longitudinal Survey of Youth. *American Journal of Public Health, 92,* 799–804. http://dx.doi.org/10.2105/AJPH.92.5.799

Lee, B. J., & Mackey-Bilaver, L. (2007). Effects of WIC and Food Stamp Program participation on child outcomes. *Children and Youth Services Review, 29,* 501–517. http://dx.doi.org/10.1016/j.childyouth.2006.10.005

Lee, C. P., Chertow, G. M., & Zenios, S. A. (2009). An empiric estimate of the value of life: Updating the renal dialysis cost-effectiveness standard. *Value in Health, 12,* 80–87. http://dx.doi.org/10.1111/j.1524-4733.2008.00401.x

Marshall, C., Gavin, L., Bish, C., Winter, A., Williams, L., Wesley, M., & Zhang, L. (2013). WIC participation and breastfeeding among White and Black mothers: Data from Mississippi. *Maternal and Child Health Journal, 17,* 1784–1792. http://dx.doi.org/10.1007/s10995-012-1198-1

Matthews, T. J., MacDorman, M. F., & Thoma, M. E. (2015). Infant mortality statistics from the 2013 period linked birth/infant death data set. *National Vital Statistics Reports, 64*(9), 1–30. Retrieved from Centers for Disease Control and Prevention, National Center for Health Statistics website: https://www.cdc.gov/nchs/data/nvsr/nvsr64/nvsr64_09.pdf

Meckel, K. (2017). *Is the cure worse than the disease? Unintended consequences of fraud reduction in transfer programs.* Unpublished manuscript, University of California, San Diego.

Metallinos-Katsaras, E., Brown, L., & Colchamiro, R. (2015). Maternal WIC participation improves breastfeeding rates: A statewide analysis of WIC participants. *Maternal and Child Health Journal, 19,* 136–143. http://dx.doi.org/10.1007/s10995-014-1504-1

Moffitt, R. (1983). An economic model of welfare stigma. *The American Economic Review, 73,* 1023–1035.

Rogowski, J. (1998). Cost-effectiveness of care for very low birth weight infants. *Pediatrics, 102,* 35–43. http://dx.doi.org/10.1542/peds.102.1.35

Rossin-Slater, M. (2013). WIC in your neighborhood: New evidence on the impacts of geographic access to clinics. *Journal of Public Economics, 102,* 51–69. http://dx.doi.org/10.1016/j.jpubeco.2013.03.009

Rossin-Slater, M. (2015). Promoting health in early childhood. *The Future of Children, 25,* 35–64. http://dx.doi.org/10.1353/foc.2015.0002

Saitone, T. L., Sexton, R. J., & Volpe, R. J. (2014). *Cost containment in the WIC program: Vendor peer groups and reimbursement rates* (Report No. 171). Retrieved from USDA Economic Research website: https://papers.ssrn.com/sol3/papers.cfm?abstract_id=2504048

Sonchak, L. (2016). The impact of WIC on birth outcomes: New evidence from South Carolina. *Maternal and Child Health Journal, 20,* 1518–1525. http://dx.doi.org/10.1007/s10995-016-1951-y

Stabile, M., & Allin, S. (2012). The economic costs of childhood disability. *The Future of Children, 22*(1), 65–96. http://dx.doi.org/10.1353/foc.2012.0008

Tiehen, L., & Frazao, E. (2016). *Where do WIC participants redeem their food benefits? An analysis of WIC food dollar redemption patterns by store type* (EIB No. 152). Retrieved from the United States Department of Agriculture website: https://www.ers.usda.gov/webdocs/publications/44073/57246_eib152.pdf?v=0

UNICEF. (2014). *Low birthweight*. Retrieved from https://data.unicef.org/topic/nutrition/ %20low-birthweight/

U.S. Central Intelligence Agency. (2017). *Country comparison: Infant mortality rate*. Retrieved from https://www.cia.gov/library/publications/the-world-factbook/ rankorder/2091rank.html

U.S. Department of Agriculture, Food and Nutrition Service. (2014). *USDA finalizes changes to the WIC program, expanding access to healthy fruits and vegetables, whole grains, and low-fat dairy for women, infants, and children* (Release No. 0031.14). Retrieved from https://www.fns.usda.gov/pressrelease/2014/003114

U.S. Department of Agriculture, Food and Nutrition Service. (2018). *National WIC 2015 eligibility and coverage rates by year and participant category*. Retrieved from https:// www.fns.usda.gov/wic/wic-2015-eligibility-and-coverage-rates

U.S. Department of Agriculture, Food and Nutrition Service. (2019). WIC data tables. Retrieved from https://www.fns.usda.gov/pd/wic-program

Woelfel, M. L., Abusabha, R., Pruzek, R., Stratton, H., Chen, S. G., & Edmunds, L. S. (2004). Barriers to the use of WIC services. *Journal of the American Dietetic Association*, *104*, 736–743. http://dx.doi.org/10.1016/j.jada.2004.02.028

Womack, L. S., Rossen, L. M., & Martin, J. A. (2018). *Singleton low birthweight rates, by race and Hispanic origin: United States, 2006–2016* (NCHS Data Brief No. 306). Retrieved from Centers for Disease Control and Prevention, National Center for Health Statistics website: https://www.cdc.gov/nchs/products/databriefs/db306.htm

Yunzal-Butler, C., Joyce, T., & Racine, A. D. (2010). Maternal smoking and the timing of WIC enrollment. *Maternal and Child Health Journal*, *14*, 318–331.

3

How Do Early-Life Health Experiences Affect Future Generations' Equality of Opportunity?

Chloe N. East and Marianne E. Page

A large literature documents that early-life health environments can have long-lasting impacts on individuals' well-being. Existing literatures in biology, epidemiology, psychology, child development, and economics also predict that the effects of early environments should persist beyond the exposed generation. This chapter considers what is known about the extent to which first-generation effects persist to later generations, with a focus on studies that use randomized experiments and natural experiment research designs that can help isolate causal effects from correlations. In addition to documenting persistent effects of early-life environments from one generation to the next, we argue that the presence and magnitude of multigenerational linkages have important implications for the evaluation of public policies intended to promote equality of opportunity. The emerging evidence on positive interventions' multigenerational impacts suggests that existing cost–benefit analyses typically underestimate the programs' true value.

It is well known that there are significant health differences between high- and low-income children and that health disparities across income groups are present even very early in life (e.g., Case, Lubotsky, & Paxson, 2002). Over the past decade, social scientists have come to appreciate that these health differences may also be important contributors to the persistence of income disparities across generations. A rapidly expanding literature harnessing *natural experiment* research designs has established causal relationships between a variety of measures of early-life health and later life health and economic

http://dx.doi.org/10.1037/0000187-004
Confronting Inequality: How Policies and Practices Shape Children's Opportunities, edited by
L. Tach, R. Dunifon, and D. L. Miller

success (Almond & Currie, 2011a, 2011b; Almond, Currie, & Duque, 2017). Importantly, although the majority of studies are based on negative shocks to children's health environments (e.g., disease outbreak, famine), studies that focus on positive early-life health interventions also find that they can lead to substantive improvements in adult health, education, and earnings.

By extension, existing literatures in biology, psychology, epidemiology, and economics predict that the effects of early-life environments should echo beyond the exposed generation. Indeed, Almond et al. (2017) noted that multi-generational studies are "a particularly exciting direction for future work, given that, thus far, there is not a great deal of research on intergenerational effects of in utero shocks in humans, although they are known to exist in animal models."

We begin by briefly describing what is known about the long-term effects of early-life health environments on treated-cohorts' well-being. In doing so, we discuss the usefulness of natural experiment research designs and common issues regarding the interpretation of estimates. Next, we describe why it is that we might expect the effects of early-life health environments to persist to later generations. We provide a brief overview of the evidence on multi-generational processes based on animal experiments that take place in a laboratory setting. We then describe recent studies that have extended the natural experiment methodology to consider similar multigenerational processes in humans. In addition to highlighting this work, our goal is to draw connections and provide insights that extend our thinking about the importance of early-life interventions.

EVIDENCE FROM ANIMAL EXPERIMENTS

Studies proposing that predictors of adult health might originate in the fetal and early-life periods existed as early as the 1930s, but interest became more widespread following the work of epidemiologist David Barker (1990). The basic idea behind Barker's fetal origins hypothesis is that, while in utero, a growing organism absorbs molecular information from the mother, treats this information as a signal about the postnatal environment, and programs itself in response to those signals. A key feature of the fetal origins hypothesis is that the observed health effects of the in utero environment can remain latent for many years.

Although there is ongoing debate about causal pathways, an abundance of animal experiments have generated substantive scientific support for the fetal origins hypothesis (e.g., Gluckman, Hanson, Cooper, & Thornburg, 2008). One heavily studied manipulation of the prenatal environment is nutritional deprivation, where researchers have consistently found that pregnant rats that are intentionally malnourished produce offspring that are more prone to metabolic disease (i.e., conditions such as obesity, diabetes, hypertension, and heart disease) and other chronic health conditions in later life, even if the offspring receive sufficient nutrition after birth (e.g., Gluckman et al., 2008). Similarly, rats that are malnourished before or during pregnancy have produced offspring with smaller brains and reduced cognition (e.g., Hunter & Sadler, 1987).

Animal experiments have also generated substantive evidence that in utero exposure to infectious disease has long-term impacts on well-being. Like studies of nutritional deprivation, the effects of such exposure extend beyond physical health. For example, several studies have documented that the offspring of pregnant rats who have been injected with the influenza (flu) virus are more likely to grow up to exhibit behavioral abnormalities similar to those of schizophrenia patients (Brown, 2012). Importantly, some studies suggest that, rather than being due to the pathogen itself, this outcome is due to the mother's excessive immune function (Canetta & Brown, 2012). This has wider implications for child development, as immune-system activation has been linked to poverty and stress. Animal experiments have also documented direct links between *in utero* stress and later life measures of physical health, mental health, and cognition (Weinstock, 2017), with additional evidence that the impacts of *in utero* stress can be reversed through interventions (e.g., Wakshlak & Weinstock, 1990). As well, there is substantive evidence that the developing fetus is affected by exposure to smoke and other pollutants (Shea & Steiner, 2008; U.S. Environmental Protection Agency, National Center for Environmental Assessment, 2009).

EVIDENCE FROM NATURAL EXPERIMENTS

Isolating causal effects of the early-life environment in humans is challenging, because unlike the physical and biological sciences, in which experiments and clinical trials are common, social scientists' opportunities to manipulate early-life conditions in truly experimental settings have been more constrained. It may be tempting to interpret correlations between the early-childhood environment and later generations' outcomes as causal, but these associations may reflect the effects of other family and parental characteristics. For example, among adults who were nutritionally deprived in utero, there is a higher incidence of economic disadvantage, so differences between their health and the health of adults with adequate nutrition in utero could actually be due to differences in childhood economic circumstances (which are also known correlates of later life health). Distinguishing causal effects from correlations is important for understanding the full range of processes that contribute to child development, however, and is imperative to the design of effective interventions.

To overcome this challenge, researchers have looked for naturally occurring variation that generates *quasi* treatment and control groups. These natural experiment research designs have tried to emulate real experimental settings by comparing outcomes across individuals who are very similar, but who are differentially exposed to potentially important environmental conditions that vary across space and/or time. The likely randomness of the variation in the health environment is often most believable when it is generated by an unanticipated health shock, such as a widespread famine or disease epidemic.[1]

As one example of a natural experiment, a series of studies investigated the long-term effects of early-life exposure to the Dutch Hunger Winter, which occurred during the winter of 1944–1945 as the result of the German occupying force placing an embargo on food transports to the western Netherlands. Prior to October 1944, caloric intake in the Netherlands was considered adequate, but in the wake of the embargo, official rations fell to 1,000 calories per day and then fell further to 500 calories per day in April 1945. Many *first-generation* studies have analyzed the long-term health consequences of in utero malnutrition by using variation in exposure to the Dutch Hunger Winter, based on the individual's date and place of birth relative to distributed food rations. The abrupt beginning and ending of the Dutch Hunger Winter ensures a necessary assumption for any valid natural experiment research design: that, in the absence of the famine, the health environments experienced by the "treatment" and "control" cohorts would have been similar. Researchers analyzing the Dutch Hunger Winter have found evidence that in utero exposure to malnutrition affects later life risk of obesity, high blood pressure, cardiovascular disease, schizophrenia, and hospitalization and has a negative impact on employment outcomes (e.g., Lumey, Stein, & Susser, 2011; Painter, Roseboom, & Bleker, 2005; Scholte, van den Berg, & Lindeboom, 2015). Importantly, all of these outcomes are known predictors of the next generation's health.

As another example, following Almond's (2006) pioneering work on the 1918 flu pandemic, a number of researchers have investigated the long-term effects of early-childhood exposure to infectious disease by making use of the abrupt spike in flu-related deaths that occurred in 1918. Like the Dutch Hunger Winter, the short nature of the epidemic's abrupt shock to the local disease environment has enabled outcome comparisons between cohorts who were prenatally exposed and cohorts who were born right before, or soon after, the outbreak (with limited concerns about other time-varying contaminators). As with studies of the Dutch Hunger Winter, analyses of the 1918 pandemic and other flu outbreaks have found substantive reductions in later life educational attainment, earnings, and health (e.g., Almond & Mazumder, 2005; Lin & Liu, 2014; Mazumder, Almond, Park, Crimmins, & Finch, 2010; Neelsen & Stratmann, 2012; Nelson, 2010; Parman, 2015; Schwandt, 2018).

Using similar research strategies, researchers have also investigated the long-term effects of in utero exposure to other diseases, nutritional deprivation resulting from seasonal variation in the observance of Ramadan, radiation

[1]We do not attempt to review every paper in this extensive literature on first-generation effects. For excellent reviews of the first-generation literature, see Almond and Currie (2011a, 2011b) and Almond et al. (2017).

and other pollutants, and maternal stress. Importantly, the set of considered outcomes in humans has included measures of later life well-being that extend beyond health, particularly measures of educational success and earnings. Recent surveys of this extensive literature are available in Almond and Currie (2011a, 2011b) and Almond et al. (2017), and they point to substantive effects of early-life health shocks on later life health, educational attainment, and economic outcomes.

A smaller literature, also summarized in the above survey articles, has begun to harness natural experiment research designs to investigate the impact of positive, and generally less dramatic, early-life health interventions. These studies are important because, in addition to contributing to our knowledge about the long-term impacts of childhood environments, they also provide evidence on the potential for policy to reduce disparities. Treatment and control groups are formed by using variation in policies that generate differential access to health inputs among otherwise nearly identical individuals. Examples include differential changes in Medicaid[2] eligibility rules across states and over time and county-by-county variation in the original adoption of the Food Stamp and Head Start programs.[3] By using this type of policy variation to identify program effects, researchers can disentangle the effects of family characteristics that affect take-up of health services from the effects of the program itself. This is critical as, even conditional on observable characteristics such as income and education, families who choose to participate in programs are generally less advantaged (and therefore have worse outcomes) than those who do not.

Similar to studies that exploit negative shocks to the childhood environment, studies focusing on the effects of positive health interventions find that they improve later life health and economic success. In utero and childhood access to the Medicaid program is associated with improvements in adolescent health status (Currie, Decker, & Lin, 2008), reductions in Black adolescents' mortality rates (Wherry & Meyer, 2016), reductions in metabolic syndrome–related illnesses and hospitalizations (Miller & Wherry, 2018), and adult mortality (Brown, Kowalski, & Lurie, 2017). Looking beyond health outcomes, childhood exposure to Medicaid has also been found to increase test scores (Levine & Schanzenbach, 2009), educational attainment (Brown et al., 2017; Cohodes, Grossman, Kleiner, & Lovenheim, 2016; Miller & Wherry, 2018), and earnings (Brown et al., 2017). Similarly, several studies of the Head Start preschool program, which provides both educational and health services, have documented that, like Medicaid, Head Start also yields important long-term

[2]Medicaid is the primary federal program that provides health insurance to American children living in low-income families.
[3]The Food Stamp Program (currently called the Supplemental Nutrition Assistance Program) is a federal program that provides food-purchasing assistance to low-income American families. The Head Start program is the largest early-childhood education program in the United States and has historically also provided an array of health-related services to low-income children.

health and economic benefits (Carneiro & Ginja, 2014; Deming, 2009; Garces, Thomas, & Currie, 2002; Ludwig & Miller, 2007). In the same vein, Bütikofer, Løken, and Salvanes (2019) examined the adoption of mother and child health centers in Norway; Glied and Neidell (2010) investigated the impacts of water fluoridation; Bhalotra and Venkataramani (2015) looked at the long-term effects of antibiotic therapies; Bharadwaj, Løken, and Neilson (2013) examined surfactant and related treatments; Fitzsimons and Vera-Hernandez (2013) looked at the effects of breast feeding encouragement programs; and Hoynes, Schanzenbach, and Almond (2016) examined the effects of the Food Stamp Program. All of these natural experiments provide strong evidence that early-life health and nutrition interventions generate long-term benefits on treated generations.

EVIDENCE OF MULTIGENERATIONAL EFFECTS

Taken as a whole, a wealth of biological- and social-science research generates two broad conclusions. First, early-life health environments have long-term impacts on the health and economic outcomes of those who experience them. Second, widespread public-health interventions targeted at children have scope to reduce later life disparities.

Potential Mechanisms

It is easy to imagine how multigenerational effects might persist to later generations, as there is substantial evidence that healthier, more educated, and higher income parents raise children who do better on a variety of measures than children whose parents are unhealthy, have low levels of education, or low incomes. This may be because families who benefit from a positive intervention have more resources to transfer onto their children, because improvements in health and socioeconomic status are accompanied by changes in behavior (e.g., reduced smoking, differences in parenting practices), or because of reductions in parental stress (Becker & Tomes, 1979; Conger & Conger, 2007; Heckman, 2007).

Direct biological mechanisms may also play a role. For example, several studies discussed above have found that there is an association between the early-life health environment and the incidence of metabolic syndrome in adulthood. In turn, maternal metabolic-syndrome conditions are associated with increased risk of gestational diabetes, pregnancy complications related to high blood pressure, preterm birth, and low birth weight (Catalano & Ehrenberg, 2006), which are predictive of offspring's future health and economic trajectories (Black, Devereux, & Salvanes, 2007; Hsin, 2012; Royer, 2009). Moreover, an abundance of animal experiments find that prenatal health shocks have persistent effects beyond the first generation, although exact biological processes underlying this transmission are not yet fully understood.[4] Many researchers believe that epigenetic processes, which change the way information in genes is transcribed, underlie these long-run effects. Unlike genes, epigenomes adjust much more rapidly to environmental insults. Epigenetic processes are also consistent with the observation that, among treated cohorts, resulting health outcomes are often not apparent until many years after birth. At the molecular level, the particular ways in which epigenetic reprogramming occurs is through the silencing of certain genes through impaired inheritance of genes, the addition of chemical compounds to the DNA, and through spatial reorganization of genes within the chromosomes (Hochberg et al., 2011; Jirtle & Skinner, 2007).

In addition to these mechanisms, environmental effects on the treated generation's survival may lead to differences in future generations' observed outcomes. Among the treated generation, any additional (fewer) deaths resulting from a decline (increase) in the quality of the health environment are most likely to occur among those who are least healthy. This will lead to a mechanical increase (decrease) in average health among survivors, which is often referred to as the selection, or "culling" effect, and that will work in the opposite direction from the direct health effect—often called the "scarring" effect (e.g., Elo & Preston, 1992). Importantly, if culling occurs among treated cohorts, then we would expect a mechanical spillover onto the next generation's observed health as well. As in the treated generation, the effects of culling on the second generation will work in the opposite direction from the direct health effects.

Finally, the same (or related) biological processes that generate improvements in the treated-generation's later life health may directly affect the treated generation's fecundity. Moreover, effects of the early-life environment on treated cohorts' human capital may be accompanied by deliberate changes in the timing of childbearing or completed family size.

Research Challenges

Although an ever-expanding number of animal experiments indicate that the effects of prenatal and childhood environments can be transmitted to later generations,[5] human studies are nearly nonexistent. Social scientists have documented that health and economic status persist across multiple generations (Clark, 2014; Solon, 2015) but, as with first-generation studies, isolating causal mechanisms in humans is challenging because social scientists' opportunities

[4]Examples include Zamenhof, van Marthens, and Grauel (1971), Cowley and Griesel (1966), Aerts and Van Assche (2006), Dunn and Bale (2009), Jimenez-Chillaron et al. (2009), and Martínez et al. (2014). Recent reviews of the literature on transgenerational epigenetic inheritance include: Daxinger and Whitelaw (2010, 2012), Grossniklaus, Kelly, Ferguson-Smith, Pembrey, and Lindquist (2013), and Heard and Martienssen (2014).
[5]Useful reviews of this literature include Daxinger and Whitelaw (2010, 2012), Heard and Martienssen (2014), Hochberg et al. (2011), and Nadeau (2009).

to manipulate early-life conditions are more constrained. A second challenge is that data availability is limited. Multigenerational studies require information spanning many years and containing detail on both individuals' outcomes and their parents' childhood circumstances. There are currently few such datasets in the United States, most of which are small, so given the sources of variation that are typically used in natural experiment estimation strategies, it is difficult to obtain statistically precise estimates. Some researchers are beginning to link administrative data—mostly outside of the United States—but to date, the opportunities for multigenerational data analyses within a causal research framework have been limited.

Evidence

In this section, we describe current natural experiment research regarding the extent to which the effects of early-life environments persist to later generations. We include all multigenerational studies that we are aware of that employ the types of research designs described previously, but we note that, due to the data challenges associated with analyzing multigenerational effects, the extent to which researchers have been able to employ the full range of robustness tests that prevail in the best first-generation studies varies—this is very much an emerging literature. We summarize the empirical evidence in Table 3.1 and briefly describe the studies here. Our discussion focuses on how the emerging literature speaks to the potential linkages laid out in the section of this chapter entitled Potential Mechanisms and highlights issues that are relevant to obtaining a better understanding of generational persistence.

Famine

A few studies have been able to extend the use of historical famines to examine how such nutritional shocks to the childhood environment affected the next generation. Using a research design similar to the natural experiments described above, Painter et al. (2008) investigated the multigenerational impacts of the Dutch Hunger Winter. They found no evidence that in utero exposure to the famine affected mothers' reports of the next generation's birth weight or incidence of prematurity, but they did find that mothers reported reductions in the second-generation's birth length and increases in predictors of the second-generation's later life obesity (e.g., neonatal adiposity). Mothers who were exposed in the first generation also reported that their offspring experienced poor health in adulthood at nearly twice the rate as the children whose mothers were not exposed.

These estimates should be interpreted with a degree of caution, because they are based on a small sample and parents' recollections of their children's health. Nevertheless, patterns in the estimates may provide clues to the underlying mechanisms: the effects were largest among first-generation mothers who were exposed to the famine near the beginning of gestation, and the authors found no evidence that fathers' exposure to famine affected

TABLE 3.1. Multigenerational Papers

Study	Data	Empirical strategy	Results	Interpretation/mechanisms/ heterogeneity
Painter et al. (2008) Examined effect of Dutch Hunger Winter on children of individuals exposed in utero.	Interviewed the Dutch Famine Birth Cohort, which were individuals born in Amsterdam between 1943 and 1947. First generation $N = 655$.	Difference-in-difference design using the Dutch Hunger Winter start and end dates to examine effects of parents' in utero exposure to famine on children's short- and long-run outcomes. During this period, the food consumption of a previously well-nourished population was reduced by more than 75%, with rations limited to 1,000 calories per day by the end of November 1944 and 500 calories per day by May 1945 (when the war ended).	No effect on next generation's birth weight or incidence of prematurity. Reductions in the second generation's birth length, increased ponderal index, and neonatal adiposity, a predictor of later life obesity. Doubling of poor health in adulthood, and the differences in poor health were not from conditions related to metabolic syndrome or psychiatric conditions (which have been generationally linked to nutritional deprivation in animal studies).	Exposure to the famine during the period of early gestation was most important to the next generation's health in later life. No evidence of transmission from first generation men who were exposed to the famine to their children.
van den Berg & Pinger (2016) Examined long-run effects of adolescent exposure to the German famine on the second and third generations' outcomes.	The German Socioeconomic Panel. Sample was second- and third-generation individuals whose parents/grandparents were born in 1902–1913. Third generation sample $n = 2,670$. Second generation sample $n = 6,548$.	Difference-in-difference design using the German famine start and end dates to examine effects of the first generation's exposure to famine just before adolescence on their children and grandchildren's adulthood outcomes.	No statistically significant effects on the third generation's height or education. Gendered effect on mental health outcomes—famine during the paternal grandfather's (grandmother's) prepubescent period was associated with worse mental health outcomes for grandsons (granddaughters). 16% of a SD effect for males. 22% of a SD effect for females.	No evidence of effects on the second generation. Controlling for family economic circumstances did not reduce the magnitude of the coefficient estimates, suggesting that the effects were due to direct biological mechanisms.

(continues)

TABLE 3.1. Multigenerational Papers (*Continued*)

Study	Data	Empirical strategy	Results	Interpretation/mechanisms/ heterogeneity
Almond et al. (2010) Studied the long-run consequences of in utero exposure to the Chinese famine on birth outcomes of the second generation.	China Census of Population in 2000 Sample was those born 1954–1964, $n = \sim 750{,}000$. Hong Kong Natality data Sample was those born 1957–1965, $N = \sim 600{,}000$.	Difference-in-difference design using the Chinese famine. The authors' modelled the intensity of the famine based on mortality rates around the date of birth, as well as location-specific mortality rates matched to the individuals' place of birth for some outcomes. Among residents of Hong Kong, the authors compared migrants from mainland China to nonmigrants.	Famine-exposed women had offspring who were 0.4 percent-age points less likely to be male. Among migrants to Hong-Kong, famine-exposed women had offspring that were 8% more likely to be low birth weight and 1.2% less likely to be male.	
Kim et al. (2014) Studied the effects of Chinese famine exposure in utero on second generations' medium-run outcomes.	China Census of Population in 2000. Sample was children ages 13–15 whose mothers were born 1954–1966. $n = \sim 40{,}000$ second-generation children.	Difference-in-difference design using the Chinese famine. The authors' modelled the intensity of the famine based on parents' location and date of birth using local mortality rates. Also used 2SLS and instrument for mortality rates with weather.	One SD increase in mothers' mortality rate exposure reduced sons' junior high attendance by 1.6%–6% and reduced female attendance by 1.4%–7%.	Largest effects from in utero exposure to famine. Results similar when controlled for parental education. Effect of fathers' mortality rate exposure not robust to 2SLS.

Study	Data/Sample	Method	Findings
Fung & Ha (2010) Examined the effect of parental exposure to the Chinese Famine on second-generation outcomes during childhood.	Chinese Health and Nutrition Survey. Sample was parents born in 1954–1966 and their children observed at ages 0–18. $n = \sim 6{,}000$ second-generation children.	Difference-in-difference design using the Chinese famine. The authors interacted cohort-fixed effects with location-specific excess mortality rates at the height of the famine (i.e., 1960), matched to the parents' place of residence. Assumed minimal migration across locations. Examined exposure to the famine in first few years of life.	Mother's exposure to the famine in early life reduced her children's height-for-age (0.2 of an *SD* for girls and 0.08 of an *SD* for boys). No effect of father's exposure on the second generation.
Richter & Robling (2013) Examined effects of the 1918 influenza pandemic on children of individuals exposed in utero.	Statistics Sweden multigenerational register. Sample was individuals with both parents born between 1915 and 1920. $N = \sim 60{,}000$ second-generation individuals.	Difference-in-difference design using the 1918–1919 influenza pandemic. Variation in exposure came from birth date relative to start and end dates of the pandemic, as well as geographic variation in influenza incidence in the parents' location of birth.	Reduced second-generation offspring's educational attainment by 1.8%–2.1%, and probability of college attendance by 12%. No effect on earnings. This effect was gendered: only maternal (paternal) exposure affected daughters' (sons') outcomes. The effects were largest for parents exposed in the second trimester while in utero. Similarly sized effects on educational attainment of first generation as in second generation. Accounting for the changes in the first generations' educational outcomes explained most of the effects found on the second generation for men, but not for women.

(continues)

TABLE 3.1. Multigenerational Papers (*Continued*)

Study	Data	Empirical strategy	Results	Interpretation/mechanisms/ heterogeneity
Almond et al. (2012) Investigated the relationship between infant mortality rate in state–year of first generations' birth and first generation mother's long-run outcomes, as well as second-generation health at birth.	1989–2006 U.S. vital statistics data. Number of births, $N = \sim 16$ million.	State-by-year variation in infant mortality rates (IMR) with state and year fixed effects. Looked at the effect of IMR in year before, during, and after birth of the first generation.	An additional postneonatal death in the year after the mother is born was associated with a 0.6% increase in the probability that her baby will be born below the low birth-weight threshold.	Effects on Whites' low birth incidence was 0.5% and effects on Blacks was −0.1%. Authors posited that differences by race may be due to differences in the effect of IMR on selective survival of first generation across races. Found changes in mother's incidence of diabetes, as well as educational attainment, marital status, weight gain during pregnancy, and smoking during pregnancy. Including these in the model slightly diminished the effect on low birth weight for Whites but increased (in absolute value) the effect for Blacks.
Black et al. (2019) Studied long-run effects of radiation exposure in first and second generation.	Norwegian Registry Data. Included cohorts born 1956–1966 and their children. First generation males, $N = 19,079$, second generation males, $N = 24,281$.	Difference-in-difference design using variation across locations and over time in exposure to radioactivity with location and time fixed effects. Variation across locations came from wind, rainfall, and topography.	In utero exposure during pregnancy months 3 and 4 (but not other months) led to a decline in the exposed generation's and second generation's IQ score for men. Effects sizes were 0.04 IQ points for exposed generation and 0.025 IQ points for the second generation. This implied an intergenerational transmission coefficient of 0.625.	Data on IQ score unavailable for women as only in military records.

Lee (2014) Examined the outcomes of second-generation children whose mothers and fathers were exposed to stress from the Kwangju Uprising.	Korean vital statistics in 2000 and 2002. Sample was mothers' who were in utero at time of uprising and age 20–22 when giving birth. Second generation, $N = \sim 1$ million.	Difference-in-difference design comparing outcomes of children born in city of Kwangju to those in other locations and comparing outcomes of children based on whether their mother was in utero at time of Kwangju Uprising (i.e., 10 days in May 1980).	Maternal prenatal exposure to the Kwangju Uprising reduced birth weight of the next generation by 56 g, reduced gestation by 2 days, increased likelihood of low birth weight and preterm birth.	Adding controls for mother's and father's socioeconomic status did not change the results. Largest effects from exposure in second trimester. Larger effects for second generation boys.
East et al. (2019) Studied the effect of early-life Medicaid on second-generation infant health outcomes.	1994–2015 U.S. Vital Statistics data. Sample was children of mothers born in 1979–1986.	State-by-year variation in eligibility rules for Medicaid and State Children's Health Insurance Program with state and year fixed effects. Looked at the effect of generosity in utero and at ages 1–18.	Mothers' early-life Medicaid eligibility positively impacted their children's birth weight. 1 year of mother's in utero exposure increased average birth weight by 30 g. 1 year of mother's childhood exposure increased average birth weight by 2.5 g.	No evidence of changes in overall fertility or timing of births. Early-life Medicaid increased the fraction of White births relative to minority births, and the fraction of births to high school dropout women. Accounting for changes in mother's characteristics explained about a third of the health effects.
Almond & Chay (2006) Investigated the relationship between first-generation access to racially integrated hospitals after birth and second-generation infant health.	1979–2000 U.S. Vital Statistics data.	Double-difference estimates comparing Black and White women before and after Title VI of the Civil Rights Act of 1964, and triple difference adding in a comparison with foreign-born women.	Black women born after hospital integration were less likely to have low birth–weight infants than Black women born earlier. Reduced the Black-White gap in very low birth-weight incidence among the second generation by 30%.	Found reductions in medical risk factors for mothers.

(continues)

TABLE 3.1. Multigenerational Papers (*Continued*)

Study	Data	Empirical strategy	Results	Interpretation/mechanisms/ heterogeneity
Bütikofer et al. (2019) Studied the long-run effects of Norwegian mother and child health centers.	Norwegian Registry Data. Sample was cohorts born 1936–1960 still alive in 1967, $N = \sim 300,000$.	Used differential timing of rollout of Norwegian mother and child health centers across locations with location and time-fixed effects.	Centers reduced the inter-generational persistence of educational attainment by 10%.	Effects were only statistically significant for father–son educational transmission.
Bütikofer & Salvanes (2015) Studied the long-run effects of Norwegian Tuberculosis control campaign.	Norwegian Registry Data. Sample was cohorts born 1930–1945, $N = \sim 440,000$.	Studied the Tuberculosis control campaign in Norway. Variation in exposure came from birth date relative to start date of program, as well as geographic variation in tuberculosis incidence in the location of birth.	14% reduction in intergenerational persistence in education from fathers to sons.	
Barr & Gibbs (2017) Studied the effect of Head Start on second-generation adult outcomes.	National Longitudinal Survey of Youth (NLSY; 1979) and Children of the NLSY. First generation, $n = \sim 2,400$, Second Generation, $n = \sim 3,500$.	Used differential timing of rollout of Head Start across locations with location and time-fixed effects.	A significant impact of Head Start availability for mothers on a summary measure of well-being that combined the next generation's educational attainment, incidence of teen pregnancy, and interaction with the criminal justice system. Mother's access to Head Start increased this index by 0.25–0.45 SDs.	Also estimate effects on first generation for the same outcomes and find similar magnitudes for first and second generation.
Rossin-Slater & Wüst (2016) Examined the long-run effects of preschools in Denmark.	Administrative population register data in Denmark. First generation, $N = \sim 900,000$.	Used differential timing of rollout of preschools across locations with location and time fixed effects.	Children of women who had access to preschool by age 3 had 0.4% more years of schooling (not significant in all models) and were 6% less likely to only have a compulsory level of education at age 25.	Little evidence of selection into fertility. Results suggested transmission coefficient of education from first to second generation of 0.27–1, depending on the outcome.

Note. 2SLS = 2 stage least squares.

later offspring. Interestingly, the differences in poor health were not clearly due to conditions related to metabolic syndrome or psychiatric conditions, which have been generationally linked to nutritional deprivation in animal studies.

Van den Berg and Pinger (2016) invoked a related identification strategy based on the German famine of 1916–1918 to investigate generationally persistent effects resulting from food restrictions experienced during the period just before adolescence (often called the slow-growth period).[6] Notably, this is one of only a few studies to examine the effect of a negative childhood shock outside of the first few years of life: the authors' focus on this later developmental period stemmed from a series of small sample[7] studies of data from the Overkalix region of northern Sweden; the results suggested that the slow-growth period may be a period of increased sensitivity for epigenetic imprinting (Cooney, 2006; Pembrey, 2002). Also motivated by the Overkalix studies' findings and previous research suggesting that some heritable epigenetic modifications may be sex dependent (e.g., Hochberg et al., 2011; Pembrey et al., 2006), van den Berg and Pinger explored gendered linkages between low maternal grandmothers' (paternal grandfathers') food access during the years right before adolescence and granddaughters' (grandsons') outcomes. They hypothesized that, because the period immediately prior to adolescence is a sensitive period for the methylation of male sperm (but not for the development of female eggs), only male slow-growth period famine exposure should affect later generations.

The authors compared second and third generations' adult height, mental health,[8] and educational outcomes based on the age of the first generation at the time of famine exposure. Importantly, their analyses relied on the assumption that there were no differences in survival between those who were exposed during their slow-growth period and those who were exposed at earlier or later stages of development. In contrast to Painter et al. (2008), van den Berg and Pinger's second-generation analyses were more mixed, with no evidence that maternal exposure affected later offspring outcomes and inconsistent patterns associated with paternal exposure. In addition, the authors did not find statistically significant effects on the third generation's height or education. However, when they focused on mental health, they did find evidence of the types of gendered relationships described earlier. Specifically, paternal grandfather exposure to the famine during his slow-growth period was positively associated with grandsons' mental health, while maternal grandmother exposure was positively associated with the mental health of granddaughters. Controlling for family economic circumstances did not reduce the magnitude

[6]Like the Dutch Hunger Winter, the German famine was severe and sharply delineated in time, making it a useful natural experiment.
[7]Approximately 300 offspring and grandchildren of parents and grandparents born in 1890, 1905, and 1920.
[8]Mental health is measured by the Mental Component Summary Scale, which is based on a factor analysis of inputs measuring general mental health, emotional functioning, social functioning, and vitality.

of the coefficient estimates, suggesting that the effects were due to direct biological processes that, because of the gender-specific patterns, the authors interpreted as evidence of epigenetic mechanisms.

Several studies of the Chinese famine found evidence of multigenerational effects. These studies all used a similar approach of comparing the offspring of cohorts conceived before, during, and after the 1959–1961 Chinese famine and used geographic variation in the famine's intensity. Almond, Edlund, Li, and Zhang (2010) found that treated generation's fetal exposure to malnutrition increased the likelihood of female births in the second generation, which is consistent with the Trivers and Willard (1973) prediction that poor fetal conditions should favor daughters. Extending the research design to consider later life outcomes, Kim, Deng, Fleisher, and Li (2014) found that the second generation was less likely to attend junior high school, and Fung and Ha (2010) found that the second generation had lower height-for-age and weight-for-age. Given that mortality was high during the famine period, Kim et al. also considered selective survival as a potential mechanism and determined this would bias against their findings, because the evidence suggested that mortality was higher among the less advantaged, whose baseline health was generally lower than other groups.

Disease Exposure
Several researchers have extended the first-generation literature on the long-term effects of early-life exposure to infectious disease to consider effects on later generations. Using generationally linked Swedish administrative data, Richter and Robling (2013) analyzed outcomes among the children of those who were differentially exposed to the 1918–1919 influenza pandemic in utero. The sheer number of observations (a 35% random sample of all individuals born in Sweden between 1932 and 1967) gave the researchers the statistical power they needed to identify the effects of exposure at different stages of fetal development. Like van den Berg and Pinger (2016), they found evidence of gendered linkages across generations. Specifically, they found that mothers' (fathers') in utero exposure to the Spanish flu reduced educational attainment among female (male) offspring by 1.8% (2.1%) and reduced the probability of college attendance by 12% (12%). They found no evidence that these effects translated into lower earnings, however, which could be due to the fact that Sweden has a compressed earnings distribution. The effect seemed to be driven by the first generation's exposure during the second trimester.

Also like van den Berg and Pinger (2016), Richter and Robling (2013) compared multigenerational estimates based on analyses that did and did not control for parents' schooling levels. Their results are somewhat harder to interpret, however, as they found no evidence that mothers' education explained the persistent effect on daughters, but controlling for father's education did eliminate the estimated link between father–son pairs. Thus, a superficial interpretation of their results would be that biological processes underlie the transmission from mothers to daughters, whereas socioeconomic processes underlie the transmission from fathers to sons. Another point of interest is that, when the authors found significant effects on the treated generation (only in some specifications), it was first-trimester exposure that appeared to be important, in contrast to the primary influence of second-trimester exposure on the second generation. The authors argued that if nonbiological mechanisms were driving the generationally persistent effects of in utero flu exposure, then the relevant trimester would be the same for both generations.

Almond, Currie, and Herrmann (2012) used U.S. vital statistics data to investigate generationally persistent impacts of broader disease exposure. They examined how state-level variation in infant mortality rates at the time of the mothers' birth related to their offspring's likelihood of being low birth weight. Among Whites, they found that higher infant mortality in the year after the mother was born was associated with an increase in the probability that her baby would be born below the low birth-weight threshold. Among Blacks, the estimates were opposite in sign. The authors posited that these racial differences in health effects were driven by racial differences in selective survival as described previously. Specifically, the observed improvement in Black infants' health was consistent with processes where the selection effect dominated the scarring effect, whereas, for Whites, the scarring effect dominated the selection effect. The dominating processes may have differed across racial groups because of differences in underlying health or access to health services.

Radiation Exposure

Black, Bütikofer, Devereux, and Salvanes (2019) built on an existing medical literature documenting the detrimental effects of exposure to acute radiation (previously based on the survivors of the atomic bombs at Hiroshima and Nagasaki), by investigating the effects of in utero exposure to low-dose levels of radioactivity on later life cognitive functioning. The authors' research design was based on regional variation within Norway of in utero exposure to low levels of radioactivity that resulted from extensive nuclear weapons testing in Russia during the 1950s and 1960s. Norway's proximity to Russia made it particularly vulnerable to nuclear fallout, with differences in treatment intensity across locations due to differences in locations' wind, rainfall, and topography. This variation was applied to administrative data that included IQ scores. A key feature of the research design was that there was little public awareness of exposure, so regional differences in outcomes were unlikely to be driven by individuals' stress about the effects of radiation or by avoidance behaviors.

Black et al.'s (2019) main analyses focused on the impacts of in utero exposure on the treated generation. Consistent with the medical literature, they found that in utero exposure during the third and fourth months of gestation (but not other months) led to a decline in first-generation males'

IQ scores.[9] In addition, they found an effect on the IQ of later sons that was about 60% as large as the first-generation effect. This suggests that a substantial part of the adverse cognitive effects of in utero radiation exposure is passed from one generation to the next.

Stress

Lee (2014) examined whether the first-generation effects of stress exposure during the in utero period spilled over onto later generations. His natural experiment was based on the Kwangju Uprising in South Korea, which was unanticipated, short-lived (i.e., 10 days), and geographically concentrated. He found evidence that maternal exposure to stress while in utero had detrimental impacts on the next generation's birth outcomes, and that the effects were particularly strong when exposure occurred in the second trimester. There was no evidence that the changes were driven by changes in mothers' or fathers' socioeconomic status.

Several drawbacks to Lee's data are worth noting because they highlight broader challenges in this literature. First, because there was limited information about fathers on the birth certificate, the analysis focused on the effects of mother's exposure to the uprising. This is a common limitation encountered by analyses of administrative natality data—although they aid researchers' ability to identify precise effects by providing large samples, they provide limited parental information, particularly for fathers. Second, because the data did not provide information on mothers' location of birth, it must be inferred based on the child's location of birth. We discuss the potential impacts of these data issues below.

Positive Policy Interventions

An even smaller number of studies investigate multigenerational effects of positive health interventions, although these too find consistent evidence that the effects of early-life environments persist to later generations. Analyses of positive interventions are particularly important because, along with providing additional information on the persistent effects of early-life environments, they can provide important insights toward the design of effective antipoverty policies by helping to more fully quantify the range of long-run program benefits.

To date, only one study has investigated the effects of an intervention that targets the prenatal period. East, Miller, Page, and Wherry (2019) built on the existing literature documenting Medicaid's substantive positive effects on children's long-term health and labor market outcomes by further investigating the health of treated-cohorts' offspring at the time of their birth. Like many first-generation studies of Medicaid, their natural experiment was based on changes in eligibility rules during the 1980s and 1990s that lead to dramatic

---

[9]IQ information is only available for men. However, similar effects are found for first-generation women's exposure in utero on their son's IQ.

FIGURE 3.1. Change in Medicaid Prenatal Coverage Across Cohorts Born 1979-1986

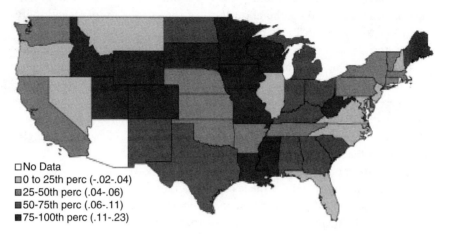

☐No Data
◻0 to 25th perc (-.02-.04)
▨25-50th perc (.04-.06)
▩50-75th perc (.06-.11)
■75-100th perc (.11-.23)

Note. From *Multigenerational Impacts of Childhood Access to the Safety Net: Early Life Exposure to Medicaid and the Next Generation's Health* (pp. 69–70), by C. N. East, S. Miller, M. Page, and L. M. Wherry, 2019, Cambridge, MA: National Bureau of Economic Research. Copyright by National Bureau of Economic Research. Adapted with permission.

increases in individuals' prenatal and early-childhood coverage—changes that were adopted differentially across states and time. Figure 3.1 provides some intuition about the treatment and control groups created through this research design. The states with the darkest shading are those that expanded coverage by the largest amount; states with the lightest shading are those that expanded coverage the least.

East et al. (2019) linked first-generation in utero and childhood Medicaid eligibility to later generation's outcomes through the information on the mothers' date of birth and state of birth that was available in the U.S. Vital Statistics Natality files. This allowed them to determine mothers' likely eligibility for Medicaid at each stage of childhood. They found that mothers' early-life Medicaid eligibility positively impacted their children's birth weight. The estimated effects of treated cohorts' in utero eligibility on later offspring were about 10 times as large as the estimated effects associated with one additional year of eligibility later in childhood. Strong patterns in the estimates also pointed toward beneficial effects on offspring's incidence of low birth weight, very low birth weight, and likelihood of being born prematurely.

Other natural experiments investigated multigenerational effects of early-life health interventions targeting older children. All of these studies also found evidence of positive effects, which has the important implication that generational trajectories can be altered even after birth. Almond and Chay (2006) studied the multigenerational impact of Title VI of the Civil Rights Act of 1964, which prohibited segregation and discrimination in hospitals receiving federal funds. Prior to Title VI, Southern Blacks were excluded from full access to hospital resources. Earlier work by Almond, Chay, and Greenstone (2006) documented a strong association between Title VI and reductions in racial gaps in infant mortality due to diarrhea and pneumonia, which made up a large fraction of infants' hospital treatments. Their experimental variation rested on the abruptness of the change in infant mortality after 1964, the sharp decline in death from specific conditions that were treatable in hospitals, and the contrast with small changes in infant mortality among Whites. This same natural experiment was employed by Almond and Chay to examine the health of the descendants of Black and White women who were differentially exposed to Title VI. Applying this strategy to the outcomes of the next generation, Almond and Chay found that Black women born after hospital integration were less likely to have low birth-weight infants than Black women born earlier: specifically, the treated generation's access to better quality healthcare reduced the Black–White gap in very low birth-weight incidence among the second generation by 30%.

Two studies by Bütikofer and coauthors (2015, 2019) examined the effects of public health interventions on the intergenerational persistence of educational attainment. Estimating the impact of an intervention on the *intergenerational transmission* of outcomes is a related, but different, concept from estimating the direct effect on later generations' outcomes. Specifically, the intergenerational transmission coefficient for a particular outcome can be thought of as the correlation in that outcome between fathers and sons. High correlations between fathers and sons indicate that family background is a strong predictor of the next generation's success, whereas small correlations indicate that parents' status is not as important—in other words, there is more equality of opportunity when intergenerational correlations are low.[10] Bütikofer et al. (2019) considered the introduction of Norwegian mother and child health centers, exploiting the fact that the timing of center openings varied substantially across locations, whereas Bütikofer and Salvanes (2015) studied the effects of a Norwegian tuberculosis control campaign making use of the fact that the campaign should have had a bigger effect in geographic areas that had higher precampaign tuberculosis levels. Although both studies focused on how the interventions improved treated cohorts' later life health and earnings, they also found that the interventions reduced the intergenerational persistence of educational attainment by 10% to 14%.

Two recent analyses of early-life interventions that provided a combination of health and education services also found evidence of generationally persistent effects (Barr & Gibbs, 2017; Rossin-Slater & Wüst, 2016). These studies built on an existing literature documenting that cohorts exposed to high-quality

---

[10]In many ways, a policy's effect on equality of opportunity is more directly measured by its effect on the intergenerational correlation than by its effect on later generation's aggregate outcomes. However, estimating intergenerational correlations requires data that contains information on the same outcome for both children and their parents. Most U.S. data sets that contain generationally linked outcomes are small, which limits the extent to which natural experiments can be applied to produce precise estimates. Several Scandinavian countries have linked administrative data across generations, which has allowed for more progress on this front.

preschool programs (especially Head Start) experience better long-term effects (e.g., higher levels of schooling and earnings, better health, and lower likelihood of engaging in risky behaviors). Both studies created comparison groups using geographic variation in the rollout of targeted, high-quality preschools that improved poor children's health environments by providing nutritional, dental, and other health-related services. Barr and Gibbs (2017) investigated the effects of the U.S. Head Start program, which was adopted by different counties in different years throughout the 1960s as part of the U.S. War on Poverty. They found evidence of a significant impact of Head Start availability on a summary measure of well-being that combined the next generation's educational attainment, incidence of teen pregnancy, and interaction with the criminal justice system. Specifically, the children of women who lived in counties with a Head Start program during their preschool years scored about 0.25 to 0.45 standard deviations (*SD*s) higher on the index than the children of women who did not have access to Head Start when they were young. Rossin-Slater and Wüst (2016) exploited variation across municipalities in the timing of government-approved preschool openings between 1930 and 1960. They found that children of women who had access to high-quality preschool by age 3 had 0.4% more years of schooling and were 6% less likely to only have a compulsory level of education at age 25.

DISCUSSION

Taken as a whole, there is emerging evidence that early-childhood environments have substantive spillover effects onto later generations. This is apparent not only for severe negative health shocks but also for positive policy interventions. In terms of magnitudes, second-generation estimates are typically smaller, or similar in magnitude, to first-generation estimates. East et al. (2019), for example, found the effect of early-life access to Medicaid on low birthweight incidence in the next generation was about 40% of the effect on the same outcome for the treated generation. This is roughly consistent with Currie and Moretti (2007), who found that the probability of being a low birth-weight infant was nearly 50% higher among children whose mothers were themselves below the low birth-weight threshold. Similarly, Rossin-Slater and Wüst (2016) found that the effects of access to high-quality preschool on the second-generation's educational outcomes were 27% to 107% of the magnitude of the effect on the first generation. Their estimates are roughly in line with estimates of the intergenerational correlation in parent–child schooling in the United States and Denmark (the source country for Rossin-Slater and Wüst's study).[11] Black et al. (2019) found that about 60% of the effect of radiation on the first-generation's IQ score was transmitted to the second

---

[11]Estimated intergenerational correlations in the United States and Denmark are typically between 0.4 and 0.5 (Hertz et al., 2008).

generation, while Painter et al. (2008), Richter and Robling (2013), and Barr and Gibbs (2017) estimated first- and second-generation effects that were similar in magnitude to each other.[12]

Another important implication of these studies is that cost–benefit ratios based only on cohorts immediately affected by program interventions are likely to underestimate their overall efficacy—*even when taking the treated generation's long-run benefits into account.* For example, in their study of the multigenerational effects of early-life access to Medicaid, East et al. (2019) estimated that even when benefit calculations are restricted to those associated with low birth weight in the first year of life, the medical cost savings generated by the second generation's improved health in the first year of life alone may be roughly 30% of the cost of the initial investment.[13] This calculation ignored the additional medical cost savings beyond the first year of life that may result from any health improvements that are associated with reductions in low birth weight, and they ignored increases in later life earnings and tax revenues that accompany higher birth weights (e.g., Bharadwaj et al., 2013; Black et al., 2007).

To our knowledge, this is the only multigenerational study to date that explicitly considered the dollar value of second-generation benefits relative to program costs, but the magnitude of second-generation effects estimated for some other U.S. early-life interventions also hints that there may be high returns. Barr and Gibbs (2017), for example, estimated that the first generation's participation in the Head Start program increased the second generation's probability of completing high school by roughly 25%. Tamborini, Kim, and Sakamoto (2015) estimated that the difference in the average present discounted value of lifetime earnings for a female completing high school, compared with dropping out of high school, is $0.14 million (in 2012 dollars). Using this descriptive evidence, a very rough estimate of the expected earnings benefit to the second generation is 0.14 million × 0.25 or equal to $35,000.[14]

---

[12]An additional point of interest is that van den Berg and Pinger (2016) found no evidence of first-generation famine exposure on second-generation outcomes, although they did find effects on third-generation outcomes. As a reminder, this is the only study we know of that analyzed the multigenerational effects of adolescent exposure, and the processes driving their estimates were, therefore, likely to be quite different from those described elsewhere in this chapter.

[13]East et al. (2019) used the 3% discount rate chosen by the U.S. Government Interagency Working Group on the Social Cost of Carbon to obtain present value estimates of medical expenses averted in the future. The dollar value ascribed to future benefits will actually strongly depend on how the future benefits are discounted. There is an active literature in economics that considers appropriate discount rates with respect to interventions with long-run impacts, especially regarding climate change (e.g., Weitzman et al., 2013), but using discount rates in the mid-range of this literature suggests that the magnitude of these previously ignored multigenerational benefits may be nontrivial.

[14]The gain for males earning a high school degree is $0.18 million, so the benefits are similar for males. Note that these are not *causal* estimates of the effect of a high school degree. Additionally, Barr and Gibbs (2017) found changes in college attendance, so the benefits may be even larger than implied by this back of the envelope calculation focusing only on changes in high school graduation.

In contrast, in 2013, federal per-pupil Head Start expenditures were about $8,000 (U.S. Department of Health and Human Services, Administration for Children and Families, 2013). Of course, even the most thoughtful cost–benefit calculations should be interpreted cautiously, as the time lags required to measure multigenerational spillovers mean that present-day program parameters and contextual environments will likely be different from those at play during the treatment period.

Because the causal literature on the multigenerational effects of early-life environments is still in its infancy, we are still very far from pinpointing underlying processes. As described earlier, an extensive literature has documented that a variety of environmental conditions affect treated-generations' physical health, mental health, education levels, and earnings—all of which have the potential to influence the well-being of later offspring and most of which are likely to be correlated with each other. This, together with many data constraints, has prevented thorough analyses of the candidate mechanisms.

The literature to date does provide suggestive evidence that there may be important mechanisms in addition to the early environment's effects on treated-generations' socioeconomic status. Most studies that have controlled for the first-generation's education and/or earnings have found that their estimated effects on later generations' outcomes are robust to the inclusion of these variables.[15]

Some studies of multigenerational effects find suggestive evidence that changes in maternal health and health behaviors may play a role. Almond et al. (2012), for example, documented that the local infant mortality rate in early childhood is positively associated with later incidence of diabetes, high weight gain, and smoking during pregnancy, although controlling for these maternal outcomes does not explain all of the estimated effect of the disease environment on later generations. On the other hand, East et al. (2019) found no changes in maternal health or behaviors among mothers who had in utero Medicaid access. Almond and Chay (2006) found that hospital integration reduced mothers' medical risk factors, but they did not investigate the extent to which this explains their second-generation effects.

Another possible channel—one that is relatively easy to observe—is changes in fertility. However, many of the studies described above do not directly examine how the early-life environment alters the first-generation's fertility. Among those that do, there is little evidence that early-life environments change overall fertility (East et al., 2019; Rossin-Slater & Wüst, 2016), but this possible mechanism deserves further investigation.

Another channel that can often be observed is a change in the composition of women giving birth. Even if aggregate later life fertility is unaffected by the early-life health environment, the types of women giving birth may be affected. Many of the multigenerational studies described in this chapter try

---

[15]As noted earlier, an exception is Richter and Robling (2013), who found that controlling for fathers' education eliminates the persistent effects of flu exposure between fathers and sons (but not mothers and daughters).

to get a sense of the importance of this potential mechanism by including controls for the first-generation's demographic characteristics—the goal being to see how much the inclusion of these controls changes the estimated effect on future generations. The results are wide-ranging, with some studies finding that compositional changes may drive part of, but not all of, the generationally persistent effect (Almond et al., 2012; East et al., 2019) and others' finding little supportive evidence (van den Berg & Pinger, 2016).

Finally, as discussed before, selective survival could be another important channel influencing later generations' observed health. In particular, the extreme negative shocks that some studies have harnessed to create treatment and control groups also affected contemporaneous mortality rates. This may have had a mechanical, positive influence on the next generation's observed health (through selection into birth). To date, however, Almond et al. (2012) are the only authors to find suggestive evidence that this type of selection plays a role.

Thus far, data constraints have limited our ability to fully investigate early-life environments' generationally persistent effects and potential underlying mechanisms. Data sets that include information on both parents and their children are typically small, limiting ability to precisely detect multigenerational linkages. As the United States moves towards other countries' willingness to invest in linked administrative data, we may be able to learn more, but administrative data often lack sufficient detail to speak to mechanisms. Efforts to move forward on this front will require creativity. Meanwhile, we make several recommendations for future analyses. First, to the extent the data allow, researchers should always investigate the direct effects of the early-life environment on both the first and the second generations, focusing in particular on first-generation outcomes that are known to be predictive of offspring outcomes, and exploring the extent to which these first-generation effects can explain the second-generation effects. Gaining an understanding of these types of early warning indicators can provide insights into potentially important mediating processes and allow researchers to make stronger statements about the potential effect of current programs on future generations.[16] Second, when possible, researchers should analyze first-generation fertility responses to the early-life intervention, along with potential changes in the composition of second-generation births. The results of such analyses will provide information that is critical to understanding the role of selection versus. direct-health effects. Finally, whenever possible, direct comparisons should be made between the magnitudes of the effects experienced by the different generations (using information available either within or across studies). These steps will help to build a more complete picture about the processes underlying the intergenerational transmission of health and economic outcomes.

Although there is still much to be learned, the analyses described in this chapter offer an important perspective on persistent inequalities and the

---

[16]We thank Jens Ludwig for making this point.

potential role for government intervention. Generational persistence in the impacts of early-life environments suggest that historical differences in fetal health conditions between advantaged and disadvantaged groups may undermine contemporaneous efforts to close health and economic gaps. At the same time, these early results indicate that early-life health investments have payoffs that extend well beyond those that social policymakers usually consider.

REFERENCES

Aerts, L., & Van Assche, F. A. (2006). Animal evidence for the transgenerational development of diabetes mellitus. *The International Journal of Biochemistry & Cell Biology, 38*, 894–903. http://dx.doi.org/10.1016/j.biocel.2005.07.006

Almond, D. (2006). Is the 1918 influenza pandemic over? Long-term effects of in utero influenza exposure in the post-1940 U.S. population. *Journal of Political Economy, 114*, 672–712. http://dx.doi.org/10.1086/507154

Almond, D., & Chay, K. Y. (2006, February). *The long-run and intergenerational impact of poor infant health: Evidence from cohorts born during the Civil Rights era* (Working Paper). Retrieved from http://www.nber.org/~almond/chay_npc_paper.pdf

Almond, D., Chay, K. Y., & Greenstone, M. (2006, December). *Civil Rights, the war on poverty, and black-white convergence in infant mortality in the rural South and Mississippi* (MIT Working Paper No. 07-04). Boston, MA: MIT Department of Economics. Retrieved from https://dspace.mit.edu/handle/1721.1/63330

Almond, D., & Currie, J. (2011a). Human capital development before age five. In D. Card & O. Ashenfelter (Eds.), *Handbook of labor economics* (Vol. 4B, pp. 1315–1486). Amsterdam, The Netherlands: North Holland.

Almond, D., & Currie, J. (2011b). Killing me softly: The fetal origins hypothesis. *The Journal of Economic Perspectives, 25*, 153–172. http://dx.doi.org/10.1257/jep.25.3.153

Almond, D., Currie, J., & Duque, V. (2017). *Childhood circumstances and adult outcomes: Act II* (NBER Working Paper No. 23017). Cambridge, MA: National Bureau of Economic Research.

Almond, D., Currie, J., & Herrmann, M. (2012). From infant to mother: Early disease environment and future maternal health. *Labour Economics, 19*, 475–483. http://dx.doi.org/10.1016/j.labeco.2012.05.015

Almond, D., Edlund, L., Li, H., & Zhang, J. (2010). Long-term effects of early-life development: Evidence from the 1959–1961 Chinese famine. In T. Ito & A. K. Rose (Eds.), *The economic consequences of demographic change in East Asia* (pp. 321–345). Chicago, IL: University of Chicago Press.

Almond, D., & Mazumder, B. (2005). The 1918 influenza pandemic and subsequent health outcomes: An analysis of SIPP data. *The American Economic Review, 95*, 258–262. http://dx.doi.org/10.1257/000282805774669943

Barker, D. J. (1990). The fetal and infant origins of adult disease. *British Medical Journal, 301*, 1111. http://dx.doi.org/10.1136/bmj.301.6761.1111

Barr, A., & Gibbs, C. R. (2017, August). *Breaking the cycle? The intergenerational effects of an anti-poverty program in early childhood* (Working Paper).

Becker, G. S., & Tomes, N. (1979). An equilibrium theory of the distribution of income and intergenerational mobility. *Journal of Political Economy, 87*, 1153–1189. http://dx.doi.org/10.1086/260831

Bhalotra, S. R., & Venkataramani, A. (2015, August). *Shadows of the captain of the men of death: Early life health interventions, human capital investments, and institutions* (Working Paper). http://dx.doi.org/10.2139/ssrn.1940725

Bharadwaj, P., Løken, K. V., & Neilson, C. (2013). Early life health interventions and academic achievement. *The American Economic Review, 103*, 1862–1891. http://dx.doi.org/10.1257/aer.103.5.1862

Black, S. E., Bütikofer, A., Devereux, P. J., & Salvanes, K. G. (2019). This is only a test? Long-run and intergenerational impacts of prenatal exposure to radioactive fallout. *Review of Economics and Statistics, 101*, 531–546.

Black, S. E., Devereux, P. J., & Salvanes, K. G. (2007). From the cradle to the labor market? The effect of birth weight on adult outcomes. *The Quarterly Journal of Economics, 122*, 409–439. http://dx.doi.org/10.1162/qjec.122.1.409

Brown, A. S. (2012). Epidemiologic studies of exposure to prenatal infection and risk of schizophrenia and autism. *Developmental Neurobiology, 72*, 1272–1276. http://dx.doi.org/10.1002/dneu.22024

Brown, D. W., Kowalski, A. E., & Lurie, I. Z. (2017). *Medicaid as an investment in children: What is the long-term impact on tax receipts* (NBER Working Paper No. 20835)? Cambridge, MA: National Bureau of Economic Research.

Bütikofer, A., Løken, K. V., & Salvanes, K. G. (2019). Infant health care and long-term outcomes. *Review of Economics and Statistics, 101*, 341–354. http://dx.doi.org/10.1162/rest_a_00790

Bütikofer, A., & Salvanes, K. G. (2015, November). *Disease control and inequality reduction: Evidence from a tuberculosis testing and vaccination campaign* (NHH Working Paper No. 28/2015). http://dx.doi.org/10.2139/ssrn.2719441

Canetta, S. E., & Brown, A. S. (2012). Prenatal infection, maternal immune activation, and risk for schizophrenia. *Translational Neuroscience, 3*, 320–327. http://dx.doi.org/10.2478/s13380-012-0045-6

Carneiro, P., & Ginja, R. (2014). Long term impacts of compensatory preschool on health and behavior: Evidence from Head Start. *American Economic Journal: Economic Policy, 6*, 135–173. http://dx.doi.org/10.1257/pol.6.4.135

Case, A., Lubotsky, D., & Paxson, C. (2002). Economic status and health in childhood: The origins of the gradient. *The American Economic Review, 92*, 1308–1334. http://dx.doi.org/10.1257/000282802762024520

Catalano, P. M., & Ehrenberg, H. M. (2006). The short-and long-term implications of maternal obesity on the mother and her offspring. *BJOG: An International Journal of Obstetrics & Gynaecology, 113*, 1126–1133. http://dx.doi.org/10.1111/j.1471-0528.2006.00989.x

Clark, G. (2014). *The son also rises: Surnames and the history of social mobility*. Princeton, NJ: Princeton University Press.

Cohodes, S. R., Grossman, D. S., Kleiner, S. A., & Lovenheim, M. F. (2016). The effect of child health insurance access on schooling: Evidence from public insurance expansions. *The Journal of Human Resources, 51*, 727–759. http://dx.doi.org/10.3368/jhr.51.3.1014-6688R1

Conger, R. D., & Conger, K. J. (2007). Understanding the processes through which economic hardship influences families and children. In D. R. Crane & T. B. Heaton (Eds.), *Handbook of families and poverty* (pp. 64–81). Thousand Oaks, CA: Sage.

Cooney, C. A. (2006). Germ cells carry the epigenetic benefits of grandmother's diet. *Proceedings of the National Academy of Sciences, 103*, 17071–17072. http://dx.doi.org/10.1073/pnas.0608653103

Cowley, J. J., & Griesel, R. D. (1966). The effect on growth and behaviour of rehabilitating first and second generation low protein rats. *Animal Behaviour, 14*, 506–517. http://dx.doi.org/10.1016/S0003-3472(66)80052-0

Currie, J., Decker, S., & Lin, W. (2008). Has public health insurance for older children reduced disparities in access to care and health outcomes? *Journal of Health Economics, 27*, 1567–1581. http://dx.doi.org/10.1016/j.jhealeco.2008.07.002

Currie, J., & Moretti, E. (2007). Biology as destiny? Short- and long-run determinants of intergenerational transmission of birth weight. *Journal of Labor Economics, 25,* 231–264. http://dx.doi.org/10.1086/511377

Daxinger, L., & Whitelaw, E. (2010). Transgenerational epigenetic inheritance: More questions than answers. *Genome Research, 20,* 1623–1628. http://dx.doi.org/10.1101/gr.106138.110

Daxinger, L., & Whitelaw, E. (2012). Understanding transgenerational epigenetic inheritance via the gametes in mammals. *Nature Reviews: Genetics, 13,* 153–162. http://dx.doi.org/10.1038/nrg3188

Deming, D. (2009). Early childhood intervention and life-cycle skill development: Evidence from Head Start. *American Economic Journal: Applied Economics, 1,* 111–134. http://dx.doi.org/10.1257/app.1.3.111

Dunn, G. A., & Bale, T. L. (2009). Maternal high-fat diet promotes body length increases and insulin insensitivity in second-generation mice. *Endocrinology, 150,* 4999–5009. http://dx.doi.org/10.1210/en.2009-0500

East, C. N., Miller, S., Page, M., & Wherry, L. R. (2019, February). *Multigenerational impacts of childhood access to the safety net: Early life exposure to Medicaid and the next generation's health* (NBER Working Paper No. 23810). Cambridge, MA: National Bureau of Economic Research.

Elo, I. T., & Preston, S. H. (1992). Effects of early-life conditions on adult mortality: A review. *Population Index, 58,* 186–212. http://dx.doi.org/10.2307/3644718

Fitzsimons, E., & Vera-Hernandez, M. (2013). *Food for thought? Breastfeeding and child development* (IFS Working Paper No. W13/31). London, England: Institute for Fiscal Studies. http://dx.doi.org/10.1920/wp.ifs.2013.1331

Fung, W., & Ha, W. (2010). Intergenerational effects of the 1959–61 China famine. In R. Fuentes-Nieva & P. A. Sack (Eds.), *Risks, shocks, and human development: On the brink* (pp. 222–254). Basingstoke, England: Palgrave Macmillan.

Garces, E., Thomas, D., & Currie, J. (2002). Longer term effects of Head Start. *The American Economic Review, 92,* 999–1012. http://dx.doi.org/10.1257/00028280260344560

Glied, S., & Neidell, M. (2010). The economic value of teeth. *The Journal of Human Resources, 45,* 468–496. http://dx.doi.org/10.3368/jhr.45.2.468

Gluckman, P. D., Hanson, M. A., Cooper, C., & Thornburg, K. L. (2008). Effect of in utero and early-life conditions on adult health and disease. *The New England Journal of Medicine, 359,* 61–73. http://dx.doi.org/10.1056/NEJMra0708473

Grossniklaus, U., Kelly, W. G., Ferguson-Smith, A. C., Pembrey, M., & Lindquist, S. (2013). Transgenerational epigenetic inheritance: How important is it? *Nature Reviews Genetics, 14,* 228–235. http://dx.doi.org/10.1038/nrg3435

Heard, E., & Martienssen, R. A. (2014). Transgenerational epigenetic inheritance: Myths and mechanisms. *Cell, 157,* 95–109. http://dx.doi.org/10.1016/j.cell.2014.02.045

Heckman, J. J. (2007). The economics, technology, and neuroscience of human capability formation. *Proceedings of the National Academy of Sciences, 104,* 13250–13255. http://dx.doi.org/10.1073/pnas.0701362104

Hertz, T., Jayasundera, T., Piraino, P., Selcuk, S., Smith, N., & Verashchagina, A. (2008). The inheritance of educational inequality: International comparisons and fifty-year trends. *The B.E. Journal of Economic Analysis & Policy, 7.* http://dx.doi.org/10.2202/1935-1682.1775

Hochberg, Z., Feil, R., Constancia, M., Fraga, M., Junien, C., Carel, J. C., . . . Albertsson-Wikland, K. (2011). Child health, developmental plasticity, and epigenetic programming. *Endocrine Reviews, 32,* 159–224. http://dx.doi.org/10.1210/er.2009-0039

Hoynes, H., Schanzenbach, D. W., & Almond, D. (2016). Long-run impacts of childhood access to the safety net. *The American Economic Review, 106,* 903–934. http://dx.doi.org/10.1257/aer.20130375

Hsin, A. (2012). Is biology destiny? Birth weight and differential parental treatment. *Demography, 49*, 1385–1405. http://dx.doi.org/10.1007/s13524-012-0123-y

Hunter, E. S., III, & Sadler, T. W. (1987). D-(–)-beta-hydroxybutyrate-induced effects on mouse embryos in vitro. *Teratology, 36*, 259–264. http://dx.doi.org/10.1002/tera.1420360214

Jimenez-Chillaron, J. C., Isganaitis, E., Charalambous, M., Gesta, S., Pentinat-Pelegrin, T., Faucette, R. R., . . . Patti, M. E. (2009). Intergenerational transmission of glucose intolerance and obesity by *in utero* undernutrition in mice. *Diabetes, 58*, 460–468. http://dx.doi.org/10.2337/db08-0490

Jirtle, R. L., & Skinner, M. K. (2007). Environmental epigenomics and disease susceptibility. *Nature Reviews. Genetics, 8*, 253–262. http://dx.doi.org/10.1038/nrg2045

Kim, S., Deng, Q., Fleisher, B. M., & Li, S. (2014). The lasting impact of parental early life malnutrition on their offspring: Evidence from the china great leap forward famine. *World Development, 54*, 232–242. http://dx.doi.org/10.1016/j.worlddev.2013.08.007

Lee, C. (2014). Intergenerational health consequences of *in utero* exposure to maternal stress: Evidence from the 1980 Kwangju uprising. *Social Science & Medicine, 119*, 284–291. http://dx.doi.org/10.1016/j.socscimed.2014.07.001

Levine, P. B., & Schanzenbach, D. (2009). The impact of children's public health insurance expansions on educational outcomes. *Forum for Health Economics & Policy, 12*, 1–26. http://dx.doi.org/10.2202/1558-9544.1137

Lin, M.-J., & Liu, E. M. (2014). Does in utero exposure to illness matter? The 1918 influenza epidemic in Taiwan as a natural experiment. *Journal of Health Economics, 37*, 152–163. http://dx.doi.org/10.1016/j.jhealeco.2014.05.004

Ludwig, J., & Miller, D. L. (2007). Does Head Start improve children's life chances? Evidence from a regression discontinuity design. *The Quarterly Journal of Economics, 122*, 159–208. http://dx.doi.org/10.1162/qjec.122.1.159

Lumey, L. H., Stein, A. D., & Susser, E. (2011). Prenatal famine and adult health. *Annual Review of Public Health, 32*, 237–262. http://dx.doi.org/10.1146/annurev-publhealth-031210-101230

Martínez, D., Pentinat, T., Ribó, S., Daviaud, C., Bloks, V. W., Cebrià, J., . . . Jiménez-Chillarón, J. C. (2014). In utero undernutrition in male mice programs liver lipid metabolism in the second-generation offspring involving altered Lxra DNA methylation. *Cell Metabolism, 19*, 941–951. http://dx.doi.org/10.1016/j.cmet.2014.03.026

Mazumder, B., Almond, D., Park, K., Crimmins, E. M., & Finch, C. E. (2010). Lingering prenatal effects of the 1918 influenza pandemic on cardiovascular disease. *Journal of Developmental Origins of Health and Disease, 1*, 26–34. http://dx.doi.org/10.1017/S2040174409990031

Miller, S., & Wherry, L. R. (2018). The long-term effects of early life Medicaid coverage. *Journal of Human Resources*. Advance online publication. http://dx.doi.org/10.3368/jhr.54.3.0816.8173R1

Nadeau, J. H. (2009). Transgenerational genetic effects on phenotypic variation and disease risk. *Human Molecular Genetics, 18*, R202–R210. http://dx.doi.org/10.1093/hmg/ddp366

Neelsen, S., & Stratmann, T. (2012). Long-run effects of fetal influenza exposure: Evidence from Switzerland. *Social Science & Medicine, 74*, 58–66. http://dx.doi.org/10.1016/j.socscimed.2011.09.039

Nelson, R. E. (2010). Testing the fetal origins hypothesis in a developing country: Evidence from the 1918 influenza pandemic. *Health Economics, 19*, 1181–1192. http://dx.doi.org/10.1002/hec.1544

Painter, R. C., Osmond, C., Gluckman, P., Hanson, M., Phillips, D. I. W., & Roseboom, T. J. (2008). Transgenerational effects of prenatal exposure to the Dutch famine on neonatal adiposity and health in later life. *BJOG: An International Journal of Obstetrics & Gynaecology, 115*, 1243–1249. http://dx.doi.org/10.1111/j.1471-0528.2008.01822.x

Painter, R. C., Roseboom, T. J., & Bleker, O. P. (2005). Prenatal exposure to the Dutch famine and disease in later life: An overview. *Reproductive Toxicology, 20,* 345–352. http://dx.doi.org/10.1016/j.reprotox.2005.04.005

Parman, J. (2015). Childhood health and sibling outcomes: Nurture reinforcing nature during the 1918 influenza pandemic. *Explorations in Economic History, 58,* 22–43. http://dx.doi.org/10.1016/j.eeh.2015.07.002

Pembrey, M. E. (2002). Time to take epigenetic inheritance seriously. *European Journal of Human Genetics, 10,* 669–671. http://dx.doi.org/10.1038/sj.ejhg.5200901

Pembrey, M. E., Bygren, L. O., Kaati, G., Edvinsson, S., Northstone, K., Sjöström, M., . . . The ALSPAC Study Team. (2006). Sex-specific, male-line transgenerational responses in humans. *European Journal of Human Genetics, 14,* 159–166. http://dx.doi.org/10.1038/sj.ejhg.5201538

Richter, A., & Robling, P. O. (2013). *Multigenerational effects of the 1918–19 influenza pandemic in Sweden* (Working Paper). Retrieved from https://www.sole-jole.org/14329.pdf

Rossin-Slater, M., & Wüst, M. (2016, October). *What is the added value of preschool? Long-term impacts and interactions with a health intervention* (NBER Working Paper No. 22700). Retrieved from http://ftp.iza.org/dp10254.pdf

Royer, H. (2009). Separated at girth: U.S. twin estimates of the effects of birth weight. *American Economic Journal: Applied Economics, 1,* 49–85. http://dx.doi.org/10.1257/app.1.1.49

Scholte, R. S., van den Berg, G. J., & Lindeboom, M. (2015). Long-run effects of gestation during the Dutch Hunger Winter famine on labor market and hospitalization outcomes. *Journal of Health Economics, 39,* 17–30. http://dx.doi.org/10.1016/j.jhealeco.2014.10.002

Schwandt, H. (2018, January). *The lasting legacy of seasonal influenza: In-utero exposure and labor market outcomes* (CEPR Discussion Paper No. DP12563). Retrieved from https://ssrn.com/abstract=3098159

Shea, A. K., & Steiner, M. (2008). Cigarette smoking during pregnancy. *Nicotine & Tobacco Research, 10,* 267–278. http://dx.doi.org/10.1080/14622200701825908

Solon, G. (2015, March). *What do we know so far about multi-generational mobility* (NBER Working Paper No. 21053)? Cambridge, MA: National Bureau of Economic Research.

Tamborini, C. R., Kim, C., & Sakamoto, A. (2015). Education and lifetime earnings in the United States. *Demography, 52,* 1383–1407. http://dx.doi.org/10.1007/s13524-015-0407-0

Trivers, R. L., & Willard, D. E. (1973). Natural selection of parental ability to vary the sex ratio of offspring. *Science, 179,* 90–92. http://dx.doi.org/10.1126/science.179.4068.90

U.S. Department of Health and Human Services, Administration for Children and Families. (2013). Head Start program facts: Fiscal year 2013. Retrieved from https://eclkc.ohs.acf.hhs.gov/about-us/article/head-start-program-facts-fiscal-year-2013

U.S. Environmental Protection Agency, National Center for Environmental Assessment. (2009, December). Integrated Science Assessment (ISA) for particulate matter (Final Report No. EPA/600/R-08/139F). Washington, DC: Author. Retrieved from http://cfpub.epa.gov/ncea/CFM/recordisplay.cfm?deid=216546

van den Berg, G. J., & Pinger, P. R. (2016). Transgenerational effects of childhood conditions on third generation health and education outcomes. *Economics and Human Biology, 23,* 103–120. http://dx.doi.org/10.1016/j.ehb.2016.07.001

Wakshlak, A., & Weinstock, M. (1990). Neonatal handling reverses behavioral abnormalities induced in rats by prenatal stress. *Physiology & Behavior, 48,* 289–292. http://dx.doi.org/10.1016/0031-9384(90)90315-U

Weinstock, M. (2017). Prenatal stressors in rodents: Effects on behavior. *Neurobiology of Stress, 6,* 3–13. http://dx.doi.org/10.1016/j.ynstr.2016.08.004

Weitzman, M. L., Arrow, K., Cropper, M., Gollier, C., Groom, B., Heal, G., . . . Tol, R. S. J. (2013). Determining benefits and costs for future generations. *Science, 341*, 349–350.

Wherry, L. R., & Meyer, B. D. (2016). Saving teens: Using a policy discontinuity to estimate the effects of Medicaid eligibility. *The Journal of Human Resources, 51*, 556–588. http://dx.doi.org/10.3368/jhr.51.3.0913-5918R1

Zamenhof, S., van Marthens, E., & Grauel, L. (1971). DNA (cell number) in neonatal brain: Second generation (F2) alteration by maternal (F0) dietary protein restriction. *Science, 172*, 850–851. http://dx.doi.org/10.1126/science.172.3985.850

FAMILY

4

Behavioral Insights and Parental Decision-Making

Susan E. Mayer, Ariel Kalil, and Nadav Klein

Economic advantage is correlated across generations. In the United States, 43% of adults who were raised in the poorest fifth of the income distribution now have an income in the poorest fifth of the income distribution, and 70% have incomes in the poorest half of the distribution. Among adults raised in the richest income quintile, 40% have incomes in the richest quintile, and 53% have incomes in the richest half of the income distribution (Pew Charitable Trusts, 2012). Although a variety of factors play a role in the correlation in outcomes of adults and their parents, evidence suggests that parental decision-making plays a crucial role. Parents make decisions that affect their children in a variety of domains including, for example, where to live, to how much time to spend with their children in various activities, what time to put their children to bed, whether their children brush their teeth each night, and whether to immunize their children against communicable diseases. Parental decision-making interpreted in this way probably accounts for around half of the variance in adult outcomes and is, therefore, an important contributor to the level of intergenerational mobility in a country (Björklund, Lindahl, & Lindquist, 2010).

Across disciplines, dozens of studies have demonstrated differences in the way advantaged and disadvantaged parents raise their children and how these differences matter to children's adult success. Among other things, advantaged parents spend more time in educational activities with their children (Guryan, Hurst, & Kearney, 2008; Kalil, Ryan, & Corey, 2012), produce

http://dx.doi.org/10.1037/0000187-005
Confronting Inequality: How Policies and Practices Shape Children's Opportunities, edited by
L. Tach, R. Dunifon, and D. L. Miller

more cognitively stimulating home learning environments (Harris, Terrel, & Allen, 1999), are more likely to read to their children (Noel, Stark, & Redford, 2016), and to do math-related activities with their children (Lazarides, Harackiewicz, Canning, Pesu, & Viljaranta, 2015). Furthermore, because highly educated mothers have increased the amount of time they spend in educational activities with their children more than mothers with less education have increased that time, the gap between the amount of time that advantaged and disadvantaged parents spend with their children overall and in educationally relevant activities has widened over the last 20 years (Altintas, 2012; Hurst, 2010; Ramey & Ramey, 2010).

James Heckman and his colleagues find that more engaged parents have greater success in producing both cognitive and non-cognitive skills in their children, and that both types of skills are crucial to social and economic success (e.g., Cunha, Heckman, Lochner, & Masterov, 2006; Heckman & Masterov, 2007). Other research finds that the amount of time that parents spend with their children has a direct and causal effect on children's cognitive test scores (Fiorini & Keane, 2014; Villena-Rodán & Ríos-Aguilar, 2011). Price and Kalil (2018) find that a 1.0 standard deviation (*SD*) increase in mother–child reading time increases children's reading achievement by 0.80 *SD*s on average.

In this chapter, we propose that applying behavioral science to the study of parenting can potentially yield new insights into why parents make (or fail to make) decisions to spend time, money, attention, or affection promoting their children's development and why these decisions are likely to differ by parental advantage. The assumption that we make is that, if advantaged and disadvantaged parents made equally optimal parenting decisions, differences in future academic and financial outcomes of their children would also narrow and intergenerational mobility would increase. In domains as varied as financial services, medicine, education, and the law, both experts and laypersons systematically make decisions that are, by their own evaluation, suboptimal due to cognitive biases (e.g., Castleman & Page, 2014; Chabris, Laibson, Morris, Schuldt, & Taubinsky, 2008; Gilovich, Griffin, & Kahneman, 2002; Meier & Sprenger, 2010; Rodgers et al., 2005; Sharek, Schoen, & Loewenstein, 2012). Parental decision-making is no different. However, advantaged and disadvantaged parents make different decisions about how to raise their children, and these differences account for differences in children's success. Understanding differences in cognitive biases by parental advantage can point to low-cost ways to narrow the parenting differences and, hence, the differences in child outcomes.

In what follows, we first describe the differences between our approach and traditional approaches to the study of parenting. We then describe characteristics of parental decision-making that make it subject to cognitive biases and why the experience of cognitive biases may differ by parental advantage. We then discuss how using behavioral insights can point to new directions for research and the development of new programs and policies to support parents.

MECHANISMS LINKING PARENT AND CHILD OUTCOMES

Theories across several disciplines try to explain why child outcomes are highly correlated with parent outcomes. The dominant theories fail to adequately explain this correlation. One of the most prevalent theories is that poor parents cannot afford the goods and services that can improve their children's life chances, including high-quality education and health-care. Other prevalent theories are that due to their social and economic circumstances, advantaged and disadvantaged parents have access to different information about parenting, or different parent groups estimate the returns to the time they spend in parenting activities differently.

Economic and social structural factors undoubtedly play a role in the intergenerational transmission of advantage. But how large that role is remains unclear. Although parental income consistently has a substantial correlation with important child outcomes, the causal impact of parental income in rich countries is much less certain. Most studies find small or no average causal effect of parental income on child outcomes, including cognitive and noncognitive skills, and even smaller effects on adult outcomes, including income and education (for reviews on this literature, see Cooper & Stewart, 2013; Mayer, 2010). However, studies that examine nonlinearities in the effect of income usually find greater effects for families with less income (e.g., Dahl & Lochner, 2012; Shea, 2000; but cf. Blau, 1999, who finds no additional effects for children from low-income families).

Although raising the income of the poorest parents might increase their children's adult income, there is uncertainty about the potential size of this increase. For example, Akee, Copeland, Keeler, Angold, and Costello (2010) studied the effect of an income windfall from casino earnings on members of a Native American tribe. They find no effect of an increase in parental income on high school graduation or educational attainment for children who were never poor; however, for children in poor families, additional parental income increased schooling by nearly one year and increased the chance of graduating high school by 30%. However, the average income increase for poor families in that study was very large—as much as 100%—and out of the range likely to be implemented by public policies in the United States.

In our own survey of parents of children in Head Start programs in Chicago, over 95% of parents report that they have all the materials that they need to help their children learn math. Almost no parents report that they ever failed to read to their child because they had no books to read (Mayer, Kalil, Oreopoulos, & Gallegos, 2018).

In the United States, differences in access to and quality of schooling may also play a role in intergenerational mobility; again, the size of the effect is unclear. The education of parents is highly correlated with the education of their adult children, which suggests that differences in school quality in the parents' generation is replicated in the children's generation or that having highly educated parents conveys other advantages. However, the substantial differences between advantaged and disadvantaged children in cognitive skills emerge well before the start of formal schooling (Washbrook & Waldfogel, 2011), and conventional measures of school quality (e.g., teacher/pupil ratios and teacher salaries) have small effects on creating or eliminating gaps after the first few years of schooling (Cunha & Heckman, 2007; Heckman & Carneiro, 2003). The importance of family influences relative to schooling is perhaps not surprising, considering children in the United States will spend only about 13% to 15% of their waking hours in school between birth and the age of 18 (Mayer et al., 2018). Finally, school outcomes reflect many child characteristics, such as orientation toward the future, sense of personal efficacy, work ethic, and other characteristics sometimes referred to as *noncognitive skills* (e.g., Cunha & Heckman, 2007; Heckman & Carneiro, 2003; Heckman & Kautz, 2012). These skills are largely shaped by family influences and not by schools. This body of research suggests that differences in what schools do does not account for a large portion of differences in educational outcomes.

Other research shows that increasing the schooling level of parents does not necessarily increase schooling levels for children. Black, Devereux, and Salvanes (2005) use a policy change in Norway that exogenously changed schooling levels for a cohort of students to estimate the effect of that change on the schooling level of their children. They found little causal relationship between the education of parents and their children with the possible exception of a modest effect of maternal education on sons' education.

Differences in information about parenting by parental advantage also do not seem to play a large role in creating differences in parenting. We use the 1998 and 2010 Early Childhood Longitudinal Survey (ECLS) data to estimate the percentage of parents who rated various child skills as "very important" or "essential." We categorized parents by socioeconomic status (SES), using a composite of mothers' and fathers' educational attainment, occupational prestige, and family income. The results for the lowest and highest SES quintiles are shown in Table 4.1. Between 1993 and 2010, the proportion of parents in the lowest SES quintile rating each of these skills as important increased. For every skill, the proportion of parents who say the skill is important is greater for parents in the lowest SES quintile than for parents in the highest quintile

TABLE 4.1. Parents' Beliefs About the Importance of Children Acquiring Various Skills Before Entering Kindergarten

Fall outcomes*	Lowest SES quintile		Highest SES quintile	
	1998	2010	1998	2010
Counting to 20	73.6	85.2	50.5	68.4
Taking turns/sharing	93.5	95	92.6	93.3
Using pencil/paintbrush	77.9	86.8	66.9	78.7
Sitting still/pays attention	90.6	92.8	74.8	79.3
Knowing letters of the alphabet	80.5	88.7	55.7	75.9
Communicating needs/wants verbally	93	95.8	93.8	94.8

Note. SES = socioeconomic status. *Percent who rated the following as "very important" or "essential." Data from the 1998 and 2010 Early Childhood Longitudinal Survey (ECLS; National Center for Education Statistics, n.d.).

in both 1998 and 2010. From this, we can conclude that the large differences by SES in the actual skills of children entering kindergarten do not arise because disadvantaged parents lack information about the importance of the skills. Recent work by Ryan, Kalil, Ziol-Guest, and Hines (2019) also shows that rich and poor parents' ideas about the characteristics children need to succeed in life (e.g., work hard, be helpful, think for oneself) have converged substantially in the last three decades.

Differences in parenting also do not seem to arise because disadvantaged parents do not know what to do to foster their child's skills. For example, surveys show that virtually all parents say that reading to their preschool-aged child is important or very important. Yet substantial numbers of disadvantaged parents do not read to their children on a regular basis (Aud et al., 2012). Some parents with basic reading skills may expect a lower return from reading to their children. Our research (Mayer et al., 2018) and research by Cunha, Elo, and Culhane (2013) found that low-income parents expect a substantial return from the time they spend in educational activities with their children. Agee and Crocker (1996) used an instrument for the parents' discount rate on time investments in their children and found that less educated and lower-income parents discount their investments at about twice the rate as more advantaged parents. However, in a survey of British parents of school aged children in England, Attanasio, Boneva, and Rauh (2019) found no difference in expected returns to time or money investments in children by parental income or education. In a companion survey, Boneva and Rauh (2018) found that low-income parents expect a lower rate of return from investments during early childhood compared to higher income parents, but they found no difference in the expected rate of return for parental investments at older ages. In any case, a lower expected rate of return could lead to either less or more investment in children, depending on whether parents try to make up for a lower expected return by spending more time engaging their children or forego investing because of the lower expected return.

Another explanation for the gap in the amount of time that advantaged and disadvantaged parents invest in their children is that disadvantaged parents have less time to engage their children. However, evidence from time diary data shows that, even when researchers account for the number and ages of children in the home, whether the parent is married, and how much time the parent works, differences by education in the amount of time that parents spend with their children persist (Guryan et al., 2008). National Center for Education Statistics data show that the proportion of parents who report that they or someone else in the household read to their three-year-old children at least three times a week does not vary by the employment status of the mother, except that the proportion of parents reading to their children was lower when the mother was *un*employed (Winquist Nord, Lennon, Liu, & Chandler, 1999).

Developmental psychology is perhaps the academic discipline that has been most influential in setting the agenda for how researchers think about parenting. A primary tenet of developmental psychology is that good parenting cannot be understood in purely quantitative terms, and that the quality of parent–child engagement is equally if not more important than the quantity.

There is little consensus about how to measure quality except by using classifications of *parenting style* as first described by Baumrind (1991). Her classifications included Authoritarian/Disciplinarian, Permissive/Indulgent, Uninvolved or Authoritative, with authoritative thought to be the most effective style. Developmental psychology has long focused on classifying parent behaviors into these parenting styles (or their variants) and correlating the different typologies with child outcomes. Darling and Steinberg (1993) noted that parenting style is a characteristic of the parent that is distinct from specific parenting practices; the former represents a constellation of parent attributes and attitudes that interacts with specific parental socialization practices to shape children's development. Notable in this conceptualization, however, is the thesis that the influence of specific parent behaviors on children's development can only be understood in the context of the emotional milieu or parenting style in which they occur.

Nevertheless, developmental psychology has not had as a primary objective explaining either why parenting styles differ or explaining the decision-making process that leads to differences in specific, measurable behaviors, such as reading to young children, enrolling children in early education programs, or taking children to school on time every day. Research on parenting styles acknowledges that, in this definition of parental behavior, the influence of any one specific parenting practice cannot be disaggregated due to its being part of a typology of other behaviors (Darling & Steinberg, 1993). But the aggregation of parental behavior across a wide range of dimensions into a global parenting characteristic, or style, hinders our understanding of how the behavior arises and what can change the behavior short of changing parents' style of interaction with their children, a task that has proven to require intensive and often expensive interventions.

Increasing intergenerational mobility requires narrowing the differences in how advantaged and disadvantaged parents raise their children. However, evidence on why parenting practices differ by parent advantage leads to a puzzle: advantaged and disadvantaged parents seem to know what is important for their children, and both groups have the time and resources to do what is important for their children, but advantaged parents are more likely to actually do the things that are important. We argue that this difference arises in large part because of differences by parental advantage in the experience of cognitive biases, and that using behavioral tools to reduce these differences can greatly narrow the gap in child outcomes. We now turn to our argument in favor of this view.

A BEHAVIORAL LENS ON PARENTAL DECISION-MAKING

Behavioral tools are intended to help people make optimal decisions by overcoming cognitive biases. Because what parents need to do to protect and nurture their children may differ in some respects by parental advantage (e.g., some research shows that harsher parenting may be required in a dangerous neighborhood; e.g., Ceballo & McLoyd, 2002), when we refer to *optimal decision-making* we do not necessarily mean that disadvantaged parents should make the same decisions as advantaged parents. Instead, by optimal decision-making, we mean the decision that the parent believes is optimal or, put another way, the decision the parent would make in the absence of a cognitive bias. Disadvantaged parents seem to want to do the same things that advantaged parents do but are less likely to actually do those things. That is, there is a wider gap between what parents aspire to do and what they actually do among disadvantaged than among advantaged parents. Behavioral tools can help narrow the gap between aspirational and actual parenting.[1] If this gap narrows, so will the outcomes of children from advantaged and disadvantaged families, increasing intergenerational mobility.

The gap between knowing what one ought to do and actually doing it is not unique to parenting. In many situations, people's intentions are not matched by their actions. For example, people often intend to complete tasks on time but routinely miss their self-imposed deadlines, a phenomenon known as the *planning fallacy* (Buehler, Griffin, & Ross, 1994; Kahneman & Tversky, 1979). Similarly, most people understand the importance of maintaining a healthy diet and taking medications as prescribed. However, research finds that large numbers of people fail to follow a healthy diet or to take medicine as prescribed because of a variety of decision errors and biases (for review, see John, Loewenstein, & Volpp, 2012).

Behavioral science has documented biases that characterize much of human decision-making. By understanding how these impede parental decision-making and how this differs by parental advantage, researchers can design low-cost interventions to manage the biases, thereby narrowing the gap in the decisions that advantaged and disadvantaged parents make. Like many other decisions, parenting decisions are complex, constraining parents' capacity to make optimal decisions simply because human judgment cannot readily master the complexity associated with parenting. For this reason, parents are prone to rely on heuristics (cognitive shortcuts) to simplify their decisions and make them "computationally cheap" (e.g., Gigerenzer & Selten, 2001). Advantaged and disadvantaged parents can experience this complexity differently, resulting in different patterns of decision-making. Here we describe four potentially important characteristics of parenting that make it especially susceptible to cognitive biases and to differential adaptions to biases by parental advantage.

Parenting Requires Making Temporal Tradeoffs

The payoff to many parenting decisions does not materialize until many years into the future. Decisions about spending money and time on educational activities with children, their children's schooling, health-promoting behaviors,

---

[1]The cost of a wrong decision may also be greater for disadvantaged parents, who have fewer resources to allow recovery from such decisions as do advantaged parents. For example, a middle-class, but not low-income, parent may be able to hire a tutor for her child to make up for not spending enough time reading to her child.

and other activities meant to improve child outcomes can be likened to investments with uncertain returns. Research suggests that people systematically overweigh present outcomes compared to future outcomes, often leading to suboptimal choices (Castillo, Ferraro, Jordan, & Petrie, 2011; Chabris et al., 2008; Meier & Sprenger, 2010; Sutter, Kocher, Glätzle-Rützler, & Trautmann, 2013). Present bias can result in parents prioritizing spending time on activities that provide immediate gratification, rather than on investing in time with their children that has a payoff sometime in the future, and then regretting those decisions once their children have grown up.

Time preference varies across countries and within countries. Although present bias is present in the populations of every country where it has been measured (Wang, Rieger, & Hens, 2016), the discount rate varies across countries and within countries (see Frederick, Loewenstein, & O'Donoghue, 2002, for a survey of this literature). There is no consensus on what causes differences in time preference. However, Becker and Mulligan (1997) proposed that the more financial resources one has to imagine the future, the lower the discount rate on the future, and empirical evidence supports the hypothesis that lower income adults have a greater discount rate on the future (Dohmen, Falk, Huffman, & Sunde, 2010; Eckel, Grundy, & Zimmet, 2005; Golsteyn, Grönqvist, & Lindahl, 2014; Harrison, Lau, & Williams, 2002; Hausman, 1979; Lawrance, 1991; Pabilonia & Song, 2013). Many early studies in sociology provide observational evidence that time preference is culturally acquired (Banfield, 1974; Cohen & Hodges, 1963; Leshan, 1952; Lewis, 1966; O'Rand & Ellis, 1974). Not deferring gratification may be useful when the future is uncertain, suggesting that children raised in poor families may become more present-oriented adults, even if this results in suboptimal decision-making.

Parenting Requires Attribution

Parents must motivate their children to engage in desirable behaviors and dissuade them from undesirable behaviors. Motivating another person requires understanding his or her preferences, thoughts, and feelings. Parents must also interpret and respond to the motivations behind the behavior of their children. A parent of a three-year-old who throws a tantrum is likely to respond differently if she thinks that the child is just doing what any three-year-old does or if she thinks the child is being willfully defiant.

Inferring the cause of another person's behavior is perhaps one of the most difficult social judgments to perform accurately (Epley, 2014). Ironically, this is especially true when the person whose perspective people try to adopt is that of a loved one (Savitsky, Keysar, Epley, Carter, & Swanson, 2011). Married couples, for example, exhibit a remarkable inability to predict each other's preferences despite being quite confident in their ability to do so (Davis, Hoch, & Ragsdale, 1986; Kruger & Gilovich, 1999). For parents, the difficulty is compounded because children's preferences are often a moving target, and children sometimes lack the ability to articulate their motivations.

The need to interpret behavior and respond to preferences opens the door for attribution biases. Attribution bias refers to systematic errors people make when they attempt to explain others' behaviors. Errors in attribution are due both to limitations in information processing and to individuals' own motivations (Gilbert & Malone, 1995; Kunda, 1990). Attribution bias arises from cognitive shortcuts that individuals use to process complex information. But people are also likely to favor attributions that are consistent with their own goals and sense of identity and to disfavor attributions that injure their self-esteem.

People's imperfect attribution processes create a number of different attribution biases. Among the most pervasive is self-serving attribution bias—the tendency to attribute our successes to our own internal traits and our failures to others or to the situation. A parent of a child who behaves well may attribute the child's behavior to his or her own good parenting. But when the child misbehaves, the parent may attribute that behavior to the child being bad or having bad influences. Self-serving attributions arise from our desire to see ourselves positively (Mezulis, Abramson, Hyde, & Hankin, 2004). The magnitude of the self-serving bias varies across countries and is on average lower in Asian countries compared to the United States (Mezulis et al., 2004). It may also vary across groups in the United States, but we have no evidence on this possibility.

As another example, the *fundamental attribution error* is the tendency to overweigh others' internal characteristics and personality and underweigh external and situational circumstances when explaining others' behavior. For instance, parents may be more likely to attribute their child's failure to do her homework to a personality trait, such as laziness, rather than to a situational factor, such as lack of sufficient time. Although fundamental attribution error is present in every culture where it has been measured, the pervasiveness and depth of the bias differs across countries (Hong, Morris, Chiu, & Benet-Martínez, 2000; Masuda & Nisbett, 2001; Mezulis et al., 2004; Miller, 1984). The magnitude of the biases also varies within countries by age and psychopathology. In addition, parents' attributions of child behavior and school success varies across countries (Bornstein, Putnick, & Lansford, 2011).

We do not know why attribution biases vary across and within cultures. People may be culturally primed to invoke certain attributions (Shweder & Bourne, 1982); people may have different needs to bolster their own self-esteem (Taylor & Brown, 1988); and other factors. However, the fact that attribution biases vary by cultural groups suggests that these biases may also vary by parental advantage.

A large research literature documents that parental attributions influence parent–child interactions. For example, parents who attribute hostile intent to their children's behavior are more likely to have interactions with the children that are characterized by conflict (Mackinnon-Lewis, Lamb, Arbuckle, Baradaran, & Volling, 1992). Mothers with inaccurate expectations about their child's development tend to be harsher with their child (Azar, Robinson, Hekimian, & Twentyman, 1984; Twentyman & Plotkin, 1982). Parent attributions are also implicated in child maltreatment and physical punishment of children (Dix, Ruble, & Zambarano, 1989; Strassberg, 1995).

We know little about why some parents are more prone to bias in the attributions they make about their child's behavior. Attribution bias is more likely to occur when information about the target of perspective-taking is lacking. Indeed, studies indicate that mothers with greater knowledge of child development and, therefore, more accurate attributions of their child behavior demonstrate more effective parenting skills, at least as they are measured by researchers (Azar et al., 1984; Benasich & Brooks-Gunn, 1996; Damast, Tamis-LeMonda, & Bornstein, 1996; Fry, 1985; Stevens, 1984; Twentyman & Plotkin, 1982). However, this evidence is from observational studies, so they do not imply that giving parents more information about child development would change parents' attributions and parenting decisions, especially if the source of the attribution bias is parents' own motivations.

As we have already noted, disadvantaged parents do not seem to lack information about the things they should do to improve their children's outcomes or how to do those things. Although information about child development may be a necessary first step to overcoming attribution bias with respect to one's child, it is unlikely to be sufficient to change parental behavior by much. Additional research is needed to understand how attribution bias influences parental decisions and the extent to which is varies by parental advantage.

Parenting Decisions Are Often Automatic Rather Than Deliberate

Parenting often requires quick and on-the-spot decisions. When a child runs toward a busy street, a parent must react rather than contemplate. When a child screams in the checkout lane because the parent says no to his request for candy, the parent seldom has time to reflect on what to do. The need to act quickly and on-the-spot results in automaticity. Automaticity is a response done with minimal cognitive processing; it is useful in that it reduces cognitive load. An automatic response can be beneficial if it is efficacious but costly when it is not. Because automatic responses can be likened to habits and habits are hard to break, ineffective automatic responses can lead to ineffective parenting.

Automaticity is the result of learning, repetition, and practice. Which automatic behaviors a parent adopts is likely to depend on the parent's own experiences. Behaviors that have been repeatedly observed or experienced as a child are likely to become the default behavior of the adult. An adult whose parents always spanked him when he misbehaved as a child is more likely to automatically spank his own children in response to their misbehavior, with little thought about alternative ways to discipline the child. We do not have a lot of evidence about how parents learn to parent. However, the little evidence that we do have (usually from small surveys) suggests that parenting behaviors are primarily learned from one's own parents, relatives, and friends (Berkule-Silberman, Dreyer, Huberman, Klass, & Mendelsohn, 2010; Koepke & Williams, 1989; Shwalb, Kawai, Shoji, & Tsunetsugu, 1995).

Automaticity reduces cognitive demands, leads to rapid responses, and is useful for many parenting situations. But automaticity can also create barriers to eliminating costly parental behaviors (e.g., yelling at a child, hitting a child, letting the child watch television before bed). Advantaged and disadvantaged parents may have the same goals for their children and even share the same information about how to achieve those goals, but because of differences in their own upbringings, they might have different parenting habits. Any habit is hard to break, but if the automatic behavior is reinforced in the in-group where parents learn and practice parenting behaviors, it is even more difficult to change.

To the extent that spheres of parenting influence differ greatly for different groups and to the extent that they fail to intersect, different groups will develop distinctive parenting habits and behaviors. This is not a problem if the different parenting decisions have little impact on children's success; however, to the extent that they do, automaticity can result in very different child outcomes.

Parenting Decisions Are Experienced as Identity-Relevant

Most parents are unlikely to experience parenting as simply a competency or a skill. Instead, parenting is experienced as meaningful and identity-relevant (Kalil, Mayer, Delgado, & Gennetian, 2019). Being a good parent is a normatively valued identity.

People often hold multiple, sometimes conflicting, identities, and different identities can create different values, preferences, and decisions (Akerlof & Kranton, 2000). In addition, different identities can be primed in different contexts. Similarly, to student–athletes, whose performance is affected by whether their student or athlete identity is activated (Yopyk & Prentice, 2005), a mother's decision to work late or to spend more time with her child depends in part on whether she thinks of herself in the moment of decision as a career woman or as a good mother. Moreover, the identities accessible to advantaged and disadvantaged parents may differ, which may partly explain different decisions across socioeconomic groups. Identities, such as wife, husband, or career professional, may be more accessible to advantaged parents, whereas identities, such as single parent or unemployed, may be more accessible to disadvantaged parents. The identities available to advantaged and disadvantaged parents may differ, and the salience of common identities may also differ. A single parent may be more likely to have the identity of girlfriend, whereas a married mother may be more likely to have the identity of wife. The identity of wife may correspond more to the identity of good mother. Consequently, there may be less competition among identities for advantaged parents.

Although there is a considerable amount of research on the role that parents play in developing children's identities, there is little research on the role that parents' identities play in parenting decisions or child outcomes. Understanding the relationship between identity and behavior points to a new way that preferences can be changed. Notions of identity evolve within a society, and they can be changed by incentives and other policies that can change or prime social categories, giving some identities great returns (see Akerlof & Kranton, 2000).

INTERVENTIONS TO MANAGE COGNITIVE BIASES IN PARENTING

Although the foregoing list of cognitive biases influencing parenting is far from exhaustive, it illustrates the potential of the behavioral perspective to improve parent decision-making. Cognitive processes can prevent parents from rationally analyzing their decisions and force them instead to rely on biases. Adopting a behavioral approach can allow us to decompose parenting behaviors into a series of decisions, and help researchers and practitioners identify and intervene when cognitive biases are likely to result in parenting decisions that are suboptimal from the parent's own point of view.

As an example of a way that a program could mitigate the effects of cognitive bias, consider the Parents and Children Together (PACT) Study, a field experiment that we conducted at the Behavioral Insights and Parenting Lab at the University of Chicago (Mayer et al., 2018). This field experiment was designed to test the ability of a behaviorally informed intervention to increase parent–child reading time among parents of children in the federally funded Head Start preschool program. This is an important outcome, because reading to one's child at an early age is associated with improved literacy and social skills (Hale, Berger, LeBourgeois, & Brooks-Gunn, 2011; Kloosterman, Notten, Tolsma, & Kraaykamp, 2011; Mol & Bus, 2011; Price & Kalil, 2018; Raikes et al., 2006).

Extensive survey work conducted as part of this study revealed that parents in this population: (a) understood the importance of reading to children (in part, this may be due to their attending Head Start, which strongly emphasizes parental reading to children), (b) had access to reading materials (again, possibly due to Head Start making books available to borrow), (c) understood the "production function" of their time investment (i.e., they reported on surveys that the more time they invested reading to their children, the greater would be the likelihood of their children's success in kindergarten), and (d) reported that it was just as much if not more their responsibility (as opposed to the teacher's responsibility) to stimulate their child's development. Our other work, moreover, shows that low-income parents enjoy spending time in developmentally relevant activities with their children to the same extent as do high-income parents, and that low-income parents do not report feeling particularly stressed or unhappy engaging in learning and teaching activities with their children (Kalil et al., 2019).

What, then, leads to infrequent book reading among low-income families? We hypothesized that present bias may be key, so the PACT intervention was designed specifically to overcome this bias with a set of behavioral tools (goal setting, feedback, reminders, and social rewards) designed to "bring the future to the present" and help parents form a habit of regular book reading. On average, the PACT intervention had a very large treatment impact (about 1.0 *SD*) on the amount of time parents spent reading with their children (the study measured time use objectively using digital tools). But even more important was the study's finding that the intervention was substantially more effective for those parents who were more present biased. In short, parents who suffer from present bias are the very ones who benefit from an intervention designed to overcome it. Those parents who were not present biased were already reading at higher levels to their children and the intervention had little impact on them.

These findings suggest that parents' difficulty with making temporal trade-offs is partly responsible for their failure to read to their children. In addition, these findings provide a blueprint for reducing the effects of this cognitive bias. By using a set of known behavioral tools, parents are able to improve parental decision-making. Moreover, the costs of the PACT program per family were relatively low, dwarfing the per-capita costs of current policy interventions designed to improve preschool children's educational outcomes, which suggests that behaviorally based interventions can feasibly be adapted for policy purposes.

As a second example, we implemented a behaviorally informed field experiment called Show Up to Grow Up, which was designed to increase attendance and diminish chronic absences at subsidized preschool programs in Chicago. We sent personalized text messages to parents, targeting behavior driving children's absences from preschool. The text messages focused on, among other things, *loss aversion* by emphasizing the learning that children miss out on when they miss Head Start. Using administrative records from preschools, we find that our intervention increased attended days by 2.5 (0.15 *SD*) and decreased chronic absenteeism by 9.3 percentage points (20%) over an 18-week period. We found that parents who benefited the most were the ones who reported lower preferences for attendance in our baseline survey. These are the parents who are less likely than other parents to report that their child would be worse off in terms of their academic and social skills if they missed many days of preschool. In short, parents who have less strong beliefs in the importance of preschool benefit most from messages that emphasize its importance through prompting parents to focus on what their child is missing out on if they don't attend.

CONCLUSION

An important determinant of the intergenerational correlation in life outcomes is the decisions that parents make regarding how to raise their children. Rethinking the challenge of increasing economic and social mobility as requiring a change in the decisions that parents make allows us to reframe the challenge as one of overcoming cognitive biases that interfere with decision-making. By conceiving of parenting as a series of decisions, researchers can identify and investigate specific constraints that prevent parents from following through on behaviors that they believe can help their children. The behavioral approach to parenting holds substantial promise for improving the decisions of all parents and especially of disadvantaged parents.

Behavioral science currently has many limitations. It often seems more like a classification system than a true theory. It is plagued by contradictions and inconsistencies in the classifications. But it still promises to be a powerful new way to understand parental behavior and especially differences in behavior by parental advantage. Although this field is still in its infancy, a number of studies have demonstrated how behavioral tools can help to manage the cognitive biases that interfere with parent engagement (see, e.g., Gennetian, Darling, & Aber, 2016; Kalil, 2014; Mayer et al., 2018; Robinson, Lee, Dearing, & Rogers, 2018; Rogers & Feller, 2018).

Despite our enthusiasm for this approach, it is important to raise some relevant cautions. For one, we do not yet know much about which parental decisions are driven by cognitive biases and which are due solely to economic and social deprivations or other social structural barriers. If parents cannot afford books, they will not read to their children no matter how many times they are nudged. We also know little about behavioral spillovers, or whether subjecting parents to multiple behavioral tools to drive a single behavior will have synergistic or antagonistic effects on other behaviors. Most importantly, we do not yet know how to make a habit of new behaviors so that cognitive biases are overcome in the long run. A theory-driven approach to integrating behavioral tools into parenting interventions has the potential to answer these questions, thereby advancing science at the same time as it improves children's life chances.

REFERENCES

Agee, M. D., & Crocker, T. D. (1996). Parental altruism and child lead exposure: Inferences from the demand for chelation therapy. *The Journal of Human Resources, 31,* 677–691. http://dx.doi.org/10.2307/146271

Akee, R. K., Copeland, W. E., Keeler, G., Angold, A., & Costello, E. J. (2010). Parents' incomes and children's outcomes: A quasi-experiment. *American Economic Journal: Applied Economics, 2,* 86–115. http://dx.doi.org/10.1257/app.2.1.86

Akerlof, G. A., & Kranton, R. E. (2000). Economics and identity. *The Quarterly Journal of Economics, 115,* 715–753. http://dx.doi.org/10.1162/003355300554881

Altintas, E. (2012). *Parents' time with children: Micro and macro perspectives* (Unpublished doctoral dissertation). Nuffield College, University of Oxford, Oxford, England.

Attanasio, O., Boneva, T., & Rauh, C. (2019, January). *Parental beliefs about returns to different types of investments in school children* (NBER Working Paper No. 25513). Cambridge, MA: National Bureau of Economic Research.

Aud, S., Hussar, W., Johnson, F., Kena, G., Roth, E., Manning, E., . . . Zhang, J. (2012). *The condition of education 2012* (NCES Annual Report No. 2012-045). Washington, DC: U.S. Department of Education, National Center for Education Statistics.

Azar, S. T., Robinson, D. R., Hekimian, E., & Twentyman, C. T. (1984). Unrealistic expectations and problem-solving ability in maltreating and comparison mothers. *Journal of Consulting and Clinical Psychology, 52,* 687–691. http://dx.doi.org/10.1037/0022-006X.52.4.687

Banfield, E. C. (1974). *The unheavenly city revisited.* Boston, MA: Little, Brown and Company.

Baumrind, D. (1991). The influence of parenting style on adolescent competence and substance use. *The Journal of Early Adolescence, 11,* 56–95. http://dx.doi.org/10.1177/0272431691111004

Becker, G. S., & Mulligan, C. B. (1997). The endogenous determination of time preference. *The Quarterly Journal of Economics, 112,* 729–758. http://dx.doi.org/10.1162/003355397555334

Benasich, A. A., & Brooks-Gunn, J. (1996). Maternal attitudes and knowledge of child-rearing: Associations with family and child outcomes. *Child Development, 67,* 1186–1205. http://dx.doi.org/10.2307/1131887

Berkule-Silberman, S. B., Dreyer, B. P., Huberman, H. S., Klass, P. E., & Mendelsohn, A. L. (2010). Sources of parenting information in low SES mothers. *Clinical Pediatrics, 49,* 560–568. http://dx.doi.org/10.1177/0009922809351092

Björklund, A., Lindahl, L., & Lindquist, M. J. (2010). What more than parental income, education and occupation? An exploration of what Swedish siblings get from their parents. *The B.E. Journal of Economic Analysis & Policy, 10*(1). http://dx.doi.org/10.2202/1935-1682.2449

Black, S. E., Devereux, P. J., & Salvanes, K. G. (2005). Why the apple doesn't fall far: Understanding intergenerational transmission of human capital. *The American Economic Review, 95,* 437–449. http://dx.doi.org/10.1257/0002828053828635

Blau, D. M. (1999). The effect of income on child development. *The Review of Economics and Statistics, 81,* 261–276. http://dx.doi.org/10.1162/003465399558067

Boneva, T., & Rauh, C. (2018). Parental beliefs about returns to educational investments—The later the better? *Journal of the European Economic Association, 16,* 1669–1711. http://dx.doi.org/10.1093/jeea/jvy006

Bornstein, M. H., Putnick, D. L., & Lansford, J. E. (2011). Parenting attributions and attitudes in cross-cultural perspective. *Parenting: Science and Practice, 11,* 214–237. http://dx.doi.org/10.1080/15295192.2011.585568

Buehler, R., Griffin, D., & Ross, M. (1994). Exploring the "planning fallacy": Why people underestimate their task completion times. *Journal of Personality and Social Psychology, 67,* 366–381. http://dx.doi.org/10.1037/0022-3514.67.3.366

Castillo, M., Ferraro, P., Jordan, J., & Petrie, R. (2011). The today and tomorrow of kids: Time preferences and educational outcomes of children. *Journal of Public Economics, 95,* 1377–1385. http://dx.doi.org/10.1016/j.jpubeco.2011.07.009

Castleman, B. L., & Page, L. C. (2014). Summer nudging: Can personalized text messages and peer mentor outreach increase college going among low-income high school graduates? *Journal of Economic Behavior & Organization, 115,* 144–160.

Ceballo, R., & McLoyd, V. C. (2002). Social support and parenting in poor, dangerous neighborhoods. *Child Development, 73,* 1310–1321. http://dx.doi.org/10.1111/1467-8624.00473

Chabris, C. F., Laibson, D., Morris, C. L., Schuldt, J. P., & Taubinsky, D. (2008). Individual laboratory-measured discount rates predict field behavior. *Journal of Risk and Uncertainty, 37,* 237–269. http://dx.doi.org/10.1007/s11166-008-9053-x

Cohen, A. K., & Hodges, H. M., Jr. (1963). Characteristics of the lower-blue-collar-class. *Social Problems, 10,* 303–334. http://dx.doi.org/10.2307/799204

Cooper, K., & Stewart, K. (2013). *Does money affect children's outcomes? A systematic review.* York, England: Joseph Rowntree Foundation.

Cunha, F., Elo, I., & Culhane, J. (2013, June). *Eliciting maternal expectations about the technology of cognitive skill formation* (NBER Working Paper No. 19144). Cambridge, MA: National Bureau of Economic Research.

Cunha, F., & Heckman, J. (2007). The technology of skill formation. *The American Economic Review, 97,* 31–47. http://dx.doi.org/10.1257/aer.97.2.31

Cunha, F., Heckman, J. J., Lochner, L., & Masterov, D. V. (2006). Interpreting the evidence on life cycle skill formation. In E. A. Hanushek & F. Welch (Eds.), *Handbook of the economics of education* (Vol. 1, pp. 697–812). Amsterdam, Netherlands: North-Holland.

Dahl, G., & Lochner, L. (2012). The impact of family income on child achievement: Evidence from the Earned Income Tax Credit. *The American Economic Review, 102,* 1927–1956. http://dx.doi.org/10.1257/aer.102.5.1927

Damast, A. M., Tamis-LeMonda, C. S., & Bornstein, M. H. (1996). Mother-child play: Sequential interactions and the relation between maternal beliefs and behaviors. *Child Development, 67,* 1752–1766. http://dx.doi.org/10.2307/1131729

Darling, N., & Steinberg, L. (1993). Parenting style as context: An integrative model. *Psychological Bulletin, 113,* 487–496. http://dx.doi.org/10.1037/0033-2909.113.3.487

Davis, H. L., Hoch, S. J., & Ragsdale, E. E. (1986). An anchoring and adjustment model of spousal predictions. *Journal of Consumer Research, 13,* 25–37. http://dx.doi.org/10.1086/209045

Dix, T., Ruble, D. N., & Zambarano, R. J. (1989). Mothers' implicit theories of discipline: Child effects, parent effects, and the attribution process. *Child Development, 60,* 1373–1391. http://dx.doi.org/10.2307/1130928

Dohmen, T., Falk, A., Huffman, D., & Sunde, U. (2010). Are risk aversion and impatience related to cognitive ability? *The American Economic Review, 100,* 1238–1260. http://dx.doi.org/10.1257/aer.100.3.1238

Eckel, R. H., Grundy, S. M., & Zimmet, P. Z. (2005). The metabolic syndrome. *Lancet, 365,* 1415–1428. http://dx.doi.org/10.1016/S0140-6736(05)66378-7

Epley, N. (2014). *Mindwise: How we understand what others think, believe, feel, and want.* New York, NY: Knopf.

Fiorini, M., & Keane, M. (2014). How the allocation of children's time affects cognitive and noncognitive development. *Journal of Labor Economics, 32,* 787–836. http://dx.doi.org/10.1086/677232

Frederick, S., Loewenstein, G., & O'Donoghue, T. (2002). Time discounting and time preference: A critical review. *Journal of Economic Literature, 40,* 351–401. http://dx.doi.org/10.1257/jel.40.2.351

Fry, P. S. (1985). Relations between teenagers' age, knowledge, expectations and maternal behaviour. *British Journal of Developmental Psychology, 3,* 47–55. http://dx.doi.org/10.1111/j.2044-835X.1985.tb00954.x

Gennetian, L., Darling, M., & Aber, J. L. (2016). Behavioral economics and developmental science: A new framework to support early childhood interventions. *The Journal of Applied Research on Children, 7*(2). Retrieved from https://digitalcommons.library.tmc.edu/childrenatrisk/vol7/iss2/2/

Gigerenzer, G., & Selten, R. (2001). Rethinking rationality. In G. Gigerenzer & R. Selten (Eds.), *Bounded rationality: The adaptive toolbox* (pp. 1–12). Cambridge, MA: MIT Press.

Gilbert, D. T., & Malone, P. S. (1995). The correspondence bias. *Psychological Bulletin, 117,* 21–38. http://dx.doi.org/10.1037/0033-2909.117.1.21

Gilovich, T., Griffin, D. W., & Kahneman, D. (Eds.). (2002). *Heuristics and biases: The psychology of intuitive judgment.* Cambridge, England: Cambridge University Press. http://dx.doi.org/10.1017/CBO9780511808098

Golsteyn, B. H. H., Grönqvist, H., & Lindahl, L. (2014). Adolescent time preferences predict lifetime outcomes. *Economic Journal, 124,* F739–F761. http://dx.doi.org/10.1111/ecoj.12095

Guryan, J., Hurst, E., & Kearney, M. (2008). Parental education and parental time with children. *The Journal of Economic Perspectives, 22,* 23–46. http://dx.doi.org/10.1257/jep.22.3.23

Hale, L., Berger, L. M., LeBourgeois, M. K., & Brooks-Gunn, J. (2011). A longitudinal study of preschoolers' language-based bedtime routines, sleep duration, and well-being. *Journal of Family Psychology, 25,* 423–433. http://dx.doi.org/10.1037/a0023564

Harris, Y. R., Terrel, D., & Allen, G. (1999). The influence of education context and beliefs on the teaching behavior of African American mothers. *Journal of Black Psychology, 25,* 490–503. http://dx.doi.org/10.1177/0095798499025004002

Harrison, G. W., Lau, M. I., & Williams, M. B. (2002). Estimating individual discount rates in Denmark: A field experiment. *The American Economic Review, 92,* 1606–1617. http://dx.doi.org/10.1257/000282802762024674

Hausman, J. A. (1979). Individual discount rates and the purchase and utilization of energy-using durables. *The Bell Journal of Economics, 10*, 33–54. http://dx.doi.org/10.2307/3003318

Heckman, J., & Carneiro, P. (2003, February). *Human capital policy* (NBER Working Paper No. 9495). Cambridge, MA: National Bureau of Economic Research.

Heckman, J. J., & Kautz, T. (2012). Hard evidence on soft skills. *Labour Economics, 19*, 451–464. http://dx.doi.org/10.1016/j.labeco.2012.05.014

Heckman, J. J., & Masterov, D. V. (2007, Fall). The productivity argument for investing in young children. *Applied Economic Perspectives and Policy, 29*, 446–493. http://dx.doi.org/10.1111/j.1467-9353.2007.00359.x

Hong, Y. Y., Morris, M. W., Chiu, C. Y., & Benet-Martínez, V. (2000). Multicultural minds. A dynamic constructivist approach to culture and cognition. *American Psychologist, 55*, 709–720. http://dx.doi.org/10.1037/0003-066X.55.7.709

Hurst, E. (2010, Spring). *Comments and discussion for The Rug Rat Race. Brookings papers on Economic Activity*, 177–184. Retrieved from https://www.brookings.edu/wp-content/uploads/2010/03/2010a_bpea_ramey.pdf

John, L. K., Loewenstein, G., & Volpp, K. G. (2012). Empirical observations on longer-term use of incentives for weight loss. *Preventive Medicine, 55*(Suppl.), S68–S74. http://dx.doi.org/10.1016/j.ypmed.2012.01.022

Kahneman, D., & Tversky, A. (1979). Prospect theory: An analysis of decision under risk. *Econometrica, 47*, 263–291. http://dx.doi.org/10.2307/1914185

Kalil, A. (2014). Addressing the parenting divide and children's life chances. *Policies to address poverty in America*. Retrieved from The Brookings Institution website: https://www.brookings.edu/research/addressing-the-parenting-divide-to-promote-early-childhood-development-for-disadvantaged-children/

Kalil, A., Mayer, S., Delgado, W., & Gennetian, L. (2019). *The education gradient in parental time use: Investment or enjoyment?* Manuscript submitted for publication.

Kalil, A., Ryan, R., & Corey, M. (2012). Diverging destinies: Maternal education and the developmental gradient in time with children. *Demography, 49*, 1361–1383. http://dx.doi.org/10.1007/s13524-012-0129-5

Kloosterman, R., Notten, N., Tolsma, J., & Kraaykamp, G. (2011). The effects of parental reading socialization and early school involvement on children's academic performance: A panel study of primary school pupils in the Netherlands. *European Sociological Review, 27*, 291–306. http://dx.doi.org/10.1093/esr/jcq007

Koepke, J. E., & Williams, C. (1989). Child-rearing information: Resources parents use. *Family Relations, 38*, 462–465. http://dx.doi.org/10.2307/585754

Kruger, J., & Gilovich, T. (1999). "Naive cynicism" in everyday theories of responsibility assessment: On biased assumptions of bias. *Journal of Personality and Social Psychology, 76*, 743–753. http://dx.doi.org/10.1037/0022-3514.76.5.743

Kunda, Z. (1990). The case for motivated reasoning. *Psychological Bulletin, 108*, 480–498. http://dx.doi.org/10.1037/0033-2909.108.3.480

Lawrance, E. C. (1991). Poverty and the rate of time preference: Evidence from panel data. *Journal of Political Economy, 99*, 54–77. http://dx.doi.org/10.1086/261740

Lazarides, R., Harackiewicz, J., Canning, E., Pesu, L., & Viljaranta, J. (2015). The role of parents in students' motivational beliefs and values. In C. M. Rubie-Davies, J. M. Stephens, & P. Watson (Eds.), *The Routledge international handbook of social psychology of the classroom* (pp. 81–94). Abingdon, England: Routledge.

Leshan, L. L. (1952). Time orientation and social class. *Journal of Abnormal Psychology, 47*, 589–592. http://dx.doi.org/10.1037/h0056306

Lewis, O. (1966). The culture of poverty. *Scientific American, 215*, 19–25.

Mackinnon-Lewis, C., Lamb, M. E., Arbuckle, B., Baradaran, L. P., & Volling, B. L. (1992). The relationship between biased maternal and filial attributions and the aggressiveness of their interactions. *Development and Psychopathology, 4*, 403–415. http://dx.doi.org/10.1017/S0954579400000869

Masuda, T., & Nisbett, R. E. (2001). Attending holistically versus analytically: Comparing the context sensitivity of Japanese and Americans. *Journal of Personality and Social Psychology, 81*, 922–934. http://dx.doi.org/10.1037/0022-3514.81.5.922

Mayer, S. E. (2010). The relationship between income inequality and inequality in schooling. *Theory and Research in Education, 8*, 5–20. http://dx.doi.org/10.1177/1477878509356346

Mayer, S. E., Kalil, A., Oreopoulos, P., & Gallegos, S. (2018). Using behavioral insights to increase parental engagement: The parents and children together intervention. *The Journal of Human Resources*. Advance online publication. http://dx.doi.org/10.3368/jhr.54.4.0617.8835R

Meier, S., & Sprenger, C. (2010). Present-biased preferences and credit card borrowing. *American Economic Journal. Applied Economics, 2*, 193–210. http://dx.doi.org/10.1257/app.2.1.193

Mezulis, A. H., Abramson, L. Y., Hyde, J. S., & Hankin, B. L. (2004). Is there a universal positivity bias in attributions? A meta-analytic review of individual, developmental, and cultural differences in the self-serving attributional bias. *Psychological Bulletin, 130*, 711–747. http://dx.doi.org/10.1037/0033-2909.130.5.711

Miller, J. G. (1984). Culture and development of everyday social explanation. *Journal of Personality and Social Psychology, 46*, 961–978. http://dx.doi.org/10.1037/0022-3514.46.5.961

Mol, S. E., & Bus, A. G. (2011). To read or not to read: A meta-analysis of print exposure from infancy to early adulthood. *Psychological Bulletin, 137*, 267–296. http://dx.doi.org/10.1037/a0021890

National Center for Education Statistics. (n.d.). *Early Childhood Longitudinal Studies (ECLS) Program: Kindergarten class of 1998–99 (ECLS-K)*. Washington, DC: U.S. Department of Education, Institute of Education Sciences. Retrieved from https://nces.ed.gov/ecls/kindergarten.asp

Noel, A., Stark, P., & Redford, J. (2016). *Parent and family involvement in education, from the National Household Education Surveys Program of 2012* (Report No. NCES 2013-028. REV2). Washington, DC: U.S. Department of Education, National Center for Education Statistics.

O'Rand, A., & Ellis, R. A. (1974). Social class and social time perspective. *Social Forces, 53*, 53–62. http://dx.doi.org/10.2307/2576837

Pabilonia, S., & Song, Y. (2013). Single mothers' time preference, smoking, and enriching childcare: Evidence from time diaries. *Eastern Economic Journal, 39*, 227–255. http://dx.doi.org/10.1057/eej.2013.7

Pew Charitable Trusts. (2012). *Pursuing the American dream: Economic mobility across generations.* Washington, DC: Author. Retrieved from https://www.pewtrusts.org/~/media/legacy/uploadedfiles/pcs_assets/2012/pursuingamericandreampdf.pdf

Price, J., & Kalil, A. (2018). The effect of mother-child reading time on children's reading skills: Evidence from natural within-family variation. *Child Development*. Advance online publication. http://dx.doi.org/10.1111/cdev.13137

Raikes, H., Alexander Pan, B., Luze, G., Tamis-LeMonda, C. S., Brooks-Gunn, J., Constantine, J., . . . Rodriguez, E. T. (2006). Mother–child bookreading in low-income families: Correlates and outcomes during the first three years of life. *Child Development, 77*, 924–953. http://dx.doi.org/10.1111/j.1467-8624.2006.00911.x

Ramey, G., & Ramey, V. A. (2010). The Rug Rat Race. *Brookings Papers on Economic Activity*, 129–176. Retrieved from https://www.brookings.edu/wp-content/uploads/2010/03/2010a_bpea_ramey.pdf

Robinson, C. D., Lee, M. G., Dearing, E., & Rogers, T. (2018). Reducing student absenteeism in the early grades by targeting parental beliefs. *American Educational Research Journal, 55*, 1163–1192. http://dx.doi.org/10.3102/0002831218772274

Rodgers, A., Corbett, T., Bramley, D., Riddell, T., Wills, M., Lin, R.-B., & Jones, M. (2005). Do u smoke after txt? Results of a randomised trial of smoking cessation using mobile phone text messaging. *Tobacco Control, 14*, 255–261. http://dx.doi.org/10.1136/tc.2005.011577

Rogers, T., & Feller, A. (2018). Reducing student absences at scale by targeting parents' misbeliefs. *Nature Human Behaviour, 2,* 335–342. http://dx.doi.org/10.1038/s41562-018-0328-1

Ryan, R., Kalil, A., Ziol-Guest, K., & Hines, C. (2019). *Parental values by income and education during a period of labor market change, 1986–2016.* Manuscript submitted for publication.

Savitsky, K., Keysar, B., Epley, N., Carter, T., & Swanson, A. (2011). The closeness-communication bias: Increased egocentrism among friends versus strangers. *Journal of Experimental Social Psychology, 47,* 269–273. http://dx.doi.org/10.1016/j.jesp.2010.09.005

Sharek, Z., Schoen, R. E., & Loewenstein, G. (2012). Bias in the evaluation of conflict of interest policies. *The Journal of Law, Medicine & Ethics, 40,* 368–382. http://dx.doi.org/10.1111/j.1748-720X.2012.00670.x

Shea, J. (2000). Does parents' money matter? *Journal of Public Economics, 77,* 155–184. http://dx.doi.org/10.1016/S0047-2727(99)00087-0

Shwalb, D. W., Kawai, H., Shoji, J., & Tsunetsugu, K. (1995). The place of advice: Japanese parents' sources of information about childrearing and child health. *Journal of Applied Developmental Psychology, 16,* 629–644. http://dx.doi.org/10.1016/0193-3973(95)90008-X

Shweder, R. A., & Bourne, E. (1982). Does the concept of the person vary cross-culturally? In A. J. Marsella & G. M. White (Eds.), *Cultural conceptions of mental health and therapy* (pp. 97–137). Dordrecht, Netherlands: D. Reidel. http://dx.doi.org/10.1007/978-94-010-9220-3_4

Stevens, J. H. (1984). Child development knowledge and parenting skills. *Family Relations, 33,* 237–244. http://dx.doi.org/10.2307/583789

Strassberg, Z. (1995). Social information processing in compliance situations by mothers of behavior-problem boys. *Child Development, 66,* 376–389. http://dx.doi.org/10.2307/1131584

Sutter, M., Kocher, M. G., Glätzle-Rützler, D., & Trautmann, S. T. (2013). Impatience and uncertainty: Experimental decisions predict adolescents' field behavior. *The American Economic Review, 103,* 510–531. http://dx.doi.org/10.1257/aer.103.1.510

Taylor, S. E., & Brown, J. D. (1988). Illusion and well-being: A social psychological perspective on mental health. *Psychological Bulletin, 103,* 193–210. http://dx.doi.org/10.1037/0033-2909.103.2.193

Twentyman, C. T., & Plotkin, R. C. (1982). Unrealistic expectations of parents who maltreat their children: An educational deficit that pertains to child development. *Journal of Clinical Psychology, 38,* 497–503. http://dx.doi.org/10.1002/1097-4679(198207)38:3<497::AID-JCLP2270380306>3.0.CO;2-X

Villena-Rodán, B., & Ríos-Aguilar, C. (2011). *Causal effects of maternal time-investment on children's cognitive outcomes* (Documentos de Trabajo No. 285), Centro de Economía Aplicada, Universidad de Chile, Santiago, Chile.

Wang, M., Rieger, M. O., & Hens, T. (2016). How time preferences differ: Evidence from 53 countries. *Journal of Economic Psychology, 52,* 115–135. http://dx.doi.org/10.1016/j.joep.2015.12.001

Washbrook, E. V., & Waldfogel, J. (2011, December). *On your marks: Measuring the school readiness of children in low-to-middle income families* (Briefing). London, England: Resolution Foundation.

Winquist Nord, C., Lennon, J., Liu, B., & Chandler, K. (1999). *Home literacy activities and signs of children's emerging literacy, 1993 and 1999* (Report No. NCES 2000-026rev). Washington, DC: U.S. Department of Education, National Center for Education Statistics.

Yopyk, D. J. A., & Prentice, D. A. (2005). Am I an athlete or a student? Identity salience and stereotype threat in student–athletes. *Basic and Applied Social Psychology, 27,* 329–336. http://dx.doi.org/10.1207/s15324834basp2704_5

5

"Whatever They Need"

Helping Poor Children Through In-Kind Support

Timothy Nelson and Kathryn Edin

In 1975, Congress authorized the creation of the Office of Child Support Enforcement (OCSE), a nationwide system designed to ensure that fathers who did not live with their children would share in the cost of caring for them. In 2017, the program collected roughly $28 billion on behalf of 15.1 million noncustodial children across the United States, providing support to about one of every five children in the country (Morales, 2017; U.S. Department of Health & Human Services, Administration for Children & Families, 2018). The benefits of this system are substantial, as it is well established that child support reduces hardship and positively impacts child well-being.

Yet there are several signs that the child support system may be broken. First, studies that separate out formal from informal and in-kind support show that most, if not all, of the positive effects on well-being accrue from informal, not formal, contributions (Amato & Gilbreth, 1999; Argys, Peters, Brooks-Gunn, & Smith, 1998; Nepomnyaschy, Miller, Garasky, & Nanda, 2014; Waller, Emory, & Paul, 2018). Second, although the system has become more effective in collecting on behalf of those with formal orders, it has gotten less effective in recent years at convincing custodial parents to participate (Schroeder, 2016; Solomon-Fears, 2014).

Our analysis of in-depth qualitative interviews with over 400 low-income, noncustodial fathers in four cities offers some clue as to why. These fathers often express a deep dislike for, and distrust in, the child support system (Edin, Nelson, Butler, & Francis, 2019). Fathers do not associate formal child support

http://dx.doi.org/10.1037/0000187-006
Confronting Inequality: How Policies and Practices Shape Children's Opportunities, edited by L. Tach, R. Dunifon, and D. L. Millers

with "providing"; they instead view their support order as "just another bill to pay." Most fathers prefer to provide support informally—through cash contributions to the mother—or in-kind—through direct provision of goods. This is, in part, because they believe these forms of support do more to enhance the father–child bond, a theme evident in prior qualitative research (Edin & Nelson, 2013; Kane, Nelson, & Edin, 2015; Waller, 2002; Waller & Plotnick, 2001). New quantitative evidence backs up these claims, although the theoretical mechanisms are not known (Waller et al., 2018).

This chapter builds on these analyses, examining the narratives of 428 low-income, nonresident fathers to more deeply uncover processes and mechanisms that may underlie these results. We identify key aspects of the formal system that trigger the overwhelmingly negative valence fathers have toward the program. We also identify aspects of informal (i.e., cash directly to the mother) and in-kind support that yield positive associations with provision—of "whatever they need"—and with the father–child bond.

On the basis of this analysis, we contend that fundamental changes to the system are needed. Specifically, we argue that all states should consider unmarried fathers eligible for joint custody, and that all orders be paired with parenting-time agreements (with good cause exemptions). We also recommend that all noncustodial parents participate in coparenting education aimed at enhancing cooperation but also to validate "coparent" as a key social role. This should be followed by guided mediation, in which parents work together to construct support orders and parenting-time agreements that they believe are in the best interest of their child. Further, we endorse allowing in-kind support, which is already practiced by some Tribal child-support systems (Solomon-Fears, 2016c), to count toward fathers' child-support obligations, if mothers agree. We believe that these reforms will succeed in delivering more overall financial resources to the child, while at the same time improving cooperation among coparents and cultivating stronger father–child bonds.

BACKGROUND

It is no secret that children's family lives have become more unstable over the past half century. In the 1960s and 1970s, a rising rate of divorce was the primary driver of family change, whereas in the 1980s and beyond, as divorce rates held steady, nonmarital childbearing played an increasingly significant role (Cherlin, 2010). Currently, more than half of all children live apart from one of their biological parents at some point during their childhood (A. Cherlin, personal communication, March 6, 2019). For these children, society faces a key challenge: How to get paternal resources—both money and time—to those whose fathers don't live with them.

The federal government established the OCSE in 1975 to reimburse the government for welfare costs in the face of burgeoning welfare rolls. Over the years, the office's mission has expanded; it now seeks to ensure that all children with a noncustodial parent receive financial support. Services are provided to all custodial parents for either no cost (in the case of welfare recipients) or for a token fee.

By 2013, OCSE caseloads covered fully half of the poor children in the United States (Solomon-Fears, 2016a; Turetsky, 2014). Child support comprises a considerable portion of poor custodial parents' income. Payments for poor custodial parents who received them made up half (49%) of their annual personal income (Solomon-Fears, 2014). Among poor custodial parents who received the full amount owed, child support accounted for over two thirds (70.3%) of average annual personal income (Grall, 2016). Although child support payments are only rarely large enough to lift children out of poverty (Short, 2015), they lessen hardship (Nepomnyaschy & Garfinkel, 2011; Nepomnyaschy et al., 2014).

Despite the significance of child support payments for custodial parents' household finances, in 2013, half of all children living apart from a parent still lacked an enforcement order. Even among those with one, about a quarter received nothing in the prior year, and fewer than 50% got the full amount owed (Solomon-Fears, 2016b). This is not necessarily due to an unwillingness to pay; many fathers struggle to satisfy their orders, because award amounts can be set unreasonably high due to failure to adjust an order when a father's income falls or due to penalties assessed when they fall into arrears (Hahn, Edin, & Abrahams, 2018).

Despite these limitations, child support is the only institution our nation has devised to ensure the flow of resources from noncustodial parents to their children. Not only do those who receive it benefit financially, but receipt of child support, broadly conceived, has positive impacts that extend beyond economic well-being. The effect of child support on noneconomic aspects of child well-being has been subjected to a meta-analysis of 14 studies (Amato & Gilbreth, 1999), plus several additional analyses (Argys et al., 1998; Nepomnyaschy, Magnuson, & Berger, 2012). This research shows that child support significantly bolsters cognitive skills, emotional development, and educational attainment.

But there is an irony in this literature as well—one that signals that the system may have fundamental flaws. In studies that separate out formal from more informal contributions (i.e., cash paid directly to the mother and the provision of in-kind goods), the positive benefits of child support flow primarily from less formal contributions, especially the direct provision of goods, which is often referred to as *in-kind* support (Amato & Gilbreth, 1999; Argys et al., 1998; Nepomnyaschy et al., 2012). Newer studies drawing on contemporary samples have shown that in-kind support is more predictive of closeness in the father–child relationship and is associated with fewer internalizing, externalizing, and delinquent behavior problems in adolescence than formal support (Nepomnyaschy, Miller, Waller, & Emory, 2019). It is also more strongly associated with the quality and quantity of the time fathers spend with children than is formal support (Nepomnyaschy & Garfinkel, 2011; Nepomnyaschy et al., 2014; Waller et al., 2018).

More worrisome is one study that found finds that involvement with the formal system may have deleterious effects on child well-being (Nepomnyaschy et al., 2012), possibly due to the corrosive effects of parental conflict that involvement with the system engenders (Edin, 1995; Waller, 2002; Waller & Plotnick, 2001). Another signal is the recent marked decline in the rate of participation among custodial parents (Schroeder, 2016). When asked about reasons for nonparticipation, results have indicated that parents may be voting with their feet because they no longer feel the system meets their needs. although the precise theoretical mechanisms underlying these results are not known, we believe our analysis will provide new insight into these perplexing findings.

Sweeping demographic and cultural changes in the family and in family roles provide a further mandate for rethinking child support. A growing body of evidence shows that today's fathers conceive of their parental roles and relate to their children differently than did prior generations. Among less educated men, the father–child bond may have eclipsed the father–mother bond in importance (Edin & Nelson, 2013; Edin et al., 2019; Waller, 2002).

The child support system was designed to insure the well-being of children living away from one of their parents. The system's mandate is currently focused on achieving this goal solely through securing financial support, but due to these considerable changes in how fathers relate to their children and conceive of their parental roles, this approach is out of synch with these new norms. We believe that this crucial institution will fall short of its potential if it does not adopt a broader mandate: Responding to new family realities by working to ensure that as many resources as possible—both financial and emotional—flow to children living apart from one of their parents.

Embracing this broader definition of support is vital to the well-being of the children whom child support seeks to serve. Although early research showed few, if any, positive outcomes for children whose fathers have spent time with them (Amato & Gilbreth, 1999; Harris, Furstenberg, & Marmer, 1998; King, 1994), these studies were often cross-sectional and based on small, nonrepresentative samples. Subsequent research has typically drawn on nationally representative samples and has often considered not just the quantity, but the quality, of time spent. These studies have generally found significant positive, albeit modest, results on a broad range of outcomes (Carlson, 2006; Coley & Medeiros, 2007). But this research has weaknesses as well: Analyses are usually based on cross-sectional data or rely on longitudinal observations collected only a year or 2 apart. Further, all rely on data sources (i.e., the National Longitudinal Survey of Youth, 1997 Cohort [see https://www.bls.gov/nls/nlsy97.htm]; the National Longitudinal Study of Adolescent Health [https://www.icpsr.umich.edu/icpsrweb/DSDR/studies/21600]) that measured key outcomes 2 or more decades ago, bringing into question their relevance to current family realities.

New analyses of adolescent outcomes deploying extended longitudinal designs and drawing on a contemporary, nationally representative sample (i.e., the Fragile Families and Child Wellbeing Study) have found that father involvement during middle childhood has relatively large payoffs by mid-adolescence. Internalizing, externalizing, and delinquent behavior are all reduced significantly by fathers' investments of time, even when those investments are modest. Perceived closeness with fathers—a measure that is distinct from measures of father–child contact—also yields significant positive results (Gold, Edin, & Nelson, 2019), as does social involvement (i.e., the frequency of time spent, engagement, and number of days seen; Nepomnyaschy et al., 2019). Furthermore, the evidence for the benefits of nonresident father involvement are more strongly associated than that of such fathers' cash contributions, whether formal or informal (Nepomnyaschy et al., 2019). In other words, investments of time may be more important than financial investments for adolescent well-being.

The stronger salience of fathers' involvement found in these new studies could be due to improved study design but may also suggest—consistent with the in-depth qualitative studies—that the importance of father involvement in children's lives is increasing over time as the salience of role of the father has grown in men's lives. Time-use data add validity to findings of these qualitative studies. They show that, in recent decades, American fathers, both resident and nonresident, have increased the amount of time they invest in parenting tasks (Bianchi, 2011).

In sum, it is time for the child support system to come to terms with what's not working, but also to consider whether its mandate should be broadened in ways that make it fully responsive to the new ways in which fathers are seeking to relate to their children. Although the system succeeds in delivering significant financial resources, this success may be coming at a price. We also need to understand why some forms of support (i.e., informal and in-kind support) *are* delivering when it comes to child well-being.

Furthermore, we need to examine what is lost when the system sidesteps the responsibility of ensuring that all children have access to the full range of paternal resources—both financial and emotional—that they need. When jurisdictions fail to consider joint custody arrangements for nonmarital children, as 18 states currently do, or fail to automatically adjudicate parenting-time agreements for unmarried parents when child support orders are set—which is the case in all but two states—they may be selling children short. Father involvement and child support payment go together (Nepomnyaschy, 2007). This suggests there will be synergistic benefits in pursuing both forms of support at once.

This chapter reports on findings from repeated, in-depth interviews with roughly 400 low-income noncustodial fathers in four U.S. metropolitan areas. In a prior analysis of these data (Edin et al., 2019), all portions of men's narratives regarding child support, whether formal, direct (cash to the mother), or in-kind (the provision of in-kind goods), were inductively coded, sorted into categories, and ranked by how often they occurred. This analysis found that fathers associated formal child support with a loss of power and autonomy and with involvement with the legal system. In contrast, informal and in-kind support were strongly associated with provision to the child and positive coparenting. The most striking finding in this analysis was that in-kind support—and only in-kind support—was strongly associated with the father–child bond.

This chapter takes this analysis a step further, identifying key dilemmas that the formal support system raises from the father's point of view—problems that may be partly or fully resolved via informal and, especially, in-kind support. We also identify the potential downsides of these more informal support arrangements. In the end, we advocate for a system that resolves these challenges, including (a) whenever possible, considering joint custody arrangements for all fathers; (b) offering all parents coparenting education and guided mediation with the goal of setting orders and parenting-time agreements that both parents believe are in the best interests of the child; and (c) creating a registry that would allow in-kind contributions to count toward a father's formal child support obligation, if the mother agrees. These prescriptions don't surmount all of Child Support's challenges, particularly the problems of unsustainable awards and arrears (Edin et al., 2019; Hahn et al., 2018), but they offer a fresh vision of what benefits could ensue if child support became a truly family building institution for the 21st century.

METHODS

This analysis is based on a study of 428 low-income, nonresident fathers across four locations: Philadelphia/Camden, NJ; Charleston, SC; and two Texas cities—Austin and San Antonio. Interviews with these men were conducted in the late 1990s and early 2000s and included Black, White, and Latino fathers (except in Charleston). Here "low income" refers to men with formal-sector earnings over the 6 months prior to initial interview totaling less than the poverty line for a family of four in that year.

These interviews took place after significant changes to the child support system were implemented in the mid-1990s. Until December 2016, no major national policy shifts occurred; in December 2016, the final rule issued by the OCSE encouraged states to pursue right-sized orders (U.S. Department of Health & Human Services, Administration for Children & Families, 2016). Views of the system captured in our study are consistent with recent interviews with men participating in fatherhood programs across the nation (Clary, Holcomb, Dion, & Edin, 2017).

Sites were chosen because they varied in labor-market strength and the stringency of the child support enforcement system. Although not nationally representative, these cities represent some of the range of economic and policy climates low-income fathers must operate within.

Low-income fathers are hard to sample and, therefore, a large percentage are missed by even the most carefully conducted surveys. This is both because such men are missed in large numbers (presumably because they are not stably attached to households or are in jail or prison) and because many don't admit to survey researchers that they have fathered children (Garfinkel, McLanahan, Meyer, & Seltzer, 1998). Thus, rather than attempt a random sample, we selected census tract clusters within each city where at least 20% of individuals were poor. We then worked through local intermediaries (i.e., nonprofits, grassroots community organizations, local employers) to identify study participants; but we included no more than five through any given source. Because many fathers are not connected to local institutions, we sampled in two additional ways: We asked each father to refer us to one or two other fathers they thought we would not find via local intermediaries. We also walked the major streets of each area in varied intervals and approached men directly, asking them if they were noncustodial parents and offering them the chance to participate. In each city, our goal was to recruit 50 men of each race–ethnicity (Blacks, Whites, and Latinos in Philadelphia, Austin, and San Antonio; Blacks and Whites in Charleston), and to recruit even numbers of men age 30 and under and over age 30 within each study cell (or in each city and race–ethnic group). The later criteria insured that we captured the experiences of fathers across the life course. By and large, we met these targets.

Each interview typically lasted between 90 minutes and 4 hours, resulting in extensive dialogue spanning numerous dimensions of their lives—both past and present. In addition, most fathers were interviewed at least two times. Respondents were asked to describe their childhood experiences, romantic relationships, employment history, expenses and income, criminal history, current relationships with children, past and current relationships with mothers of their children, visitation, and child support.

We defined *formal child support* as monies paid through the formal child support enforcement system and informal support as cash given directly to the mother (or child). In-kind support included noncash contributions made to the child's household or given directly to the child. Consistent with the set of items commonly defined as in-kind goods (Garasky, Stewart, Gundersen, & Lohman, 2010; Grall, 2016; Waller & Plotnick, 2001), interviewers asked fathers to list all in-kind contributions offered over the last 6 months. We began with a series of open-ended questions regarding in-kind support and then probed systematically for specific contributions of the following: baby products (e.g., diapers, formula, strollers, cribs), clothing, shoes, school expenses (e.g., school trips, school uniforms, school supplies, after-school program costs), gifts (e.g., Christmas, birthday), food, child care tuition expenses, and "other" expenses (e.g., medical expenses, miscellaneous items). Interviewers asked fathers to estimate how much they had spent for each item and how often they provided it in a 6-month period. We created a separate quantitative database containing this information. Fathers were able to recall this information easily, perhaps because their own budgets were tight and even small contributions often required some level of sacrifice. In cases in which fathers were not able to remember how much an item cost (e.g., a pack of diapers), we estimated the value using prices reported by other fathers in the study for these same items. For example, on average, fathers who were able to recall a specific amount said they paid $17 for a pack of disposable diapers.

In what follows, we first document the proportion of nonresident children of the fathers in our study who received financial support from formal child support payments, informal cash contributions, through in-kind expenditures, or some combination of the above. Second, we use interviews with these fathers to show how they experienced each of these channels of financial support and the problems and potential pitfalls inherent in each type of support which might inhibit father involvement, therefore, suppressing potentially better child outcomes.

FINDINGS

We asked each father about all the children he had fathered, or had played a father role with, at some point in his life. For this analysis, we limited the sample to only those children who lived apart from their father and to whom he would have been obligated to support, if child support was sought. As a result, any child over age 18 residing with their father, or any child who was not the biological or adoptive child of the father was not included in this analysis. From the interview transcripts, we created a database for each father in the study (all of whom had at least one qualifying child) and a separate database for each of the 695 children who fit the above criteria.

Table 5.1 shows that, of the 695 children of these 428 fathers, one third (33.5%) were receiving no monthly financial support of any kind from their fathers at the time of our interview. Just over half (54%) received $50 or more in average monthly support from one of the child support streams (i.e., formal support, direct cash payments to the custodial parent, or in-kind support). The remaining children (12.5%) received only minimal support, with average monthly amounts of less than $50.

Table 5.2 shows that of the 375 children who received over the minimal monthly amount, just over two thirds (70.1%) were being supported through a single support stream (defined as those receiving 90% or more of their monthly support from one stream). Of the remaining 30%, two combinations (i.e., formal plus in-kind and cash plus in-kind) make up the bulk of the cases (i.e., 99 children or 26.4% of the total). Overall, just over half of the

TABLE 5.1. All Children by Support Levels

Support level	N	%
Nonsupport	233	33.5
Minimal support	87	12.5
Support	375	54.0
Total	695	100

Note. "Minimal support" = $1–$49 per month; "Support" = minimum of $50 per month in total support.

TABLE 5.2. Support by Type

Type	N	%	Mean monthly $	Mean age of child
Cash only*	65	17.3	215.96	7.9
In-kind only	88	23.5	112.31	7.0
Formal only	110	29.3	179.85	9.8
Formal + In-kind	41	10.9	256.60	7.8
Formal + Cash	6	1.6	295.33	9.0
In-kind + Cash	58	15.5	230.36	6.2
All three types	7	1.9	211.29	9.0
Total	375	100	193.15	8.0

Note. *"Only" = > 90% of total monthly support from that source.

children (51.7%) were receiving in-kind support as either their sole source of financial support or combined with cash and/or formal support; 43.7% received formal support either solely or combined with other sources. Direct cash payments were provided to the custodial parents of 36.3% of children (most often mothers but sometimes relatives of either the mother or father).

Each contribution stream reached a substantial number of children. If we limited our analyses only to those receiving formal support, we would dramatically underestimate the number of children with low-income nonresident fathers who supported them above a minimal level. In fact, we would miss 60% of such children. As important as these figures are, they provide only a thin understanding of what is happening on the ground. In the analysis that follows, we utilize our in-depth interviews with fathers to illuminate their views and experiences with each kind of support. We sought to identify aspects of each form of support that might facilitate or inhibit the salience of fathers' identities as providers and whether it threatened or strengthened the father–child bond. We pay attention not only to the stories these men told but also to the language they used in describing the various kinds of support. Our analysis identifies six problems inherent in formal and—to a lesser extent— direct cash support that are resolved, or at least mitigated against, by in-kind support.

PROBLEMS OF FORMAL SUPPORT

As indicated earlier, just under a third of the children in our study received financial contributions only through the formal system. As Table 5.2 shows, this is the most common single source of support. The mean age of children who receive only formal support is higher (9.8 years) than the average for all children (8.0 years), likely because fathers tend to be put on the formal system by the mother only after relations with the custodial parent break down (Edin, 1995; Waller & Plotnick, 2001). The primary problem fathers associated with formal support was what—using the words of one respondent—we call the "Just Another Bill" problem. When a father has a child support order, the federal government mandates that the monthly obligation be deducted from his paycheck and sent either to the custodial parent or, in the case of mothers receiving benefits from the Temporary Assistance to Needy Families (TANF) program, to the state to reimburse the government for welfare costs. Although fathers often complained about the amount of the award, the issue here is the process through which the money is extracted.

According to fathers' accounts, when support for a child is automatically withheld from a paycheck by a government agency, it has the effect of stripping the father's sense of power and autonomy. It does not allow a father to do what custodial fathers typically do—take responsibility to set aside resources for one's child and ensure that they benefit from those resources. This might seem a small matter, yet many fathers in our study experienced wage withholding as a signal that the government did not trust them to provide for their children. More than a quarter of the fathers in the full sample spoke directly about how they felt powerless in their dealings with the child support system, and they often blamed the mother for deploying the state to extract resources from them. When mothers chose to participate in the formal system, it often sparked significant conflict between the mother and father, conflict that might have corroded the benefits of formal support for child well-being. Representative phrases in this regard included "I was demanded to pay," "They took every last cent," "She turned me in," "She's coming at me," "She's got the power." Feelings of loss of autonomy were evident in phrases such as, "they take it," "jacking me up," "they come looking for you," "[makes me feel like I'm] not man enough," "hounding me," "at their mercy," "put me under a microscope," and "crushing [my] manhood."

Because of the impersonal and indirect nature of the process, fathers typically experienced participation in the formal system not as a form of provision, but simply as another bill that must be paid. In our prior analysis of the words and phrases fathers used regarding the different forms of support, the theme of parental provision is found in only a handful of discussions regarding formal support. In contrast, discussions of direct cash contributions by 50 fathers linked this form of support to notions of provision. Phrases such as "I take care of my kid," "my child gets what she needs," "I did my part," "I give to my children first," and "give them the best support that I can" were typical of those that are used in these discussions.

When a White Philadelphia father was asked about formal support, he replied, "I don't really want to do it that way because it's sort of degrading if you think about it." When asked to expand on his views, he replied, "It [would] make me feel like I'm not responsible enough to send her the money like I do." A White father from Austin dispensed small amounts of cash to his exwife in addition to being subject to wage withholding for a formal order. Of the direct cash contributions, he said, "She doesn't ever really ask me for it, but I give it to her. I'll just hand her twenty dollars and say, 'Here, get them something, an ice cream. Buy them a movie.'" These small direct contributions allowed this father to play the role of benefactor, in contrast to the formal support withheld from his paycheck.

Yet in reality, child support is much more than just another bill fathers must pay monthly. It is a financial obligation that carries potentially severe penalties if not met. One Black respondent in Charleston emphasized this fact: "I've come to the conclusion that it is just another bill that you're late on, *except on that kind of bill you can go to jail* [emphasis added]." Indeed, "court" was the most common word associated with formal support in men's narratives and "jail" was the next most common. Other words and phrases from these narratives give more texture to this theme: "order/ordered," "file," "sue," "the attorney general has my name," "didn't give me no rights," "charged me/ pressing charges," "warrant," and "take me downtown." One father shared that his participation in the formal system "makes me feel like I need a *judge* to make me responsible!" Another father said the system made him feel like "some kind of criminal."

What gets lost in this process of formal support, then, is a key aspect of what fathers think should be inherent when contributing to their children—the connection between payment and a sense of parental provision. Our interviews suggest that the "Just Another Bill" problem adheres to formal child support in part because of the process through which support is extracted and distributed.

PROBLEMS OF DIRECT CASH SUPPORT

As Table 5.2 indicates, about one in five children received financial support only through direct cash payments from their fathers to their custodial parents, usually their mothers. Another third (37%) received direct cash support in combination with formal of in-kind support. Unlike formal support, which was disliked by almost all fathers, direct cash support was viewed in a mostly positive light. Men who contributed in this way were especially likely to link direct support to notions of cooperative parent, a theme that is nearly absent in discussions of formal support. Sometimes, fathers' narratives about direct cash support invoked an implicit contrast to being forced to pay through the formal OCSE system: "We worked it out like civilized people," "she trusted me to bring her money," "we made an agreement without going to court," "we have an understanding," "a verbal agreement." And, as noted earlier, fathers often talked about their cash contributions in terms of paternal provision. Phrases like, "I'm there for them," "I love my daughter—I want her to have things," "my son comes first" exemplify this category.

But our interviews revealed downsides to direct cash contributions as well. The first is what we call the "Congenial Ex" problem. Direct support usually depends upon a relatively good relationship between parents or on situations in which someone other than the biological mother has custody (in rare cases, a trusted go-between is used). Perhaps for this reason, longitudinal survey data show that direct cash contributions fall off dramatically over time (Nepomnyaschy & Garfinkel, 2010).

Second, cash contributions are subject to what we call the "Gift" problem, the reverse of the "Just Another Bill" problem. Although paying through the formal OCSE system strips fathers of agency, fathers who pay in cash may be tempted to treat the transaction as a *gift relationship*, in which the father attempts to use his contributions to exert control over the mother. For example, some fathers insisted that their children's mother, or older children, had no automatic right to support. Rather, they had to ask him for money and offer a rationale. A White father from Charleston said of his ex, "If she needs it, and tells me she needs it, then I'll go buy it or give her the money to go buy it." A Black father from Camden also insisted on being asked first: "You want something, you ask me for it. Don't take it from me. You don't take it from someone." This father was implicitly condemning the formal system, which "takes" rather than allowing him to "give," one of the most common words used in discussions of direct cash contributions.

A Black Philadelphia father of a teenager tried to assert his paternal authority through his direct contributions in a way that paying through the formal system could never allow. When his 17-year-old son's mother asked him for support, he responded, "Troy about to be a man, he don't need nothing. If Troy wants something, he can talk to me direct." A Black father from Austin espoused a similar philosophy: "If they ask, and I know they need it, and I have it, then it happens." This father applied three conditions to his direct cash contributions: (a) their asking, (b) his assessment whether the request constitutes a need, and (c) his ability to satisfy it.

PROBLEMS COMMON TO BOTH FORMAL AND DIRECT CASH CONTRIBUTIONS

Three additional problems are commonly discussed in relation to formal and direct cash contributions: (a) the "Mistrust," (b) "Pay to Play," and (c) "Invisibility" problems. Some fathers who contributed in cash, either directly or through the formal system, trusted their children's mother to deploy their contributions in the best interests of the child. One told us, "I realize she's got bills to pay too," and said, "Even if she does want to spend it on herself, that's on her. She still got to provide the 40 dollars or whatever it may take for the baby." However, most did not, and were frustrated over the fact that they had little, if any, control over how their child's mother spent their contributions. In particular, many seemed fixated on the possibility that the mother was spending his hard-earned contributions on herself. A Black father in Philadelphia sighed, and then said of his daughter's mother, "Oh God, she went shopping. She might spend some on her friends, some on our daughter, her daughter [from another relationship], spend the rest on herself." He also named "alcohol and drugs" as items she might purchase with his child support. One Latino father from San Antonio contacted the Texas attorney general's office due to his concern that his child support would be used to further his child's mother's addiction. "'Look, this lady has a history of going to jail and using drugs,'" he reportedly told them. But to his dismay, they informed him that there was no way to ensure she spent the money on his kids.

Several fathers worried about their child's mother's current boyfriend and how he might appropriate and use their support. A White Austin father, for example, said he "had a problem" sending his child's mother any money because of a guy she was living with, "and I knew what kind of life he lived, so. . . ."

One strategy that fathers sometimes used in the case of cash contributions was to try and earmark their support in some way. One Black father in Charleston put his daughter's name on the monthly money order he sent to his own father, who had custody of the teenager, "to make her feel more important." He did this even though he knew that, "Pops takes it and puts it in his account anyway." A White Austin father that had a child support order but flouted it (which he could do because he worked informally), instead chose to provide cash directly to the mother. He also liked to earmark his contributions by writing the checks payable to his 5-year-old daughter, even though he knew the money would go into his daughter's mothers' account. "I want my daughter to have it," he told us, "I don't want [my ex] to have it."

Some fathers drew on these fears to justify not supporting their children at all at present, but claimed that they are "saving up" support for when their children were older. A White father in Austin claimed to have set up a bank account in his son's name, "so when he gets old enough, he'll have some money." He said that he put money into that account regularly, though he also occasionally gave "a little money to [my child's] mother." Another White Austin father boasted to having a gold coin that he believed might be worth as much as $250,000. He planned to give it to his daughter when she turned 18. He was adamant that the proceeds were only for her and not her mother. "It's in her name; the mom can't touch it." Meanwhile, he paid no regular support.

The reverse of the "Gift" problem is the "Pay to Play" problem; here, allowing access to children becomes a bargaining chip for the custodial parent, who can insist on formal or cash contributions as a condition for visitation. For example, one White Austin father claimed that his child's mother "hasn't been letting me see him because I am a little bit behind [in formal support], you know." When asked, "How often are you able to see your daughter?," a Black Philadelphia father answered, "When I have the money." A White father from Charleston was resigned to the fact that, "If I don't bring money or food [to his child's mother], then I'm pretty much SOL [shit out of luck]." He told us that, when he managed to get enough cash, "I'll call her up and say, 'Hey, how're you doing? I've got [something] for you. Can I see the kids now?" Similarly, a White San Antonio father claimed, it was only when he brought money to his expartner that "she'll let me spend time with the kids." Recognizing his vulnerability to the "Pay to Play" problem but still wishing to avoid a formal order, one White Charleston father made an explicit bargain with his exwife over payment and visitation. "I said, 'can't we work this out where I'll pay you directly every week, and if I don't, then I won't have no visitation rights to my children?'"

Some fathers were so frustrated with the limited access they had to their children that they considered volunteering to pay through the formal system, due to their erroneous belief that visitation is always automatically adjudicated when a formal order is set. A White Charleston father told us, "I don't really want to have a judge involved or anything like that, but I do want to see my kids." In an exceptional case that proves the rule, one Black Philadelphia father, whose children's mother had remarried and had moved out of the area, believed that she wanted him out of his daughter's life. Thus, he claimed that she refused to accept any contributions that exceeded the small amount she had stipulated. Although emphasizing that he would like to do more, this father told us, "I do as much as I can and as much as she will allow me to do."

The final problem that often applied to both formal and direct cash contributions is the "Invisibility" problem. Fathers often noted that cash support is often deployed in ways that are unseen and unacknowledged by the child. The abstractness and fungibility of cash may make it the most valuable form of support in the eyes of the custodial parent, who must pay rent, and procure and pay utility bills. Yet fathers wanted their contributions to be seen and appreciated by their children, particularly when they lived far away or were otherwise unable to be involved in their day-to-day lives.

Studies have consistently found that children's feelings of closeness to their nonresident fathers have positive developmental outcomes. For example, several studies have shown that perceived closeness protects against adolescent behavioral problems (Carlson, 1999; Gold et al., 2019). In another analysis of the data gathered in this chapter, we find that fathers intentionally sought to deploy their support in ways that they believed would foster feelings of closeness. Although fathers sometimes managed to render their contributions more visible through various forms of earmarking, as described earlier, the primary way they do so is via direct provision of goods to the household or child—in-kind support (Kane et al., 2015).

IN-KIND SUPPORT: A (PARTIAL) SOLUTION?

Table 5.2 shows that almost half (47.9%) of children who received any support received at least some of it in-kind. For just under a quarter of the total receiving any support, in-kind contributions are their only source. Furthermore, in-kind support is by far the most common channel of contribution for the children receiving what we call "minimal support"—contributions worth between $5 and $49 in the average month, as Table 5.3 shows.

What fathers provide varies widely, and what a given father provides changes over time as the needs and circumstances of his children evolve. When children are infants and toddlers, the most common items purchased are diapers, formula, clothing, and direct payment of daycare bills. When children reach school age, fathers typically provide sneakers, school supplies,

TABLE 5.3. Minimal Support by Type

Type	N	Percent	Mean monthly $	Mean age of child
Cash only	23	26.4	23.65	8.8
In-kind only	43	49.4	19.86	9.0
Formal only	15	17.2	24.00	7.6
Formal + In-kind	1	1.1	37.00	10
Formal + Cash	0	0	0	
In-kind + Cash	5	5.7	35.60	9.4
All three types	0	0	0	
Total	87	100	22.68	8.7

Note. Calculations are based on National Survey of Family Growth data from Andersson, Thomson, and Duntava (2017).

winter coats, or take their children shopping for clothes or out to meals. As we and others have indicated elsewhere (Edin, 1995; Kane et al., 2015; Waller & Plotnick, 2001), these items have not only practical but symbolic significance. The provision of Pampers and formula not only insures that a child's most basic needs are provided for, but it is a symbol to the community that the father has claimed the child and accepted paternal responsibility (i.e., a social form of paternity establishment). Here, the audience is the mother and the community at large. But as a child grows older, the purchase of that special pair of Jordans not only meets a material need, the pricey items are also a highly visible symbol of a father's love and devotion, a "repository of parental sentiment" (Kane et al., 2015). In-kind contributions usually involve face-to-face interaction, which keeps them in contact with their children and allows them to directly observe, and respond to, a child's needs. For example, the White Philadelphia father who paid for his sons' karate lessons not only made a financial contribution but also was offered a window into the boy's interests and activities—information that facilitated conversation and further engagement.

For these reasons, discussions of in-kind support often contained themes of provision (as was the case with direct contributions, but not with formal support). The following phrases are representative of how fathers involved the provision theme when discussing in-kind support: "I had to buy him everything he needed," "I'm responsible for everything she needs," "anything they need, they'll have before I have," "the kid has so much stuff because of me," "buy him what he needs; I try to provide for him the best I can."

Another strong theme in discussions of in-kind support is coparenting (also common in discussions of direct cash contributions but not formal support). Phrases indicating coparenting included "We take care of the baby together" and "Whenever she needs something, she calls me." Particularly when the children are young, in-kind provision is just as subject to the "Congenial Ex" problem as direct cash support is, but as children get older and can establish independent relationships with their fathers, their children can and do ask them directly for things they need. And when fathers come through, the exchange often involves face-to-face contact and opportunities to spend time together. Perhaps for this reason, the language used to describe in-kind support was especially likely to emphasize the father–child bond. In fact, the father–child bond is the theme most strongly associated with in-kind support (but virtually absent from discussions of formal support and only sometimes mentioned in discussions of direct cash support). Examples included "I buy him a pizza and just talk, you know"; "We go to the movies, go out to dinner, buy more toys, gifts, clothes. I try to buy her a pair of 'tennies' [tennis shoes] every time she comes down [to visit]"; "I wanna show them the love [by buying them things]"; "I'd rather buy the stuff for my little girl"; and "Bringing my kids what they need."

A Black Philadelphia father, whose own father had custody of his teenage daughter, expressed the connection between in-kind support and the parent–child bond in this way:

> As far as giving [my father] money . . . I know he would do the right thing with the money, but I feel better getting Nicole what she needs when she's here rather than just handing him the money. It's more personal. You know, instead of just saying, "Okay, I am paying my child support, now here's this much for the month." [My father] would rather me do it that way, but it's more personal for me [to give things to her directly] and I think it's more bonding for her and I. When the money's sent . . . she doesn't see it, so she wouldn't remember it. [But when I buy her things], I feel like there's a bond there when I when I do that. I only get her every other weekend, so I know that I'm going to spend that [money]. I always buy her something.

As this quote illustrates, fathers who give in-kind contributions do not face the "Just Another Bill" problem, because their contributions are responses to children's needs. In-kind support is also not as prone to the "Congenial Ex" problem (except when the children are young) or the "Gift" problem as are other forms of support, because in-kind support is usually predicated on a direct relationship between a father and his child, especially as the child grows older. Finally, in-kind support addresses the more serious problems of "Mistrust," "Pay to Play," and "Invisibility." By definition, in-kind support allows fathers to earmark their contributions. Usually (except in cases where fathers are paying day care bills), the contributions involve goods that directly benefit the child and not the household. The lack of fungibility does not allow mothers—or mothers' new boyfriends—to divert it to other uses. Although fathers may still experience the problem of "Pay to Play," as children age, fathers can circumvent the mother and provide in-kind goods directly to the child. This form of provision is both visible to, and acknowledged by, the child.

In solving, or at the least mitigating, problems inherent in other forms of support, we believe that in-kind support provides the best opportunity to ensure that a father contributes to his child *and* creates stronger father–child bonds simultaneously. As indicated earlier, both have been shown to boost child well-being significantly, but in-kind support is more strongly associated with these benefits than formal support. As we argue later in this chapter, encouraging and allowing in-kind contributions to count toward a father's support obligation (if mothers agree) could create a positive feedback loop, as each strand amplifies the others rather than dampening or forcing trade-offs between them.

Finally, we consider children who receive only minimal monthly support, most of it through in-kind contributions. A closer look at these cases reveals that these are primarily fathers a who are in the worst circumstances: homeless or in halfway houses, addicted to alcohol or drugs, unemployed or working only sporadically (see also Kane et al., 2015). Their contributions are especially likely to be in-kind and usually consist of small items that serve as a reminder—to themselves and to their children—that the relationship has not been forgotten. Contributions are usually tied to special occasions or to seasonal expenses: Christmas and birthday gifts, back-to-school clothes, and the like. Although the cash value of their support is not significant compared with the costs of raising a child, these contributions may have an emotional weight that extends beyond their financial value and might serve to keep communication channels open until fathers are in a position to provide more. If feelings of closeness to one's father is indeed beneficial to children, then these token contributions—symbols that their fathers have not forgotten them—could constitute worth far beyond their face value.

CONCLUSION AND POLICY IMPLICATIONS

Because informal contributions often diminish as children age (Nepomnyaschy, 2007), the current system should not be abandoned but should be reformed in ways that minimize its harms and capitalize on some of the benefits to both fathers and children that inhere to in-kind support. We've shown that one irony of automatic wage withholding is that this procedure seems to reduce child support to "Just Another Bill" in fathers' minds. This is reinforced by the feelings of loss of power and autonomy men experience while participating in the formal system, which they feel "strips me of my manhood" because "I need a *judge* to make me feel responsible." The fact that parenting time is only rarely adjudicated when a child support order is set seems to compound men's sense that child support is not providing for their children but is merely paying a bill.

As our earlier inductive analysis of these men's narratives regarding child support showed (Edin et al., 2019), the contributions of fathers who give cash directly to the mother are not viewed in this way and, in fact, evoke positive expressions of positive coparenting. Rather than the court taking his contributions from him and delivering them to the mother, he is giving her these contributions. In this chapter, we showed that for fathers with trusting, supportive relationships with the mother (i.e., what we call the "Congenial Ex"), informal arrangements seem to work well. But not all relationships are, or remain, congenial.

We've also shown that cash contributions can also tempt fathers to view their contributions as gifts rather than provision. As anthropologists have shown, when transformed into a gift exchange, the giver gains control over the recipient. In our data, fathers who view their contributions as gifts often try to control the mothers' behavior or gain control of decisions regarding the child.

Three additional problems that adhere to both formal and direct cash contributions are (a) "Mistrust," (b) "Pay to Play," and (c) "Invisibility." Mistrust ensues because fathers have no way of earmarking the money's use. Fathers commonly fear that the mother spends child-support dollars on herself or, even worse, a new boyfriend (Weiss & Willis, 1993). Our evidence suggests that this fear both lowers fathers' motivation to pay and serves as a justification for nonpayment (Craigie, 2015). In our data, we observe several attempts to symbolically earmark direct cash contributions, such as the father who wrote the check directly to his 5-year-old child.

Meanwhile, the other side of the coin of the "Gift" problem, which may allow fathers excessive control, is the "Pay to Play" problem, in which mothers feel justified in prohibiting contact when fathers fail to pay. This problem, one variant of a larger issue known as "maternal gatekeeping," is commonly noted among fathers in a variety of studies (Claessens, 2007; Edin & Nelson, 2013; Waller, 2002). The other side of the coin is that custodial mothers often claim that lack of visitation is due to lack of interest on the father's part. One study drew upon the Fragile Families study to adjudicate these rival claims, and found evidence that gatekeeping may, in fact, be common, particularly when mothers transition to new partners (Tach, Mincy, & Edin, 2010). However, they also found that the intensity of fathers' visitation falls off over time, particularly after the birth of a subsequent child. Regardless of the veracity of men's claims, their perception that they have to pay in order to play adds to their impression that they are viewed by the system (i.e., for those who pay formally) and by the mothers as merely a paycheck and not as a parent.

Finally, both formal and direct cash support are subject to the "Invisibility" problem—contributions that flow to the mother will often be invisible to the child. This is likely why in-kind support is most strongly associated with a sense of provision in our prior analysis of these men's' child support narratives. As we have documented elsewhere (Kane et al., 2015), in-kind support has different meanings as children age. For infants and toddlers, providing Pampers, formula, and "little outfits" is a powerful signal to the community that a father accepts responsibility for a child, as a kind of informal paternity establishment. The symbolic value is amplified by the fact that the items in question address the child's most basic needs. But above and beyond these features, the exchange of these items usually involves frequent face-to-face interaction and direct observation of a child's needs, thus cementing the relationship between his contributions and his sense that he is providing for his child. As the child ages, in-kind items shift to direct payment of daycare expenses, purchases of school clothes, money for field trips, and the like—all clear needs—but some wants as well, such as Jordans or designer clothes. Although the provision of wants can stir conflict with the mother, who by necessity must focus first on needs, these small extravagances are symbols to the child that a father cares, what we have called "a repository of paternal sentiment," that children can draw on, even if their dads are separated from them by incarceration, addiction, or death. And this may well have vital significance, as several studies have shown that adolescents' perceived closeness to them in middle childhood (Gold et al., 2019) is strongly associated with reduced behavioral problems.

Reviewing the problems discussed here, how might child support be transformed to address them? One critical task is to transform the meaning of child support from "Just Another Bill"—predicated on the perceived stripping of power and autonomy—to provision. We recommend that local agencies look to examples such as the Minnesota Co-Parenting Court, in which unmarried parents were invited to participate in a co-parenting curriculum and engage in guided mediation to form a child-support and parenting-time agreement that they felt was in the best interest of the child—agreements that were later incorporated into the formal support order. Such an approach would honor the role of fathers as parents, not as mere paychecks, and would presumably restore a sense of power and autonomy, while still ensuring that resources flow to the mother and child. It might also build more positive coparenting (more "Congenial Exes"), which could mitigate against mistrust and lower conflict levels.

To address the Pay to Play problem, which may be significant, states should consider all fathers for joint custody and should adjudicate parenting time for all fathers when the support order is set. Although older research on the value of paternal visitation on children's outcomes was mixed, newer research on contemporary samples of fathers and children show that even modest levels of contact experienced earlier in a child's life can have substantial impacts on adolescent well-being. States should recognize that men's value lay not only in their wallets but in their hearts and actions as well. If such agreements are set in the context of a guided mediation between both coparents, as was the case in the Minnesota Co-Parenting Court, it might also send the signal to mothers and fathers that the father's presence is, and will continue to be, vital in his child's life.

To guard against the Gift and Invisibility problems, states and locales should move in-kind support into the formal system and recognize it as one form of formal support. We and other child support experts have suggested that family resource programs could develop registries of children's needs and parents' varied contributions (Hahn et al., 2018). These registries could work in various ways. They could function like wedding or other gift registries, whereby parents could direct their court-ordered financial contributions toward specific items on their children's lists of needs, if both parents agree. The lists could include discretionary items, like a new toy, as well as the child's portion of basic household expenses. Or, registries could track parents' nonfinancial as well as financial contributions. For example, parenting time, in-kind contributions (e.g., diapers, home repairs), and direct cash payments to the mother could be formally credited. Should parents agree to use the registry to establish a college fund for the child and fathers were to contribute, states, the federal government, or private entities could consider providing some level of match. The match could be coupled with an extensive advertising campaign to help fathers feel more involved with their children's financial support and later life success. The value of the registries is: (a) the autonomy and power they offer to the paying parent without stripping control from the receiving parents, and (b) their framing of fathers' contributions as going directly to the children, rather than to the mother who may use them in ways that do not directly benefit the child, which is the cause of the mistrust problem discussed above.

We note that these innovations would not address what is perhaps the most fundamental problem with the system for low-income men: that it often shoulders them with little means with unsustainable financial demands, which then leads to unsupportable arrears. We and our collaborators have written about this crisis elsewhere (Edin et al., 2019: Hahn et al., 2018). Although reform in this area is necessary, it would not, in our judgement, be sufficient to make fathers view the formal system as a means of providing whatever they need rather than just another bill to pay.

REFERENCES

Amato, P. R., & Gilbreth, J. G. (1999). Nonresident fathers and children's well-being: A meta-analysis. *Journal of Marriage and the Family, 61*, 557–573. http://dx.doi.org/10.2307/353560

Andersson, G., Thomson, E., & Duntava, A. (2017). Life-table representations of family dynamics in the 21st century. *Demographic Research, 37*, 1081–1230. http://dx.doi.org/10.4054/DemRes.2017.37.35

Argys, L. M., Peters, H. E., Brooks-Gunn, J., & Smith, J. R. (1998). The impact of child support on cognitive outcomes of young children. *Demography, 35*, 159–173. http://dx.doi.org/10.2307/3004049

Bianchi, S. M. (2011). Family change and time allocation in American families. *The Annals of the American Academy of Political and Social Science, 638*, 21–44. http://dx.doi.org/10.1177/0002716211413731

Carlson, M. J. (1999). *Do fathers really matter? Father involvement and social-psychological outcomes for adolescents.* Center for Research on Child Wellbeing, Princeton University, Princeton, NJ.

Carlson, M. J. (2006). Family structure, father involvement, and adolescent behavioral outcomes. *Journal of Marriage and Family, 68*, 137–154. http://dx.doi.org/10.1111/j.1741-3737.2006.00239.x

Cherlin, A. (2010). Demographic trends in the United States: A review of research in the 2000s. *Journal of Marriage and Family, 72*, 403–419. http://dx.doi.org/10.1111/j.1741-3737.2010.00710.x

Claessens, A. (2007). Gatekeeper moms and (un)involved dads: What happens after a breakup? In P. England & K. Edin (Eds.), *Unmarried couples with children* (pp. 204–227). New York, NY: Russell Sage Foundation. Retrieved from https://www.jstor.org/stable/10.7758/9781610441865.12

Clary, E., Holcomb, P., Dion, R., & Edin, K. (2017). *Providing financial support for children: Views and experiences of low-income fathers in the PACT evaluation* (OPRE Report No. 2017-14). Retrieved from the Office of Planning, Research and Evaluation website: https://www.acf.hhs.gov/opre/resource/providing-financial-support-children-views-and-experiences-low-income-fathers-pact-evaluation

Coley, R. L., & Medeiros, B. L. (2007). Reciprocal longitudinal relations between non-resident father involvement and adolescent delinquency. *Child Development, 78,* 132–147. http://dx.doi.org/10.1111/j.1467-8624.2007.00989.x

Craigie, T.-A. L. (2015). Multipartner fertility and child support. *Eastern Economic Journal, 41,* 571–591. http://dx.doi.org/10.1057/eej.2014.46

Edin, K. (1995). Single mothers and child support: The possibilities and limits of child support policy. *Children and Youth Services Review, 17,* 203–230. http://dx.doi.org/10.1016/0190-7409(95)00009-2

Edin, K., & Nelson, T. J. (2013). *Doing the best I can: Fatherhood in the inner city.* Berkeley: University of California Press.

Edin, K., Nelson, T. J., Butler, R., & Francis, R. (2019). Taking care of mine: Can child support become a family-building institution? *Journal of Family Theory & Review, 11,* 79–91. http://dx.doi.org/10.1111/jftr.12324

Garasky, S., Stewart, S. D., Gundersen, C., & Lohman, B. J. (2010). Toward a fuller understanding of nonresident father involvement: An examination of child support, in-kind support, and visitation. *Population Research and Policy Review, 29,* 363–393.

Garfinkel, I., McLanahan, S., Meyer, D., & Seltzer, J. (Eds.). (1998). *Fathers under fire: The revolution in child support enforcement.* New York, NY: Russell Sage.

Gold, S., Edin, K., & Nelson, T. J. (2019). *Does time with dad in childhood pay off in adolescence?* Manuscript submitted for publication.

Grall, T. (2016). *Custodial mothers and fathers and their child support: 2013* (Current Population Reports No. P60-255). Washington, DC: U.S. Census Bureau. Retrieved from https://www.census.gov/content/dam/Census/library/publications/2016/demo/P60-255.pdf

Hahn, H., Edin, K., & Abrahams, L. (2018). *Transforming child support into a family-building system* (Idea paper). Washington, DC: U.S. Partnership on Mobility from Poverty. Retrieved from https://www.mobilitypartnership.org/transforming-child-support-family-building-system

Harris, K. M., Furstenberg, F. F., Jr., & Marmer, J. K. (1998). Paternal involvement with adolescents in intact families: The influence of fathers over the life course. *Demography, 35,* 201–216. http://dx.doi.org/10.2307/3004052

Kane, J. B., Nelson, T., & Edin, K. (2015). How much in-kind support do low-income nonresident fathers provide? A mixed-method analysis. *Journal of Marriage and Family, 77,* 591–611. http://dx.doi.org/10.1111/jomf.12188

King, V. (1994). Variation in the consequences of nonresident father involvement for children's well-being. *Journal of Marriage and Family, 56,* 963–972. http://dx.doi.org/10.2307/353606

Morales, M. (2017). *The child support program provides more support to families in 2016.* Washington, DC: U.S. Department of Health & Human Services, Administration for Children & Families. Retrieved from the Office of Child Support Enforcement website: https://www.acf.hhs.gov/css/ocsedatablog/2017/12/the-child-support-program-provides-more-support-to-families-in-2016

Nepomnyaschy, L. (2007). Child support and father–child contact: Testing reciprocal pathways. *Demography, 44,* 93–112. http://dx.doi.org/10.1353/dem.2007.0008

Nepomnyaschy, L., & Garfinkel, I. (2010). Child support enforcement and fathers' contributions to their nonmarital children. *Social Service Review, 84,* 341–380.

Nepomnyaschy, L., & Garfinkel, I. (2011). Fathers' involvement with their nonresident children and material hardship. *Social Service Review, 85,* 3–38. http://dx.doi.org/10.1086/658394

Nepomnyaschy, L., Magnuson, K., & Berger, L. M. (2012). Child support and young children's development. *Social Service Review, 86,* 3–35. http://dx.doi.org/10.1086/665668

Nepomnyaschy, L., Miller, D. P., Garasky, S., & Nanda, N. (2014). Nonresident fathers and child food insecurity: Evidence from longitudinal data. *Social Service Review, 88,* 92–133. http://dx.doi.org/10.1086/674970

Nepomnyaschy, L., Miller, D. R., Waller, M. R., & Emory, A. D. (2019). *The role of fathers in reducing socioeconomic inequalities in adolescent behavioral outcomes.* Unpublished manuscript.

Schroeder, D. (2016). *The limited reach of the child support enforcement system.* Washington, DC: American Enterprise Institute. Retrieved from https://www.aei.org/research-products/report/the-limited-reach-of-the-child-support-enforcement-system/

Short, K. (2015). *The supplemental poverty measure, 2014* (Current Population Reports No. P60-254). Washington, DC: U.S. Census Bureau. Retrieved from https://www.census.gov/content/dam/Census/library/publications/2015/demo/p60-254.pdf

Solomon-Fears, C. (2014). *Nonmarital births: An overview* (Report No. R43667). Washington, DC: Congressional Research Service. Retrieved from https://fas.org/sgp/crs/misc/R43667.pdf

Solomon-Fears, C. (2016a). *Child support: An overview of census bureau data on recipients* (Report No. RS224990). Washington, DC: Congressional Research Service. Retrieved from https://fas.org/sgp/crs/misc/RS22499.pdf

Solomon-Fears, C. (2016b). *Child support enforcement: Program basics.* Washington, DC: Congressional Research Service.

Solomon-Fears, C. (2016c). *Child support enforcement: Tribal programs* (Report No. 41204). Washington, DC: Congressional Research Service. Retrieved from https://greenbook-waysandmeans.house.gov/sites/greenbook.waysandmeans.house.gov/files/R41204%20-%20Child%20Support%20Enforcement%20-%20Tribal%20Programs_0.pdf

Tach, L., Mincy, R., & Edin, K. (2010). Parenting as a "package deal": Relationships, fertility, and nonresident father involvement among unmarried parents. *Demography, 47*, 181–204. http://dx.doi.org/10.1353/dem.0.0096

Turetsky, V. (2014). History demonstrates child support lifts children out of poverty. *Child Support Report, 36*, 1–2. Retrieved from https://www.acf.hhs.gov/sites/default/files/programs/css/february_2014_child_support_report.pdf

U.S. Department of Health & Human Services, Administration for Children & Families. (2016). Flexibility, efficiency, and modernization in child support enforcement programs final Rule, 81 Fed. Reg. 93492 (rule adopted December 20, 2016). Retrieved from https://www.govinfo.gov/app/details/FR-2016-12-20/2016-29598

U.S. Department of Health & Human Services, Administration for Children & Families. (2018). FY 2017 Child support enforcement preliminary report. Retrieved from https://www.acf.hhs.gov/sites/default/files/programs/css/fy_2017_preliminary_data_report.pdf?nocache=1529610354

Waller, M. R. (2002). *My baby's father: Unmarried parents and paternal responsibility.* Ithaca, NY: Cornell University Press.

Waller, M. R., Emory, A. D., & Paul, E. (2018). Money, time, or something else? Measuring nonresident fathers' informal and in-kind contributions. *Journal of Family Issues, 39*, 3612–3640. http://dx.doi.org/10.1177/0192513X18783801

Waller, M. R., & Plotnick, R. (2001). Effective child support policy for low-income families: Evidence from street level research. *Journal of Policy Analysis and Management, 20*, 89–110. http://dx.doi.org/10.1002/1520-6688(200124)20:1<89::AID-PAM1005>3.0.CO;2-H

Weiss, Y., & Willis, R. J. (1993). Transfers among divorced couples: Evidence and interpretation. *Journal of Labor Economics, 11*, 629–679. http://dx.doi.org/10.1086/298310

NEIGHBORHOODS AND SCHOOLS

6

Promoting Equality of Educational Opportunity by Investing Early

Recommendations for Longitudinal Research

Tyler W. Watts and C. Cybele Raver

POVERTY AND THE PROMISE OF EARLY-CHILDHOOD EDUCATION PROGRAMS

During a time when the top 1% of earners have laid claim to an unprecedented amount of wealth and income in the United States (Saez, 2017), 13.3 million children still live below the poverty line (approximately 18% of the population, according to estimates taken from the Current Population Reports; see Semega, Fontenot, & Kollar, 2017).

Poverty and Early Child Development

Although results from longitudinal studies suggest that many low-income children demonstrate long-term socioemotional resilience, research has also shown that a substantial fraction of children in poverty are likely to face higher rates of emotional, behavioral, and mental health problems throughout their lives. These difficulties include, but are not limited to, depression, anxiety, and greater levels of health- and behavioral risk-taking (Aber, Jones, & Cohen, 2000; Berenson, Wiemann, & McCombs, 2001; Browning, Burrington, Leventhal, & Brooks-Gunn, 2008). Likewise, children growing up in economically underresourced, ethnic-minority neighborhoods face major disparities in access to higher quality education, with high school graduation rates for African American and Latino students severely lagging behind the national average (Heckman & LaFontaine, 2010; Stetser & Stillwell, 2014).

http://dx.doi.org/10.1037/0000187-007
Confronting Inequality: How Policies and Practices Shape Children's Opportunities, edited by L. Tach, R. Dunifon, and D. L. Miller

143

Even more troubling, research clearly indicates that spending the early-childhood years (typically defined as ages 0–5) in poverty substantially increases the risk of detrimental effects on long-term development. Longitudinal studies suggest that exposure to poverty during early childhood, even when accounting for exposure during middle childhood and adolescence, strongly predicts a host of negative adult outcomes, including lower earnings and poor labor-market success (Duncan, Ziol-Guest, & Kalil, 2010), fewer years of completed schooling (Duncan, Yeung, Brooks-Gunn, & Smith, 1998), and higher levels of obesity (Ziol-Guest, Duncan, & Kalil, 2009).

Several decades of research highlight the multiple systems of child development affected by poverty, as limited access to economic resources impacts how the family, neighborhood, and education systems function (see Brito & Noble, 2014; Duncan & Magnuson, 2005; Ludwig et al., 2013). Within households that are financially strapped due to low or falling income, parents experience greater psychological distress while trying to manage a host of stressors (see Blair & Raver, 2012, for a review). In turn, findings across several nationally representative data sets consistently illustrate that such stressors place children's early cognitive and self-regulation skills at risk through the toll these stressors take on parents' well-being, emotional reactivity, and psychological bandwidth for responsive parenting (Gershoff, Aber, Raver, & Lennon, 2007; Mistry, Stevens, Sareen, De Vogli, & Halfon, 2007; Raviv, Kessenich, & Morrison, 2004). Indeed, these grave findings are accompanied by the important proviso that many low-income parents maintain a pattern of warm, sensitive, and cognitively stimulating caregiving, and that such parenting approaches can serve as a key environmental buffer across both neurobiological and behavioral levels of measurement (Blair et al., 2011; Luby et al., 2013).

From a multiple systems perspective, researchers should also consider factors outside the home that make a difference in children's chances of academic difficulty versus success. Poverty restricts families' choices and access to higher quality housing and safer neighborhoods, with fewer community supports and higher chronic exposure to neighborhood crime found to be biologically stressful to both adults and children (Gianaros, Marsland, Sheu, Erickson, & Verstynen, 2013). Our own work, as well as the work of others, suggests that children's neurocognitive development and cognitive function are placed at greater risk as a result of higher exposure to crime in urban, underresourced neighborhoods (McCoy, Raver, & Sharkey, 2015; Sharkey, Tirado-Strayer, Papachristos, & Raver, 2012). In addition, low-income neighborhoods offer children and their parents fewer high-quality alternatives for stable forms of cognitively enriching out-of-home early care (Phillips, Voran, Kisker, Howes, & Whitebook, 1994; Zhai, Brooks-Gunn, & Waldfogel, 2014). Stated another way, poverty may not only compound children's risk of experiencing greater stress in home and neighborhood contexts, but it also lowers children's likelihood of receiving high levels of stable, enriching, and responsive care outside the home.

Across these systems, children's neurocognitive and emotional outcomes have been found to be placed in jeopardy, with clear behavioral and biopsychological evidence that higher levels of material hardship, greater exposure to poverty-related stressors, and lower quality caregiving robustly predict disadvantages in children's brain and behavioral development (Blair & Raver, 2012; Brito & Noble, 2014; Hanson, Chandra, Wolfe, & Pollak, 2011; Tottenham & Sheridan, 2010). Importantly, evidence of early brain plasticity has also been cited as motivation for substantial investments in high-quality early childcare. Researchers have argued that time spent in high quality out-of-home classrooms with emotionally supportive adult caregivers can serve a reparative or boosting function, as some programs have produced significant improvements in young children's neurocognitive function (Blair & Raver, 2014; Raver et al., 2011). In some cases, the largest benefits of early intervention have been found for children at greatest socioeconomic risk, fueling the hope that high-quality preschool interventions might offer a means of closing gaps in children's longer-term academic trajectories (Blair & Raver, 2012; Bloom & Weiland, 2015; Brooks-Gunn, Gross, Kraemer, Spiker, & Shapiro, 1992). In short, although the past 2 decades of research has underscored the costs of poverty to children's developmental potential, researchers have also outlined a developmental rationale for taking policy action to reduce the risk of those negative consequences.

Evidence for Early Childhood Education Programs

Drawing on this evidence of early plasticity and the detrimental effects of early poverty exposure, policymakers and researchers have long turned to early-childhood interventions as a potential means of offsetting the adverse effects of poverty exposure on development (e.g., see Gillies, Edwards, & Horsley, 2017, for a history of this rationale in the United States and United Kingdom dating back to early 20th century). The interest in early-childhood interventions, particularly targeted public preschool programs, has grown during recent decades. This regenerated interest has been spurred partly in response to growing economic inequality (see the review by Duncan, Ludwig, & Magnuson, 2007) and also because of the promising longitudinal evidence from early intervention studies that grew out of the war on poverty policies of the late 1960s (e.g., see the review in Elango, García, Heckman, & Hojman, 2015). Although the evidence base connecting early poverty exposure to long-term developmental outcomes has grown precipitously since the 1960s, the rationale for early interventions has changed surprisingly little. Namely, researchers and policymakers argue that if high-quality interventions can change children's early environmental experiences in a manner that positively supports cognitive and socioemotional development, then these effects should place children on better lifelong trajectories (e.g., Heckman, 2011; Ramey et al., 1976).

Indeed, research has accumulated showing the positive long-term returns to early-childhood interventions, especially on outcomes related to educational attainment (for reviews, see Camilli, Vargas, Ryan, & Barnett, 2010; McCoy et al., 2017). Unfortunately, almost all of these studies have depended upon nonexperimental, data-dependent designs to compare program participants with nonparticipants, limiting our ability to draw strong causal inferences. Consequently, the best evidence concerning the long-run effects of early-childhood interventions still stems from two small and intensive intervention evaluations, both conducted over 40 years ago: (a) The HighScope Perry Preschool Program (PPP; Heckman, Moon, Pinto, Savelyev, & Yavitz, 2010; Schweinhart, Barnes, Weikart, Barnett, & Epstein, 1993) and (b) the Carolina Abecedarian Early Intervention Project (ABC; Campbell, Ramey, Pungello, Sparling, & Miller-Johnson, 2002; Ramey et al., 1976). Both programs were evaluated through random assignment designs, and both programs offered access to exceptionally high-quality early child care. Further, PPP and ABC each targeted African Americans living in severely impoverished conditions, and the programs introduced children to instruction that was intensive, individualized, and child-centered to support positive socioemotional and cognitive development. The scope of the programs somewhat differed, as PPP offered high-quality preschool to children at age 4, and ABC offered services from birth through age five. Nevertheless, evaluations have shown that both PPP and ABC had strong short-run effects on children's cognitive functioning and socioemotional development, and long-run, beneficial, effects were found on adult measures of educational attainment, economic success, and criminal behavior (see Elango et al., 2015, for estimates for both interventions).

The success of PPP helped fuel the growth of Head Start, which now constitutes the largest source of federal investment in early childhood education (ECE). In 2017, Head Start was budgeted to receive over $9 billion in federal funds, and it annually enrolls approximately 1 million American children from low-income families (U.S. Department of Health and Human Services, 2018). Yet, the findings from evaluations of Head Start have been much more sobering when compared with the promising results of PPP and ABC. The Head Start Impact Study (HSIS) was commissioned by Congress in 1998 and was designed as a random-assignment experiment that would test the effectiveness of Head Start with longitudinal follow-up. Data were collected between 2002 and 2006, and the study found that assignment to Head Start produced short-term positive effects on prereading skills, and children who attended Head Start were less likely to struggle with problem behaviors measured at the end of the program. However, follow-up analyses showed that these positive cognitive and behavioral effects faded to zero by age 9 (Puma et al., 2012).

A number of follow-up studies have attempted to explain this pattern of fadeout using additional sources of data that shed light on the environmental experiences of children in both the treatment (i.e., Head Start attendees) and control group, which we discuss at greater length below. Nevertheless, the

HSIS is far from the only early-childhood intervention evaluation that has reported disappointing fadeout effects. A recent meta-analysis of 67 high-quality, early-childhood interventions (Bailey, Duncan, Odgers, & Yu, 2017) reported a similar decline in the meta-analytic average treatment effect in the years following program completion. Unlike other recent meta-analyses that have reported positive long-term findings for ECE programs (e.g., Camilli et al., 2010), Bailey et al. (2017) limited their meta-analytic sample to studies that included a randomized control design with measured impacts on child cognitive skills. Across the studies included in their analysis, they found that the average treatment impact measured at the end of preschool was approximately 0.25 standard deviations (*SD*s) in favor of the treated group, yet this impact declined by approximately 40% in the year immediately following the end of treatment and was indistinguishable from zero by 3 years posttreatment.

This disappointing fadeout effect begs the question: If most early-childhood intervention impacts fade over time, then should we continue to make early investments in intervention programs with the expectation that these programs will produce long-lasting effects on children's lives? Even more confounding, how do we make sense of the promising findings from early studies, like ABC and PPP, given the recent evidence of fadeout? Were these studies simply outliers in a larger body of literature, or were they somehow qualitatively different from the interventions that came later?

RECOMMENDATIONS FOR CONTINUED ECE RESEARCH

In the following sections, we grapple with these questions and provide recommendations for future research that we argue could shed light on this puzzling body of evidence. In so doing, we draw on our own experiences implementing and evaluating a recent large-scale, early-childhood intervention, the Chicago School Readiness Project (CSRP).

The Need for More Longitudinal Research

Although the recent pattern of fadeout reported in studies like the HSIS and the Bailey et al. (2017) meta-analysis may be troubling, the discussion around fadeout masks a more fundamental problem in the literature: the dearth of longitudinal evidence following randomly-assigned, early-childhood interventions. Surprisingly, of the 67 interventions reviewed in Bailey et al., less than one third of the followed subjects beyond program completion, and only a handful of studies followed participants beyond 4 years. Given that promising long-run effects reported for ABC and PPP were detected well into adulthood, the fadeout pattern reported by Bailey et al. and the HSIS would be best characterized as "medium-term" fadeout, as neither report estimated impacts past elementary school. This lack of longitudinal evidence has also plagued the literature on public Prekindergarten programs. In a recent consensus statement by leaders in the various research fields focused on early childhood interventions, Phillips et al. (2017) noted the almost total lack of Pre-K randomized controlled trials (RCTs) with longitudinal follow-up.[1]

However, theoretically and empirically compelling reasons remain to continue testing whether ECE investments may pay off in adolescence or early adulthood, even when medium-term fadeout on cognitive test scores is detected. First, although researchers predict that early-childhood intervention programs will affect indicators of adult functioning, such as economic productivity, health, and educational attainment, the mediating mechanisms through which early interventions operate are still not well understood. Certainly, modern theories of *skill-building* (i.e., Cunha & Heckman, 2007) have posited that early interventions affect later life outcomes through a process of skill acquisition that unfolds and compounds over time. Such theories would predict that early interventions affect later outcomes through changing the cognitive and socioemotional capacities of children themselves, and these newly-developed skills should compound into other skill advancements that gradually build in later periods.

However, evidence from PPP and ABC gives little indication that this process explained the full set of adult impacts reported in those studies. In PPP, IQ benefits faded during middle childhood, suggesting that much like the set of studies included in the Bailey et al. (2017) meta-analysis, the treatment and control group were no different in terms of cognitive functioning by the middle of primary school (see Elango et al., 2015). Thus, although PPP apparently affected adult outcomes such as earnings and criminal behavior, the evidence from the few years after the Pre-K program ended suggested that changes in cognitive skills were unlikely the sole cause of these later benefits.

Interestingly, we have also seen a similar pattern in our recent evaluation work of the CSRP, an early-childhood intervention program implemented in inner-city Head Start centers spread throughout Chicago. The program was designed to improve the quality of Head Start classrooms, and teachers randomly assigned to the treatment group were offered professional development intended to help them assist students in their behavioral and emotional regulation. Teachers were also provided access to mental health consultants, who supported teachers' efforts to implement the intervention and worked with teachers to relieve stress and burnout. Thus, the program was fairly comprehensive, targeting aspects of student behavioral regulation, teacher professional development, as well as teacher and student mental health.

Initial evaluation work of CSRP showed that the program was largely successful at meeting its immediate goals. Teachers in the intervention group were rated as having more supportive and well-managed classrooms by the end of the preschool year (Raver et al., 2008), and children who received the

---

[1]The notable exception being the evaluation of the Tennessee Voluntary Pre-Kindergarten Program, which found evidence of fadeout and some negative long-run effects following random assignment to the Tennessee Pre-K program (see Lipsey et al., 2018; Watts et al., 2019).

intervention also scored higher on assessments of neurocognitive function and early academic skills (Raver et al., 2011). Furthermore, students in the intervention group were rated as better behaved by both their teachers and parents (Raver et al., 2009). But, despite these promising early results, CSRP was not immune to the fadeout pattern found in other studies, as the impacts on student capacities largely faded in the year immediately following program completion (Zhai et al., 2014). Subsequent follow-up analyses in later elementary school suggested that CSRP-enrolled students' lower levels of executive control, behavioral regulation, and academic performance were significantly predicted by higher exposure to a host of poverty-related factors, yet no evidence for the impact of CSRP intervention was found (Friedman-Krauss & Raver, 2015; Roy, McCoy, & Raver, 2014).

Despite these disappointing results, we continued to collect longitudinal data on the children who participated in CSRP, and we recently estimated program impacts on a host of outcomes—all measured during adolescence. Perhaps surprisingly, we found evidence that children who originally participated in the intervention performed better on our primary measure of adolescent executive function and had moderately higher self-reported GPAs (Watts, Duncan, Clements, & Sarama, 2018). However, we found no difference on measures of behavioral problems, and we found interesting results on a measure of emotional regulation, suggesting that children who participated in the Pre-K intervention had heightened sensitivity to negative emotional stimuli as adolescents.

These results were surprising given the fadeout effects detected in early elementary school, and they certainly warrant further examination before strong conclusions can be drawn. To that end, we have attempted to better understand how these long-term effects might have arisen, and our analyses have led us in some unexpected directions. We have found compelling evidence supporting the need for greater attention to the multiple systems in which children are embedded. Specifically, we uncovered clear evidence that children who participated in the Pre-K intervention found their way into higher-performing schools upon leaving Head Start. They enrolled in slightly better elementary schools in kindergarten and, by high school, they enrolled in schools with higher graduation rates and lower race-based achievement gaps (Watts et al., 2019). These analyses further suggest that, if CSRP affected long-run academic achievement and cognitive ability, the program impact may have materialized by affecting changes in other subsequent environmental exposures.

Indeed, others have hypothesized that subsequent environmental experiences could be a key factor in producing long-lasting impacts from early programs (e.g., Clements, Sarama, Wolfe, & Spitler, 2013; Johnson & Jackson, 2018), yet such impacts have little chance of being detected if intervention follow-up ends 1 or 2 years posttreatment. For this reason, we need more intervention evaluations that continue to follow students well after the intervention ends, even in cases where medium-term fadeout on cognitive measures is detected. If causal theories predict that interventions will have long-lasting effects on developmental outcomes, then we should continue to evaluate intervention impacts into adolescence and adulthood. Such efforts would likely yield substantial benefits for the field, even if null effects are found in later periods. At present, we still know relatively little regarding the likely long-term outcomes of successful early interventions, including the mediational processes that might be at work. Our field could make substantial progress on this front by continuing to evaluate randomly-assigned, high-quality, early interventions with truly long-term follow-up.

Understanding the Treatment and Control Contrast

A central challenge facing early-intervention evaluators and designers concerns the changing nature of the counterfactual condition present in most early-intervention studies. Most researchers recognize the RCT to be the gold standard for evaluation evidence, and this design requires randomly assigning some children to a control condition. In evaluations of programs such as Head Start or state-funded Pre-K, the control group is typically denied enrollment at a given program, but the family is then free to enroll their child in any number of other services, often including alternative sites of the same program in question. In one sense, this design answers a policy-relevant question. Namely, how does the chance to attend the focal program affect children in comparison with any other local care arrangement available to parents? However, we are often interested in other comparisons for theoretical reasons, as comparing the effectiveness of a single program against other similar programs does not necessarily answer the question, Do high quality early interventions have long-lasting effects on children's lives? Indeed, this issue sheds light on an historical trend that makes early-intervention evaluations harder to interpret today than in the years when PPP and ABC were first implemented: the number of services available to families has grown substantially since the late 1960s. Thus, evaluation studies today often compare one intervention against a set of alternative interventions of unknown quality and intensity.

This issue has been a focal point of recent work on Head Start, as multiple recent studies have attempted to estimate the impact of attending Head Start against receiving no organized formal childcare (i.e., staying at home or relative care). This work has received substantial interest in recent reviews of the Head Start evaluation literature (e.g., Elango et al., 2015; Morris et al., 2018), because an estimated 40% of children in the control condition in the HSIS attended some kind of formal center-based care. To address the question of Head Start's effectiveness against no other formal care arrangement, researchers have taken multiple approaches to generating comparisons between similar groups of children who opted into varying child care arrangements. However, it should be noted that all of these methods lose the benefits of random assignment and instead depend on statistical approaches to form comparable groups. Even so, in their studies, Kline and Walters (2016) and Feller,

Grindal, Miratrix, and Page (2016) attempted to estimate effect sizes measuring the difference between attending the program and no formal care arrangement, and they found substantial positive impacts on cognitive scores measured at the end of the program. Similarly, Zhai and colleagues (2014) used a matching technique and also found larger effects on a range of cognitive scores for treatment children who were matched to control children who stayed home, and they found some evidence that these gains lasted during early elementary school.

Although these studies used data-driven approaches to make comparisons, they all suggest that Head Start was most effective when the contrast between the treatment and control group was substantial. Unfortunately, these studies do not elucidate whether impacts persist in the long-run when comparisons are made between children who attended Head Start and children who attended no formal center-based preschool. To answer this question, evidence from PPP and ABC should again be brought to bear. In both of these demonstration programs, the contrasts between the treatment and control groups were substantial and likely much larger than the contrasts present in any early childhood intervention evaluations conducted in the United States today.

Consider the treatment and control contrast present in ABC (see a full description in Campbell et al., 2002; Ramey et al., 1976). First, ABC was designed to test the extent to which early intervention could prevent *developmental compromise* among children growing up in extreme poverty in the late 1960s. As part of the study, families were screened for substantial markers of disadvantage, and only children with mothers scoring at 75 or below on an IQ test were enrolled in the study. Children randomly assigned to the intervention group received extensive services from birth through age 5. Most children in the intervention group began attending center-based care run at the University of North Carolina at the age of 4 months; this included year-round childcare with individualized instruction designed to meet the specific developmental needs of each child. Children in the intervention group also received onsite pediatric attention, access to a full-time nurse practitioner, and full meals throughout the day (breakfast, lunch, and a snack). Parents also received intervention services, which included consultations about available government services (especially pertaining to help finding employment), and home visits by the center-based caregiver.

In contrast, children in the control group also had contact with the center for the purposes of data collection, and they were given free iron-fortified formula for the first 15 months of life and free diapers. However, the alternative services available to these families were probably much poorer than the services that would have been available today. Head Start was in its earliest phase and would not have offered full services until control children were 3 or 4 years of age depending on the site. Even so, it is unlikely that ABC-control-group children would have enrolled in formal center-based care once age eligible. Today, approximately 60% of children enroll in some type of formal care setting by age 3 but, in 1970, only 20% of children ever enrolled in center-based care (see Ludwig & Miller, 2007). Further, the Food Stamp program was also in its infancy and would not reach all 50 states until 1975 (see Hoynes, Schanzenbach, & Almond, 2016).

Thus, it remains likely that the substantial positive outcomes estimated for ABC were in part due to the substantial contrast in the environmental experiences of the children in the treatment and control groups. This type of contrast would be much more difficult to produce today, which should be seen as an accomplishment given that the expansion of early services has also coincided with a substantial drop in the child mortality rate among low-income families (see Ludwig & Miller, 2007). Perhaps not surprisingly, recent work from developing countries, where services are limited, has continued to suggest that long-term effects can be expected when the treatment and control contrast is substantial. For example, Gertler and colleagues' (2014) evaluation of an early-childhood program in Jamaica, which offered both cognitively stimulating instruction and nutritional assistance to severely disadvantaged children, found substantial impacts on both health-related outcomes and labor market returns over 20 years after the intervention ended.

Interestingly, studies of modern interventions tested in the United States have also found some indication that more focus should be placed on the treatment/control contrast, as analyses of treatment impact heterogeneity typically find that program benefits are largest for the most disadvantaged children in the sample (see reviews by Barnett, 2011; Camilli et al., 2010). Indeed, state-funded Pre-K has been shown to produce the strongest benefits for students who qualify for free or reduced-price lunch (e.g., Camilli et al., 2010), suggesting that students who experience the strongest disadvantage without access to Pre-K benefit the most from ECE services. This pattern of findings has also been replicated in the HSIS, as language minority status, family characteristics, and poverty exposure have all been found to be significant moderators of the Head Start effect on cognitive scores—with students possessing substantial markers of disadvantage again benefiting the most from the program (Bloom & Weiland, 2015; Morris et al., 2018).

Similar analyses of impact variation at the site level have also revealed interesting sources of heterogeneity, again indicating that, as the treatment and control contrast grows, treatment impacts tend to become more substantial. Recent follow-up work on the HSIS has shown that estimated effect sizes were up to 0.25 *SD*s larger for higher performing Head Start programs (Morris et al., 2018), and other recent work on state-funded Pre-K has shown that children in the poorest communities may gain the largest advantages from access to early Pre-K (Pearman, 2019).

It may also be important to maintain a strong developmental focus on the age of children at the time of intervention, as the timing may determine whether the treatment and control contrast stands to benefit the affected child in the most productive manner possible. For example, recent findings by Chetty, Hendren, and Katz (2016) from the Moving to Opportunities (MTO) study suggest that being given the chance to move out of a poor neighborhood to a middle-class neighborhood benefited only children who were very young at the time of the move. Children who were older seemed to incur greater cost from being dislocated from one's community, which likely outweighed the benefits of moving to a higher income neighborhood.

For researchers, knowing when to focus on heterogeneity can be a complicated question. Is it better to know the impact of an intervention estimated across all types of children in all types of settings or to know whether the intervention benefits some children more than it does others? The answer to this question largely depends on the investigators' aims. If those aims are focused on addressing policy-relevant questions of whether programs work and are worth the investment, issues of treatment heterogeneity will likely serve as second-order concerns. But, if those aims are to detect for whom the intervention is and is not working, it is of great value to test for the role of both child and setting characteristics as statistical moderators. Further, these tests can help us understand when the treatment and control contrast is substantial enough to produce large benefits for targeted populations.

Although providing the kind of treatment/control contrast present in a study such as ABC might be difficult today, we believe researchers and policymakers should view this new reality as a challenge instead of a source of discouragement. It remains an open question whether the effect of early-childhood experiences operates by threshold (i.e., whether there is a point at which quality becomes "good enough"; see Burchinal, Vandergrift, Pianta, & Mashburn, 2010) or whether the returns are continuous across various levels of quality (see Vandell, Belsky, Burchinal, Steinberg, & Vandergrift, 2010). Nevertheless, if we continue to evaluate programs that make only marginal changes to children's experiences, then we should expect marginal returns to these investments, especially in the long-term. If we hope to attain the kind of long-lasting effects reported by studies such as ABC, then we should challenge ourselves to provide the kind of early-care experiences that will produce similar (and large) contrasts between children in the treatment and control groups that were once typical of early-intervention studies.

Moving Beyond Test Scores

Most research work on early-childhood intervention programs focuses on outcomes pertaining to child cognitive functioning. This focus reflects aforementioned theories of skill-building (e.g., Cunha & Heckman, 2007) and matches the overall tendency to view educational outcomes through the prism of achievement test scores (e.g., Hanushek, 2010). Yet, early-childhood intervention programs, especially programs like state-funded Pre-K or Head Start, have a much broader set of goals in mind. According to the U.S. Department of Health and Human Services, Head Start was created to promote early learning, child social skills, health, and family well-being (Hudson, 2015; U.S. Department of Health and Human Services, 2019). Each of us has made the case in prior work that early interventions should balance focus between both cognitive and socioemotional development, as such an approach is grounded in the recognition that learning and academic performance are both cognitively and emotionally mediated at neurobiological and interpersonal levels (Blair & Raver, 2012; Raver & Blair, 2016; Watts, Gandhi, Ibrahim, Masucci, & Raver, 2018).

The challenge remains that because our field has fewer widely known, low-cost, age-normed, direct assessments of key socioemotional skills, especially when compared with measures of cognitive performance, investigators struggle to incorporate measures of these *soft skills* in many long-term evaluations of early intervention. Certainly, the HSIS directly assessed a broad set of well-measured child cognitive outcomes, but measures relating to social skills, health, and family well-being were far less robust (see Puma, Bell, Cook, Heid, & Lopez, 2005). Measures of child behavior and social skills during the Pre-K year were only collected from parent surveys, leaving questions as to whether ratings accurately assess children's school-related behaviors. Measures of health and family well-being were even less robust, as no direct child health outcomes were recorded. Family well-being was not directly assessed, although the study did survey parents regarding parenting practices, such as bedtime reading and spanking. When compared with the cognitive outcomes, which were all measured via direct assessment of children using standardized tests that had been validated and shown to have good reliability, the measures of Head Start's other stated goals pale.

The field's focus on cognitive outcomes is well-placed given that early cognitive skills have been shown to be highly predictive of later life outcomes (e.g., Duncan, Dowsett, et al., 2007; Watts, Duncan, Siegler, & Davis-Kean, 2014). Yet evaluation efforts should also take seriously the other stated goals of early-intervention programs. For investigators testing the impact of early socioemotional interventions on outcomes through elementary school, this is not news: Extensively cited reviews of smaller-scale socioemotional learning interventions have provided persuasive evidence that early intervention can increase children's positive socioemotional outcomes in middle childhood (e.g., Durlak, Weissberg, Dymnicki, Taylor, & Schellinger, 2011).

For those exposed to more socioemotionally supportive classrooms, benefits have been shown to include improved relationships with teachers, more competent profiles of emotional and behavioral self-regulation, and lower risk of long-term profiles of internalizing and externalizing behavioral problems (Durlak et al., 2011; McCoy et al., 2017; Nix, Bierman, Domitrovich, & Gill, 2013). Even recent ECE studies relying on administrative data from school districts have found ways to incorporate socioemotional skills into their outcome measures, as indicators for emotional and behavioral individualized education program placements or referrals for serious disciplinary offenses can be used as rough proxies for socioemotional development (e.g., Dobbie & Fryer, 2015; Imberman, 2011; Lipsey, Farran, & Durkin, 2018). Further, this case has been bolstered by findings from longitudinal studies, such as the Dunedin Study, which suggest that children's early profiles of self-control (assessed from toddlerhood through age 8) significantly predict a range of positive life outcomes in adulthood, including better parenting (e.g., later age at first birth) and lower involvement in the criminal justice system (Moffitt et al., 2011).

Calls for broader frameworks and definitions of success in K–12 education have also been highlighted in recent work by Brighouse, Ladd, Loeb, and Swift (2018). Brighouse et al. argued that U.S. society expects schools to provide a host of benefits to schools and communities, including the capacity for economic productivity, personal autonomy, democratic competence, healthy and personal relationships, treating others as equals, and personal fulfillment. Achievement test scores likely capture only a portion of the variation related to this broad set of outcomes, yet our long-run evaluation work unduly places a heavy emphasis on test scores alone. Needless to say, the evaluation evidence for early-intervention programs also faces this same challenge.

Fortunately, some recent work estimating the impact of early intervention into young adulthood has seriously taken into account broader outcomes beyond measures of student cognitive performance. For example, Cascio and Schanzenbach (2013) used variation in the rollout of public Pre-K programs to estimate the effect of Pre-K enrollment on a broad set of outcomes reflecting both child functioning and family well-being. They found that Pre-K program access was related to increases in the amount of time parents spent with their children on activities like reading, increases in mother participation in the labor market, and decreases in family expenses on childcare. In addition, long-run analysis of large-scale policy interventions targeting other domains of low-income families' lives, such as the MTO experiment have highlighted the importance of early interventions not only on academic outcomes, such as high school graduation and college-going, but also on avoiding trouble with law enforcement, greater economic self-sufficiency, and more supportive profiles of family formation (Chetty et al., 2016; Sanbonmatsu et al., 2012).

The remaining challenge for several of these studies is that putative socioemotionally-based mediators such as students' hypothesized profiles of greater emotional, motivational, and behavioral skills, better peer relationships, or more positive social networks with mentoring adults cannot be satisfactorily explored if they are not well-measured. Such measures can be equally helpful in trying to uncover possible reasons for negative or iatrogenic effects of intervention, should they be found (see Lipsey et al., 2018). In our own work, we have attempted to remedy this measurement challenge by including students' self-reports of socioemotional function, as well as low-cost, computerized direct assessments of students' emotional self-regulation and executive control at multiple time points, including adolescence. Inclusion of those assessments has proven invaluable in detecting long-term treatment impacts of CSRP, not only on students' grades but also on their executive function and rapid processing of emotional information (Watts, Gandhi, et al., 2018).

Further, ECE evaluations should also focus more attention on systems external to child functioning that could also be affected by improved access to ECE. For example, access to free child care has long been promoted as a benefit to working mothers, as childcare can be a prohibitive factor limiting employment opportunities in the years between childbirth and the start of formal K–12 schooling. The influence of access to publicly funded early care on maternal labor participation has been examined most extensively in international settings, with quasi-experimental work in Germany (Bauernschuster & Schlotter, 2015), Canada (Lefebvre & Merrigan, 2008), and Argentina (Berlinski & Galiani, 2007) finding positive effects of increased access to ECE on the mother labor-force supply. However, some quasi-experimental work in the United States has found small or null effects (Fitzpatrick, 2010), raising some question as to how robust such findings may be in U.S. settings and highlighting the need for more work in this area.

In short, we severely lack RCTs with the broad set of outcome measures needed to fully assess the extent to which early programs meet their diverse goals. Of course, to the extent that the promise of early-childhood intervention programs pertains to producing impacts on child developmental outcomes, then it stands to reason that we should continue to focus on child-oriented measures. However, as argued earlier, we still know relatively little about the various mechanisms through which early programs might affect child outcomes, providing further reason to assess impacts on the multiple systems potentially affected by early interventions.

CONCLUSION

Early-childhood education programs have received substantial research and policy attention because they have been promised to affect long-term developmental outcomes. The large research base on the developmental effects of early exposure to poverty also suggests that such programs should have long-lasting effects, yet recent research on early interventions has been marked by confounding evidence, as many studies show precipitous fadeout after the intervention ends. In this chapter, we argued that researchers should adopt a more expansive view when evaluating ECE investments, as the current program evaluation literature on ECE has largely failed to produce a rigorous body of experimentally evaluated interventions and programs with long-term follow-up. Moreover, we argued that our intervention investments have become more incremental over time, limiting the treatment and control contrast present in most modern evaluation studies and curbing the potential of these studies to make strong long-lasting impacts. Finally, we proposed that researchers should expand the set of outcomes considered following ECE programs, as our research has become too focused on theories of cognitive skill-building and ignored other factors that could be affected by increased access to high-quality ECE.

If researchers can expand their perspective in the ways we recommend, we believe that the benefits to both research and practice would be substantial. Such efforts will not come without cost, as most of our recommendations would require broadening our evaluations of ECE programs in ways that would require serious commitment. In particular, continuing to follow evaluation samples, even after fadeout has been detected, could be risky to both funders and researchers, as such efforts may yield statistically insignificant findings that funders may have little appetite to pursue. However, the availability of longitudinal data from secondary sources has substantially decreased the cost associated with following samples into later periods. For example, new longitudinal research on the Tennessee Star Experiment and the MTO studies leveraged tax return records to measure participant's earnings without the need for researcher-developed measurement and data collection (Chetty, Friedman, et al., 2011, Chetty, Hendren, & Katz, 2016). Both examinations yielded critical findings that substantially contributed to our understanding of both studies, and these conclusions were reached with data sources readily available for other early-intervention studies that stopped following participants years ago.

Certainly, broadening the scope of outcomes considered by early evaluations can also create unwieldy research designs that could lead to Type I errors if researchers attempt to focus attention on too many variables. Yet, our ability to draw strong causal inference from well-designed evaluations has never been greater. Recent work from diverse early-childhood interventions has made strides by using econometric techniques, like instrumental variables, to estimate the causal effect of targeting certain environmental characteristics or child skills in ECE programs. For example, Auger, Farkas, Burchinal, Duncan, and Vandell (2014) relied on a set of early–child care interventions to estimate the causal effect of spurring changes in early-childcare quality on later academic and socioemotional outcomes, and Watts, Duncan, et al. (2018) used a similar instrumental variables approach to estimate the causal effect of gaining early mathematical skills on later achievement. These approaches can substantially sharpen our ability to pinpoint which early levers should be targeted by interventions.

Similarly, we should not shrug off intense and comprehensive interventions, such as the famous PPP or ABC Programs, as historical anachronisms that could never be replicated today. Indeed, designing a program that achieved such a large treatment and control contrast would be difficult and costly today, yet it was also difficult and costly in the 1960s and 1970s (e.g., see Ramey et al., 1976). Moreover, other recent programs have set high aspirations and many have achieved substantial results. For example, the Harlem Children's Zone, which was designed as a comprehensive intervention that included home, neighborhood, and educational components beginning at birth found substantial sustained impacts on educational and socioemotional outcomes (e.g., Dobbie & Fryer, 2011). Similar outcomes have also been reported for evaluations of KIPP charter schools, which also take a comprehensive and intensive approach to K–12 education (e.g., Angrist, Dynarski, Kane, Pathak, & Walters, 2012).

Certainly, bringing these programs to scale presents a challenge, yet the staggering research on fadeout from recent ECE evaluations should send a clear message to ECE researchers: If we hope to replicate the successes of the foundational programs that we continue to cite as proof that ECE investments can pay off, then we should set our aspirations in line with what these programs hoped to achieve.

REFERENCES

Aber, J. L., Jones, S., & Cohen, J. (2000). The impacts of poverty on the mental health and development of very young children. In C. H. Zeanah, Jr. (Ed.), *Handbook of infant mental health* (2nd ed., pp. 113–128). New York, NY: Guilford Press.

Angrist, J. D., Dynarski, S. M., Kane, T. J., Pathak, P. A., & Walters, C. R. (2012). Who benefits from KIPP? *Journal of Policy Analysis and Management, 31*, 837–860. http://dx.doi.org/10.1002/pam.21647

Auger, A., Farkas, G., Burchinal, M. R., Duncan, G. J., & Vandell, D. L. (2014). Preschool center care quality effects on academic achievement: An instrumental variables analysis. *Developmental Psychology, 50*, 2559–2571. http://dx.doi.org/10.1037/a0037995

Bailey, D., Duncan, G. J., Odgers, C. L., & Yu, W. (2017). Persistence and fadeout in the impacts of child and adolescent interventions. *Journal of Research on Educational Effectiveness, 10*, 7–39. http://dx.doi.org/10.1080/19345747.2016.1232459

Barnett, W. S. (2011). Effectiveness of early educational intervention. *Science, 333*, 975–978. http://dx.doi.org/10.1126/science.1204534

Bauernschuster, S., & Schlotter, M. (2015). Public child care and mothers' labor supply—Evidence from two quasi-experiments. *Journal of Public Economics, 123*, 1–16. http://dx.doi.org/10.1016/j.jpubeco.2014.12.013

Berenson, A. B., Wiemann, C. M., & McCombs, S. (2001). Exposure to violence and associated health-risk behaviors among adolescent girls. *Archives of Pediatrics & Adolescent Medicine, 155*, 1238–1242. http://dx.doi.org/10.1001/archpedi.155.11.1238

Berlinski, S., & Galiani, S. (2007). The effect of a large expansion of pre-primary school facilities on preschool attendance and maternal employment. *Labour Economics, 14*, 665–680. http://dx.doi.org/10.1016/j.labeco.2007.01.003

Blair, C., Granger, D. A., Willoughby, M., Mills-Koonce, R., Cox, M., Greenberg, M. T., . . . Fortunato, C. K. (2011). Salivary cortisol mediates effects of poverty and parenting on executive functions in early childhood. *Child Development, 82*, 1970–1984. http://dx.doi.org/10.1111/j.1467-8624.2011.01643.x

Blair, C., & Raver, C. C. (2012). Child development in the context of adversity: Experiential canalization of brain and behavior. *American Psychologist, 67*, 309–318. http://dx.doi.org/10.1037/a0027493

Blair, C., & Raver, C. C. (2014). Closing the achievement gap through modification of neurocognitive and neuroendocrine function: Results from a cluster randomized controlled trial of an innovative approach to the education of children in kindergarten. *PLoS One, 9*, e112393. http://dx.doi.org/10.1371/journal.pone.0112393

Bloom, H. S., & Weiland, C. (2015, March). *Quantifying variation in Head Start effects on young children's cognitive and socio-emotional skills using data from the National Head Start Impact Study* (Working Paper). New York, NY: MDRC. Retrieved from https://www.mdrc.org/sites/default/files/quantifying_variation_in_head_start.pdf

Brighouse, H., Ladd, H. F., Loeb, S., & Swift, A. (2018). *Educational goods: Values, evidence, and decision-making*. Chicago, IL: University of Chicago Press. http://dx.doi.org/10.7208/chicago/9780226514208.001.0001

Brito, N. H., & Noble, K. G. (2014). Socioeconomic status and structural brain development. *Frontiers in Neuroscience, 8*, 276. http://dx.doi.org/10.3389/fnins.2014.00276

Brooks-Gunn, J., Gross, R. T., Kraemer, H. C., Spiker, D., & Shapiro, S. (1992). Enhancing the cognitive outcomes of low birth weight, premature infants: For whom is the intervention most effective? *Pediatrics, 89*, 1209–1215.

Browning, C. R., Burrington, L. A., Leventhal, T., & Brooks-Gunn, J. (2008). Neighborhood structural inequality, collective efficacy, and sexual risk behavior among urban youth. *Journal of Health and Social Behavior, 49,* 269–285. http://dx.doi.org/10.1177/002214650804900303

Burchinal, M., Vandergrift, N., Pianta, R., & Mashburn, A. (2010). Threshold analysis of association between child care quality and child outcomes for low-income children in pre-kindergarten programs. *Early Childhood Research Quarterly, 25,* 166–176. http://dx.doi.org/10.1016/j.ecresq.2009.10.004

Camilli, G., Vargas, S., Ryan, S., & Barnett, W. S. (2010). Meta-analysis of the effects of early education interventions on cognitive and social development. *Teachers College Record, 112,* 579–620.

Campbell, F. A., Ramey, C. T., Pungello, E., Sparling, J., & Miller-Johnson, S. (2002). Early childhood education: Young adult outcomes from the Abecedarian Project. *Applied Developmental Science, 6,* 42–57. http://dx.doi.org/10.1207/S1532480XADS0601_05

Cascio, E. U., & Schanzenbach, D. W. (2013). The impacts of expanding access to high-quality preschool education. *Brookings Papers on Economic Activity, 2013,* 127–192. http://dx.doi.org/10.1353/eca.2013.0012

Chetty, R., Friedman, J. N., Hilger, N., Saez, E., Schanzenbach, D. W., & Yagan, D. (2011). How does your kindergarten classroom affect your earnings? Evidence from Project Star. *The Quarterly Journal of Economics, 126,* 1593–1660. http://dx.doi.org/10.1093/qje/qjr041

Chetty, R., Hendren, N., & Katz, L. F. (2016). The effects of exposure to better neighborhoods on children: New evidence from the Moving to Opportunity experiment. *The American Economic Review, 106,* 855–902. http://dx.doi.org/10.1257/aer.20150572

Clements, D. H., Sarama, J., Wolfe, C. B., & Spitler, M. E. (2013). Longitudinal evaluation of a scale-up model for teaching mathematics with trajectories and technologies: Persistence of effects in the third year. *American Educational Research Journal, 50,* 812–850. http://dx.doi.org/10.3102/0002831212469270

Cunha, F., & Heckman, J. (2007). The technology of skill formation. *The American Economic Review, 97,* 31–47. http://dx.doi.org/10.1257/aer.97.2.31

Dobbie, W., & Fryer, R. G., Jr. (2011). Are high-quality schools enough to increase achievement among the poor? Evidence from the Harlem Children's Zone. *American Economic Journal: Applied Economics, 3,* 158–187. http://dx.doi.org/10.1257/app.3.3.158

Dobbie, W., & Fryer, R. G., Jr. (2015). The medium-term impacts of high-achieving charter schools. *Journal of Political Economy, 123,* 985–1037. http://dx.doi.org/10.1086/682718

Duncan, G. J., Dowsett, C. J., Claessens, A., Magnuson, K., Huston, A. C., Klebanov, P., . . . Japel, C. (2007). School readiness and later achievement. *Developmental Psychology, 43,* 1428–1446. http://dx.doi.org/10.1037/0012-1649.43.6.1428

Duncan, G. J., Ludwig, J., & Magnuson, K. A. (2007). Reducing poverty through preschool interventions. *The Future of Children, 17,* 143–160. http://dx.doi.org/10.1353/foc.2007.0015

Duncan, G. J., & Magnuson, K. A. (2005). Can family socioeconomic resources account for racial and ethnic test score gaps? *The Future of Children, 15,* 35–54. http://dx.doi.org/10.1353/foc.2005.0004

Duncan, G. J., Yeung, W. J., Brooks-Gunn, J., & Smith, J. R. (1998). How much does childhood poverty affect the life chances of children? *American Sociological Review, 63,* 406–423. http://dx.doi.org/10.2307/2657556

Duncan, G. J., Ziol-Guest, K. M., & Kalil, A. (2010). Early-childhood poverty and adult attainment, behavior, and health. *Child Development, 81,* 306–325. http://dx.doi.org/10.1111/j.1467-8624.2009.01396.x

Durlak, J. A., Weissberg, R. P., Dymnicki, A. B., Taylor, R. D., & Schellinger, K. B. (2011). The impact of enhancing students' social and emotional learning: A meta-analysis of school-based universal interventions. *Child Development, 82*, 405–432. http://dx.doi.org/10.1111/j.1467-8624.2010.01564.x

Elango, S., García, J. L., Heckman, J. J., & Hojman, A. (2015, December). *Early childhood education* (NBER Working Paper No. 21766). Cambridge, MA: National Bureau of Economic Research. http://dx.doi.org/10.3386/w21766

Feller, A., Grindal, T., Miratrix, L., & Page, L. C. (2016). Compared to what? Variation in the impacts of early childhood education by alternative care type. *The Annals of Applied Statistics, 10*, 1245–1285. http://dx.doi.org/10.1214/16-AOAS910

Fitzpatrick, M. D. (2010). Preschoolers enrolled and mothers at work? The effects of universal prekindergarten. *Journal of Labor Economics, 28*, 51–85. http://dx.doi.org/10.1086/648666

Friedman-Krauss, A. H., & Raver, C. C. (2015). Does school mobility place elementary school children at risk for lower math achievement? The mediating role of cognitive dysregulation. *Developmental Psychology, 51*, 1725–1739. http://dx.doi.org/10.1037/a0039795

Gershoff, E. T., Aber, J. L., Raver, C. C., & Lennon, M. C. (2007). Income is not enough: Incorporating material hardship into models of income associations with parenting and child development. *Child Development, 78*, 70–95. http://dx.doi.org/10.1111/j.1467-8624.2007.00986.x

Gertler, P., Heckman, J., Pinto, R., Zanolini, A., Vermeersch, C., Walker, S., . . . Grantham-McGregor, S. (2014). Labor market returns to an early childhood stimulation intervention in Jamaica. *Science, 344*, 998–1001. http://dx.doi.org/10.1126/science.1251178

Gianaros, P. J., Marsland, A. L., Sheu, L. K., Erickson, K. I., & Verstynen, T. D. (2013). Inflammatory pathways link socioeconomic inequalities to white matter architecture. *Cerebral Cortex, 23*, 2058–2071. http://dx.doi.org/10.1093/cercor/bhs191

Gillies, V., Edwards, R., & Horsley, N. (2017). *Challenging the politics of early intervention: Who's "saving" children and why*. Bristol, England: Policy Press.

Hanson, J. L., Chandra, A., Wolfe, B. L., & Pollak, S. D. (2011). Association between income and the hippocampus. *PLoS One, 6*, e18712. http://dx.doi.org/10.1371/journal.pone.0018712

Hanushek, E. A. (2010). The economic value of education and cognitive skills. In G. Sykes, B. Schneider, & D. N. Plank (Eds.), *Handbook of education policy research* (pp. 39–56). New York, NY: Routledge.

Heckman, J. J. (2011). The economics of inequality: The value of early childhood education. *American Educator, 35*, 31.

Heckman, J. J., & LaFontaine, P. A. (2010). The American high school graduation rate: Trends and levels. *The Review of Economics and Statistics, 92*, 244–262. http://dx.doi.org/10.1162/rest.2010.12366

Heckman, J. J., Moon, S. H., Pinto, R., Savelyev, P. A., & Yavitz, A. (2010). The rate of return to the HighScope Perry Preschool Program. *Journal of Public Economics, 94*, 114–128. http://dx.doi.org/10.1016/j.jpubeco.2009.11.001

Hoynes, H., Schanzenbach, D. W., & Almond, D. (2016). Long-run impacts of childhood access to the safety net. *The American Economic Review, 106*, 903–934. http://dx.doi.org/10.1257/aer.20130375

Hudson, D. (2015, May 18). *This day in history: The creation of Head Start*. Retrieved from https://obamawhitehouse.archives.gov/blog/2015/05/18/day-history-creation-head-start

Imberman, S. A. (2011). The effect of charter schools on achievement and behavior of public school students. *Journal of Public Economics, 95*, 850–863. http://dx.doi.org/10.1016/j.jpubeco.2011.02.003

Johnson, R. C., & Jackson, C. K. (2018, February). *Reducing inequality through dynamic complementarity: Evidence from Head Start and public school spending* (NBER Working Paper No. 23489). Cambridge, MA: National Bureau of Economic Research.

Kline, P., & Walters, C. R. (2016). Evaluating public programs with close substitutes: The case of Head Start. *The Quarterly Journal of Economics, 131,* 1795–1848. http://dx.doi.org/10.1093/qje/qjw027

Lefebvre, P., & Merrigan, P. (2008). Child-care policy and the labor supply of mothers with young children: A natural experiment from Canada. *Journal of Labor Economics, 26,* 519–548. http://dx.doi.org/10.1086/587760

Lipsey, M. W., Farran, D. C., & Durkin, K. (2018). Effects of the Tennessee Pre-kindergarten Program on children's achievement and behavior through third grade. *Early Childhood Research Quarterly, 45,* 155–176. http://dx.doi.org/10.1016/j.ecresq.2018.03.005

Luby, J., Belden, A., Botteron, K., Marrus, N., Harms, M. P., Babb, C., . . . Barch, D. (2013). The effects of poverty on childhood brain development: The mediating effect of caregiving and stressful life events. *JAMA Pediatrics, 167,* 1135–1142. http://dx.doi.org/10.1001/jamapediatrics.2013.3139

Ludwig, J., Duncan, G. J., Gennetian, L. A., Katz, L. F., Kessler, R. C., Kling, J. R., & Sanbonmatsu, L. (2013). Long-term neighborhood effects on low-income families: Evidence from Moving to Opportunity. *The American Economic Review, 103,* 226–231. http://dx.doi.org/10.1257/aer.103.3.226

Ludwig, J., & Miller, D. L. (2007). Does Head Start improve children's life chances? Evidence from a regression discontinuity design. *The Quarterly Journal of Economics, 122,* 159–208. http://dx.doi.org/10.1162/qjec.122.1.159

McCoy, D. C., Raver, C. C., & Sharkey, P. (2015). Children's cognitive performance and selective attention following recent community violence. *Journal of Health and Social Behavior, 56,* 19–36. http://dx.doi.org/10.1177/0022146514567576

McCoy, D. C., Yoshikawa, H., Ziol-Guest, K. M., Duncan, G. J., Schindler, H. S., Magnuson, K., . . . Shonkoff, J. P. (2017). Impacts of early childhood education on medium- and long-term educational outcomes. *Educational Researcher, 46,* 474–487. http://dx.doi.org/10.3102/0013189X17737739

Mistry, R., Stevens, G. D., Sareen, H., De Vogli, R., & Halfon, N. (2007). Parenting-related stressors and self-reported mental health of mothers with young children. *American Journal of Public Health, 97,* 1261–1268. http://dx.doi.org/10.2105/AJPH.2006.088161

Moffitt, T. E., Arseneault, L., Belsky, D., Dickson, N., Hancox, R. J., Harrington, H., . . . Caspi, A. (2011). A gradient of childhood self-control predicts health, wealth, and public safety. *Proceedings of the National Academy of Sciences, 108,* 2693–2698. http://dx.doi.org/10.1073/pnas.1010076108

Morris, P. A., Connors, M., Friedman-Krauss, A., McCoy, D. C., Weiland, C., Feller, A., . . . Yoshikawa, H. (2018). New findings on impact variation from the Head Start Impact Study: Informing the scale-up of early childhood programs. *AERA Open, 4.* Advance online publication. http://dx.doi.org/10.1177/2332858418769287

Nix, R. L., Bierman, K. L., Domitrovich, C. E., & Gill, S. (2013). Promoting children's social–emotional skills in preschool can enhance academic and behavioral func-tioning in kindergarten: Findings from Head Start REDI. *Early Education and Devel-opment, 24,* 1000–1019. http://dx.doi.org/10.1080/10409289.2013.825565

Pearman, F. A., II. (2019, September). The moderating effect of neighborhood poverty on preschool effectiveness: Evidence From the Tennessee Voluntary Prekinder-garten Experiment. *American Educational Research Journal.* http://dx.doi.org/10.3102/0002831219872977

Phillips, D. A., Lipsey, M., Dodge, K., Haskins, R., Bassok, D., Burchinal, P., . . . Weiland, C. (2017). *The current state of scientific knowledge on pre-kindergarten effects.* Retrieved from https://www.brookings.edu/wp-content/uploads/2017/04/duke_prekstudy_final_4-4-17_hires.pdf

Phillips, D. A., Voran, M., Kisker, E., Howes, C., & Whitebook, M. (1994). Child care for children in poverty: Opportunity or inequity? *Child Development, 65,* 472–492. http://dx.doi.org/10.2307/1131397

Puma, M., Bell, S., Cook, R., Heid, C., Broene, P., Jenkins, F., . . . Downer, J. (2012, October). *Third grade follow-up to the Head Start Impact Study: Final Report* (OPRE Report No. 2012-45). Washington, DC: U.S. Department of Health and Human Services, Administration for Children and Families. Retrieved from https://www.acf.hhs.gov/sites/default/files/opre/head_start_report.pdf

Puma, M., Bell, S., Cook, R., Heid, C., & Lopez, M. (2005, May). *Head Start Impact Study: First year findings*. Washington, DC: U.S. Department of Health and Human Services, Administration for Children and Families. Retrieved from https://www.acf.hhs.gov/sites/default/files/opre/first_yr_finds.pdf

Ramey, C. T., Collier, A. M., Sparling, J. J., Loda, F. A., Campbell, F. A., Ingram, D. L., & Finkelstein, N. W. (1976). The Carolina Abecedarian Project: A longitudinal and multidisciplinary approach to the prevention of developmental retardation. In T. Tjossem (Ed.), *Intervention strategies for high-risk infants and young children* (pp. 629–665). Baltimore, MD: University Park Press.

Raver, C. C., & Blair, C. (2016). Neuroscientific insights: Attention, working memory, and inhibitory control. *The Future of Children, 26*, 95–118. http://dx.doi.org/10.1353/foc.2016.0014

Raver, C. C., Jones, S. M., Li-Grining, C. P., Metzger, M., Smallwood, K., & Sardin, L. (2008). Improving preschool classroom processes: Preliminary findings from a randomized trial implemented in Head Start settings. *Early Childhood Research Quarterly, 63*, 253–255. http://dx.doi.org/10.1016/j.ecresq.2007.09.001

Raver, C. C., Jones, S. M., Li-Grining, C., Zhai, F., Bub, K., & Pressler, E. (2011). CSRP's impact on low-income preschoolers' preacademic skills: Self-regulation as a mediating mechanism. *Child Development, 82*, 362–378. http://dx.doi.org/10.1111/j.1467-8624.2010.01561.x

Raver, C. C., Jones, S. M., Li-Grining, C., Zhai, F., Metzger, M. W., & Solomon, B. (2009). Targeting children's behavior problems in preschool classrooms: A cluster-randomized controlled trial. *Journal of Consulting and Clinical Psychology, 77*, 302–316. http://dx.doi.org/10.1037/a0015302

Raviv, T., Kessenich, M., & Morrison, F. J. (2004). A mediational model of the association between socioeconomic status and three-year-old language abilities: The role of parenting factors. *Early Childhood Research Quarterly, 19*, 528–547. http://dx.doi.org/10.1016/j.ecresq.2004.10.007

Roy, A. L., McCoy, D. C., & Raver, C. C. (2014). Instability versus quality: Residential mobility, neighborhood poverty, and children's self-regulation. *Developmental Psychology, 50*, 1891–1896. http://dx.doi.org/10.1037/a0036984

Saez, E. (2017). Income and wealth inequality: Evidence and policy implications. *Contemporary Economic Policy, 35*, 7–25. http://dx.doi.org/10.1111/coep.12210

Sanbonmatsu, L., Marvokov, J., Potter, N., Yang, F., Adam, E., Congdon, W. J., . . . McDade, T. W. (2012). The long-term effects of Moving to Opportunity on adult health and economic self-sufficiency. *Cityscape, 14*, 109–136.

Schweinhart, L. J., Barnes, H. V., Weikart, D. P., Barnett, W. S., & Epstein, A. S. (1993). *Significant benefits: The HighScope Perry Preschool Study through age 27*. Ypsilanti, MI: The HighScope Educational Research Foundation.

Semega, J. L., Fontenot, K. R., & Kollar, M. A. (2017). Income and poverty in the United States: 2016. *Current Population Reports, 2017*. U.S. Census Bureau. Retrieved from https://www.census.gov/library/publications/2017/demo/p60-259.html

Sharkey, P. T., Tirado-Strayer, N., Papachristos, A. V., & Raver, C. C. (2012). The effect of local violence on children's attention and impulse control. *American Journal of Public Health, 102*, 2287–2293. http://dx.doi.org/10.2105/AJPH.2012.300789

Stetser, M. C., & Stillwell, R. (2014, April). *Public high school four-year on-time graduation rates and event dropout rates: School years 2010–1 and 2011–12, first look* (NCES No. 2014-391). Washington, DC: Institute for Educational Sciences, National Center for Education Statistics.

Tottenham, N., & Sheridan, M. A. (2010). A review of adversity, the amygdala and the hippocampus: A consideration of developmental timing. *Frontiers in Human Neuroscience, 3*, 68. http://dx.doi.org/10.3389/neuro.09.068.2009

U.S. Department of Health and Human Services. (2018). Office of Head Start: Data and reports. Retrieved from https://www.acf.hhs.gov/ohs/reports

U.S. Department of Health and Human Services. (2019). Office of Head Start: Head Start programs. Retrieved from https://www.acf.hhs.gov/ohs/about/head-start

Vandell, D. L., Belsky, J., Burchinal, M., Steinberg, L., & Vandergrift, N. (2010). Do effects of early child care extend to age 15 years? Results from the NICHD study of early child care and youth development. *Child Development, 81*, 737–756. http://dx.doi.org/10.1111/j.1467-8624.2010.01431.x

Watts, T. W., Duncan, G. J., Clements, D. H., & Sarama, J. (2018). What is the long-run impact of learning mathematics during preschool? *Child Development, 89*, 539–555. http://dx.doi.org/10.1111/cdev.12713

Watts, T. W., Duncan, G. J., Siegler, R. S., & Davis-Kean, P. E. (2014). What's past is prologue: Relations between early mathematics knowledge and high school achievement. *Educational Researcher, 43*, 352–360. http://dx.doi.org/10.3102/0013189X14553660

Watts, T. W., Gandhi, J., Ibrahim, D. A., Masucci, M. D., & Raver, C. C. (2018). The Chicago School Readiness Project: Examining the long-term impacts of an early childhood intervention. *PLoS ONE, 13*, e0200144. http://dx.doi.org/10.1371/journal.pone.0200144

Watts, T. W., Ibrahim, D. A., Khader, A., Li, C., Gandhi, J., & Raver, C. C. (2019). The impact of an early childhood intervention on later school selection. Manuscript submitted for publication.

Zhai, F., Brooks-Gunn, J., & Waldfogel, J. (2014). Head Start's impact is contingent on alternative type of care in comparison group. *Developmental Psychology, 50*, 2572–2586. http://dx.doi.org/10.1037/a0038205

Ziol-Guest, K. M., Duncan, G. J., & Kalil, A. (2009). Early childhood poverty and adult body mass index. *American Journal of Public Health, 99*, 527–532. http://dx.doi.org/10.2105/AJPH.2007.130575

7

Does School Spending Matter?

The New Literature on an Old Question

C. Kirabo Jackson

There has been a long-standing debate regarding whether increasing the financial resources available to public schools can improve child outcomes in general and low-income children's outcomes in particular. Shedding light on this issue, in 1966, James Coleman and coauthors conducted the first large-scale U.S. study to link student achievement outcomes to family background and school characteristics. The report used data from a cross section of students in 1965 and examined the cross-sectional relationship (i.e., at a given point in time) between school spending, family background, and test scores. The report concluded that "it is known that socioeconomic factors bear a strong relation to academic achievement. When these factors are statistically controlled, however, it appears that differences between schools account for only a small fraction of differences in pupil achievement" (Coleman et al., 1966, pp. 21–22). Since Coleman et al. (1966), many social scientists have estimated the relationship between school spending and student outcomes in order to better ascertain whether increased financial resources for public schools improve child outcomes.

THE OLD LITERATURE

Prior to 1995, all U.S.-based studies relating student outcomes to measures of per-pupil spending were observational (i.e., correlational) in nature. These studies either (a) estimated the relationship between school spending and

http://dx.doi.org/10.1037/0000187-008
Confronting Inequality: How Policies and Practices Shape Children's Opportunities, edited by
L. Tach, R. Dunifon, and D. L. Miller

student outcomes after accounting for family background, (b) estimated the relationship between changes in school spending over time within a particular geographical area (e.g., state, district) and changes in student outcomes after accounting for family background, or (c) some combination of the two.

Spending and Outcomes Tend to Move Together

Summarizing these older studies, in an influential literature review, Hanushek (2003) examined the findings of 163 studies relating school resources to student achievement that were published prior to 1995. When assessing the results of several studies, it is helpful to consider what one would observe if school spending were indeed unrelated to student outcomes. If school spending and student outcomes were unrelated (and each study were independent), then 2.5% of studies should be significant and positive and 2.5% should be significant and negative (with a two-sided p-value < .05).[1] However, Hanushek found that 27% of these early studies were statistically significant and positive, whereas 7% were significant and negative—there were more than 10 times as many positive and significant studies than would be expected by random chance alone if the true effect were zero.

It is important to point out that the 163 studies included both single-state studies and those that combined multiple states. This distinction is important. If school-spending effects are heterogeneous, they may be large in some states and nonexistent in others. Accordingly, if school spending matters on average, but the effects are heterogeneous, one should see larger impacts in multistate studies (which may reflect the average of positive effects and some null effects) than in individual state studies (some of which could have real null effects). This is exactly what Hanushek's (2003) data showed. Among the 74 studies that used multiple states, 35% were statistically significant and positive, whereas only 1% were statistically significant and negative. Although Hanushek looked at this and concluded that there was little association between resources and outcomes, the statistical reasoning dictates otherwise. Indeed, Hedges, Laine, and Greenwald (1994) conducted a formal meta-analysis of much of the data studied in Hanushek (2003) and concluded that the older studies on school spending and student outcomes suggested a strong association between school spending and student outcomes. To put it bluntly, any claim that there is little evidence of a statistical link between school spending and student outcomes is demonstrably false.

The Old Literature Should Not be Taken as Causal

Although the literature on school spending and student outcomes published prior to 1995 indicated a real and economically meaningful *association* between increased school spending and improved student outcomes, these studies did

---

[1]Although all of the individual studies are likely not statistically independent, this is a useful benchmark. Importantly, a lack of statistical independence across studies does not lead one to expect a higher proportion of false positives.

not provide strong evidence of a *causal* relationship between increased school spending and improved student outcomes This is for two key reasons.

The first reason is straightforward. The older studies compared students from different households across schools, so that the observed relationships were correlational. Simply comparing outcomes among families that attend schools with different levels of spending does not yield a causal relationship, because there may be many other differences between these families and schools. Although one can always include additional controls to help mitigate omitted variables bias, if there are any remaining unobserved student characteristics that predict achievement and are correlated with school spending (or family background, or any other covariate in the models) then the estimated relationship will be biased. As the common saying goes "correlation does not imply causation," and similarly "lack of correlation does not imply lack of causation." To complicate this approach further, adding additional controls can, in some cases, exacerbate any underlying biases and influence the result in unpredictable and counterintuitive ways (see Elwert & Winship, 2014; Lechner, 2008). The second reason is subtler. Even if there are no omitted variables nor confounding, because school spending is a function of family background (i.e., families select into neighborhoods based on schools, and school spending is based, in part, on property values that are a function of wealth), it can be difficult to disentangle the two. If one does not appropriately model the relationships between school spending, family background, and student outcomes, a regression model using observational variation is unlikely to correctly attribute "blame" to the correct variable.[2]

One can overcome these limitations of the older literature by relying on exogenous (i.e., external) shocks to school spending that are both (a) unrelated to other determinants of student outcomes, and (b) not driven by the decisions of the individual families under study. With such independent variation in school spending, one can then credibly disentangle school spending from family background and disentangle variation in school spending from other underlying differences. This is the approach taken in the new literature on school spending.

THE NEW LITERATURE ON SCHOOL SPENDING

The "credibility revolution" (Angrist & Pischke, 2010) in empirical economics started to take root in the mid-1990s. The vast majority of the studies examined in Hanushek (2003) were undertaken before this revolution and would

---

[2]The intuition is as follows. If one does not properly specify the relationship between school resources and family background (say one uses a contemporaneous measure of school spending as opposed to a cumulative measure of school spending or, alternatively, one includes spending in levels as opposed to logs), because school spending is often endogenous to family income in observational data, the specification errors in school spending are likely to be correlated with family income. In this scenario, the model may attribute the benefits of school spending to family income. I have verified this with simulated data.

not be deemed credible by existing standards of evidence. This is not to say that all studies on school spending written before 1995 are "wrong" or that the authors of these studies made mistakes. The point is that the older studies are not based on the most up-to-date or credible research designs and should, therefore, not be taken as causal. Accordingly, to determine whether there is a causal relationship between school spending and student outcomes, one should only examine studies that can be deemed credibly causal by current standards.

In the past 5 years, a new literature relating school spending to student outcomes has emerged. This new literature is heavily influenced by the credibility revolution, and the studies rely on empirical models that employ exogenous independent variation in school spending in order to disentangle the influence of school spending from that of family background and other influences. What distinguishes the new research from the old research is that is it design based. That is, the new studies lay out a clear comparison group to which some treated group will be compared. These studies do not simply use any variation in school spending, but rather rely on changes in school spending that are known and understood. The ability to identify exactly why one family is exposed to more school spending than another is critical to assessing the extent to which the results in each study can be interpreted causally. In each of these newer studies, the source of variation in school spending is transparent, and that source can credibly be argued to be unrelated to family background and other attributes. Although none of these studies is perfect, each study is clear about the possible sources of any bias, and each study conducts considerable sensitivity analysis on the main results. The results from this more credibly causal set of studies are summarized here and some conclusions are drawn.

School Finance Reforms (National Studies)

Ideally, one would want to run an experiment in which money was randomly dropped on some school districts but not on others. To ensure that one makes comparisons among similar populations, one could then compare the outcomes of cohorts that were in school during and after the money drop to the outcomes of cohorts from the same school district before the money drop. Note that the fact that the money is dropped from above ensures that it is not driven by the decisions of the individual school districts or parents. The fact that the timing and location of the money drop is random ensures that the places that received the money drop were not also areas in which families were becoming richer or poorer, etc. Although such a money drop does not exist in reality, school finance reforms (SFRs) provide a context that approximates this idealized experiment.

A key source of variation used in many studies is SFRs. In most states, before the 1970s, local property taxes accounted for most resources spent on K–12 schooling (Howell & Miller, 1997). Because the local property tax base is typically higher in areas with higher home values, and there are high levels of residential segregation by socioeconomic status, heavy reliance on local financing contributed to affluent districts' ability to spend more per student. In response to large within-state differences in per-pupil spending across wealthy/high-income and poor districts, state supreme courts overturned school-finance systems in 28 states between 1971 and 2010. Because of these court decisions, many states implemented SFRs that led to important changes in public education funding. Most of these court-ordered SFRs changed the parameters of spending formulas to reduce inequality in public-school spending and weaken the relationship between per-pupil school spending and the wealth and income level of the district.

Jackson, Johnson, and Persico (2015) examined SFRs that occurred between 1971 and 1990. They compared the changes in spending in previously low-spending and high-spending districts in years before and after a court-mandated SFR. They classified districts as low- or high-spending based on whether their average per-pupil spending levels were in the bottom or top 25% of districts in their state as of 1972, before any reforms were implemented. Figure 7.1 shows that in states that passed SFRs, low-spending districts experienced greater increases in per-pupil spending than similar districts in nonreform states, while high-spending districts experienced decreases—reducing spending gaps between previously low- and high-spending districts in reform states.

FIGURE 7.1. School Finance Reform Event Study on Log Spending by Prereform Spending

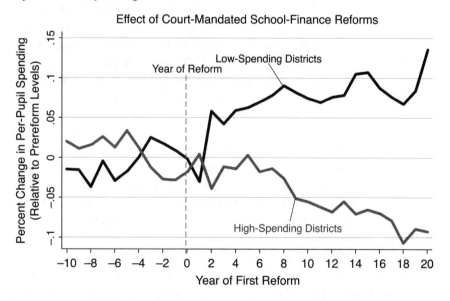

The outcome variable is the natural log of per-pupil spending relative to the average spending levels in the 10 years prior to the court order. Negative values on the X-axis indicate years prior to the court order, whereas positive values indicate years after the court order. Low- and high-spending directs are those in the bottom and top 25% of the per-pupil spending distribution within the state in 1972, respectively. Data from Jackson, Johnson, and Persico (2015).

Having established that court-mandated SFRs affected school spending differently in different kinds of districts, Jackson, Johnson, and Persico (2016) used more detailed information about the specific reforms enacted in each state to predict how much of an increase each district would receive based on the behaviors of similar districts in other states passing similar kinds of reforms. The basic idea behind this approach is as follows: if certain kinds of reforms have systematic and predictable effects on certain kinds of school districts, then one can predict district-level changes in school spending after a court-ordered SFR based only on factors that are unrelated to potentially confounding changes in unobserved determinants of school spending and student outcomes (e.g., local commitment to education or the state of the local economy). With this clean, predicted variation in spending, one can then test whether in those districts that are predicted (based on prereform characteristics) to experience larger reform-induced spending increases, cohorts exposed to the reform have better outcomes than unexposed cohorts. The increased financial resources that suddenly become available to some cohorts, but not others, within some districts but not available to other districts due to the statewide passage of a SFR, approximates the money drop analogy laid out above. By relating outcomes with only the quasirandom reform-induced variation in school spending (rather than all variation in spending), one removes the confounding effect of unobserved factors that might influence both school spending and student outcomes (e.g., other local policies or changes in family background).

Figure 7.2 shows that exposed cohorts in reform districts predicted to experience larger per-pupil school spending increases during their school-age years did experience larger spending increases, whereas exposed cohorts in reform districts predicted to experience smaller spending increases saw little change in school spending. Importantly, the figure also shows that predicted increases in per-pupil spending induced by SFRs are also correlated with increased years of educational attainment among exposed cohorts (relative to the unexposed cohorts). Using this variation in an instrumental variables framework, Jackson et al. (2016) found that a 10% increase in per pupil spending each year for all 12 years of public school led to 0.31 more completed years of education, about 7% higher wages, and a 3.2 percentage-point reduction in the annual incidence of adult poverty. They also found that the effects were more pronounced for children from low-income families.

Unlike an observational study, this was a design-based study in which the source of the variation in school spending was well-defined and understood. Because the school-spending changes used in this study were driven by state-level legislative action, they did not reflect individual family's decisions. Also, because the changes induced by the SFRs were outside of the control of local policymakers (because it was a statewide policy change), they were unrelated to other polices that may have been implemented by local authorities. Although this empirical approach lends itself to credible causal inference, this was but a single study. To better understand if school spending matters, it is

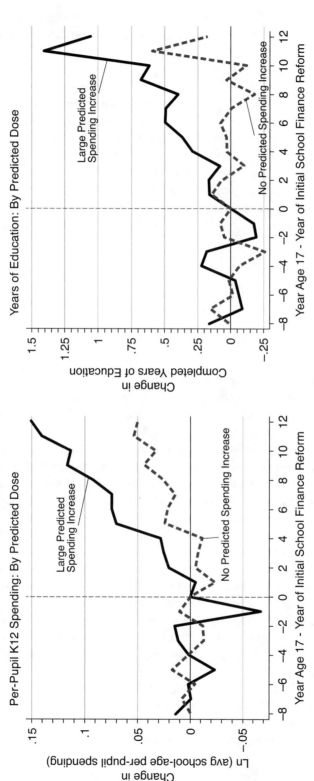

FIGURE 7.2. School Finance Reform Event Study by Predicted Dose

Areas with no predicted spending increase and those with large predicted spending increase dose are those in the bottom and top 25% of the distribution of predicted school finance reform impacts (i.e., dose), respectively. Adapted from "The Effects of School Spending on Educational and Economic Outcomes: Evidence From School Finance Reforms," by C. K. Jackson, R. C. Johnson, and C. Persico, 2016, *The Quarterly Journal of Economics, 131,* pp. 181–182, 188–189. Copyright 2015 by C. K. Jackson, R. C. Johnson, and C. Persico.

important to look at a range of different studies, each of which is similarly credible, but that used different data, different methods, and different samples.

Recent SFRs (National Studies)

Jackson et al. (2016) examined school-spending impacts using variation due to court-ordered SFRs that occurred between 1972 and 1990. Because current school-spending levels are more than twice as high than during the 1970s, and school spending may exhibit diminishing marginal returns, it is reasonable to wonder if one would observe positive school-spending impacts at current school-spending levels. Speaking to this question, there are a number of studies that analyze the impacts of recent school finance reforms that occurred between 1990 and the present day. For example, Lafortune, Rothstein, and Schanzenbach (2018) studied the impact of post-1990 SFRs on absolute and relative spending and achievement in low-income school districts. Using an event-study design that exploited the quasirandomness of reform timing, they showed that reforms led to sharp, immediate, and sustained increases in school spending in low-income school districts. Using test score data from the National Assessment of Educational Progress, they found that SFRs increased student achievement in these low-income districts. They concluded that a one-time $1,000 increase in per-pupil annual spending sustained for 10 years increased test scores by between 0.12 and 0.24 standard deviations (*SD*s).

In another recent study, Brunner, Hyman, and Ju (in press) examined recent SFRs and explored their impacts by union strength. They examined whether or not teacher unions affected the fraction of reform-induced state aid that passed through to local spending and the allocation of these funds. They found that districts with strong teacher unions increased spending nearly dollar-for-dollar with state aid, spending the funds primarily on teacher compensation. In contrast, districts with weak unions used aid primarily for property tax relief and spent remaining funds on hiring new teachers. Importantly, the greater expenditure increases in strong union districts led to larger increases in student achievement.

In another study, Candelaria and Shores (2019) provided evidence on the effect of 1989–2010 court-ordered SFRs on per-pupil revenues and high school graduation rates. They used event-study models that were similar to those employed in the other above studies. They found that 7 years after reform, the highest poverty districts in a reform state experienced an 11.5% to 12.1% increase in per-pupil spending and a 6.8 to 11.5 percentage-point increase in graduation rates. Consistent with diminishing marginal returns to school spending, these impacts were smaller than those documented in Jackson et al. (2016). However, these estimated impacts are large, economically important, and statistically significant. The estimated impacts indicate that increased school spending may have economically important effects even at current school-spending levels.

In one of the few studies to examine the long-run impacts of recent SFRs, Biasi (2015) showed that equalizing school expenditure between high- and low-income districts increased income mobility for low-income students, with small negative effects on high-income pupils. These results are in line with Jackson et al. (2016), who showed that increasing school spending improves long-run outcomes of disadvantaged students.

Changes in Underlying Revenue Sources (National Studies)

Given that SFRs are the result of some legislative action, it is helpful to have studies that rely on variation that is not a direct consequence of legislative action (which could potentially be endogenous to other policies). To address this critique, researchers have approximated the ideal experiment by taking the school-funding formulas as given and then examining what happens when the underlying variables of the formulas change. One such study was undertaken by Jackson, Wigger, and Xiong (2018). In their study, the authors relied on the fact that during the Great Recession state tax receipts (state income taxes and sales taxes) fell very suddenly relative to receipts for local or federal taxes. As a result, states in which funding formulas relied much more heavily on state taxes to fund education were also those that experienced the largest drops in their per-pupil revenues. Importantly, these changes were beyond the control of parents and policymakers. Also, because the reliance of states on state revenues was unrelated to recession intensity (i.e., states that were more reliant on state taxes to fund public schools were no more or less likely to experience large economic downturns during the recession), these changes were unrelated to changes in underlying family characteristics.

To show the patterns visually, Jackson et al. (2018) plotted the trajectory over time in both per-pupil spending and standardized test scores before and after the Great Recession for states that were more heavily reliant on state revenues for public education (relative to those that were less reliant). See the left panel of Figure 7.3. Those states that were most heavily reliant on state taxes were those for which the declines in per-pupil spending were most severe after the recession. The figure also shows that these states had larger declines in standardized scores than other states. A similar result is presented in the right panel of Figure 7.3, which shows that affected cohorts in these states also experienced lower high school completion rates. Using this recession-induced variation in an instrumental variables framework, Jackson et al. found that exposure to 10% lower per-pupil spending over the previous four years led to an approximately 5.0% *SD* lower test scores and 1.4 percentage-point lower graduation rates. The test score effects were similar in magnitude to those in studies based on spending increases.

The results of another similar study were reported by Miller (2018), where the funding formulas as given were scrutinized. Miller then asked what happens when state property values rise and fall. The investigator found that, because state funding formulas treat districts differently (by income levels, housing values, etc.), the same state-level change in house prices translated into different changes in per-pupil spending across individual districts within a state. Also, because different states used different funding formulas, the same

FIGURE 7.3. Event Study by Reliance on State Revenues

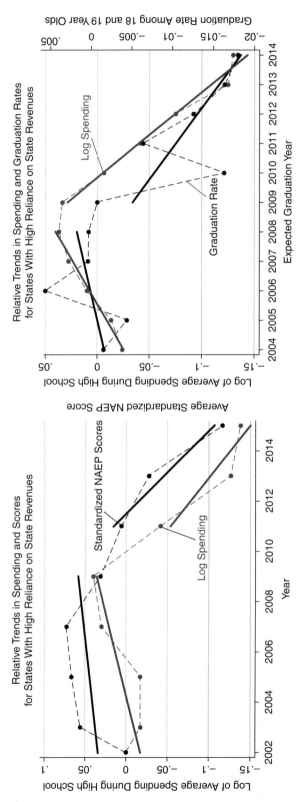

Relative Trends in Spending and Scores
for States With High Reliance on State Revenues

Relative Trends in Spending and Graduation Rates
for States With High Reliance on State Revenues

States with a high reliance on state revenues are those with had more than one-third of the public school revenue from state sources. The solid lines represent the linear fit during the prerecession period during the prerecession period/cohorts (negative values of exposure) and postrecession periods/cohorts (non-negative values of exposure). NAEP = National Assessment of Educational Progress. Adapted from "Do School Spending Cuts Matter? Evidence From the Great Recession," by C. K. Jackson, C. Wigger, and H. Xiong, 2018 (https://www.nber.org/papers/w24203.pdf). Copyright 2018 by C. K. Jackson, C. Wigger, and H. Xiong.

increase or decrease in home values translated into different changes in the level of per-pupil spending across states. Miller then estimated the effect of education spending on district-level student outcomes in 24 states by leveraging changes in revenue driven by property value variation. To do this, he fed state-level changes in property values into the fixed school-finance formulas that determined how state aid and local revenue responded to those changes to create a simulated instrument for school spending. Importantly, because the changes driven by the formulas were beyond districts and parents' control, the simulated school-spending changes were highly predictive of real changes in revenue and spending but were unrelated to other district policies and underlying changes within districts. Using these simulated changes as instruments, a 10% increase in spending increased graduation rates by 3 to 5 percentage points and student test scores by 0.07 to 0.09 *SD*s. These estimated impacts were similar to those found in Jackson et al. (2018).

Overview of Multistate Studies

The studies discussed thus far all rely on data from multiple states. As such, these studies do not answer the question of whether school spending matters in all states, or in all contexts, but rather provide estimates of whether school spending improves student outcomes on average. To gain a sense of all such recent U.S. studies, I compiled a list of all studies on the impact of school spending on student outcomes that use some sort of quasi-experimental design (i.e., any nonobservational study). I compiled this list employing a Google search, citation searches, and through consultation with active researchers in the field. To examine whether school spending matters on average, I first examined the estimated impacts for multistate studies. See Table 7.1.

In the top half of Table 7.1, I summarize all of the national-level studies or multistate studies. Of the 13 multistate studies, 12 (92%) find a positive and statistically significant relationship between school spending and student outcomes.[3] If each study was independent (which is perhaps an implausible scenario), one would not even expect a single study to be statistically significant and positive by random chance. If one were to be conservative, one could treat each source of variation independently. There are school-finance studies, tax-limit studies, recession-based studies, house-price-based studies, and studies that use the rollout of Title I. The single study that was not significant was an SFR study, but there were several positive estimated impacts. As such, using all five sources of variation, on average, the evidence points to a causal positive impact of increased school spending on outcomes.[4]

---

[3]Card and Payne (2002), Figlio (1997), Hoxby (2001), and Husted and Kenny (2000) are listed in the summary table but are not referenced in the main text.
[4]As in all overviews, there is the concern that the set of published studies may reflect some publication bias where only the positive impacts are accepted for publication. I will explore this possibility using formal statistical techniques in future work.

TABLE 7.1. List of Studies

Study	Positive and Significant	Negative and Significant	Not Significant	Outcomes	Variation	State	Type of Spending
				Multi-State Studies			
Jackson, Johnson, & Persico (2015)	Y			Education, Wages	CO-SFR	ALL	Any
Johnson & Jackson (2018)	Y			Education, Wages, other	CO-SFR	ALL	Any
Lafortune, Rothstein, & Schanzenbach (2018)	Y			Test Scores	SFR	ALL	Any
Candelaria & Shores (2019)	Y			Graduation Rates	CO-SFR	ALL	Any
Brunner, Hyman, & Ju (in press)	Y			Test Scores	SFR	ALL	Any
Biasi (2015)	Y			Income mobility	SFR	ALL	Any
Card & Payne (2002)	Y			SAT score inequality	CO-SFR	ALL	Any
Hoxby (2001)			Y	Dropout rates	SFR	ALL	Any
Figlio (1997)	Y			Test Scores	DiD-Tax Limit	ALL	Any
Johnson (2015)	Y			Graduation Rates	DiD	ALL	Title I
Jackson, Wigger, & Xiong (2018)	Y			Test Scores	IV-Recession	ALL	Any
Miller (2018)	Y			Test Scores	IV-House Values	ALL	Any
Cascio, Gordon, & Reber (2013)	Y			Dropout	Event Study	SOUTH	Title I

Single-State Studies

Study		Outcome	Method	State	Category
Hyman (2017)	Y	College-going	Rules-Based IV	MI	Any
Gigliotti & Sorensen (2018)	Y	Test Scores	Rules-Based IV	NY	Any
Papke (2008)	Y	Test Scores (pass rates)	IV-SFR	MI	Any
Roy (2011)	Y	Test Scores	Policy (SFR)	MI	Any
Guryan (2001)	Y	Test Scores	Rules-Based IV	MA	Any
Clark (2003)		Test Scores	Rules-Based IV	KY	Any
Lee & Polachek (2018)	Y	Graduation Rates	RD-Referenda	NY	Any
Holden (2016)	Y	Test scores	RD	CA	Textbooks
Husted & Kenny (2000)	Y	SAT Scores	DiD	CA	Any
Cellini, Ferreira, & Rothstein (2010)	Y	Test Scores	RD-Bonds	CA	Capital
Lafortune & Schönholzer (2018)	Y	Test Scores	Event-Study	CA	Capital
Martorell, Stange, & McFarlin (2016)	Y	Test Scores	RD-Bonds	TX	Capital
Conlin & Thompson (2017)	Y	Test Scores	IV	OH	Construction
Goncalves (2015)	Y	Test Scores	Event-Study	OH	Construction
Hong & Zimmer (2016)	Y	Test Scores	RD-Bonds	MI	Capital
Kogan, Lavertu, & Peskowitz (2017)	Y	Test Scores	RD-Referenda	OH	Any
Neilson & Zimmerman (2014)	Y	Test Scores	Event-study	New Haven, CT	Construction
van der Klaauw (2008)	Y	Test Scores	RD-Title I	NY City (NYC)	Title-I
Matsudaira, Hosek, & Walsh (2012)	Y	Test Scores	RD-Title I	NYC*	Title-I
Weinstein, Stiefel, et al. (2009)	Y	Test Scores	RD-Title I	NYC*	Title-I

Note. DiD = Difference in Difference; IV = Instrumental Variables; RD = Regression Discontinuity; SFR = School Finance Reform; CO-SFR = Court-Ordered School Finance Reform.
*These studies are not reported as being based in New York City. However, this location can be inferred.

The fact that the early (and less credibly causal) multistate studies indicate a positive relationship between school spending and student outcomes suggests that the on-average positive association is real. The fact that this is also true using only the more recent credible design-based studies that rely on different samples, sources of variation, and time periods is compelling evidence that there is a positive causal relationship and that, on average, money does matter.

MONEY DOES NOT ALWAYS MATTER: WITHIN-STATE STUDIES

Although individual state-level and district-level studies cannot answer the question of whether, on average, money matters, they *can* answer the question of whether money matters in particular contexts and not in others. Most of the state-level studies not only examine a particular location but are also based on a particular kind of spending (as opposed to overall budget increases as in the national studies). Given that spending effects will likely depend on how the money is spent, one might expect studies based on different geographic locations and based on different kinds of spending to be less consistent with each other, even if spending matters on average. To gain a handle on the heterogeneity by spending type and location, it is helpful to consider the state-level or city-level studies by the type of spending examined.

Unrestricted Spending

Although many single-state studies examine specific forms of spending, not all of them do. Three studies explored different sources of variation to examine the impact of increased school spending in Michigan. Papke (2008) used a difference-in-difference (before vs. after) analysis of outcomes in Michigan after the passage of a 1994 SFR. She found that increases in spending have nontrivial, statistically significant effects on math test pass rates. The effects were larger for districts with initially poor performance. Roy (2011) examined this same reform somewhat more extensively and came to largely the same conclusions. Hyman (2017) used a different approach, exploring the fact that the school funding formulas set into motion a predictable time path of additional allowances that was equalizing over time—thus providing plausibly exogenous variation in spending. The basic idea was that, for reasons outside the control of districts and parents, initially low-spending districts received large initial allowances from the state that fell over time as school-spending levels became more equal. Using the time path of the size of the state allowance to individual districts, he found that students exposed to 10% more spending were 3 percentage points (7%) more likely to enroll in college and 2.3 percentage points (11%) more likely to earn a postsecondary degree. In contrast to some other studies finding that school spending has larger impacts for disadvantaged children, these effects were concentrated among districts that were lower poverty, higher achieving at baseline.

Using data from New York State, Gigliotti and Sorensen (2018) leveraged variation in per-pupil expenditures from a specific provision of the state-aid formula in New York State that allowed districts to maintain prior levels of total state aid even as their student enrollment declined. Because of this provision, districts with declining enrollments tended to have systematically higher per-pupil expenditures over time. To isolate the influence of declining enrollment itself, Gigliotti and Sorensen controlled directly for demographic changes associated with these enrollment losses. Using this variation, they found that $1,000 in additional per-pupil spending led to achievement gains of approximately 0.047 *SD*s in math and 0.042 *SD*s in English.

Relying on discontinuities inherent in the funding formulas in Massachusetts, Guryan (2001) found that increased school spending improved test scores. Similarly, using a regression-discontinuity design, Lee and Polachek (2018) found that increased school spending led to increased high school graduation rates. The only single-state study of unrestricted funds not to find positive and statistically significant effects was reported in Clark (2003). She examined the Kentucky Education Reform Act (KERA) and found that the increased spending induced by KERA did not improve test scores. Finally, Kogan, Lavertu, and Peskowitz (2017) used a regression-discontinuity design to examine the impact of passing a referendum to increase school spending in Ohio. They found that referendum failure (as opposed to passage) led to lower instructional spending and lower student achievement growth.

Overall, of the nine single-state studies that examined the impacts of unrestricted spending, seven (77%) found a positive and statistically significant relationship between school spending and student achievement.[5] This suggests that budget increases (that are unrestricted in the use of funds) will tend to improve student outcomes in most contexts.

Textbook Spending

Some of the credible studies have been based on quirks in the school finance formulas that generate discontinuities in policies that can be exploited. One of the clearest examples of these studies was described by Holden (2016). That study explored the effects of a one-time payment of $96.90 per student for textbooks, which was available if the students' school fell below a predetermined threshold of academic performance. The threshold for this payment allowed for variation in textbook spending that was unrelated to family background and not under the control of policymakers. Specifically, among schools with very similar achievement levels around the thresholds, whether a school had performance just above the threshold or just below

---

[5]Note that Husted and Kenny (2000) find a positive statistically significant impact of spending in some specifications. Because they do not have statistically significance in all models, I take the conservative approach and do not include this study as a positive impact.

was essentially random. Accordingly, any systematic difference in outcomes among those just above and below the cutoff could reasonably be attributed to the effect of the additional textbook spending. Exploiting this variation, Holden found that textbook funding had significant positive effects on school-level achievement in elementary schools. In her preferred estimates, a one-time increase in funding of $96.90 per student improved school-average test scores by about 0.07 student-level *SD*s.

This estimated impact is larger than most in the literature. However, this could potentially be rationalized by a model in which spending on textbooks was inefficiently low. One implication of this is that the result of this study is unlikely to generalize to all other forms of spending. However, this study is a valuable contribution and a useful data point that helps us understand the relationship between school spending and student achievement.

Capital and Construction Spending

Looking at another particular type of spending, Martorell, Stange, and McFarlin (2016) used a regression-discontinuity design to examine the impacts of having additional capital spending in Texas. They studied the achievement effects of nearly 1,400 capital campaigns initiated and financed by local school districts, comparing districts where school capital bonds were either narrowly approved or defeated by district voters. Overall, they found little evidence that school capital campaigns improved student achievement. Similar null impacts were found for capital spending (using a very similar design) in California (Cellini, Ferreira, & Rothstein, 2010) and Ohio (Goncalves, 2015). However, Conlin and Thompson (2017) found positive impacts of capital spending toward new school construction in Ohio, and Hong and Zimmer (2016) found positive impacts of capital spending (again using an regression-discontinuity design) in Michigan. Looking at an even smaller unit of analysis, Neilson and Zimmerman (2014) used an event-study framework to study a new school construction policy in New Haven, CT, and found positive impacts on student achievement. Using an event-study design, Lafortune and Schönholzer (2018) found similar benefits of new school construction in Los Angeles, California.

As a whole, studies on the impact of capital spending in different states are mixed. Of the seven studies that were identified, four were positive and three were null impacts. The fact that none were negative suggests that the average impact of capital spending is positive, but that there may be considerable heterogeneity in that impact (and it may be zero in many cases).[6]

---

[6]It is worth noting that, even in those studies that find no effect in the short run, some of them point to potential long-run benefits (i.e., Cellini et al., 2010; Martorell et al., 2016).

Title I Spending

Many of the school spending papers that have relied on within-state variation examine Title I spending. Coincidentally, these studies all use data from New York City (NYC), all use the same regression-discontinuity design, and all come to the same conclusion. Title I provides financial assistance to schools and districts with high numbers or high percentages of children from low-income families. Often, there is some cutoff percentage of low-income children above which additional funds are provided and below which they are not. Researchers have used this discontinuous jump in school funding through the cutoff to identify the causal impact of additional school funding on student outcomes. Importantly, Title I funds are not unrestricted because schools must focus "Title I services to children who are failing, or most at risk of failing, to meet challenging State academic standards" (U.S. Department of Education, 2018). Also, by definition, schools receiving Title I funds are among the lowest income schools in the state.

In an influential study, van der Klaauw (2008) examined the impact of Title I funding on school finances and student performance in NYC public schools. Using a regression-discontinuity approach, he found that Title I eligibility did not improve student outcomes in high-poverty schools. However, he also found that gaining Title I eligibility does not lead to a statistically significant increase in average per-pupil expenditures. As such, while van der Klaauw's study is a good test of the Title I program, it is not a good test of whether money matters. Weinstein, Stiefel, Schwartz, and Chalico (2009) also examined the Title I program in NYC and found that, although Title I changed the mix of spending for high schools, it had very little impact on spending in elementary and middle schools. Not surprisingly, they found that Title I spending did not improve the achievement of students and may even reduce schoolwide average test scores in elementary and middle schools. Matsudaira, Hosek, and Walsh (2012) found the same result using a similar approach in NYC. They found that Title I eligibility raised total revenues by between 3% and 4% relative to that those that were not eligible. However, they found no statistically significant increase in average test scores.

Although the results from NYC might lead one to conclude that Title I spending does not improve child outcomes, note that not all Title I studies find null impacts. Cascio, Gordon, and Reber (2013) examined the rollout of Title I using an event-study framework in multiple Southern states. They documented considerable supplanting of Title I funds, such that receiving Title I money did not necessarily lead to increases in overall spending. However, they did find that White cohorts exposed to higher levels of Title I spending while in school had decreased dropout rates. Similarly, using nationally representative data, Johnson (2015) found that county-level Title I spending was associated with increased educational attainment. One potential explanation for this difference is that Title I was unsuccessful in New York City but generally improved outcomes elsewhere. Also, it is possible that Title I improved longer-run outcomes that were not well detected by test scores (see Jackson, 2018;

see also Beuermann & Jackson, 2019, for discussions of this). Yet another plausible explanation is that Title I funds are often offset by reductions in taxes, such that overall spending levels are often largely unchanged (Gordon, 2004). In such cases, a lack of a Title I effect does not speak to the broader impacts of school spending per se. Whatever the reasons, it is clear that increased Title I spending may not always improve student outcomes in all settings.

Overview of Single-State Studies

Although the national studies almost uniformly point to an on average positive causal relationship between school spending and student achievement, it is helpful to examine all of the single-state studies to gain a sense of whether this is true in all states or cities. There have been 20 studies that examine relationships within an individual state (or city within a state). Of these, 13 (65%) found positive and significant relationships between spending and outcomes, and none found negative and significant impacts. If, in fact, there was no relationship, assuming that each study was independent, one would expect one study to be positive and significant. Given that there are more than 12 times that number, this pattern is consistent with positive overall impacts, in an average sense. However, the fact that, in about one third of the cases, there is no significant relationship suggests that a strong positive relationship may not exist in all settings or for all spending types.

To better understand why some studies find positive impacts but others do not, an examination of the few studies that are not positive is instructive. Three out of the seven papers that are not significant involve Title I spending and three out of the seven involve capital spending. Given that six out of seven (86%) of the studies that find no significant impact involve particular spending types, it may suggest that, although overall budget increases may improve outcomes, increased funding tied to particular uses may not improve such outcomes. In particular, the evidence is consistent with capital spending and Title I spending being less predictably effective than spending in general. Consistent with this interpretation, almost all of the national studies examine general increases in spending.

CONCLUSION

Social scientists have long sought to examine the causal impact of school spending on child outcomes. The literature on this topic can be put into two clear categories: (a) an older literature that relies on observation variation to correlate school spending and student outcomes, and (b) a newer literature that relies on quasi-experimental methods to uncover relationships that are plausibly causal.

The older literature provides strong support for there being a positive economically important association between increased school spending and improved student outcomes. That is, despite claims to the contrary, the application of reasonable statistical reasoning to the patterns across studies would lead one to conclude that there is a strong statistical link between spending and outcomes. However, because this older literature is entirely observational in nature, these studies do not speak to the causal question of whether increased school spending improves student outcomes. To do this, one must examine the more recent quasi-experimental literature.

The recent quasi-experimental literature overwhelmingly supports a causal relationship between increased school spending and student outcomes. All but one of the several multistate studies find a strong link between spending and outcomes—indicating that money matters on average. Importantly, this is true across studies that use different datasets, examine different time periods, rely on different sources of variation, and employ different statistical techniques. Although one can poke holes in each individual study, the robustness of the patterns across a variety of settings is compelling evidence of a real positive causal relationship, on average, between increased school spending and student outcomes. However, an examination of single-state studies suggests that, on average, money matters, but that this is not always so in all settings or in all contexts. In particular, studies of Title I spending and capital spending in individual states uncover null impacts in some cases.

Exactly in what contexts increased school spending are most likely to improve student outcomes remains an open question. However, recent evidence suggests that school spending is more effective in areas with well-established Head Start programs (Johnson & Jackson, 2018). Also, Brunner et al. (in press) provided some evidence that the marginal impact of school spending may vary by teacher union strength. More generally, one might expect school spending increases to improve outcomes in settings with stronger incentives to promote student outcomes. However, this is an active area of research. By and large, the question of whether money matters is essentially settled. Researchers should now focus on understanding what kinds of spending increases matter the most, and in what contexts school spending increases are most likely to improve student outcomes.

REFERENCES

Angrist, J. D., & Pischke, J. S. (2010). The credibility revolution in empirical economics: How better research design is taking the con out of econometrics. *The Journal of Economic Perspectives, 24*, 3–30. http://dx.doi.org/10.1257/jep.24.2.3

Beuermann, D. W., & Jackson, C. K. (2019, May). *The short and long-run effects of attending the schools that parents prefer* (NBER Working Paper No. 24920). Cambridge, MA: National Bureau of Economic Research.

Biasi, B. (2015). *School finance equalization and intergenerational income mobility: Does equal spending lead to equal opportunities?* Retrieved from https://www.russellsage.org/sites/all/files/conferences/Biasi_Draft.pdf

Brunner, E., Hyman, J., & Ju, A. (in press). School finance reforms, teachers' unions, and the allocation of school resources. *The Review of Economics and Statistics*. Advance online publication. http://dx.doi.org/10.1162/rest_a_00828

Candelaria, C. A., & Shores, K. A. (2019). Court-ordered finance reforms in the adequacy era: Heterogeneous causal effects and sensitivity. *Education Finance and Policy*, *14*, 31–60. http://dx.doi.org/10.1162/edfp_a_00236

Card, D., & Payne, A. A. (2002). School finance reform, the distribution of school spending, and the distribution of student test scores. *Journal of Public Economics, 83*, 49–82. http://dx.doi.org/10.1016/S0047-2727(00)00177-8

Cascio, E. U., Gordon, N., & Reber, S. (2013). Local responses to federal grants: Evidence from the introduction of Title I in the South. *American Economic Journal: Economic Policy, 5*, 126–159. http://dx.doi.org/10.1257/pol.5.3.126

Cellini, S. R., Ferreira, F., & Rothstein, J. (2010). The value of school facility investments: Evidence from a dynamic regression discontinuity design. *The Quarterly Journal of Economics, 125*, 215–261. http://dx.doi.org/10.1162/qjec.2010.125.1.215

Clark, M. A. (2003). *Education reform, redistribution, and student achievement: Evidence from the Kentucky Education Reform Act* (Unpublished doctoral dissertation). Princeton University, Princeton, NJ.

Coleman, J. S., Campbell, E. Q., Hobson, C. J., McPartland, J., Mood, A. M., Weinfeld, F. D., & York, R. L. (1966). *Equality of Educational Opportunity*. Washington, DC: U.S. Department of Health, Education, and Welfare, Office of Education.

Conlin, M., & Thompson, P. N. (2017). Impacts of new school facility construction: An analysis of a state-financed capital subsidy program in Ohio. *Economics of Education Review, 59*, 13–28. http://dx.doi.org/10.1016/j.econedurev.2017.05.002

Elwert, F., & Winship, C. (2014). Endogenous selection bias: The problem of conditioning on a collider variable. *Annual Review of Sociology, 40*, 31–53. http://dx.doi.org/10.1146/annurev-soc-071913-043455

Figlio, D. N. (1997). Did the "tax revolt" reduce school performance? *Journal of Public Economics, 65*, 245–269. http://dx.doi.org/10.1016/S0047-2727(97)00015-7

Gigliotti, P., & Sorensen, L. C. (2018). Educational resources and student achievement: Evidence from the Save Harmless provision in New York State. *Economics of Education Review, 66*, 167–182. http://dx.doi.org/10.1016/j.econedurev.2018.08.004

Goncalves, F. (2015). *The effects of school construction on student and district outcomes: Evidence from a state-funded program in Ohio* (Working Paper No. 593). Princeton, NJ: Princeton University.

Gordon, N. (2004). Do federal grants boost school spending? Evidence from Title I. *Journal of Public Economics, 88*, 1771–1792. http://dx.doi.org/10.1016/j.jpubeco.2003.09.002

Guryan, J. (2001, May). *Does money matter? Regression-discontinuity estimates from education finance reform in Massachusetts* (NBER Working Paper No. w8269). Cambridge, MA: National Bureau of Economic Research. http://dx.doi.org/10.3386/w8269

Hanushek, E. A. (2003). The failure of input-based schooling policies. *Economic Journal, 113*, F64–F98. http://dx.doi.org/10.1111/1468-0297.00099

Hedges, L. V., Laine, R. D., & Greenwald, R. (1994). An exchange: Part 1: Does money matter? A meta-analysis of studies of the effects of differential school inputs on student outcomes. *Educational Researcher, 23*, 5–14. http://dx.doi.org/10.3102/0013189X023003005

Holden, K. L. (2016). Buy the book? Evidence on the effect of textbook funding on school-level achievement. *American Economic Journal: Applied Economics, 8*, 100–127. http://dx.doi.org/10.1257/app.20150112

Hong, K., & Zimmer, R. (2016). Does investing in school capital infrastructure improve student achievement? *Economics of Education Review, 53*, 143–158. http://dx.doi.org/10.1016/j.econedurev.2016.05.007

Howell, P. L., & Miller, B. B. (1997). Sources of funding for schools. *The Future of Children, 7*, 39–50. http://dx.doi.org/10.2307/1602444

Hoxby, C. M. (2001). All school finance equalizations are not created equal. *The Quarterly Journal of Economics, 116*, 1189–1231. http://dx.doi.org/10.1162/003355301753265552

Husted, T. A., & Kenny, L. W. (2000). Evidence on the impact of state government on primary and secondary education and the equity–efficiency trade-off. *The Journal of Law & Economics, 43*, 285–308. http://dx.doi.org/10.1086/467456

Hyman, J. (2017). Does money matter in the long run? Effects of school spending on educational attainment. *American Economic Journal. Economic Policy, 9*, 256–280. http://dx.doi.org/10.1257/pol.20150249

Jackson, C. K. (2018). What do test scores miss? The importance of teacher effects on non-test score outcomes. *Journal of Political Economy, 126*, 2072–2107. http://dx.doi.org/10.1086/699018

Jackson, C. K., Johnson, R. C., & Persico, C. (2015). Boosting educational attainment and adult earnings: Does school spending matter after all? *Education Next, 15*(4), 69–76.

Jackson, C. K., Johnson, R. C., & Persico, C. (2016). The effects of school spending on educational and economic outcomes: Evidence from school finance reforms. *The Quarterly Journal of Economics, 131*, 157–218. http://dx.doi.org/10.1093/qje/qjv036

Jackson, C. K., Wigger, C., & Xiong, H. (2018, August). *Do school spending cuts matter? Evidence from the great recession* (NBER Working Paper No. w24203). Cambridge, MA: National Bureau of Economic Research. http://dx.doi.org/10.3386/w24203

Johnson, R. C. (2015). Follow the money: School spending from Title I to adult earnings. *RSF: The Russell Sage Foundation Journal of the Social Sciences, 1*, 50–76. http://dx.doi.org/10.7758/rsf.2015.1.3.03

Johnson, R. C., & Jackson, C. K. (2018, February). *Reducing inequality through dynamic complementarity: Evidence from Head Start and public school spending* (NBER Working Paper No. w23489). Cambridge, MA: National Bureau of Economic Research. http://dx.doi.org/10.3386/w23489

Kogan, V., Lavertu, S., & Peskowitz, Z. (2017). Direct democracy and administrative disruption. *Journal of Public Administration: Research and Theory, 27*, 381–399. http://dx.doi.org/10.1093/jopart/mux001

Lafortune, J., Rothstein, J., & Schanzenbach, D. W. (2018). School finance reform and the distribution of student achievement. *American Economic Journal: Applied Economics, 10*, 1–26. http://dx.doi.org/10.1257/app.20160567

Lafortune, J., & Schönholzer, D. (2018, December). *Do school facilities matter? Measuring the effects of capital expenditures on student and neighborhood outcomes.* Paper presented at the 2019 American Economic Association, Allied Social Science Associations Annual Meeting, Atlanta, GA. Retrieved from https://www.aeaweb.org/conference/2019/preliminary/paper/2iN6Hbs4

Lechner, M. (2008). A note on endogenous control variables in causal studies. *Statistics & Probability Letters, 78*, 190–195. http://dx.doi.org/10.1016/j.spl.2007.05.019

Lee, K. G., & Polachek, S. W. (2018). Do school budgets matter? The effect of budget referenda on student dropout rates. *Education Economics, 26*, 129–144. http://dx.doi.org/10.1080/09645292.2017.1404966

Martorell, P., Stange, K., & McFarlin, I., Jr. (2016). Investing in schools: Capital spending, facility conditions, and student achievement. *Journal of Public Economics, 140*, 13–29. http://dx.doi.org/10.1016/j.jpubeco.2016.05.002

Matsudaira, J. D., Hosek, A., & Walsh, E. (2012). An integrated assessment of the effects of Title I on school behavior, resources, and student achievement. *Economics of Education Review, 31*, 1–14. http://dx.doi.org/10.1016/j.econedurev.2012.01.002

Miller, C. L. (2018, July). *The effect of education spending on student achievement: Evidence from property wealth and school finance rules* (Unpublished doctoral dissertation). Cornell University, Ithaca, NY.

Neilson, C. A., & Zimmerman, S. D. (2014). The effect of school construction on test scores, school enrollment, and home prices. *Journal of Public Economics, 120*, 18–31. http://dx.doi.org/10.1016/j.jpubeco.2014.08.002

Papke, L. E. (2008). The effects of changes in Michigan's school finance system. *Public Finance Review, 36,* 456–474. http://dx.doi.org/10.1177/1091142107306287

Roy, J. (2011). Impact of school finance reform on resource equalization and academic performance: Evidence from Michigan. *Education Finance and Policy, 6,* 137–167. http://dx.doi.org/10.1162/EDFP_a_00030

U.S. Department of Education. (2018). *Improving basic programs operated by local educational agencies (Title I, Part A).* Retrieved from https://www2.ed.gov/programs/titleiparta/index.html

van der Klaauw, W. (2008). Breaking the link between poverty and low student achievement: An evaluation of Title I. *Journal of Econometrics, 142,* 731–756. http://dx.doi.org/10.1016/j.jeconom.2007.05.007

Weinstein, M. G., Stiefel, L., Schwartz, A. E., & Chalico, L. (2009). *Does Title I increase spending and improve performance? Evidence from New York City* (Working Paper No. 09-09). New York, NY: Institute for Education and Social Policy.

8

How Parents and Children Adapt to New Neighborhoods

Considerations for Future Housing Mobility Programs

Stefanie DeLuca, Anna Rhodes, and Allison Young

Interdisciplinary scholarship examining the effects of neighborhoods on families and children has grown significantly since the publication of Wilson's landmark 1987 book, *The Truly Disadvantaged* (Brooks-Gunn, Duncan, & Aber, 1997; Clampet-Lundquist & Massey, 2008; Sampson, 2012). Over the past 30 years, research has converged on the idea that neighborhoods have independent effects on child development and family functioning (Galster & Sharkey, 2017; Harding, 2003; Sharkey, 2013). However, it was Rubinowitz and Rosenbaum's (2000) groundbreaking research on Chicago's Gautreaux program that first signaled how housing policy that moved low-income families to neighborhoods with more resources, lower crime, and better schools could be more broadly used as a tool for social mobility.

Inspired by the early Gautreaux findings, the high-profile Moving to Opportunity (MTO) experiment expanded housing and neighborhood opportunities to four additional cities in the 1990s (Orr et al., 2003). Despite a pessimism that followed the mixed results from the interim evaluation of MTO, subsequent research on MTO (as well as longitudinal survey research in Chicago) supported the idea that neighborhood settings matter for children and families (Harding, 2003; Ludwig et al., 2011; Sampson, Sharkey, & Raudenbush, 2008; Sharkey, 2013). More recently, Raj Chetty and colleagues found long-term significant benefits of MTO for young children (Chetty, Hendren, & Katz, 2016) and renewed the conversation about the impacts of neighborhoods on child development. In particular, the team of economists found that children who

http://dx.doi.org/10.1037/0000187-009
Confronting Inequality: How Policies and Practices Shape Children's Opportunities, edited by L. Tach, R. Dunifon, and D. L. Miller

moved with MTO to lower poverty areas when they were younger (under age 13) earned more, went to college more often, were more likely to get married, and were more likely to raise their own children in low-poverty neighborhoods than their peers in the control group (Chetty et al., 2016).

The policy and practice response to the Chetty team's (2016) research was swift and has been gaining momentum. Presidential hopefuls, such as Jeb Bush and Hillary Clinton, sought advice from Chetty and his collaborators about such programs during their 2016 campaigns (Davis, 2015; Linskey, 2015). To date, housing mobility programs have launched or been planned in 16 new cities (Juracek et al., 2018). In 2018, local housing authorities in Seattle and King County embarked on a random assignment mobility intervention with a mixed methods experimental evaluation (Creating Moves to Opportunity; see http://creatingmoves.org/). Now, nearly 20 more housing authorities are part of a research consortium interested in pursuing mobility programs, inspired by recent research. Most recently, in February 2019, Congress passed the Housing Mobility Demonstration Act, which will provide 28 million dollars to support moves to high-opportunity neighborhoods (U.S. Government Publishing Office, 2018). The idea that housing policy is a lever for health, education and social mobility has deeply taken hold in scholarly, policy, and public circles (Badger & Bui, 2018). The issue of neighborhood effects is no longer restricted to the realm of academic evaluation—it is also central to future practice and policy that will affect the lives of thousands of families.

Given the expansion of these programs nationwide, it is a good time to reflect on past findings. If housing mobility is to be a significant policy tool, what do we need to consider if we want to help families and children benefit the most from these programs? Our team has been studying mobility programs for almost 20 years (see DeLuca, Clampet-Lundquist, & Edin, 2016; DeLuca & Rosenbaum, 2003; DeLuca & Rosenblatt, 2017), using mixed methods to reveal important insights about how policy operates within the realities and constraints of everyday life among the poor (see DeLuca, Duncan, & Keels, 2011). In this chapter, we reflect on our findings in three key areas that all suggest we must consider person–environment fit when considering housing policies that relocate families and children: (a) how housing mobility affects parenting, (b) the significance of friendships for children, and (c) parental engagement in higher performing schools. Bronfenbrenner's (1979) ecological systems theory suggests that human development occurs within a nested set of systems and contexts. Our work (and that of additional colleagues)[1] reveals that families and children who participate in housing mobility programs must adapt to changes in their environment in a number of these systems, including their households, neighborhoods, schools, and places of

---

[1]Our larger Moving to Opportunity qualitative study collaborators include Kathryn Edin, Susan Clampet-Lundquist, Rebecca Kissane, Peter Rosenblatt, Melody Boyd, Kristin Turney, Jennifer Darrah, Eva Rosen, and Phil Garboden.

work. How youth and parents negotiate these changes in context has implications for what we can assume the effects of housing mobility programs will be. Although we draw on previous research looking at Chicago's Gautreaux program and the MTO experiment, we also include data from a more recent and less well-known program in Baltimore, the Baltimore Housing Mobility Program (BHMP).

First, we discuss the impacts of housing mobility on parent mental health and well-being, bringing attention to important findings that are often pushed aside in favor of a focus on children's outcomes in general and measures of adult socioeconomic self-sufficiency in particular. Second, we consider how children transition to new neighborhoods and schools through housing mobility programs and the role of friendships in helping children benefit from better-resourced schools and communities. Last, we show that despite previous research that describes parental engagement in school as differing by social class, many low-income parents who moved through mobility programs were quite actively engaged in their children's schooling. However, their strategies for connecting with their children's schools back in the city differed markedly from practices that were accepted and encouraged in suburban schools. These differences hampered parents' efforts to support their children's academic experiences.

BRIEF OVERVIEW OF MAJOR HOUSING MOBILITY PROGRAMS[2]

Housing mobility programs, usually funded in part through subsidies from the Housing Choice Voucher Program (HCVP), have given poor families in disadvantaged neighborhoods support to move to a wider range of communities. Mobility program vouchers are similar to the HCVP in that poor families choose to sign up for a subsidy, which covers some or most of their rent in a private-market unit, and heads of household must go through an application and screening process (e.g., criminal background and credit score checks). However, these programs also differ markedly from the HCVP. For example, some programs are part of legal remedies or innovative housing programs supported by federal or local governments. This means that families' eligibility may be based on membership in a legal class or determined by a random assignment process. Mobility programs often require families to move to neighborhoods with specific demographic characteristics, such as racial composition or poverty rate. Families may also receive varying degrees of housing counseling and housing search assistance, such as financial workshops, transportation to see housing in suburban communities, or assistance in finding

---

[2]Here we only discuss four major mobility programs that have been evaluated or studied by researchers. Other housing mobility efforts in Dallas, Minneapolis, Hartford, and elsewhere have helped low-income minority families move to areas of higher opportunity, but have received less research attention (Goetz, 2004; Juracek et al., 2018; Popkin et al., 2003).

landlords in more affluent areas who are willing to accept vouchers. Although there is no standard form of counseling in mobility programs, families typically receive more assistance than is available in the HCVP.

The first of these housing mobility interventions was Chicago's Gautreaux program, resulting from a housing desegregation case that started in the late 1960s (Polikoff, 2006). Over a 20-year period, the Gautreaux program helped over 7,000 poor African American families living in public housing (and those on the public housing waiting list) move to private-sector rental housing in primarily White suburbs or revitalizing neighborhoods in the city of Chicago (Rubinowitz & Rosenbaum, 2000). When they applied for the program, families resided in some of the city's most distressed and racially isolated communities, many with poverty rates above 40% and populations that were over 80% African American. Program counselors recruited landlords to directly offer families units in higher-resource neighborhoods. Families moved to communities that were on average only 17% poor and 28% Black, and in the suburbs, the rates were even lower, at 5% poor and 10% Black (DeLuca & Rosenbaum, 2003).

Not only did the Gautreaux program help families move to safer, more racially and economically integrated neighborhoods, but the moves were durable; most families were in similar communities 15 to 20 years later (Keels, Duncan, DeLuca, Mendenhall, & Rosenbaum, 2005). For example, mothers continued to reside in low-poverty neighborhoods with a fairly even balance of Black and non-Black residents (DeLuca, Duncan, Keels, & Mendenhall, 2010). Mothers who moved to more advantaged, less segregated areas spent more time employed and less time receiving cash assistance (Mendenhall, DeLuca, & Duncan, 2006). Children who moved to the suburbs were more likely to complete high school and attend college than those placed in the city, and mortality rates were lower for boys who moved with Gautreaux to neighborhoods with more educated residents (Kaufman & Rosenbaum, 1992; Votruba & Kling, 2009). In the long run, children who moved to less segregated communities with the Gautreaux program were also more likely to live in such areas as adults (Keels, 2008).

In the mid-1990s—on the heels of Gautreaux's success—the Department of Housing and Urban Development designed a more rigorous program to test the promise of housing mobility interventions: the federally funded MTO research demonstration, which included a random-assignment experimental design in five cities (see Briggs, Popkin, & Goering, 2010). Families assigned to the experimental group were offered vouchers and housing counseling to relocate to low-poverty areas that were no more than 10% poor; unlike the Gautreaux program where counselors found units for families, MTO participants searched for housing largely on their own. Other families were assigned to the Section 8 (now known as Housing Choice Voucher Program) treatment group and were offered the standard housing voucher subsidy, or the control group, which received no additional services. After random assignment, experimental movers were living in neighborhoods with average poverty rates of only 11%, far lower than the average poverty rate of 40% or higher in their original public housing projects (Orr et al., 2003). Up to 15 years later, experimental group families were living in communities that were 27% poor on average (21% for experimental compliers); this was lower than the control group average of 31%, but higher than the low-poverty neighborhoods to which many had initially moved (Sanbonmatsu et al., 2011). Given that there were no neighborhood racial composition requirements for MTO, participating families both began and ended up in mostly minority neighborhoods. At the final impacts evaluation, experimental mover families were in neighborhoods that were almost 80% minority on average (Sanbonmatsu et al., 2011).[3]

While the initial evaluation of the MTO program was underway, the city of Chicago and a nonprofit launched a subsequent round of the Gautreaux program (Pashup, Edin, Duncan, & Burke, 2005). The program—Gautreaux Two—gave Chicago's public housing residents the opportunity to receive a voucher that they could use in a neighborhood with a poverty rate below 23.49% and a racial composition of no more than 30% Black residents. Unlike the original Gautreaux program, which offered families apartments found by housing counselors who coordinated with landlords, Gautreaux Two households searched for housing mostly on their own. Of the 549 eligible families who began the program, only 200 (36%) had successfully leased up within 18 months (Pashup et al., 2005). Four years later, nearly half had moved again, and most of these households relocated to areas that were more racially segregated and poorer than the neighborhoods to which they originally moved after joining the program (Boyd, Edin, Clampet-Lundquist, & Duncan, 2010).

In 2003, the BHMP was launched as part of a court-ordered remedy stemming from a desegregation lawsuit, *Thompson v. HUD*, filed in 1995 (see DeLuca & Rosenblatt, 2017, for more details on the case and the program). The remedy required that families receiving BHMP vouchers lease up in census tracts where less than 10% of households were below the poverty line, no more than 30% of the residents were Black, and fewer than 5% of households

---

[3]Research comparing Gautreaux and MTO suggests that several elements of program design made Gautreaux a more effective intervention for helping families move to more integrated and less poor neighborhoods. As mentioned above, Gautreaux program staff worked directly with landlords to find specific units for families. MTO experimental group families were also required to move to low-poverty census tracts, but it was primarily up to the families to find their own housing units, with relatively low levels of counseling and support from program staff. The Gautreaux program design induced much larger changes in environment for suburban movers: families moved longer distances into lower poverty neighborhoods with smaller minority populations, better schools, and higher employment rates than participants in MTO. These differences in the types of neighborhood placements the programs created likely account for at least some of the differences in the programs' individual outcomes, such as education, employment, and subsequent moves (Rosenbaum & Zuberi, 2010).

received housing assistance.[4] Like Gautreaux, BHMP placed restrictions on eligible neighborhoods on the basis of both poverty level and racial composition, but like the MTO program, families found their own housing units with the assistance of counselors. Between 2003 and 2019, the BHMP has helped over 4,000 families relocate to higher opportunity neighborhoods in the metropolitan area. These moves have been made possible through a number of important administrative features and program supports. For example, the BHMP employs regional administration (allowing participants to lease-up across six metro-area counties), higher rent payment standards (to make more units affordable), and landlord outreach. Families also receive intensive counseling before, during, and after they move, participate in a series of workshops (to support financial planning and credit repair, household management, and neighborhood education), and receive security deposit assistance. Because of these program features, the BHMP created large changes in both neighborhood and school characteristics (described below). These large changes in environment make the BHMP a strong intervention, similar to Gautreaux. We include more details about the program later in this chapter.[5]

In the sections that follow, we draw on evidence from these programs to examine how parents and children who moved with residential mobility programs negotiated the changes in their social contexts. We focus on three areas that illustrate the importance of considering person–environment fit when implementing housing policy interventions that induce large changes in neighborhood settings. Specifically, we examine: (a) the impacts of housing mobility on parent mental health and well-being, (b) the significance of friendships for children as they transition to new neighborhoods and schools,

---

[4]In July 2015, the BHMP changed its opportunity definition to a composite designation based on: the Maryland Department of Housing and Community Development Opportunity Index; the Opportunity Mapping Advisory Panel opportunity index; and supplemented by the Department of Housing and Urban Development's Picture of Subsidized Households data, Maryland school performance data (MSA test scores), American Community Survey data, and BHMP administrative data.

[5]When compared with the first Gautreaux program, we suggest that the more recent BHMP was similarly effective in shaping longer term neighborhood residence in part because it offered access to neighborhood opportunity that was much higher than other recent mobility programs. For example, BHMP participants moved to very low-poverty census tracts (< 10% poor), which was much lower than that required by Gautreaux II, which set a poverty limit of 23.49%. The BHMP also employed race and subsidized housing assistance levels to define high-opportunity neighborhoods, compared with the poverty-only criterion that was used to guide the MTO program. As DeLuca and Rosenblatt (2017) noted,

> The inclusion of the racial criterion is essential, given that predominantly African American neighborhoods have historically been more susceptible to economic decline than other areas, and because the schools in nonsegregated neighborhoods are higher quality, on average. . . . Using a lower poverty threshold than *Gautreaux II* and including the racial criterion that MTO lacked meant that BHMP families were unlikely to move to neighborhoods surrounded by other low-opportunity tracts. (p. 538)

and (c) parental engagement in their children's new higher-performing schools after moving.[6]

OFTEN OVERLOOKED BUT POWERFUL BENEFITS: THE PARENTING DIVIDENDS OF HIGHER OPPORTUNITY NEIGHBORHOODS

Recent conversations about the effects of housing mobility have tended to focus on how moves to lower poverty neighborhoods affect children's outcomes, such as academic achievement and earnings. Yet, some of the most striking MTO results were those showing improvements in mental health and well-being for mothers who moved to low-poverty neighborhoods (Kling, Liebman, & Katz, 2005; Ludwig et al., 2012). Parents who received an MTO voucher experienced reductions in psychological distress and increases in mental calm that were comparable to best practices in antidepression medication therapies (Kling, Liebman, & Katz, 2007; Ludwig et al., 2012).[7] Had it not been for the foresight of Jeffrey Kling and Jeffrey Liebman, who included exploratory qualitative research in the early phases of the Boston site of MTO experiment, we might not have discovered this connection (Kling, Liebman, & Katz, 2005). This early work convinced Kling, Liebman, and Katz (2005, 2007) to add measures of physical and mental health to the interim and final evaluation surveys. Subsequent work in this area has also found that neighborhood and housing quality affects adult psychological well-being (e.g., Jones-Rounds, Evans, & Braubach, 2014), and scholars have long argued that a family's ecological context, including their neighborhood, can influence parental mental health, parental self-efficacy, and parenting behaviors (Eccles & Harold, 1996; Pinderhughes, Nix, Foster, & Jones, 2001; Shumow & Lomax, 2002).

It is our perception that these findings tend to get far less policy attention when compared to the negative or null findings on economic self-sufficiency or educational attainment. Yet it is hard to imagine that most of the family processes that are key to child development are possible without healthy parents, and it is likely that increases in parental mental health and efficacy could make other policy interventions more effective. For example, prior research has found that improvements in parent mental health and self-efficacy—and reductions in parental stress—promote positive parenting behaviors that support children's development (Bogenschneider, Small, & Tsay, 1997; Conger et al., 1992; Hoover-Dempsey & Sandler, 1997; Jones & Prinz, 2005; Shumow

---

[6]Throughout this chapter, we use pseudonyms to protect the confidentiality of our research participants.

[7]Teenage daughters in the experimental group also experienced significant reductions in psychological distress (Kling et al., 2007). Qualitative research in three MTO cities (Los Angeles, Boston, and New York) suggests these mental health improvements may have been due in part because of increases in neighborhood safety and reduction in harassment by male peers (Popkin, Leventhal, & Weismann, 2010).

& Lomax, 2002). In this first section, we describe findings from housing mobility programs showing that moving to lower poverty, safer neighborhoods can improve parental well-being, in the hopes that such measures will continue to be included in future research on housing mobility and housing policy discussions.

Neighborhoods, Mental Health, and Substance Use

Scholars have shown that neighborhood disadvantage is negatively associated with health (Diez Roux & Mair, 2010; Ross, 2000; Ross & Mirowsky, 2001) and that both the social and physical components of neighborhoods can act as stressors that diminish physical and mental health (Diez Roux & Mair, 2010). Many studies have also found that exposure to violence is associated with an increase in depression or depressive symptoms (Curry, Latkin, & Davey-Rothwell, 2008; Cutrona, Russell, Hessling, Brown, & Murry, 2000; Wilson-Genderson & Pruchno, 2013; Yen, Yelin, Katz, Eisner, & Blanc, 2006). Across all three of the housing mobility programs we have studied, we find numerous accounts of parents who explicitly link the neighborhood change they experienced after moving with an improved sense of well-being and also report other behavioral changes, such as reductions in substance abuse.[8]

For example, Mr. K, a single father who raised his children in the former Robert Taylor homes before moving to a western suburb of Chicago with Gautreaux, remarked,

> There is a freedom that I didn't have over there in that concentration camp. It was very restrictive. I couldn't take my kids outside. . . . My kids were in peril. I feared for them. It was my main objective to get out of there.[9]

Ms. P, a mother who also moved with Chicago's Gautreaux program, compared the housing projects she left behind to a prison and connected her new suburban community with a sense of peace:

> I think it was the richness in the atmosphere that the children realized . . . they no longer had to be in the projects; they no longer had to dodge bricks and things coming in the building where they lived. Here they could just sit out and enjoy themselves, and they did. And they just fit right in.

For Ms. P, the change in neighborhood safety her family experienced after moving reduced her daily stress and worry about her children, as she explained, "Up here, it's a lot different; it's quieter, much quieter. I'm able to sleep at night."

---

[8]Although most MTO respondents reported that moves to low-poverty neighborhoods through an MTO voucher relieved their stress, some parents reported that these moves were the cause of additional worries, such as higher utility bills, increasing rents, transportation issues, and childcare challenges (see Turney, Kissane, & Edin, 2012; Talbert, 2018).
[9]See Rosenbaum, Reynolds, and DeLuca (2002) for more details.

Other members of our MTO research team (2012)—Kristin Turney, Rebecca Kissane, and Kathryn Edin—examined the mechanisms by which the MTO program might have improved the mental health of mothers in the experimental group. Using interviews conducted with mothers from the Baltimore site of MTO, the research team described how the radical increases in housing and neighborhood quality mothers experienced after their MTO moves reduced a number of psychological stressors and increased relief, hope and pride. Table 8.1 shows how some of these stressors were significantly reduced for parents after moving with MTO. For example, at the baseline survey, 48% of parents in the experimental group reported that a member of the household had been victimized in the last six months, and only 42% reported that they felt safe on the streets at night. By the time the final evaluation was conducted, the percentage of household heads reporting that a member of the household had been victimized dropped to 20%, and the percentage reporting that they felt safe at night increased to 68%.

MTO mothers in Baltimore referred to the public housing projects they left as the "danger zone," "pure unadulterated hell," and, in a particularly vivid example, Tammy described the Flag House Courts as a place that made you feel "trapped, caged, and worthless, stuck in an atmosphere of absolutely no progress . . . a house of terror." Not only did parents report significant reductions in their experiences of victimization and increases in their perceptions of safety after moving, they tied these changes directly to improvements in their well-being, some saying explicitly that they were less depressed after the moves.[10] Niecy, a mother of two who had lived in the Murphy Homes project on Baltimore's West Side, made an explicit connection between her new housing and neighborhood conditions and her sense of what could be possible in the future (Turney, Kissane, & Edin, 2012):

> [The MTO unit] wasn't a high rise, it wasn't like that. It was a single home. . . . I could see grass, and I could see trees and birds and squirrels. But [in the housing project], it wasn't nothing like that. . . . It was just like day and night. I had moved from night to day. So it was just, it was clean. The [project] was not clean. . . . I mean from me coming from [the projects] and being here like this, this is really nice. And you know, I know what, you know what, it gets better. It's gonna get better. (p. 9)

---

[10]Despite feeling positive about their new neighborhoods and expressing a desire to stay, many MTO parents ended up returning to high-poverty neighborhoods. In other research, we found that subsequent moves were often caused by housing quality failures, landlord practices, and significant changes in family circumstances— not a desire to leave their neighborhoods. Each subsequent move also presented the challenge of negotiating the housing market with a voucher and no counseling support—in most communities in the country, it is perfectly legal to refuse to rent to a voucher holder and, in more affluent communities, it can be especially challenging to find landlords who readily accept voucher tenants (Edin, DeLuca, & Owens, 2012; Rosenblatt & DeLuca, 2012).

TABLE 8.1. Safety and Victimization in Neighborhoods at Baseline Survey and Final Impact Evaluation

Safety and victimization measure[a]	Experimental-group (%)
Baseline—member of household victimized in last 6 months	48
Final—member of household victimized in last 6 months	20
Baseline—streets near home felt safe at night[b]	42
Final—streets near home felt safe or very safe at night	68

Note. [a]For the baseline survey, $N = 631$; for the final adult survey, $N = 451$; for the final youth survey, $N = 610$. [b]The survey questions at baseline and at final survey were slightly different. The baseline variable calculated those who felt very unsafe in their neighborhood at night, and we flipped the percentage around. Because this percentage now includes even those who felt unsafe in their neighborhoods, the difference in safety between baseline and final is even more profound than noted here. From *Coming of Age in the Other America* (p. 51), by S. DeLuca, S. Clampet-Lundquist, and K. Edin, 2016, New York, NY: Russell Sage Foundation. Copyright 2016 by Russell Sage Foundation. Adapted with permission.

Similarly, Amy, a mother who had long battled depression and anxiety, reported that the MTO move to a lower poverty neighborhood in the city helped her feel calmer, specifically because of the change in her physical environment.

> So moving up here, it's a whole different atmosphere, the greenery, you living in a high-rise, you got a lot [of] cement. And there's something to that effect in the psychology . . . the hardness you get from all that concrete. The greenery, it softens you. It's just so beautiful and peaceful, the space, the open space. You got more space. (Turney, Kissane, & Edin, 2012, p. 9)

We saw very similar responses to improvements in neighborhood and housing conditions among parents who moved with the BHMP (see Darrah & DeLuca, 2014). When Renee moved to a suburban neighborhood in Harford County, Maryland, she told us,

> I love it out here. I love the peace and quiet. We don't have all the . . . violence out here. . . . In the city you see it on the street or on the corner. Everywhere you go you see it. I really, really like it out here. It's safe. We can actually go outside and play without worrying about a stray bullet.

Miss Cora, a mother of two, told us that when she compared her new neighborhood in the northwest suburbs to the one she left behind, there "was a big difference from Pedestal Gardens [a neighborhood in Baltimore City], it was really rough . . . it was like leavin' Hell and goin' to Heaven." Pedestal Gardens had "a lot of killin', break-ins." She described her suburban neighborhood in Reisterstown, Maryland, saying it "was such a dream. It was the place I always wanted to be, in a far out nice place with quiet and home owners. Schools was good—it was beautiful." Unlike other neighborhoods she had lived in, "it wasn't dangerous at all out there. . . . It was so beautiful and quiet out there. You could take walks and the kids played with each other." She told us that after they settled into their new home, they were motivated to improve their physical health as well. "Me and the children had got so better about ourselves. We was less stressed out. We was less depressed. We started joinin' Curves [a local gym] when we was livin' out there. We started losing an amount of weight." Miss Cora clearly articulated how the change in her neighborhood context, and a reduction in stress about threats of violence and crime, led to an improvement in mental and physical health for her family.

Although not an explicit focus of the experimental or quantitative analyses of the mobility programs so far, we also found that parents made direct connections between their neighborhood conditions and desisting from drugs and alcohol (DeLuca, Clampet-Lundquist, & Edin, 2016). In our Baltimore MTO site, of the 44 mothers who admitted to ever using drugs, 27 claimed that they were no longer using 4 to 7 years after their move, a change many credited directly to relocating from public housing into new, lower poverty neighborhoods. Tina described her transformation:

> I'm more settled. I'm not as wild and wide-open as I was when I was in the [projects]. In the [projects], I stayed in the streets more. I did work—that's one thing. [But] it was basically all about drinking and hanging out. Out here, you gonna be responsible because everyone I'm surrounded [by] works and is responsible, you know?

Rachel, a mother of three recounted,

> I really didn't socialize with anybody down there [in the projects]. [But] that's one of the things that allowed me to continue to use drugs, 'cause I was always looking at people that was worse than me, instead of looking at people that were better, that were doing better than me.

Notably, Rachel moved to a much lower poverty neighborhood in Baltimore, albeit not through MTO, and had managed to leave drugs behind, a success she attributed to the change in her neighborhood environment.

In a particularly detailed account, Terry, a mother who moved with the BHMP to a southwestern suburb, and then to Harford County, attributed the change in how she handled alcohol when coping with stress to her move away from the city. When she was living in the city, Terry drank to excess around her children. "Because I was so adapted to the city, I was drinking . . . but when I moved out here, it just changed a lot . . . now I barely even touch a drink," she said. After leaving the city, she described a different daily routine:

> I just go to work, come home and pay the bills and have fun with my children. . . . I think the atmosphere that I was in, the friends that I had, they wasn't no help to me because when I needed a shoulder to cry on . . . it was like let's go take a drink . . . but the people I work with [here], but when I see them it's 'let's go to work' not 'let's go take a drink.'

Similarly, Ms. F reported that her move to a northern Chicago suburb with Gautreaux allowed her to be more available for her daughter and less likely to get caught up in drinking. She recalled,

> I was out, like, running around, trying to party and go out. If I hadn't moved to the suburbs, I would still have been doing that, and I probably wouldn't have

been being responsible for [my daughter]. . . . I probably wouldn't have paid any attention to things that she needed, because I probably would've been a wild person—like I was!

Although we cannot identify the precise mechanisms that explain why these parents and others we met decided to abstain from drug and alcohol use, their narratives suggest that as they moved into new neighborhoods, they were exposed to less violence and fewer neighborhood stressors, and they made social connections with fewer people who were heavily consuming drugs and alcohol.

Parenting Efficacy and Increased Bandwidth

Recent research by economists has made more explicit the connection between poverty and cognitive functioning, describing the effects of scarcity as a *bandwidth tax* (Mullainathan & Shafir, 2013). Many of the low-income parents we met routinely faced circumstances—such as bouts of extreme poverty, violence, eviction, and job loss—that reduced their capacity to cope, leaving their bandwidth, "devoted to the balls in the air that are about to fall" (Mullainathan & Shafir, 2013, p. 129). When faced with these pressures, poor parents had reduced capacity to invest in other domains, including some aspects of parenting, employment, and their own education and health. However, we also observed that parents could get some of that bandwidth back after moving to less violent neighborhoods.

Tammy, mentioned earlier, was a mother of three who left the Flag House Courts project through MTO. She reflected on how living in those projects had profoundly limited her ability to be an effective parent:

> When I was down in [the] project . . . I wouldn't even deal with my children. I couldn't provide well for them, so I was detached from them. I didn't know what to teach them, living in a place where I couldn't point out this and I couldn't point out that [to illustrate a good role model]. I was very unhappy. There was never a punishment, because I always felt like being there was their punishment.

Once away from the violence and chaos of the Flag homes and relocated to the low-poverty Frankford neighborhood on the city's northeast side, Tammy claimed that she was able to cultivate an atmosphere of discipline in the home and serve healthy meals. Tammy recounted,

> I knew I could not do anything as long as I was trapped in that situation. . . . Moving to Opportunity, it was, it's well worth, it, to whomever was there. The picture was clear that you had a chance, a way out of whatever you was going through. So I took it, took the chance.

She also spoke in detail about how the exposure to different kinds of people and shopping centers affected the food she bought and how she prepared it for her children. Instead of just the "corner store" in her old neighborhood, she had a number of grocery stores nearby. Tammy explained,

So [now] you're thinking a little broader about what to choose from. . . . You have a multitude of different people shopping and it's a better selection of different foods . . . and seeing people buy certain foods that you looked at one point and just thought they weren't edible or didn't know what to do with them. So you're exposed to um, wanting to be a little more healthier. You feel a little better, you know, and you know you have to eat better so you can look better, feel better, and it's all about exposure.

Peaches, a mother of two, also attributed her improved parenting ability to leaving the Murphy Homes for the working-class neighborhood of Evesham in Northeast Baltimore. She told us,

When I first moved in the house, I just cried. I just really cried. I was like 'Oh my God. . . . Now I can raise my family in the way I want to raise them,' you know? If I had not had that opportunity to go into the MTO program, I would not have known what it would have been like to live in a house in a positive environment . . . to see how middle class people live. . . . It just made me want that.

Freed up from the worries about violence and the challenges of supervising children in dangerous areas, parents were able to focus on employing the types of parenting strategies they thought were best for their children.

Living in safer neighborhoods also afforded parents' greater bandwidth to focus on their own futures. Miss Q, who moved to a northern suburb of Chicago through the Gautreaux program, remarked that prior to the move,

I was hanging with the wrong crowd. . . . Now I'm trying to work and better my life. . . . I have a better house, but I can't live off of this [program] forever, so now I'm trying to strive and get going back to school and trying to work and just better myself.

Living in the suburbs gave her a new perspective, the sense that she could control her life, as she explained: "I felt better about where I lived and that made me want to try to do something with my life other than just sit back and be nervous and worried all the time."

Tasha moved to Laurel, Maryland from the Latrobe Homes with the BHMP and described the noise, drug activity, and chaos she experienced all hours of the day and night when she lived in city housing projects. Since she was no longer constantly worrying about managing her environment to keep things stable for her children, she felt like she could focus more on some of her life goals, such as education:

And I'm ready to try to get myself back into some type of, like I said, some type of program and things, and I'm more focused here. Because living there [in public housing], I was like on track, off-track, on track, off-track because it is so much that was going on around me. . . . I was so much more focused on praying to get out of there, that I really couldn't focus on too much else. Of course, I'm focusing on my kids, but for the things that I wanted to do for myself, I couldn't stay focused. So now, I'm somewhere where it's peace and quiet, and now I can stay more focused.

Tasha described what she termed a "transformation" as a result of the move to Harford County, where she had a backyard, greenery, quiet, and space outside of her home to enjoy. She contrasted this with growing up in the city housing projects:

> I had to basically barricade myself in my home. . . . I couldn't go sit out my back-yard because I didn't have one. . . . I'm not going to sit on my front porch cause you had so much going on in front of you, that I choose not to want to see. . . . I didn't have bars, I could still come and go as I please, but I still felt like I was in jail. So that was the difference.

In the design and evaluation of MTO, it was assumed that moving to better neighborhoods would translate into better employment outcomes for parents. The results surprised many, when parents in the experimental group were not more likely to be working or earning more than their counterparts in the control group (Turney, Edin, Clampet-Lundquist, Kling, & Duncan, 2006). However, here we offer evidence of other benefits to parents that often gets lost in the policy discussions about MTO and neighborhood interventions—benefits that, if combined with additional job supports, could promote employment and economic stability and self-sufficiency.[11] Opportunity moves may improve mental health, parenting efficacy, decision making, and bandwidth. In other words, we find evidence of a *parenting dividend*. We also speculate that the changes in mental health and parenting bandwidth are one of the mechanisms through which MTO had positive long-term effects on children (Chetty et al., 2016; DeLuca, Clampet-Lundquist, & Edin, 2016).

NECESSARY CONDITIONS FOR NEIGHBORHOOD AND SCHOOL EFFECTS: FRIENDSHIPS

As noted earlier, housing mobility programs rest on the premise that large gains in neighborhood quality will improve children's well-being and life chances (Briggs et al., 2010; Orr et al., 2003). However, the process of moving to starkly different neighborhood contexts can also be highly disruptive, as children not only experience a substantial improvement in their neighborhood contexts but also move away from their existing peer networks. Peer

---

[11]Turney et al. (2006) examined employment patterns from the MTO Baltimore site using mixed methods data from both the interim impacts survey and the 2003–2004 qualitative study. They found several reasons why the experimental movers did not experience gains in employment/self-sufficiency. First, experimental-group mothers reported that their neighbors in low-poverty areas were more likely to work in jobs that required more training and education than they had, making them more hesitant to ask about job leads. Second, for some movers, ill health interfered with their ability to obtain and/or maintain employment. Experimental families' new neighborhoods were also further away from the jobs they would typically apply for based on their education and skill levels.

TABLE 8.2. BHMP Neighborhood Poverty Rates and Racial Composition

Move status	Poverty mean rate (%)	African American mean (%)
Pre BHMP	32.0	78.7
1-year postmove	8.4	22.3

Note. BHMP = Baltimore Housing Mobility Program. Based on analytic sample (full *N* = 1,423 excluding 154 households who made initial city moves and 144 families who faced a forced second move). Source: BHMP participant database, American Community Survey, Decennial Census.

relationships have long been offered as a mechanism through which neighborhood effects operate (Crane, 1991; Ellen & Turner, 1997; Jencks & Mayer, 1990; Leventhal & Brooks-Gunn, 2000), and prior research has shown that peers also matter for children's educational outcomes, primarily by influencing their engagement and motivation in school (Brown & Larson, 2009; Bukowski, Brendgen, & Vitaro, 2007; Connell, Spencer, & Aber, 1994; Ryan, 2001). However, mobile students may lack peer relationships that can serve to promote school participation as well as other prosocial behaviors and attitudes (Drukker, Feron, Mengelers, & Van Os, 2009; Haynie, South, & Bose, 2006). Thus, for children and youth, the potential benefits of moving into lower poverty communities may be mediated (or moderated) by the social connections they are able to form in their new neighborhoods and schools. We use examples from the BHMP to illustrate how youth navigated the disruption of their social lives and the challenge of building new friendships in their suburban communities after moving.

The BHMP has helped thousands of families move into significantly lower poverty and more racially diverse neighborhoods, primarily in the suburban counties surrounding Baltimore City. As shown in Table 8.2, on average, when they signed up for the program, families were living in neighborhoods with a poverty rate over 30% and where over 78% of their neighbors were Black. After moving with the assistance of the program, families resided in neighborhoods that were less than 10% poor on average, and 22% Black.[12] However, it was not only neighborhood demographics that changed—as we discussed earlier, mothers also experienced an increase in safety and expressed profound relief and a sense of "peacefulness" after moving to these more advantaged neighborhoods.

Youth also described their new neighborhoods as quieter and safer (in line with similar results from MTO). Beyonce, who moved to Baltimore County just before fifth grade, told us that she felt more secure in her suburban

---

[12]Participating families also continue to remain in lower poverty and more racially integrated neighborhood over time, even 7 years after receiving their vouchers (DeLuca, Rhodes, et al., 2016).

neighborhood, in comparison to the city neighborhoods where she had previously lived:

> All the other neighborhoods was like loud and violent. We was in the city, so there's more crimes down there. It's just like this [new neighborhood] is more better. Like safe. Like you can leave your stuff outside. Like [before in the city] you had to lock the doors everywhere you go. Like we had to get people to walk us to school. That's how like dangerous it was.

Although the BHMP move provided youth (and their parents) with a greater sense of neighborhood safety, youth still expressed anxiety about how to navigate social life in their new communities after moving away from their old peer networks. Prior research documents that the loss of relationships is a consequential part of moving for youth (Pribesh & Downey, 1999). When DJ moved and changed schools in second grade, one of his biggest worries was whether he would make new friends, and he said, "I had thought that I wasn't going to have any friends, it was going to be hard to make friends." Nya, who moved in eighth grade, also worried about leaving her friends in the city and not knowing anyone in the suburbs:

> It actually came to me like, 'Nya you're going to be gone. You're not going to see nobody. What are you going to do? . . . All of your best friends live in the city. What are you going to do?'

Although youth talked about their new neighborhoods as safer, the move came with a potential tradeoff as they faced the challenge of establishing new friendships in a neighborhood that was often so far away from the city that it distanced them from their prior social networks.

Role of Social Ties

If we expect that moving to safer and more resource-rich neighborhoods will positively influence youth outcomes, the benefits that youth reap from these neighborhoods are sure to be greatest when they are socially connected in their communities. Some of our recent work shows that peer relationships play a role in how youth adjust to their new schools and neighborhoods after moving with a housing mobility program (Rhodes, 2018). However, the process of making friends after moving varies by age, with adolescents forming new friendships more slowly than youth who move at younger ages. Younger children become socially connected more quickly in their new neighborhoods, while older youth more frequently rely on friends from their former city neighborhoods as a source of social support even after moving (Rhodes, 2018).

For example, John was only in the second grade when he moved with his family to the Baltimore suburbs. At first, he was worried about making friends in his suburban community because there were far fewer children playing outside than in his former city neighborhood. But he quickly made friends at the neighborhood bus stop when school started. He explained,

> Bobby and Oliver they were the first ones that I met because of the bus stop. I met Oliver first . . . and because me and him like to play football and stuff, we were, we were friends. So they showed me everything.

A common interest in the Baltimore Ravens football team provided a quick entrée to friendship for John, and these friendships helped John become more socially integrated into his new suburban community. Tiffany told us that her younger son, Thomas, who was in sixth grade when the family moved to the suburbs, formed new friendships more easily than her older daughters, who were both in high school at the time of the move. Tiffany said, "Because my girls didn't really give it a chance, but my son, he's friends with everybody, Whites, Hispanics, everybody." Her son spent time with friends in his new neighborhood, unlike his older sisters, who more frequently went back to the city to hang out with friends:

> My son, he has friends [here in the new neighborhood]. He'll go out and play ball or he'll go hang out with his friends. . . . My daughters, they'll go to the mall and they'll go, they still travel to the city to go see the people they know.

Similarly, Anthony, who moved as an adolescent, told us that his younger brother was quick to make friends in their new neighborhood: "Every time he met a new person, they always go play in the house and play the games." Anthony himself was more cautious and encouraged his brother to be careful, because "you never know. People is crazy these days." Anthony adopted a slower approach to forming friendships with new peers, telling us, "I didn't really like chill with people at first. I'd hang with them, but I wouldn't hang, hang, like all day. I'd hang with them a couple of hours, just to get to know them." Anthony said it was important to spend time with new peers and evaluate who was worthy of his trust.[13] In the meantime, he returned to the city on the weekends to hang out with friends there.

Worried that her son Lucas would get into trouble in the city as he got older, Deon's parenting strategy was to leave Baltimore and move through the BHMP. However, after moving to the northeastern suburbs, Deon told us that Lucas felt like he was missing out on things in the city, and that he never really adjusted to their suburban neighborhood. Deon told us, "he stays more in the city versus here. He hasn't adjusted. It's like, when he's here, he feels like he's missing something in the city."

These age differences in how youth adapted socially to the mobility program moves may help us better understand why the long-term evaluation of the MTO demonstration found positive and significant effects for children who moved when they were younger than 13 years old, but no significant effects for older youth (Chetty et al., 2016). As youth age and enter adolescence, peer groups and peer social support begin to play a more prominent role in their lives (Brown, 1990, 2004; Steinberg & Morris, 2001). However, when students move, they can end up more peripherally tied to peer groups in their new schools (South & Haynie, 2004), which may be driven in part by their adopting a slower and more cautious approach to establishing new friendships. Housing mobility may be more disruptive for adolescents, who are moving at a time

---

[13]Our team also heard accounts of suspicion and mistrust of new friends among young adults from the MTO program, who felt that it was easier to avoid peers, to be about yourself and your family, in order to stay away from "drama" (DeLuca, Clampet-Lundquist, & Edin, 2016; Edin, Rosenblatt, & Zhu, 2015; Koogler, 2019).

when their peer ties and the social support of their friends have heightened importance.

Our evaluations of residential mobility programs assume that all family members move to, and then stay, in their new neighborhoods, but findings from the BHMP indicate that adolescents who feel socially disconnected from their new communities, may return to the city neighborhoods where their existing social networks are located. Notably, however, as older youth begin to form social ties, this can change. Renee told us that, although her son was returning to the city to spend time with friends shortly after they moved with the BHMP, he started to spend less time in city as he began making friends in his new suburban neighborhood. She told us, "He doesn't go to the city as much. He got friends out here now. He like his friends out here."

Findings from the BHMP suggest that moving with a residential mobility program does not affect every child in the same way and highlights the difficulty that older youth may experience in this transition. Heterogeneity of treatment effects was also found for children who moved with MTO. The long-term evaluation of the MTO program also showed differences in adult outcomes by children's age at move (Chetty et al., 2016), and earlier MTO research also revealed gender differences, with significant mental health gains for adolescent girls but not for boys (Kling et al., 2007). Girls in the experimental group were also less likely to participate in risky behaviors than were boys (Kling, Ludwig, & Katz, 2005). Qualitative work by our colleagues showed that these differences were likely driven by how and where girls and boys spent time after moving: girls spent more time with friends at the mall or inside homes, and boys were more likely to socialize outside on the corner or on the neighborhood basketball court (Clampet-Lundquist, Edin, Kling, & Duncan, 2011, p. 1184).[14] Collectively, both quantitative and qualitative findings from these programs point to the continued need to explore the mechanisms that might explain heterogeneous effects for youth participating in housing mobility programs.

STUDENT AND PARENTAL ENGAGEMENT IN DIFFERENT SCHOOL SETTINGS

Like MTO and Gautreaux, many BHMP families were motivated to move by a desire for better educational opportunities for their children (Orr et al., 2003; Rubinowitz & Rosenbaum, 2000). Much like Gautreaux (see

---

[14]This may be influenced by a greater orientation among boys' friendship networks toward shared activities and their tendency to spend time in larger groups than girls' orientation (Rose & Rudolph, 2006). Boys participating in MTO also discussed experiencing greater surveillance in their neighborhoods after moving and reported more frequent questioning or harassment by the police than girls. Experimental boys, in contrast with boys in the control group, also appeared less discriminating when selecting their friends. Additionally, they did not develop the same knowledge base and set of skills for navigating neighborhoods that would allow them to actively avoid dangerous areas and risk behavior in neighborhoods, if through subsequent moves they returned to higher poverty communities (Clampet-Lundquist et al., 2011).

Popkin, Rosenbaum, & Meaden, 1993), but unlike MTO (see Sanbonmatsu, Kling, Duncan, & Brooks-Gunn, 2006), families moving with the BHMP did indeed experience large changes in children's school contexts, as most families moved out of Baltimore City and into surrounding suburban counties and school districts (DeLuca & Rosenblatt, 2017). Table 8.3 shows that before moving with the BHMP, children attended schools that were, on average, higher poverty, lower performing, and more racially segregated. In these schools, nearly 90% of their peers were African American, almost 80% of their classmates qualified for free or reduced-price lunch, and only 51% of students at their schools met the proficiency standard on the state assessment testing. After moving, youth attended schools where only half of their peers were African American, less than half of the students were eligible for free or reduced-price lunch, and almost three quarters of their classmates scored proficient or advanced on the state assessment testing.

JJ, a mother who moved into the northwestern suburb of Pikesville with the BHMP, described her poor opinion of the city schools saying, "They're not getting a good education. They're not getting something that they will be able to grow or say I got a chance to go to college or whatever." Many parents hoped the BHMP would allow them to send their children to better schools. Chanel, a mother of two who moved to suburban Baltimore County with the BHMP, told us,

> My goal was to get my son to this school out here, to get him out of city schools, get him into a county school where he had a better chance at a better education . . . and I feel like I have accomplished that.

This change, however, meant that parents and children faced the added challenge of navigating markedly different school settings as well as new neighborhoods when moving with the BHMP. In this last section, we explore how parents and children coped with school settings that differed in important ways from the ones they left behind.

Better Schools, Some Academic Challenges

In line with the administrative data presented earlier, when we interviewed parents who participated in the BHMP, they were pleased to see that their children's new schools were much higher quality than the ones they left

TABLE 8.3. BHMP School Race, Class, and Achievement Changes

Move status	African American (%)	Free and reduced lunch (%)	Proficient or advanced score (%)
Pre BHMP	89	78	51
1-year postmove	51	48	74

Note. BHMP = Baltimore Housing Mobility Program. Based on analytic sample (full *N* = 3,153 children excluding households who made initial city moves and those forced to relocate). Source: BHMP Participant Database, Maryland State Department of Education (MSDE) Student Data, Common Core of Data.

behind. Kim, a mother of four, told us that the biggest difference between her suburban neighborhood and her previous city neighborhood, where she lived in a low-rise public housing complex, was school quality:

> The education [in the suburbs]—number one—is excellent. My children always been A to Bs, but since they've been here, they've been like straight honor roll. So, out here, they pay it more attention. They pay more attention to the children in their learning skills. As opposed to, I say, in the city school system, the child could possibly get lost. And you don't know until your child fails or whatever, the rules are out there. So here, they don't even let them lose their self or get overwhelmed, they will put them in a small group really quick, so it's awesome.

Monique also told us, "I love the schools out here. I think they're phenomenal." She has lived in the same suburban neighborhood for several years and described her motivation for remaining in that unit, "Yep, to stay in the same spot, because I love the diversity that she's getting at school, and I know that the opportunity that she has now would not be afforded in the city."

Although many parents were happy with the new schools on a number of fronts—safety, diversity, academic and extracurricular programming, and teacher quality—some children faced a rocky transition, as they encountered the increase in academic intensity. Riley told us that although classes in his suburban school "had more of a purpose," they were also "getting more challenging." Similarly, Nicole explained, "Math at my old school was easy. Math here [in the suburbs] is hard. Reading at my old school was way easier than it is here." She struggled to catch up and developed strategies to improve her performance. For example, Nicole told us that,

> I just studied when I could. I asked students around for help. Got up in groups, asking teachers—raising my hand. Like, it could be a question that I didn't know, but I still raised my hand to at least try.

In her work on Chicago's Gautreaux II program, Micere Keels also found that children needed to bridge curriculum gaps in order to reap the educational benefits of attending high-achieving schools (Keels, 2013).

As noted earlier, residential and school mobility can be disruptive for children's learning, and our quantitative analysis of state standardized test scores for youth participating in the BHMP reflects such an adjustment period, with test scores dipping at first, as youth negotiate this transition. Yet, over time, the findings support parents' perceptions that their participation in the program was beneficial for their children's education; within 5 years of voucher receipt, children whose families moved with the program began performing moderately better on standardized tests than they would have in the absence of the program (DeLuca, Rhodes, & Garboden, 2016). Given the disruption school mobility brings, it may be especially important for parents to establish an active partnership with their child's school to support the transition. However, we find that many parents also faced some unexpected challenges as they navigated these school transfers.

Parent–School Engagement

Existing research has long demonstrated a positive relationship between parent involvement and children's academic achievement (Fan & Chen, 2001; Hill & Tyson, 2009; Jeynes, 2007). Yet scholars also find that middle-class parents are more likely to be involved in schools than lower income parents (Lareau, 1987, 2003; Useem, 1992). Low-income and minority parents also face greater obstacles to their school-based participation and often find ways to support their children's education at home instead, efforts which may go unrecognized by their schools (Hill & Taylor, 2004; Lee & Bowen, 2006). However, Rhodes and Young (2017) found that low-income Black parents who participated in the BHMP were often active participants in their children's city schools and were surprised to encounter resistance to their preferred forms of participation at their children's new suburban schools. Sociologists have found that low-income and minority parents may face more frequent "moments of exclusion" in schools that are oriented around dominant middle-class, White norms—schools similar to those some of the children in the BHMP attended after their move (Lareau & Horvat, 1999). These experiences can limit parents' opportunities to learn about and activate school resources for their child (Lareau, 2000; Lewis-McCoy, 2014; Useem, 1992).

We find that as families navigated the BHMP move and school transfer, some parents also faced unexpected challenges connecting with new schools. For these parents, the expected *level* of school participation in suburban schools was less of an issue than the institutional norms and policies about *how* schools expected parents to participate. In city schools, many parents had relied on informal school visits, or "popping in," as their primary form of participation. These visits allowed parents to accomplish several goals: monitoring their child's behavior in class; observing the child's teachers, classroom, and school; and establishing a presence and making connections in the school that could yield greater access to resources. However, suburban schools rarely allowed this practice of informal school visits, which some parents perceived as a barrier to their school-based participation in suburban schools.

Tee, a mother of two boys who moved to suburban Baltimore County with the BHMP, told us that, in the city,

> I could basically show up at [my son]'s school any time of the day, and I could stay all day. They had a parent room where we could go and do activities for the students. I could go visit the classroom.

However, in her son's suburban school, "you had to schedule an appointment versus just going and just pop up. You can't pop up at school. They don't want you to. I've done it, but they don't want you to. Sometimes you won't get in." Another mother, Mary, who moved to Howard County with her two children, told us,

> I understand you have rules. Everybody got rules. But when you get to a place where you don't want the parents involved—you want them involved, but you

don't want them involved. I don't want to be involved to come and be at the little parent thing. I'm the type of parent that this is my child 24/7 and will always be my child.

She was frustrated that the school would not allow her to visit informally. "I had a problem with, 'Oh, you just can't come in and just kind of peek in and see what your kids are doing just to get an idea of the environment.'"

Monica explained why she preferred to participate by visiting her child's classroom:

I want to make sure the classroom is under control, if the teacher needs assistance and things like that. For instance, if a child is being disruptive to the class, that affects my daughter. Because the teacher has to stop to get you under control, and that's why I stay in the class. I want to make sure my children gets every minute, every second, every hour.

Parents wanted to support their children and ensure that they were staying on track and getting the teacher support they needed, but suburban schools discouraged the informal type of participation parents had relied on in the city. As a result, some parents found it challenging to establish an effective connection with their children's suburban schools.

Although they were disappointed informal visits were not allowed, many parents were pleased with increased levels of communication from suburban schools compared with city schools. Tiffany told us, "If your child does something wrong out here, if my son is chewing gum in school, they're going to call me. If he does anything wrong, they're going to call me." In the city, she felt the school did not inform her about her child's misbehavior or academic struggles, until it was too late to intervene. "I wasn't getting notified until it was out of hand. Most of the time, I couldn't make it out to the school because of my work schedule." Although parents appreciated the high level of communication from suburban schools, without the option of popping in, parents sometimes became reliant on school-initiated communication as their only strategy to obtain information about their children's educational experiences. This sometimes led to missed opportunities for a more robust partnership between schools and parents.

Communication can break down due to poor practices by school administrators or teachers (something that happens in both the city and the suburbs), but when this school-initiated communication is the primary mechanism for parents to stay informed and involved in suburban schools, this disconnect can be consequential. For example, Michelle found it challenging to communicate with her daughter Demi's suburban school, which made things harder when Demi was struggling in math. Michelle's attempts to visit the school and talk to Demi's math teacher were unsuccessful. "When I went up there, it was always she was busy." Demi also had difficulty getting the extra help she needed. Even though her teacher assigned her to an extra math tutoring class, neither Demi nor Michelle knew that she had to sign up ahead of time or she would not be allowed to attend the session. Michelle described the challenge of getting extra help saying,

> When she went the—she went one time and they told her that she needed an appointment, and she's like, 'Why do I need an appointment if my teacher signed me up for this class?' And she's like, 'Well, you need an appointment to come' . . . and she went one time and then all the other times it was, 'Oh, well, the class is full now.'

The situation reached a boiling point for Michelle, when the school did not inform her that Demi could not graduate with her class because she failed her math exam—it was Demi who found out just before the graduation rehearsal. Michelle told us,

> They was graduating on a Thursday. They told her Monday, when she was going to rehearsal . . . and then the counselor was like, 'Well, you got to go to summer school to take your exam over because you failed the exam.' Really? Like who does that? No letter home, no nothing.

Michelle viewed this as both a failure on the school's part to sufficiently support her daughter's academic needs and a failure to communicate about the problem in an appropriate way, because they never called or emailed to speak with her about the issue. Michelle was frustrated that she was not informed enough to help address the issue before her daughter failed the class and was unable to graduate.

Overall, our mixed methods research suggests that the BHMP is beneficial to children's academic performance, and the long-term research on MTO shows that housing mobility can be an effective strategy to improve college attendance and earnings (Chetty et al., 2016). However, children's initial struggles to adapt to increased academic expectations and parents' reported difficulties actively partnering with their children's new schools may moderate what could otherwise be larger academic gains for children. Research shows that effective partnerships between schools, families, and communities can promote student learning (Epstein, 1995); therefore, if parents participating in residential mobility programs were able to form more effective partnerships with suburban schools, children may achieve even greater academic gains and educational attainment than seen in previous mobility programs.

DISCUSSION AND CONCLUSION

In his 1977 paper, "Toward an Experimental Ecology of Human Development," Urie Bronfenbrenner not only provided a theoretical model for how we should think about the relationships between individuals and the systems and settings they are nested in, but also recommended the research designs necessary to study them. Although he made clear the value of many different research methods, he made a crucial point: It is difficult to observe how people and their environments "fit" and observational methods alone are not adequate. He explained:

> The 'accommodation' or 'fit' between person and environment is not an easy phenomenon to recognize. Here, looking is usually not enough. . . . If looking is not enough, what is one to do? . . . The answer to this question was given' me more than 30 years ago, long before I was ready to appreciate it, by my first mentor in graduate school, Walter Fenno Dearborn. In his quiet, crisp New England accent, he once remarked: 'Bronfenbrenner, if you want to understand something, try to change it.' . . . *If you wish to understand the relation between the developing person and some aspect of his or her environment, try to budge the one, and see what happens to the other* [emphasis in original]. (pp. 517–518)

Toward the end of the article, Bronfenbrenner (1977) recommended a particular kind of ecological experiment—a *transforming* one, that profoundly changes people's settings and "activates previously unrealized behavioral potential" (p. 528). As we wrote our chapter on the experiences of parents and children who participated in housing mobility programs—certainly a kind of transforming experiment—we could not help thinking about Bronfenbrenner's call to study person–environment fit by observing what happens when things change. Without a doubt, the kinds of housing, school, and neighborhood changes the parents and children across our various studies have described had profound effects on their lives. In turn, their adaptations to these changes are extraordinarily important to observe, if we are to continue to invest in housing policy that helps families move to higher opportunity neighborhoods.

Bronfenbrenner's thinking revolutionized the field of neighborhood effects, not only by bringing together interdisciplinary researchers but also by forcing us to think about creative research designs (e.g., Brooks-Gunn et al., 1997). The lessons learned from this vast, multidisciplinary literature have sparked enormous interest in and support for policies that increase neighborhood quality (Briggs et al., 2010; Chetty & Hendren, 2018a, 2018b; Ludwig et al., 2011; Sharkey, 2013). Recent research on the long-term impacts of housing mobility programs has prompted policymakers and practitioners from around the country to consider leveraging housing subsidies so that families can move to higher opportunity neighborhoods. Although we have enough evidence to act, it makes sense to consider what we have learned from the larger research base to date on these programs, so that we can improve the experiences of families and children, capture appropriate metrics in our future research, and be realistic about what we can expect from such programs.

In our chapter, we have considered a few examples of processes that have received less attention, and each provides important insights about the benefits and challenges of moving to new places. Together our findings provide several takeaways. First, the research on mother's mental health, well-being, and parenting also suggests that we need to think clearly about our policy goals—what do we expect a housing program to accomplish? The MTO findings on mother's mental health tend to get short shrift, because the employment and economic self-sufficiency results were disappointing. But we would argue that improved mental health and efficacy is the bedrock for helping parents become self-sufficient and is a worthy outcome in its own right because improved mental health could also make other interventions more effective. Research has shown that positive mental health and parental self-efficacy is not only good for parents but can also promote better children's outcomes through improved parenting practices (Jones & Prinz, 2005). Furthermore, housing mobility alone will likely not be a panacea for unemployment when local labor markets are unfavorable to those with only a high school degree. Thus, if we hope to see increases in employment or participation in job training among parents, additional programmatic supports will be required (Briggs et al., 2010; Turney et al., 2006). Policymakers should evaluate how additional programs, policies, and resources might be coupled with housing mobility for maximum benefit (see also Turner & Briggs, 2008).

Second, although it is no doubt imperative to get children out of harm's way (see Sharkey, 2010), we have to remember that children are also social beings who need friendship and connection to thrive (Newcomb & Bagwell, 1995). However, as children enter new neighborhoods and schools, they negotiate the process of establishing new social ties differently by age (Rhodes, 2018), and by gender (Clampet-Lundquist et al., 2011). Just as parents face challenges adjusting to new environments, adolescents who have more exposure to high-poverty neighborhoods before moving bring with them a more cautious approach to friendship formation as they enter new neighborhoods (Rhodes, 2018). As a result, younger children become socially integrated into their new communities more quickly; adolescents, however, more frequently rely on existing friends for social support and end up spending more time in their former city neighborhoods. Thus, mobility programs may benefit from a focus on bolstering counseling and services that include adolescents in the process, including counseling that helps families seek out developmentally appropriate activities and spaces for youth to establish social ties in their new communities. Moving forward, mobility programs should continue to explore what children of different ages need before, during, and after the move.

Third, when considering how policies might affect children and parents, we have to remember that families' previous experiences matter; parents have learned to adapt to challenging environments, such as violent communities and lower-performing schools where they worry about the quality of their child's education (see also Rosenblatt & DeLuca, 2012; Turney et al., 2006). Although parents often participate in residential mobility programs as a strategy to provide their family with access to better-resourced environments, adjustments may still be necessary after they move. These challenges can be amplified when institutions like suburban schools have different expectations about what constitutes acceptable parent participation. Parents can be empowered by an effective and inclusive partnership with their children's schools, but when they face roadblocks, it can dampen their involvement and reduce their capacity to actively support their children's academic adjustment to these new schools. Knowing that school mobility is a disruptive process for children (Kain & O'Brien, 1999; Voight, Shinn, &

Nation, 2012), this parental support is vital. However, parents may require additional information and support as they negotiate new ways to effectively partner with their children's new schools.

If the last few years are any indicator, policymakers and housing providers will continue to expand the use of mobility programs across the country, giving thousands of families and children more choices and a chance to live in safer, more diverse communities and schools. Therefore, it is increasingly important to improve the efficacy of these programs. To do so, we must conduct research that examines these policies and practices with Bronfenbrenner's (1977) framework in mind—observing how parents and children adapt to large changes in their environments, and focusing on how aspects of new neighborhoods and schools interact with the existing assets and challenges already present in families' lives.

REFERENCES

Badger, E., & Bui, Q. (2018, October 1). Detailed maps show how neighborhoods shape children for life. *The New York Times*. Retrieved from https://www.nytimes.com/2018/10/01/upshot/maps-neighborhoods-shape-child-poverty.html

Bogenschneider, K., Small, S. A., & Tsay, J. C. (1997). Child, parent, and contextual influences on perceived parenting competence among parents of adolescents. *Journal of Marriage and the Family, 59*, 345–362. http://dx.doi.org/10.2307/353475

Boyd, M. L., Edin, K., Clampet-Lundquist, S., & Duncan, G. J. (2010). The durability of gains from the Gautreaux Two residential mobility program: A qualitative analysis of who stays and who moves from low-poverty neighborhoods. *Housing Policy Debate, 20*, 119–146. http://dx.doi.org/10.1080/10511481003599902

Briggs, X. D. S., Popkin, S. J., & Goering, J. (2010). *Moving to Opportunity: The story of an American experiment to fight ghetto poverty*. New York, NY: Oxford University Press. http://dx.doi.org/10.1093/acprof:oso/9780195393712.001.0001

Bronfenbrenner, U. (1977). Toward an experimental ecology of human development. *American Psychologist, 32*, 513–531. http://dx.doi.org/10.1037/0003-066X.32.7.513

Bronfenbrenner, U. (1979). *The ecology of human development: Experiments by nature and design*. Cambridge, MA: Harvard University Press.

Brooks-Gunn, J., Duncan, G. J., & Aber, J. L. (1997). *Neighborhood poverty: Context and consequences for children* (Vol. 1). New York, NY: Russell Sage Foundation.

Brown, B. (1990). Peer groups. In S. S. Feldman & G. R. Elliott (Eds.), *At the threshold: The developing adolescent* (pp. 171–196). Cambridge, MA: Harvard University Press.

Brown, B. (2004). Adolescents' relationships with peers. In R. Lerner & L. Steinberg (Eds.), *Handbook of adolescent psychology* (2nd ed., pp. 363–394). New York, NY: Wiley.

Brown, B. B., & Larson, J. (2009). Peer relationships in adolescence. In R. M. Lerner & L. Steinberg (Eds.), *Handbook of adolescent psychology* (Vol. 2, pp. 74–103). Hoboken, NJ: John Wiley.

Bukowski, W. M., Brendgen, M., & Vitaro, F. (2007). Peers and socialization: Effects on externalizing and internalizing problems. In J. E. Grusec & P. D. Mastings (Eds.), *Handbook of socialization: Theory and research* (pp. 255–381). New York, NY: Guildford Press.

Chetty, R., & Hendren, N. (2018a). The effects of neighborhoods on intergenerational mobility I: Childhood exposure effects. *The Quarterly Journal of Economics, 133*, 1107–1162. http://dx.doi.org/10.1093/qje/qjy007

Chetty, R., & Hendren, N. (2018b). The effects of neighborhoods on intergenerational mobility II: County level estimates. *The Quarterly Journal of Economics, 133*, 1163–1228. http://dx.doi.org/10.1093/qje/qjy006

Chetty, R., Hendren, N., & Katz, L. F. (2016). The effects of exposure to better neighborhoods on children: New evidence from the Moving to Opportunity experiment. *The American Economic Review, 106*, 855–902. http://dx.doi.org/10.1257/aer.20150572

Clampet-Lundquist, S., Edin, K., Kling, J. R., & Duncan, G. J. (2011). Moving teenagers out of high-risk neighborhoods: How girls fare better than boys. *American Journal of Sociology, 116*, 1154–1189. http://dx.doi.org/10.1086/657352

Clampet-Lundquist, S., & Massey, D. S. (2008). Neighborhood effects on economic self-sufficiency: A reconsideration of the Moving to Opportunity experiment. *American Journal of Sociology, 114*, 107–143. http://dx.doi.org/10.1086/588740

Conger, R. D., Conger, K. J., Elder, G. H., Jr., Lorenz, F. O., Simons, R. L., & Whitbeck, L. B. (1992). A family process model of economic hardship and adjustment of early adolescent boys. *Child Development, 63*, 526–541. http://dx.doi.org/10.2307/1131344

Connell, J. P., Spencer, M. B., & Aber, J. L. (1994). Educational risk and resilience in African-American youth: Context, self, action, and outcomes in school. *Child Development, 65*, 493–506. http://dx.doi.org/10.2307/1131398

Crane, J. (1991). The epidemic theory of ghettos and neighborhood effects on dropping out and teenage childbearing. *American Journal of Sociology, 96*, 1226–1259. http://dx.doi.org/10.1086/229654

Curry, A., Latkin, C., & Davey-Rothwell, M. (2008). Pathways to depression: The impact of neighborhood violent crime on inner-city residents in Baltimore, Maryland, USA. *Social Science & Medicine, 67*, 23–30. http://dx.doi.org/10.1016/j.socscimed.2008.03.007

Cutrona, C. E., Russell, D. W., Hessling, R. M., Brown, P. A., & Murry, V. (2000). Direct and moderating effects of community context on the psychological well-being of African American women. *Journal of Personality and Social Psychology, 79*, 1088–1101. http://dx.doi.org/10.1037/0022-3514.79.6.1088

Darrah, J., & DeLuca, S. (2014). Living here has changed my whole perspective: How escaping inner-city poverty shapes neighborhood and housing choice. *Journal of Policy Analysis and Management, 33*, 350–384. http://dx.doi.org/10.1002/pam.21758

Davis, B. (2015, October 20). Economist Raj Chetty's proposals on inequality draw interest on both sides of the political aisle. *The Wall Street Journal*. Retrieved from https://www.wsj.com/articles/economist-raj-chettys-proposals-on-inequality-draw-interest-on-both-sides-of-the-political-aisle-1445383469

DeLuca, S., Clampet-Lundquist, S., & Edin, K. (2016). *Coming of age in the other America.* New York, NY: Russell Sage Foundation.

DeLuca, S., Duncan, G. J., & Keels, M. (2011). The notable and the null: Using mixed methods to understand the diverse impacts of residential mobility programs. In M. van Ham, D. Manley, N. Bailey, L. Simpson, & D. Maclennan (Eds.), *Neighborhood effects research: New perspectives* (pp. 195–223). Dordrecht, Netherlands: Springer.

DeLuca, S., Duncan, G. J., Keels, M., & Mendenhall, R. M. (2010). Gautreaux mothers and their children: An update. *Housing Policy Debate, 20*, 7–25. http://dx.doi.org/10.1080/10511481003599829

DeLuca, S., Rhodes, A., & Garboden, P. M. E. (2016, March). *The power of place: How housing policy can boost educational opportunity.* Baltimore, MD: Abell Foundation. Retrieved from https://www.abell.org/sites/default/files/files/ed-power-place31516.pdf

DeLuca, S., & Rosenbaum, J. E. (2003). If low-income Blacks are given a chance to live in White neighborhoods, will they stay? Examining mobility patterns in a quasi-experimental program with administrative data. *Housing Policy Debate, 14*, 305–345. http://dx.doi.org/10.1080/10511482.2003.9521479

DeLuca, S., & Rosenblatt, P. (2017). Walking away from *The Wire*: Housing mobility and neighborhood opportunity in Baltimore. *Housing Policy Debate, 27*, 519–546. http://dx.doi.org/10.1080/10511482.2017.1282884

Diez Roux, A. V., & Mair, C. (2010). Neighborhoods and health. *Annals of the New York Academy of Sciences, 1186*, 125–145. http://dx.doi.org/10.1111/j.1749-6632.2009.05333.x

Drukker, M., Feron, F. J. M., Mengelers, R., & Van Os, J. (2009). Neighborhood socioeconomic and social factors and school achievement in boys and girls. *The Journal of Early Adolescence, 29*, 285–306. http://dx.doi.org/10.1177/0272431608320124

Eccles, J. S., & Harold, R. D. (1996). Family involvement in children's and adolescents' schooling. In A. Booth & J. F. Dunn (Eds.), *Family-school links: How do they affect educational outcomes* (pp. 3–34)? Mahwah, NJ: Erlbaum.

Edin, K., DeLuca, S., & Owens, A. (2012). Constrained compliance: Solving the puzzle of MTO's lease-up rates and why mobility matters. *Cityscape, 14*, 181–194.

Edin, K., Rosenblatt, P., & Zhu, Q. (2015). I do me: Young Black men and the struggle to resist the streets. In O. Patterson & E. Fosse (Eds.), *Bringing culture back in: New approaches to the problems of Black youth* (pp. 229–251). Cambridge, MA: Harvard University Press.

Ellen, I. G., & Turner, M. A. (1997). Does neighborhood matter? Assessing recent evidence. *Housing Policy Debate, 8*, 833–866. http://dx.doi.org/10.1080/10511482.1997.9521280

Epstein, J. L. (1995). School/family/community partnerships: Caring for the children we share. *Phi Delta Kappan, 76*, 701–712.

Fan, X., & Chen, M. (2001). Parent involvement in students' academic achievement. *Educational Psychology Review, 13*, 1–22. http://dx.doi.org/10.1023/A:1009048817385

Galster, G., & Sharkey, P. (2017). Spatial foundations of inequality: A conceptual model and empirical overview. *RSF: The Russell Sage Foundation Journal of the Social Sciences, 3*, 1–33. http://dx.doi.org/10.7758/RSF.2017.3.2.01

Goetz, E. G. (2004). Desegregation lawsuits and public housing dispersal: The case of *Hollman v. Cisneros* in Minneapolis. *Journal of the American Planning Association, 70*, 282–299. http://dx.doi.org/10.1080/01944360408976379

Harding, D. J. (2003). Counterfactual models of neighborhood effects: The effect of neighborhood poverty on dropping out and teenage pregnancy. *American Journal of Sociology, 109*, 676–719. http://dx.doi.org/10.1086/379217

Haynie, D. L., South, S. J., & Bose, S. (2006). The company you keep: Adolescent mobility and peer behavior. *Sociological Inquiry, 76*, 397–426. http://dx.doi.org/10.1111/j.1475-682X.2006.00161.x

Hill, N. E., & Taylor, L. C. (2004). Parent school involvement and children's academic achievement: Pragmatics and issues. *Current Directions in Psychological Science, 13*, 161–164. http://dx.doi.org/10.1111/j.0963-7214.2004.00298.x

Hill, N. E., & Tyson, D. F. (2009). Parental involvement in middle school: A meta-analytic assessment of the strategies that promote achievement. *Developmental Psychology, 45*, 740–763. http://dx.doi.org/10.1037/a0015362

Hoover-Dempsey, K. V., & Sandler, H. M. (1997). Why do parents become involved in their children's education? *Review of Educational Research, 67*, 3–42. http://dx.doi.org/10.3102/00346543067001003

Jencks, C., & Mayer, S. E. (1990). The social consequences of growing up in a poor neighborhood. In L. E. Lynn, Jr., & M. G. H. McGeary (Eds.), *Inner-city poverty in the United States* (pp. 111–185). Washington, DC: National Academies Press.

Jeynes, W. H. (2007). The relationship between parental involvement and urban secondary school student academic achievement. *Urban Education, 42*, 82–110. http://dx.doi.org/10.1177/0042085906293818

Jones, T. L., & Prinz, R. J. (2005). Potential roles of parental self-efficacy in parent and child adjustment: A review. *Clinical Psychology Review, 25*, 341–363. http://dx.doi.org/10.1016/j.cpr.2004.12.004

Jones-Rounds, M. L., Evans, G. W., & Braubach, M. (2014). The interactive effects of housing and neighbourhood quality on psychological well-being. *Journal of Epidemiology and Community Health, 68*, 171–175. http://dx.doi.org/10.1136/jech-2013-202431

Juracek, A., Bell, A., Rolfe, N., Tegeler, P., Kurniawan, H., & Herskind, M. (2018). Housing mobility programs in the U.S.: 2018. Retrieved from the Poverty & Race Research Action Council website: https://prrac.org/pdf/mobilityprogramsus2018.pdf

Kain, J. F., & O'Brien, D. M. (1999, July). *A longitudinal assessment of reading achievement: Evidence for the Harvard/UTD Texas Schools Project.* Dallas, TX: The Green Center for the Study of Science and Society, University of Texas at Dallas. Retrieved from https://somwritinglab.utdallas.edu/research/tsp-erc/pdf/wp_kain_1999_longitudinal_assessment_reading.pdf.pdf

Kaufman, J. E., & Rosenbaum, J. E. (1992). The education and employment of low-income Black youth in White suburbs. *Educational Evaluation and Policy Analysis, 14,* 229–240. http://dx.doi.org/10.3102/01623737014003229

Keels, M. (2008). Residential attainment of now-adult Gautreaux children: Do they gain, hold, or lose ground in neighborhood ethnic and economic segregation? *Housing Studies, 23,* 541–564. http://dx.doi.org/10.1080/02673030802101658

Keels, M. (2013). The importance of scaffolding the transition: Unpacking the null effects of relocating poor children into nonpoor neighborhoods. *American Educational Research Journal, 50,* 991–1018. http://dx.doi.org/10.3102/0002831213497247

Keels, M., Duncan, G. J., DeLuca, S., Mendenhall, R., & Rosenbaum, J. (2005). Fifteen years later: Can residential mobility programs provide a long-term escape from neighborhood segregation, crime, and poverty. *Demography, 42,* 51–73. http://dx.doi.org/10.1353/dem.2005.0005

Kling, J. R., Liebman, J. B., & Katz, L. F. (2005). Bullets don't got no name: Consequences of fear in the ghetto. In T. S. Weisner (Ed.), *Discovering successful pathways in children's development: Mixed methods in the study of childhood and family life* (pp. 243–280). Chicago, IL: University of Chicago Press.

Kling, J. R., Liebman, J. B., & Katz, L. F. (2007). Experimental analysis of neighborhood effects. *Econometrica, 75,* 83–119. http://dx.doi.org/10.1111/j.1468-0262.2007.00733.x

Kling, J. R., Ludwig, J., & Katz, L. F. (2005). Neighborhood effects on crime for female and male youth: Evidence from a randomized housing voucher experiment. *The Quarterly Journal of Economics, 120,* 87–130.

Koogler, H. (2019). *"I'm a soloist": Social strategies among disadvantaged urban youth.* Unpublished manuscript, Johns Hopkins University, Baltimore, MD.

Lareau, A. (1987). Social class differences in family–school relationships: The importance of cultural capital. *Sociology of Education, 60,* 73–85. http://dx.doi.org/10.2307/2112583

Lareau, A. (2000). *Home advantage: Social class and parental intervention in elementary education* (2nd ed.). Oxford, England: Rowman & Littlefield.

Lareau, A. (2003). *Unequal childhoods: Class, race, and family life.* Berkeley: University of California Press.

Lareau, A., & Horvat, E. M. (1999). Moments of social inclusion and exclusion: Race, class, and cultural capital in family–school relationships. *Sociology of Education, 72,* 37–53. http://dx.doi.org/10.2307/2673185

Lee, J., & Bowen, N. K. (2006). Parent involvement, cultural capital, and the achievement gap among elementary school children. *American Educational Research Journal, 43,* 193–218. http://dx.doi.org/10.3102/00028312043002193

Leventhal, T., & Brooks-Gunn, J. (2000). The neighborhoods they live in: The effects of neighborhood residence on child and adolescent outcomes. *Psychological Bulletin, 126,* 309–337. http://dx.doi.org/10.1037/0033-2909.126.2.309

Lewis-McCoy, R. L. (2014). *Inequality in the promised land: Race, resources, and suburban schooling.* Stanford, CA: Stanford University Press.

Linskey, A. (2015, April 10). Clinton taps Harvard professor's ideas on social mobility. *Boston Globe.* Retrieved from https://www.bostonglobe.com/news/politics/2015/04/10/

with-harvard-economist-raj-chetty-hillary-clinton-has-been-studying-how-encourage-upward-mobility-runup-her-campaign/OvuYUMVdb6rF5mxdnzuoeI/story.html

Ludwig, J., Duncan, G. J., Gennetian, L. A., Katz, L. F., Kessler, R. C., Kling, J. R., & Sanbonmatsu, L. (2012). Neighborhood effects on the long-term well-being of low-income adults. *Science, 337,* 1505–1510. http://dx.doi.org/10.1126/science.1224648

Ludwig, J., Sanbonmatsu, L., Gennetian, L., Adam, E., Duncan, G. J., Katz, L. F., . . . McDade, T. W. (2011). Neighborhoods, obesity, and diabetes—A randomized social experiment. *The New England Journal of Medicine, 365,* 1509–1519. http://dx.doi.org/10.1056/NEJMsa1103216

Mendenhall, R., DeLuca, S., & Duncan, G. (2006). Neighborhood resources, racial segregation, and economic mobility: Results from the Gautreaux program. *Social Science Research, 35,* 892<en.923.http://dx.doi.org/10.1016/j.ssresearch.2005.06.007

Mullainathan, S., & Shafir, E. (2013). *Scarcity: Why having too little means so much.* New York, NY: Henry Holt.

Newcomb, A. F., & Bagwell, C. L. (1995). Children's friendship relations: A meta-analytic review. *Psychological Bulletin, 117,* 306–347. http://dx.doi.org/10.1037/0033-2909.117.2.306

Orr, L., Feins, J. D., Jacob, R., Beecroft, E., Sanbonmatsu, L., Katz, L. F., . . . Kling, J. R. (2003). *Moving to Opportunity interim impacts evaluation.* Washington, DC: U.S. Department of Housing and Urban Development, Office of Policy Development and Research.

Pashup, J., Edin, K., Duncan, G. J., & Burke, K. (2005). Participation in a residential mobility program from the client's perspective: Findings from Gautreaux Two. *Housing Policy Debate, 16,* 361–392. http://dx.doi.org/10.1080/10511482.2005.9521550

Pinderhughes, E. F., Nix, R., Foster, E. M., & Jones, D. (2001). Parenting in context: Impact of neighborhood poverty, residential stability, public services, social networks, and danger on parental behaviors. *Journal of Marriage and Family, 63,* 941-953.

Polikoff, A. (2006). *Waiting for Gautreaux: A story of segregation, housing, and the Black ghetto.* Evanston, IL: Northwestern University Press.

Popkin, S. J., Galster, G. C., Temkin, K., Herbig, C., Levy, D. K., & Richer, E. K. (2003). Obstacles to desegregating public housing: Lessons learned from implementing eight consent decrees. *Journal of Policy Analysis and Management, 22,* 179–199. http://dx.doi.org/10.1002/pam.10112

Popkin, S. J., Leventhal, T., & Weismann, G. (2010). Girls in the 'hood: How safety affects the life chances of low-income girls. *Urban Affairs Review, 45,* 715–744. http://dx.doi.org/10.1177/1078087410361572

Popkin, S. J., Rosenbaum, J. E., & Meaden, P. M. (1993). Labor market experiences of low-income Black women in middle-class suburbs: Evidence from a survey of Gautreaux program participants. *Journal of Policy Analysis and Management, 12,* 556–573. http://dx.doi.org/10.2307/3325306

Pribesh, S., & Downey, D. B. (1999). Why are residential and school moves associated with poor school performance? *Demography, 36,* 521–534. http://dx.doi.org/10.2307/2648088

Rhodes, A. (2018). The age of belonging: Friendship formation after residential mobility. *Social Forces, 97,* 583–606. http://dx.doi.org/10.1093/sf/soy062

Rhodes, A., & Young, A. (2017, August). *Unanticipated tradeoffs: How school policies influence parent participation.* Presented at the annual meeting of the American Sociological Association, Montreal, Canada.

Rose, A. J., & Rudolph, K. D. (2006). A review of sex differences in peer relationship processes: Potential trade-offs for the emotional and behavioral development of girls and boys. *Psychological Bulletin, 132,* 98–131. http://dx.doi.org/10.1037/0033-2909.132.1.98

Rosenbaum, J. E., Reynolds, L., & DeLuca, S. (2002). How do places matter? The geography of opportunity, self-efficacy and a look inside the black box of residential mobility. *Housing studies, 17*, 71–82. http://dx.doi.org/10.1080/02673030120105901

Rosenbaum, J. E., & Zuberi, A. (2010). Comparing residential mobility programs: Design elements, neighborhood placements, and outcomes in MTO and Gautreaux. *Housing Policy Debate, 20*, 27–41. http://dx.doi.org/10.1080/10511481003599845

Rosenblatt, P., & DeLuca, S. (2012). "We don't live outside, we live in here": Neighborhood and residential mobility decisions among low-income families. *City & Community, 11*, 254–284. http://dx.doi.org/10.1111/j.1540-6040.2012.01413.x

Ross, C. E. (2000). Neighborhood disadvantage and adult depression. *Journal of Health and Social Behavior, 41*, 177–187. http://dx.doi.org/10.2307/2676304

Ross, C. E., & Mirowsky, J. (2001). Neighborhood disadvantage, disorder, and health. *Journal of Health and Social Behavior, 42*, 258–276. http://dx.doi.org/10.2307/3090214

Rubinowitz, L. S., & Rosenbaum, J. E. (2000). *Crossing the class and color lines: From public housing to White suburbia.* Chicago, IL: University of Chicago Press.

Ryan, A. M. (2001). The peer group as a context for the development of young adolescent motivation and achievement. *Child Development, 72*, 1135–1150. http://dx.doi.org/10.1111/1467-8624.00338

Sampson, R. J. (2012). *Great American city: Chicago and the enduring neighborhood effect.* Chicago, IL: University of Chicago Press. http://dx.doi.org/10.7208/chicago/9780226733883.001.0001

Sampson, R. J., Sharkey, P., & Raudenbush, S. W. (2008). Durable effects of concentrated disadvantage on verbal ability among African-American children. *Proceedings of the National Academy of Sciences, 105*, 845–852. http://dx.doi.org/10.1073/pnas.0710189104

Sanbonmatsu, L., Kling, J. R., Duncan, G. J., & Brooks-Gunn, J. (2006). Neighborhoods and academic achievement results from the Moving to Opportunity experiment. *The Journal of Human Resources, XLI*, 649–691. http://dx.doi.org/10.3368/jhr.XLI.4.649

Sanbonmatsu, L., Ludwig, J., Katz, L. F., Gennetian, L. A., Duncan, G. J., Kessler, R. C., . . . Lindau, S. T. (2011). *Moving to Opportunity for fair housing demonstration program: Final impacts evaluation.* Washington, DC: U.S. Department of Housing and Urban Development, Office of Policy Research and Development.

Sharkey, P. (2010). The acute effect of local homicides on children's cognitive performance. *Proceedings of the National Academy of Science, 107*, 11733–11738. http://dx.doi.org/10.1073/pnas.1000690107

Sharkey, P. (2013). *Stuck in place: Urban neighborhoods and the end of progress toward racial equity.* Chicago, IL: University of Chicago Press. http://dx.doi.org/10.7208/chicago/9780226924267.001.0001

Shumow, L., & Lomax, R. (2002). Parental efficacy: Predictor of parenting behavior and adolescent outcomes. *Parenting: Science and Practice, 2*, 127–150. http://dx.doi.org/10.1207/S15327922PAR0202_03

South, S. J., & Haynie, D. L. (2004). Friendship networks of mobile adolescents. *Social Forces, 83*, 315–350. http://dx.doi.org/10.1353/sof.2004.0128

Steinberg, L., & Morris, A. S. (2001). Adolescent development. *Annual Review of Psychology, 52*, 83–110. http://dx.doi.org/10.1146/annurev.psych.52.1.83

Talbert, E. M. (2018). *Balancing the three-legged stool: Sustainable childrearing routines, family, and work in two American cities.* (Doctoral dissertation). Retrieved from https://jscholarship.library.jhu.edu/handle/1774.2/60125

Turner, M. A., & Briggs, X. D. S. (2008). *Assisted housing mobility and the success of low-income minority families: Lessons for policy, practice, and future research.* Washington, DC: The Urban Institute.

Turney, K., Edin, K., Clampet-Lundquist, S., Kling, J. R., & Duncan, G. J. (2006). Neighborhood effects on barriers to employment: Results from a randomized housing mobility experiment in Baltimore. *Brookings–Wharton Papers on Urban Affairs, 2006,* 137–187. http://dx.doi.org/10.1353/urb.2006.0028

Turney, K., Kissane, R., & Edin, K. (2012). After Moving to Opportunity: How moving to a low-poverty neighborhood improves mental health among African American women. *Society and Mental Health, 3,* 1–21. http://dx.doi.org/10.1177/2156869312464789

U.S. Government Publishing Office. (2018). S.2945—Housing Choice Voucher Mobility Demonstration Act of 2018. Washington, DC: Author. Retrieved from https://www.congress.gov/bill/115th-congress/senate-bill/2945/text?format=txt

Useem, E. L. (1992). Middle schools and math groups: Parents' involvement in children's placement. *Sociology of Education, 65,* 263–279. http://dx.doi.org/10.2307/2112770

Voight, A., Shinn, M., & Nation, M. (2012). The longitudinal effects of residential mobility on the academic achievement of urban elementary and middle school students. *Educational Researcher, 41,* 385–392. http://dx.doi.org/10.3102/0013189X12442239

Votruba, M. E., & Kling, J. R. (2009). Effects of neighborhood characteristics on the mortality of Black male youth: Evidence from Gautreaux, Chicago. *Social Science & Medicine, 68,* 814–823. http://dx.doi.org/10.1016/j.socscimed.2008.12.018

Wilson, W. J. (1987). *The truly disadvantaged: The inner city, the underclass, and public policy.* Chicago, IL: University of Chicago Press.

Wilson-Genderson, M., & Pruchno, R. (2013). Effects of neighborhood violence and perceptions of neighborhood safety on depressive symptoms of older adults. *Social Science & Medicine, 85,* 43–49. http://dx.doi.org/10.1016/j.socscimed.2013.02.028

Yen, I. H., Yelin, E. H., Katz, P., Eisner, M. D., & Blanc, P. D. (2006). Perceived neighborhood problems and quality of life, physical functioning, and depressive symptoms among adults with asthma. *American Journal of Public Health, 96,* 873–879. http://dx.doi.org/10.2105/AJPH.2004.059253

IV

MULTIDISCIPLINARY COMMENTARY AND CONCLUSION

Concepts From the Bioecological Model of Human Development

Rochelle Cassells and Gary Evans

The core of Bronfenbrenner's bioecological model of human development is the process–person–context–time (PPCT) model (Bronfenbrenner, 1979; Bronfenbrenner & Crouter, 1983; Bronfenbrenner & Evans, 2000; Bronfenbrenner & Morris, 1998).[1]

THE PPCT MODEL

We begin our discussion by considering Process, and in particular, *Proximal Processes*, given their central position in the bioecological model.

Process

Proximal processes are exchanges of energy between the developing person and objects, symbols, and other persons in the developing person's immediate environment. To be effective, these processes have to occur on a regular basis over extended periods of time and become progressively more complex

---

[1]A brief note about bioecological model citations. Our presentation of the bioecological model is based on published (Bronfenbrenner, 1979; Bronfenbrenner & Crouter, 1983; Bronfenbrenner & Evans, 2000; Bronfenbrenner & Morris, 1998) and unpublished work between the second author and Bronfenbrenner from a joint seminar they offered for several years in the Departments of Human Development and of Design and Environmental Analysis at Cornell University.

http://dx.doi.org/10.1037/0000187-010
Confronting Inequality: How Policies and Practices Shape Children's Opportunities, edited by L. Tach, R. Dunifon, and D. L. Miller

as the developing person becomes more competent. Bronfenbrenner believed proximal processes are the engines of human development, with the ability to shape an individual's life trajectory in important ways (Bronfenbrenner & Evans, 2000; Bronfenbrenner & Morris, 1998). Two parameters of proximal processes that influence their power are intensity and exposure. The *intensity* of the process refers to the degree or amount of energy. *Exposure* refers to temporal elements and is expanded later under the section titled Time.

The preeminent proximal process is interaction between the developing child and their primary caregiver. Examples of such processes are attachment, responsiveness or sensitivity to the child, caregiver monitoring, joint engagement in activities (e.g., play or learning), neglect/abuse or violence, and degree of autonomy/decision latitude. Other forms of proximal processes include exploration and manipulation of the immediate environment, stimulation levels, and degree of mastery/control over the environment. Language is a key feature of proximal processes because it undergirds the acquisition and use of meaning and symbolism, which both support proximal processes. Bronfenbrenner and colleagues also noted that the most powerful proximal processes are reciprocal in nature, meaning that they involve energy exchanges in both directions (Bronfenbrenner & Evans, 2000; Bronfenbrenner & Morris, 1998).

Early formulations of the bioecological model considered the impact of technology on family life (Bronfenbrenner, 1977). Bronfenbrenner anticipated the growing potential of mobile technology and social media to either facilitate or interrupt proximal processes. Among his concerns in terms of child development was the addictive quality of screen devices that diverted both child and caregiver joint attention and interaction. Bronfenbrenner was also concerned about the exponential growth in sensory overload impinging on children and adolescents, which can have adverse developmental consequences (Wohlwill & Heft, 1987).

Two propositions concerning proximal processes in the bioecological model have particular relevance for interventions aimed at disadvantage children. The first states that proximal processes can be either generative or disruptive. This does not, however, suggest that proximal processes are necessarily the opposite of one another. The effectiveness of proximal processes, whether to bring forth good or bad outcomes, is heightened by extended, progressively more complex interactions. It is worth noting that lower income children are much more likely to be the recipients of less generative and more dysfunctional proximal processes (Bradley & Corwyn, 2002; Brooks-Gunn, Johnson, & Leventhal, 2010; Brooks-Gunn, Klebanov, & Liaw, 1995).

The second proposition of the bioecological model is that negative proximal processes will have greater impact among children growing up in disadvantaged environments, whereas positive proximal processes will have greater impact for those in more advantaged environments. This proposition is linked to the concept of affordance (Gibson, 1976). The social, symbolic, or physical environment typically does not dictate a developmental trajectory but instead offers opportunities and challenges that engage the developing organism. Greater personal resources better enable the developing person to take advantage of opportunities; Lower resources heighten vulnerability to challenges. This implies that attenuating or, ideally, removing negative proximal processes will be more helpful to disadvantaged children than using a buffer approach, wherein the harmful impacts of disadvantaged environments are counterbalanced by adding positive resources. It is important to bear in mind as well that children exposed to risks respond more to the amount of risk exposure than to the amount of resources available (Evans, Li, & Whipple, 2013; Sameroff, 2006).

Given that low-income children are more likely to experience a greater number of negative proximal processes, and that the amount of risk weighs more heavily on the scales of development than the number of available resources, this raises several concerns about conceptualizing interventions through a resilience lens. First, resilient poor children are the exception, not the norm. It may be shortsighted to determine variables for intervention based on a subset of children who appear to overcome disadvantage. Furthermore, it is important to delineate type and severity of adversity in any conceptualization of resilience, as the failure to do so results in potentially improper expectations of positive adaptation (Bonanno & Diminich, 2013). Second, although resilience researchers (e.g., Masten, 2015) have stressed the importance of both individual resources (e.g., good temperament, IQ) in conjunction with environmental resources (e.g., long-term, positive interactions with a dedicated caregiver, collective efficacy, and social cohesion), American citizens and policymakers usually consider resilience to be a personal attribute. Thinking about resilience in this way diverts attention away from the fundamental environmental forces that both create disadvantage in the first place and largely convey its toxic effects. Moreover, this popularization of resilience champions individual responsibility such that coping with disadvantage becomes the task of the individual only. Third, as economists are fond of saying: there is no free lunch. There is growing evidence that resilience to disadvantage comes at a high cost, indicative of elevated allostatic load and higher morbidity (Brody et al., 2013).

Person

One of Bronfenbrenner's (1977, 1979) favorite aphorisms was that the action in human development is in the interactions. What he meant by this is that although the key element of PPCT for understanding human development is Proximal Processes, their operation is almost always dependent upon the other three elements of the bioecological model (Person, Context, and Time). Thus, most of the discussion of these other three elements are in reference to their dynamic interplay with Proximal Processes. Person characteristics refer to physical characteristics, such as age, sex, or physical appearance (e.g., attractiveness, body size, skin color); personal dispositions, such as temperament or personality, gender identity; and individual resources, such as intelligence, physical health (e.g., low birth weight, premature birth, disability), executive functioning skills, or genetics.

As one can imagine, each of these person characteristics is capable of affecting human development in its own right. But Bronfenbrenner (Bronfenbrenner & Ceci, 1994) posited that the major action of person variables was to either directly shape proximal processes (e.g., a positive, happier child elicits different caregiver interactions than a child who is more difficult) or to moderate proximal processes. A child with a high IQ will respond differently to a language rich environment than a low IQ child. The harm from low linguistic input is posited to be greater for the low IQ child; the benefits of a high linguistic input environment accrue more readily to the high IQ child. The more restricted the Context, the greater the power of Person variables to affect human development. A well-researched example of this idea that is salient to programs designed to enhance development among disadvantaged children are behavioral genetic studies that find greater genetic contributions to developmental outcomes among high- versus low-socioeconomic status (SES) children (Tucker-Drob & Bates, 2016). Restricted environmental range among more privileged children relative to their disadvantaged peers is believed to be the reason for this finding.

Context

Perhaps the most widely known feature of the bioecological model is Bronfenbrenner's (1977, 1979) description of the nested spheres of environmental influence termed micro-, meso-, exo-, and macrocontext. The *microcontext* describes the set of environments the developing person occupies and has special prominence because this is where proximal processes occur. For instance, a microcontext for most people is their residential setting. For a young child this might be her or his only microcontext, whereas for an older child, additional microcontexts typically include childcare setting, school, or neighborhood. *Mesocontext* refers to the joint operation of two or more microcontexts. An example that is relevant to the present volume is the potential interplay of housing and neighborhood characteristics to jointly influence the development of a low-income child. The *exocontext* describes contexts that the developing person does not occupy but can nonetheless indirectly affect his or her development (e.g., parent's work setting). For instance, the location and scheduling of work among many low SES workers can exacerbate some of the challenges for child rearing. Moreover, the type of work demands placed upon the caregiver can readily spill over into the home in the form of fatigue, impatience, or expectations for autonomy and achievement motivations (Kohn, 1989; Repetti, Wang, & Saxbe, 2009). The *macrocontext* is the larger context wherein each of the preceding contexts is embedded. Culture (e.g., individual/collective, political and economic systems, ethnicity, religion) and socioeconomic factors are powerful, distal parts of a developing person's ecosystem that can both directly shape risks and opportunities as well as moderate how proximal processes influence development.

Two context propositions are directly related to this volume. First, proximal contexts will have more power to shape development than distal contexts because (a) proximal processes occur within settings that children inhabit (i.e., micro- and mesocontexts), and (b) proximal processes often interact with Person characteristics. For instance, infants and toddlers are more likely to be affected by characteristics of the residential setting. As children age, their activity orbit expands and thus the potential for a broader array of setting to influence them grows. Preschoolers may spend time in a daycare or nursery school, and how that social, symbolic, and physical setting is constituted can also affect the preschooler directly or through interactions with home life (i.e., in the mesocontext). Later in this chapter, we discuss how gender identity (Person) relates to parenting norms and behaviors. The second proposition states that macrocontexts, including SES, are powerful in large part because of the ways in which they affect the range of opportunities and challenges embedded in micro-, meso-, and exocontexts; the macrocontext can either support or interfere with proximal processes. Low SES parents tend to be less responsive and harsher with their children in comparison with their more privileged counterparts. This happens partly because high levels of poverty-related stress undermine important coping and regulatory processes such as social support (Conger & Donnellan, 2007; Grant et al., 2003). Moreover, parent sociocultural background can moderate how low-income parents respond to the strains associated with poverty (Cassells & Evans, 2017).

Time

Proximal processes are dynamic; in much the same way that intensity contributes to developmental outcomes, so too do temporal characteristics. Time, like Context, can be structured according to scale. *Microtime* refers to continuity with ongoing proximal processes. *Mesotime* captures broader categories of time, such as days or weeks. *Macrotime* typically refers to an historical period, societal epochs (e.g., a generation), or life stages. Life stage has the dual capacity of being considered both as a Time and Person variable, the latter case being when we talk about a person's age. The primary distinction lies in the fact that life stage emphasizes how the external world perceives and responds to the person based upon his or her age. It also situates life stage in major historical and cultural changes happening in the macrocontext (e.g., natural and human-made disasters; dramatic political, cultural, or economic shifts; Elder, 1998). On the other hand, chronological age refers more to intellectual, social, and physical growth and capabilities associated with maturation.

These temporal processes at micro-, meso-, or macro scale can moderate proximal processes. They can also be directly impacted by context as well as interact with it. For proximal processes to be effective, they need to be sustained over an extended period of time (mesotime) and become increasingly more complex with competency. Thus, the duration and frequency of proximal processes is critical to developmental efficacy. The requirement of progressively more complex with growing organism competency implies something about their timing, intensity, and potentially predictability (microtime).

As an illustration of the role of Time in Proximal Process, later in his life Urie Bronfenbrenner became increasingly concerned about the growing levels of chaos in American children's lives, which he saw as interfering with effective proximal processes (Bronfenbrenner & Evans, 2000). Instability and change in caregivers, residential instability, escalating exposure to high stimulation settings (e.g., noise, crowding, traffic), variable and unpredictable work schedule, and high intensity, developmentally inappropriate computer-mediated experiences are all contributors to suboptimal proximal processes. Note, as well, how each of these different types of chaos can be shaped by Context. Lower SES children, for instance, have greater turnover in caregivers, residential and school settings, more dramatic variations in parental work schedules, and face a daunting array of social and physical stressors that overload the system (Evans, 2004). Thinking about mesotime instead of microtime, an emerging picture in the poverty and child development literature is that the duration of poverty exposure appears to be critical in understanding its impact on children (Duncan, 2012; Wadsworth et al., 2016). With respect to macrotime, evidence is mounting that early-in-life exposure to disadvantage for some outcomes (e.g., language, mental health, HPA axis) is more consequential than exposures later in life; whereas some outcomes (e.g., executive function, cardiovascular disease, educational attainment) are more sensitive to the accumulation of disadvantage over the life course (Chen et al., 2002; Cohen, Janicki-Deverts, Chen, & Matthews, 2010; Miller & Chen, 2013).

In summary, this section has reviewed the key elements of the bioecological framework for human development. We now turn to our commentary on the ways in which select chapters in this volume reflect the legacy of this generative theory. Broadly speaking, although each chapter emphasizes a different aspect of the theory, as a whole they illustrate an important idea of the model and its relationship to interventions: Coordination is needed across all PPCT variables for maximum intervention effectiveness.

COMMENTARY

Previous studies on the effect of housing mobility programs have focused on child outcomes. By broadening the scope of analysis to include the effect of neighborhood relocation on parent well-being, DeLuca and her colleagues (in Chapter 8) demonstrate the influence of Context on Proximal Processes. Namely, they found that altering the neighborhood environment fostered a greater sense of parental self-efficacy, which then positively impacted parenting behaviors in the shared microcontext. Parental fear and hyper-vigilance gave way to freedom and agency after families relocated, and parental self-efficacy appears to be a consequence of qualitative reductions in stress, anxiety, and depression. Other theories discuss the effect of parental mental health on parenting behaviors. In particular, the family economic stress model shows that economic strain is related to greater psychological distress, which adversely impacts parenting behaviors and is associated with adverse child outcomes (Conger et al., 2002). However, what the present findings show is that poverty in the macrocontext interacts with the neighborhood in the microcontext to positively or negatively impact parenting behaviors. In other words, the physical environment of poverty seems just as influential to parental well-being as the subjective (and tangible) experience of financial strain, and both these factors have an impact on the proximal process of parenting.

Another aspect of their findings on parent well-being that is worth further interrogation is the interaction between Person characteristics and the microcontext. Mothers reported not only changes in the physical landscape (e.g., more space, more nature) but social changes as well. Jonathan Haidt's (2001) research on elevation could be extended to the way in which mothers discussed the effect of witnessing a different way of life modelled by their new neighbors. Some mothers noted different expectations in their new neighborhoods. In effect, previous neighborhoods lent themselves to more horizontal thinking, whereas new neighborhoods motivate more vertical thinking, which mothers reported as more conducive to family success. One wonders to what degree elevation is increased after moving and whether greater levels of elevation after moving contributed to the observed changes in parenting behavior. An unexplored aspect of housing mobility programs may be their impact on increasing positive emotions, like elevation, among low-income parents.

Moreover, the findings on social connection among children illustrates Bronfenbrenner's principle of "action in the interaction." Much was made of the mixed findings from the Moving to Opportunity for Fair Housing (MTO) study, until recent research showed that age moderated the observed effects (Chetty, Hendren, & Katz, 2016). Why are low-income children who moved to higher resourced neighborhoods earlier in life doing better? Because age (Person) is interacting with social relationships (Proximal Process). DeLuca and colleagues also help us understand the age-related differences in outcomes by situating the findings in the mesocontext. Adolescents are moving in and out of two microsystems (old and new neighborhoods), while younger children establish networks in the new neighborhood. One could argue that rather than age (Person), the appropriate PPCT variable is life stage (Time) because older children receive greater freedom from parents than younger children, which enables them to still engage with previous social networks. Nevertheless, future housing mobility programs should consider technology and increased social media platforms as variables that may interfere with these findings. Said differently, the effect of age or life stage may become negligible if children have access to social networks in previous communities through smartphone devices.

The power of the mesocontext to illuminate important reciprocal relationships was further illustrated in DeLuca and colleagues' discussion of the fit between parents and the school environment. What we see is that the macrocontext of poverty creates different cultural norms (Wilson, 1985), such that parents from an inner-city milieu are not accustomed to the policies regarding parental engagement in middle-income school settings. However, we must also consider what Bronfenbrenner says about reciprocal relationships; in as much as mother/child are unaware of norms, middle-income schools are also unprepared to accommodate students from different environmental contexts. In fact, the resources are often designed to suit the needs of middle-income families who are more familiar with school rules and operations. A parallel could be drawn to the research on immigrant children—who are also more likely to be poor. Many teachers are unprepared to meet the demands of students from different sociocultural backgrounds, especially teachers in suburban areas that are new destination cities for migrants (Lowenhaupt, 2016). Though their work, DeLuca and her colleagues highlight important elements of the bioecological model, specifically the power of reciprocity and interactions among PPCT variables. Together, these chapters highlight important elements of the bioecological model, specifically the power of reciprocity and interactions among PPCT variables.

As noted earlier in this commentary, Bronfenbrenner discussed the need to consider factors that interfere with proximal processes. In Chapter 5 of this volume, Nelson and Edin show that a macrocontext factor, the legal structure of child support payments, impinges on proximal processes such as coparenting, parental involvement, and the health and well-being of children. First, the issue is best contextualized by thinking about Time. Changes in union formation and nonmarital childbirths over macrotime have given rise to the need for legal regulations on child support. This societal change over time interacts with poverty in the macrocontext, such that minority families are disproportionately affected by this change. Nelson and Edin suggest that formal child support can diminish the role fathers play in the life of their noncustodial children and the ways in which informal child support can have adverse effects on children.

Their chapter also elucidates some of the complexity of the bioecological model by considering gender as both a Person variable and as a macrocontext. Ideas of motherhood and fatherhood are socially prescribed. Their qualitative analyses reveal that the legal structure of child support is designed in such a way that mothers are given priority for providing care to children, although paternal support is relegated to mainly financial contributions. These laws unintentionally distance fathers from their children. In fact, the law stresses money as a vital resource, yet Time with caregiver and the quality of the proximal processes therein are just as integral to child development. Gender as a Person variable is expressed in all the ways fathers attempt to reassert their agency in the childrearing process, either by setting up conditions for how contributions are given or by giving financial contributions over and above formal child support. The issue with this kind of arrangement is that consistent care is not being provided to all children, which was the original intent of the law. Edin and Nelson conclude by suggesting that in-kind support both empowers and increases parental efficacy for fathers, while also ensuring that children are receiving consistent, meaningful support. Future work may want to explore *when* in-kind support appears more potent. Their chapter suggests that in-kind support offers a way for fathers experiencing financial difficulties to maintain their identity as a provider, but it is unclear whether its effects on children are uniform across developmental stages. One question to resolve is whether in-kind support is more meaningful to the infant, the child, or the adolescent? And how does the relationship between child age and in-kind support relate to coparenting and the parental stress of the custodial parent? It is clear that this line of work has opened up other avenues for thinking about child support.

In Chapter 2, Currie and Rossin-Slater ask why the WIC program works. The evidence suggests that the WIC program improves health among infants and young children and may contribute to a reduction in the income-health gap, although it is unclear if the effects are overstated or understated. Principally, the chapter highlights the lack of knowledge regarding the proximal processes involved in making the program efficacious. To gain clarity on these processes, there needs to be greater consideration of Age as a personal factor because only a few studies presently examine outcomes beyond infancy. As Currie and Rossin-Slater suggest, more answers are likely to emerge with longitudinal or cohort studies that assess the impact of WIC in early life on later outcomes.

Although the evidence suggests that the program is beneficial, roughly 80% of eligible women use the program and coverage drops off quickly as children age. The use and attrition rates suggest that improvements to the program are necessary. One factor to bear in mind when designing program requirements is that many that low-income women are more likely to perform shift work with non-standard hours, which may be an obstacle to long-term participation, especially when their work hours are coupled with transportation issues. We would like to emphasize stigma as an important variable that also influences program participation. Stigma is an interaction between Person variables (e.g., personality) and the cultural norms of both the microcontext (e.g., local communities) and macrocontext (e.g., political rhetoric, media messages), which can lead to feelings of shame. Individual ideas about welfare are related to internalized notions of the Protestant work ethic, which may vary across communities. Fitchen's (1981) seminal work with low-income, rural families illustrates that long-term reliance on federal programs is seen as unacceptable. We can infer from this that some women may be deincentivized to participate based on their community membership.

More work may be needed to address if Person or Context factors (or the interaction of the two) are contributing to lower program participation. Future work may also want to explore whether better retention in places where WIC retailers are local is related to stigma or shame. If stigma and shame are related to program participation, finding ways to combat them emerge as important to the program's agenda.

CONCLUSION

We have employed a bioecological lens derived from Bronfenbrenner's theorizing about how and why child development happens to comment on the forgoing chapters. One important theme that emerges from our analysis is that, it is highly unlikely that one intervention, no matter how promising, is likely to have uniformly positive impacts on disadvantaged children. The ecological context enveloping disadvantaged children requires multifaceted interventions that address all four aspects of the bioecology of child development: Proximal Process, Person, Context, and Time. Each of the preceding chapters has introduced valuable insights about what types of interventions are needed and described to varying degrees some of the underlying dynamics of how and why these interventions can be helpful for disadvantaged children and their families.

REFERENCES

Bonanno, G. A., & Diminich, E. D. (2013). Annual research review: Positive adjustment to adversity—trajectories of minimal-impact resilience and emergent resilience. *Journal of Child Psychology and Psychiatry 54*, 378–401. http://dx.doi.org/10.1111/jcpp.12021

Bradley, R. H., & Corwyn, R. F. (2002). Socioeconomic status and child development. *Annual Review of Psychology, 53*, 371–399. http://dx.doi.org/10.1146/annurev.psych.53.100901.135233

Brody, G. H., Yu, T., Chen, E., Miller, G. E., Kogan, S. M., & Beach, S. R. H. (2013). Is resilience only skin deep? Rural African Americans' socioeconomic status-related risk and competence in preadolescence and psychological adjustment and allostatic load at age 19. *Psychological Science, 24*, 1285–1293. http://dx.doi.org/10.1177/0956797612471954

Bronfenbrenner, U. (1977). Toward an experimental ecology of human development. *American Psychologist, 32*, 513–531. http://dx.doi.org/10.1037/0003-066X.32.7.513

Bronfenbrenner, U. (1979). *The ecology of human development*. Cambridge, MA: Harvard University Press.

Bronfenbrenner, U., & Ceci, S. J. (1994). Nature–nurture reconceptualized: A bioecological model. *Psychological Review, 101*, 568–586. http://dx.doi.org/10.1037/0033-295x.101.4.568

Bronfenbrenner, U., & Crouter, A. C. (1983). Evolution of environmental models in developmental research. In P. H. Mussen (Ed.), *Handbook of child psychology* (pp. 357–414). New York, NY: Wiley.

Bronfenbrenner, U., & Evans, G. W. (2000). Developmental science in the 21st century: Emerging questions, theoretical models, research designs, and empirical findings. *Social Development, 9*, 115–125. http://dx.doi.org/10.1111/1467-9507.00114

Bronfenbrenner, U., & Morris, P. (1998). The ecology of developmental process. In W. Damon & R. Lerner (Eds.), *Handbook of child psychology* (Vol. 1, pp. 992–1028). New York, NY: Wiley.

Brooks-Gunn, J., Johnson, A. D., & Leventhal, T. (2010). Disorder, turbulence, and resources in children's homes and neighborhoods. In G. W. Evans & T. D. Wachs (Eds.), *Chaos and its influence on children's development* (pp. 155–170). Washington, DC: American Psychological Association. http://dx.doi.org/10.1037/12057-010

Brooks-Gunn, J., Klebanov, P., & Liaw, F. (1995). The learning, physical, and emotional environment of the home in the context of poverty: The Infant, Health, and Development Program. *Children and Youth Services Review, 17,* 251–276. http://dx.doi.org/10.1016/0190-7409(95)00011-Z

Cassells, R. C., & Evans, G. W. (2017). Ethnic variation in poverty and parenting stress. In K. Deater-Deckard & R. Panneton (Eds.), *Parental stress and early child development* (pp. 15–45). New York, NY: Springer. http://dx.doi.org/10.1007/978-3-319-55376-4_2

Chen, E., Matthews, K. A., & Boyce, W. T. (2002). Socioeconomic differences in children's health: How and why do these relationships change with age? *Psychological Bulletin, 128,* 295–329. http://dx.doi.org/10.1037/0033-2909.128.2.295

Chetty, R., Hendren, N., & Katz, L. F. (2016). The effects of exposure to better neighborhoods on children: New evidence from the Moving to Opportunity experiment. *The American Economic Review, 106,* 855–902. http://dx.doi.org/10.1257/aer.20150572

Cohen, S., Janicki-Deverts, D., Chen, E., & Matthews, K. A. (2010). Childhood socioeconomic status and adult health. *Annals of the New York Academy of Sciences, 1186,* 37–55. http://dx.doi.org/10.1111/j.1749-6632.2009.05334.x

Conger, R. D., & Donnellan, M. B. (2007). An interactionist perspective on the socioeconomic context of human development. *Annual Review of Psychology, 58,* 175–199. http://dx.doi.org/10.1146/annurev.psych.58.110405.085551

Conger, R. D., Wallace, L. E., Sun, Y., Simons, R. L., McLoyd, V. C., & Brody, G. H. (2002). Economic pressure in African American families: A replication and extension of the family stress model. *Developmental Psychology, 38,* 179–193. http://dx.doi.org/10.1037/0012-1649.38.2.179

Duncan, G. J. (2012). Give us this day our daily breadth. *Child Development, 83,* 6–15. http://dx.doi.org/10.1111/j.1467-8624.2011.01679.x

Elder, G. H., Jr. (1998). The life course and human development. In W. Damon & R. Lerner (Eds.), *Handbook of child psychology* (Vol. 1, pp. 939–991). New York, NY: Wiley.

Evans, G. W. (2004). The environment of childhood poverty. *American Psychologist, 59,* 77–92. http://dx.doi.org/10.1037/0003-066X.59.2.77

Evans, G. W., Li, D., & Whipple, S. S. (2013). Cumulative risk and child development. *Psychological Bulletin, 139,* 1342–1396. http://dx.doi.org/10.1037/a0031808

Fitchen, J. (1981). *Poverty in rural America: A case study.* Prospect Heights, IL: Waveland Press.

Gibson, J. J. (1976). *The theory of affordances and the design of the environment.* Paper presented at the annual meeting of the American Society for Aesthetics, Toronto, Ontario, Canada.

Grant, K. E., Compas, B. E., Stuhlmacher, A. F., Thurm, A. E., McMahon, S. D., & Halpert, J. A. (2003). Stressors and child and adolescent psychopathology: Moving from markers to mechanisms of risk. *Psychological Bulletin, 129,* 447–466. http://dx.doi.org/10.1037/0033-2909.129.3.447

Haidt, J. (2001). Elevation and the positive psychology of morality. In C. L. M. Keyes & J. Haidt (Eds.), *Flourishing: Positive psychology and the life well-lived* (pp. 275–289). Washington, DC: American Psychological Association.

Kohn, M. L. (1989). *Social class and conformity.* Chicago, IL: University of Chicago Press.

Lowenhaupt, R. (2016). Immigrant acculturation in suburban schools serving the new Latino diaspora. *Peabody Journal of Education, 91*, 348–365. http://dx.doi.org/10.1080/0161956X.2016.1184944

Masten, A. S. (2015). *Ordinary magic.* New York, NY: Guilford Press.

Miller, G. E., & Chen, E. (2013). The biological residue of childhood poverty. *Child Development Perspectives, 7*, 67–73. http://dx.doi.org/10.1111/cdep.12021

Repetti, R., Wang, S., & Saxbe, D. (2009). Bringing it all back home. *Current Directions in Psychological Science, 18*, 106–111. http://dx.doi.org/10.1111/j.1467-8721.2009.01618.x

Sameroff, A. J. (2006). Identifying risk and protective factors for healthy development. In A. Clarke-Stewart & J. Dunn (Eds.), *Families count* (pp. 53–76). New York, NY: Cambridge University Press. http://dx.doi.org/10.1017/CBO9780511616259.004

Tucker-Drob, E. M., & Bates, T. C. (2016). Large cross-national differences in gene × socioeconomic status interaction on intelligence. *Psychological Science, 27*, 138–149. http://dx.doi.org/10.1177/0956797615612727

Wadsworth, M. E., Evans, G. W., Grant, K., Carter, J. S., & Duffy, S. (2016). Poverty and the development of psychopathology. In D. Cicchetti (Ed.), *Developmental psychopathology* (3rd ed., pp. 136–179). New York, NY: Wiley.

Wilson, W. J. (1985). Cycles of deprivation and the underclass debate. *Social Service Review, 59*, 541–559. http://dx.doi.org/10.1086/644330

Wohlwill, J. F., & Heft, H. (1987). The physical environment and the development of the child. In D. Stokols & I. Altman (Eds.), *The handbook of environmental psychology* (pp. 281–328). New York, NY: Wiley.

10

Multigenerational Influences on Child Development

Jens Ludwig

I was trained as a garden-variety economist. Over the last couple of years, I, like some of the other contributors to this volume, have been trying to do more work out in the real world that actually changes things and improves social conditions. For this purpose, economics as a discipline essentially offers you just one tool—"change incentives." But changing incentives is often quite expensive, or quite disruptive, or else not feasible or relevant for the problem at hand. Having just a single tool in your policy toolkit is, in other words, a bit limiting.

In contrast, the field of psychology focuses on getting inside the incredibly complex "black box" of human cognition. The rich set of insights that have come out of this work has helped identify a much wider range of policy levers that we can start to act on, in different ways and in different settings. This understanding of human cognition greatly expands the items in our policy intervention toolkit that we can use to address different policy problems, including inequality and early childhood learning environments but certainly not limited to that.

In this sense, the work that my University of Chicago colleagues Ariel Kalil, Susan Mayer, and Nadav Klein have been doing at the Behavioral Insights and Parenting Lab is very exciting and groundbreaking. In this chapter, I want to offer a complementary view to the conceptual framework they outline in Chapter 4, one that is based on dual processing theory as summarized, for example, in wonderful books like Daniel Kahneman's (2011) *Thinking, Fast*

http://dx.doi.org/10.1037/0000187-011
Confronting Inequality: How Policies and Practices Shape Children's Opportunities, edited by
L. Tach, R. Dunifon, and D. L. Miller

233

and Slow or Timothy Wilson's (2002) *Strangers to Ourselves*. The essential idea is that we all rely on two types of cognition. Conscious thought is typically good at reasoning through problems, but it is mentally costly. To conserve mental effort, we all develop, and rely on, automatic responses to frequently encountered situations. These automatic responses that we develop are usually adaptive for most of the circumstances we tend to face, but they can sometimes be maladaptive, if we encounter a new situation or confuse what sort of situation we're in. This highlights that people can sometimes make cognitive mistakes, and that these mistakes often have some predictable structure—and so can be anticipated and hence prevented. This framework also highlights how and why the situations in which people find themselves can have such powerful impacts on behavior and policy-relevant outcomes. This opens the door to a wide range of new policy interventions as Kalil, Mayer, and Klein's work on parenting and child outcomes helps illustrate.

We now have had 20 years of behavioral science interventions in different domains, and we are starting to see a little bit of a backlash from those who wonder whether it actually has transformative potential. Behavioral science interventions often have amazing benefit–cost ratios, not because the numerators of those ratios (the benefits) are so large, but because the costs of those interventions are often so low. Anytime your denominator is very close to zero, you are going to get a ratio that looks pretty good. Any intervention that has an encouraging ratio of benefit to cost is good, and we should implement it, but behavioral science to some people sometimes can feel limited in its ability to transform the world.

The results presented in Chapter 4 make one wonder whether parenting might be one of those domains that is an exception to this concern. Their parenting intervention for reading produces a one standard deviation improvement in reading to kids. One standard deviation! The absolute amount of reading still might be low but, it is a very impressive effect size. How much might we expect that to translate in terms of child outcomes and narrowing gaps in child literacy? This would be a very useful next step to figure out in this line of research, because it would tell us whether this behavioral science intervention is worth doing, not only because it has big benefit to cost ratio, but also because it can have absolutely big impacts on the world.

Also relevant to thinking about the absolute size of the benefits that might be realized is the persistence of effects. With some of these behavioral science interventions for parenting, we might wonder also about persistence in responsiveness to the intervention itself. Do people start to tune reminders out? As the Chapter 4 authors note, we don't know very much about this right now, but it seems like an important area for future research.

To date, the behavioral science and parenting field has addressed an incredibly important set of parenting decisions: Do I take my kid to school today? Do I read to them? Looking into the future, to Behavioral Science 2.0, there is a different sort of decision that parents make that we are increasingly appreciating is very important for kids: Where should I live? What school should

I send my child to? What classes should I encourage them to take? What college should they eventually attend and what should they major in?

Behavioral science works well when there is an obviously right thing to do. You read to your kid. You get your kid to school. Eat more fruits and vegetables. Save more. If you think about the neighborhood choice question, no single neighborhood is the best neighborhood for everyone; there is some sort of personalization in what is the right choice. In Behavioral Science 2.0, we can begin to combine behavioral science insights and an understanding of where people make predictable mistakes, using big data on previous people's choices, and, via machine learning, develop personalized decision recommendations. This is a very exciting scientific frontier, and I think one that is quite relevant for the domain of parenting and child outcomes that is at the heart of Kalil, Mayer, and Klein's work.

Now transitioning to an earlier chapter in this volume, let us suppose that we have some behavioral science intervention that can change child outcomes. The key issue addressed by East and Page in Chapter 3 is that there may be important impacts not just on the children who are the direct recipients of the intervention, but by their children as well—there may be intergenerational effects. Ignoring the possibility of these intergenerational effects has the potential to lead us to substantially understate the benefits of some of our policy levers.

The logic behind their argument is, of course, compelling, but it does raise two different measurement challenges that East and Page touch on, but that I think are worth elaborating upon. First, in this intergenerational-transmission literature, identification of causal effects does not come from the long-term follow-up of participants in randomized controlled trials (RCTs), because we don't actually have that many RCTs from a long enough time to measure intergenerational impacts. So, instead, we rely on what economists call "natural experiments" that are often induced by changes in policy or programs out in the real world.

Often the relationship between the policy lever at the heart of the natural experiment and the developmental environment that someone experiences is not so large (what economists would call the "first stage" relationship). So we need very big samples to detect impacts on the outcomes we care about. That leads you down a path where you need to rely on administrative data in order to have adequate sample sizes and, hence, adequate statistical power.

The flip side of this is that we also care a lot about understanding mechanisms of action through which different policy levers affect people's life outcomes. That can help us not just refine our scientific theories about the way the world works but also enhance the effectiveness of policy design. But trying to understand mechanisms leads us down a very different path with respect to our research strategy—one that now says we might want to do original, in-person data collection so that we can have more control over the things we are measuring.

To the extent to which this two-generation literature progresses, there are going to be very high returns to careful thinking about how we strategically do in-person data collection built around natural experiments. This will require some real creativity as the field moves forward.

There is a second measurement challenge that, in some sense, is even harder. The literature reviewed in the East and Page chapter looks back a couple generations. In these rare cases, we have these data sets that show us that there was a famine or flu in the early 1900s, and that those people grew up, and then they had kids who are now adults. Essentially, we using that information to inform a very forward-looking question: today we've got a bunch of little kids, and we want to decide what interventions will help them become healthy adults so that their kids are healthy. In a world in which nature is perfectly stable, there would be no problem using 1900s information to forecast to the 2020s intervention. The problem is, we are not in a static world.

In the early childhood literature, the big return for future work is going to be figuring out what the intermediate outcomes are—the short- or medium-term indicators that predict the longer term life outcomes (or even intergenerational effects) that we care about. We don't want to wait over 100 years to find out if what we are doing today is actually having these two-generation impacts. So, we need early warning indicators. It feels enormously unsatisfying that I can't look at a program five or 10 years after it was done and tell you whether it's going to have any sort of lasting impacts on people. It is incredibly important that we figure out what to do in these early childhood interventions.

What is exciting about both Chapters 3 and 4 is that they represent very different and new directions for the early childhood literature. And these new directions are important for helping both expand the set of policy levers that we consider in improving the lives of children and families, and in understanding which of these policy levers are worth supporting with public-sector investments. Building on these two approaches will be an important part of the field moving forward.

REFERENCES

Kahneman, D. (2011). *Thinking, fast and slow*. New York, NY: Farrar, Straus and Giroux.

Wilson, T. D. (2002). *Strangers to ourselves: Discovering the adaptive unconscious*. Cambridge, MA: Belknap Press/Harvard University Press.

11

Education and Equality of Opportunity

Sean F. Reardon

Two previous chapters in this volume help us to consider the evidence about when and how to invest in education. Should we invest in early childhood education programs? Should we invest more than we currently do in the K–12 system?

In Chapter 7, "Does School Spending Matter? The New Literature on an Old Question," Jackson summarizes the school funding literature and demonstrates quite persuasively that the most rigorous studies consistently find that students benefit from increased K–12 school funding. The old received wisdom—that school spending doesn't benefit students—turns out to be based on flawed methods; it is just plain wrong.

In Chapter 6, "Promoting Equality of Opportunity by Investing Early," Watts and Raver tell us that the impacts of early childhood education programs are complicated and it matters which outcomes one looks at and when. Their chapter brings coherence to the somewhat conflicting results of rigorous evaluations of early childhood programs. Nonetheless, the literature they review does not tell us much about what spending in preschool or early childhood education does and whether or not it leads to positive benefits for children. Perhaps this is because the research on spending in preschool is not as well developed as the K–12 literature. But there is enormous variation in how much money the states spend on preschool, and there is enormous variation between public and private preschool programs. Learning more about the effect of dollar investments in preschool would complement what we have

http://dx.doi.org/10.1037/0000187-012
Confronting Inequality: How Policies and Practices Shape Children's Opportunities, edited by L. Tach, R. Dunifon, and D. L. Miller

learned about the design of high-quality programs in terms of their practices, curricula, and environments.

So, where should the research go from here? What should the next generation of studies look like? How do we design new studies so that, in 20 years, we have more satisfying answers to the questions about how to design education programs? One area that the next generation of research questions needs to consider is mechanisms. It is not enough to know that money matters. We want to know how and why it matters. How does it change the learning environment of a child? Does it change who is teaching in the classroom or how large the class is? Does it change who enrolls in public schools? Does it change the resources or facilities? Does it change the qualifications of teachers? What is changed in the experience of the child as a result of more money, and what kinds of changes occur that are consequential for that child's learning?

Answering these questions starts to move us toward questions that are central to building a scientific understanding of how individuals grow and develop in contexts. Such questions differ from social policy questions, which are about what we should do with our money. In Chapter 7, Jackson points out that we have a good answer to the policy question regarding school funding, but the literature he reviews doesn't do much to advance the science of learning and development because it doesn't tell us much about how funding changes alter children's environments and experiences. That's not to say we couldn't learn more about this, however. Some of the instrumental variables used to identify the effects of school funding could plausibly be used to explore whether and how different kinds of funding streams impact contextual features of learning; this would provide an opportunity to tease out the mechanisms through which funding affects learning.

Likewise, the mechanism question is at the core of Watts and Raver's analysis in Chapter 6. We invest a lot of money in what seems to be a good childhood educational experience, which translates into better short-term outcomes, but then something happens that leads these effects to fade. We do not really understand what causes this. The literature provides a set of candidate hypotheses and mechanisms, but the proposed mechanisms are very broad and imprecise. We need both greater specificity about hypothesized mechanisms and studies designed to test these hypotheses.

When the subject of inquiry is mechanisms, heterogeneity is our friend; we aren't so interested in average effects. What we want is a world in which there's an enormous amount of variation in effects. The discussion in Watts and Raver's chapter about treatment-control contrasts points to a type of heterogeneity that is useful for answering questions about mechanisms. Consider a meta-analysis where some studies have a big treatment-induced contrast on one dimension (one potential mediator) but a small contrast on another dimension (a different potential mediator), but other studies show the opposite pattern. This variation in treatment-control contrasts along multiple dimensions provides a way to tease out information about the mechanisms through which programs have their effects.

In order to develop better policy, we want more than answers to policy questions; we want to answer questions that help us understand development in context. Once we understand development in context, then we can design better policies. Program design can be better targeted once we understand the science behind it. If all we do is evaluate policy, we are always evaluating something we did in the past when the world was different. That might not tell us what to do now or tomorrow. But if we have a science that consists of a set of general principles about development in context, then we can adapt programs so that they are suitable to a current context. That is, we want an evaluation science, a policy analysis science, that is not just designed to ask and answer the question "did this policy work?" but that is aimed at helping us understand general principles about development in context that we can use to design, refine, and better target social policies.

What do we need to do to develop a better science of policy analysis? We need not just an expanded set of research questions but also an expanded set of tools to answer these questions. First, we need different research designs. The randomized controlled trial (RCT) is well-suited for answering the main effect question, but the standard RCT by itself is not very good at answering mechanism questions. We have to design an RCT differently to answer mechanism questions: We need multiarm RCTs, RCTs that induce variation in different hypothesized mechanisms, and dynamic, sequential RCTs.

Second, we need better data. As Watts and Raver point out in Chapter 6, if we want to learn about long-term impacts and the mechanisms that lead to them, we need data systems that enable that. The growth of administrative data systems will help us with this, but it requires thinking about how we can link administrative data systems, how we can maintain identifiers while protecting privacy, and how to effectively repurpose for research data that were collected for bureaucratic purposes.

Third, we need both good theory and good knowledge of bureaucratic program practice on the ground. What happens in early childhood programs? How do parents decide to enroll their children in a particular school? How do administrators spend the extra money they get? What are the policies and procedures that make things work? If we don't have this kind of practical knowledge, along with theory, we're not going to be able to do a great job at figuring out the mechanisms through which programs have their effects.

We often operate in a world of central tendencies. We do that often because we don't have enough data to study heterogeneity and variation. But the world is much more variable than the central tendency of any regression coefficient. If we start to think about the world as much more variable, then we need to start thinking about more targeted kinds of social policy. As my research on district variation in student test scores shows, the places where educational opportunity is low prior to third grade are not necessarily the places where educational opportunity is low from third to eighth grade (Reardon, 2019). There are some communities where poor kids come to third grade with very low test scores, but they learn a lot from third to eighth grade. And there are places where poor kids come to third grade doing fine (above the national average), but they don't learn a lot from third to eighth grade. And there are lot of communities where educational opportunity is low during both the early and middle years, as well as places where it is high at both times. One implication here is that if we are thinking about where to target our educational investments, we should probably make very different choices about when in the developmental life course to target these investments based on what community we are working in.

In conclusion, we need to think about targeting not just educational policies but social policies more broadly. We need to target not just in place-specific ways but also in developmental, age-specific ways. A smart set of education policies would figure out what is most needed at what stage. We need to think about more than the central tendency and invest in places where it's going to make the most impact. Doing that requires something well beyond where the field is now. We have neither sufficient data nor sufficient understanding of how development occurs in context to know what the right investments are at the right developmental stage. Chapters 6 and 7 help us think about ways to get there.

REFERENCES

Reardon, S. F. (2019). Educational opportunity in early and middle childhood: Using full population administrative data to study variation by place and age. *RSF: The Russell Sage Foundation Journal of the Social Sciences, 5*, 40–65. http://dx.doi.org/10.7758/RSF.2019.5.2.03

Conclusion

Invigorating Research and Practice to Promote Equality of Opportunity for Children

Laura Tach, Rachel Dunifon, and Douglas L. Miller

Although inequality of opportunity is a persistent, and in some cases growing, feature of American society, the contributions of this volume highlight the progress that social scientists have made both in understanding the origins of inequality during childhood and in charting innovative solutions in the realms of policy and practice. In some cases, the authors revisited classic debates about the roles of key settings like schools, families, and neighborhoods in generating unequal opportunities for youth. In other cases, the authors weighed in on innovative experiments in these domains, breaking down traditional barriers between basic and applied research. Taken together, these approaches reveal the power of multidisciplinary approaches and diverse methodologies to shed new light on durable social inequalities. They also point to new directions for invigorating research and practice to promote equality of opportunity for children.

HARNESSING THE POWER OF MULTIDISCIPLINARY PERSPECTIVES

The authors who contributed to this volume are exemplars of multidisciplinary engagement; they bring the best tools of their disciplines to tackle core questions of cross-disciplinary interest and policy relevance. Economists Janet Currie and Maya Rossin-Slater (Chapter 2), Chloe N. East and Marianne E. Page (Chapter 3), and C. Kirabo Jackson (Chapter 7) demonstrate the power of quasi-experimental research designs that exploit natural variation and,

http://dx.doi.org/10.1037/0000187-013
Confronting Inequality: How Policies and Practices Shape Children's Opportunities, edited by
L. Tach, R. Dunifon, and D. L. Miller

in many cases, existing data sources to understand the short- and long-run effects of major U.S. social policies related to health, income, and education. Sociologists Timothy Nelson and Kathryn Edin (Chapter 5) and Stefanie DeLuca, Anna Rhodes, and Allison Young (Chapter 8) showcase how qualitative research can provide a window into the personal experience of inequality, uncover the power of social connection, and reveal how policies work—or don't work—for families and children in their daily lives. Drawing insights from psychology, Emma Adam, Sarah Collier Villaume, and Emily Hittner (Chapter 1), Susan E. Mayer, Ariel Kalil, and Nadav Klein (Chapter 4), and Tyler W. Watts and C. Cybele Raver (Chapter 6) demonstrate the importance of proximal processes and person–environment interactions and show how inequality influences biological and cognitive processes and social–emotional development.

Insights from each chapter can also be used to enrich other chapters in this volume, pushing the frontiers of their respective disciplinary fields forward in important ways. The field of stress biology (Chapter 1) offers a number of potential biological mechanisms that could help to explain why some policies and programs—such as the federal Special Supplemental Nutrition Program for Women, Infants, and Children (WIC; Chapter 2), Medicaid and food stamps (now called SNAP; Chapter 3), or housing mobility programs (Chapter 8)—generate benefits for health and development and why others do not. The insight that people have measurable biological responses to policy and program interventions should prompt social scientists to consider how policies and programs affect human functioning in ways that may not be observable in individual behavior. This calls for novel biological data collection approaches that may not be in the toolkits of traditional social scientists, suggesting the benefit of multidisciplinary research teams to tackle these questions.

Similarly, the insights that come from the union of psychology and economics in the Mayer, Kalil, and Klein chapter ask researchers to consider the range of settings in which cognitive biases may lead to suboptimal individual decision-making—either relative to one's own values and goals or relative to societal expectations. It also prompts researchers and policymakers to consider how the tools of behavioral economics might be deployed to improve equity. For example, insights about cognitive biases could inform why take-up rates in the WIC program decline over time, what barriers nonresident fathers face in contributing time and resources to their children, or why school district administrators and teachers invest in some types of school resources rather than others. The contributions in this volume also encourage social scientists to consider the macrolevel implications of their research for durable social inequalities. For example, what are the societal costs and benefits of interventions that reduce stress disparities or increase the amount of money that nonresident fathers contribute to their children? Can behavioral nudges that increase parental reading to children or improve take-up of the WIC program reduce population-level socioeconomic gaps in children's school readiness or morbidity?

NEW INSIGHTS ABOUT CLASSIC DEBATES

The contributions in this volume ask us to revisit classic, long-standing debates in the social sciences about the role of key social institutions in creating inequality and how best to change them to equalize opportunities. Several authors revisit the classic question "What do parents do?" and update it using 21st-century perspectives. DeLuca and colleagues find that the neighborhood environment influences parental mental health and parenting efficacy, arguing that what may appear to be parenting differences among socioeconomic or racial groups are perhaps adaptive responses to external neighborhood conditions. Mayer and colleagues harness the insights of behavioral economics and show that parental decision-making is subject to cognitive biases, resulting in a gap between aspirations and actions, especially for parents lacking resources. They also argue that behavioral tools can mitigate these biases, influence parental decision-making about how they spend their time with children and ultimately reduce certain socioeconomic gaps in children's literacy. Nelson and Edin's work interrogates the meaning of this question for non-resident fathers during a historical period when a majority of less advantaged children can expect to live apart from at least one of their biological parents. The authors argue for the importance of nonresident parental involvement for healthy child development, but show how challenging it can be to maintain such involvement when parents are no longer romantically involved with each other and when the parent and child do not live together. They critique a child support system that drives families apart rather than bolstering fragile nonresidential ties.

Other authors revisit the classic question "Does schooling matter?" by providing broad synthesis and pointed critiques. Jackson argues that the question of whether increased school spending improves children's outcomes is largely settled, with strong evidence indicating that school spending does benefit children, although we know less about whether specific forms of spending are more effective than others. Watts and Raver ask us to rethink the classic early childhood intervention "fade out" finding. They argue that by pushing the boundaries of traditional cognitive and behavioral measurement, we can identify whether interventions that appear to fade out actually have long-run benefits and the mechanisms behind those long-run gains. DeLuca and colleagues focus our attention on the social connections fostered through schools, which play an important developmental role during adolescence. They caution that the strategies schools use to engage parents may not work equally well for parents of all socioeconomic and racial backgrounds.

More recently, social scientists have interrogated the biological and health consequences of inequality by asking how inequality "gets under the skin." Building on work showing that early-life health has consequences for long-term development and economic outcomes, Currie and Rossin-Slater show how social safety net programs targeting fetal and early-childhood health, like WIC, can yield positive impacts for population health disparities. They also show, however, that program take-up and persistence are far from perfect, and they call for greater attention to these issues not just for WIC but for all means-tested nutritional policies. Also building on this literature, East and Page show that program impacts accrue not only throughout the life course of the target individual; benefits also extend to the subsequent generation via both biological and behavioral mechanisms. Adam and colleagues advance this question by focusing on the unequal distribution of environmental stressors and the consequences for biological processes that, in turn, influence healthy development. Attuning to the biology of stress shapes the types of data we collect to understand the impacts of environmental stressors and, in turn, can inform the types of interventions we conduct and how we understand their effects.

CONSIDERING MULTILEVEL PROCESSES TO BUILD BETTER THEORY AND POLICY

A cornerstone of the Bronfenbrenner (1979) bioecological model is that the social environment operates at multiple levels to shape human development—from the proximal environment with which individuals interface directly to the more distal cultural, economic, and policy environments. An implication of the bioecological model is that attention to multiple levels may help a policy or intervention to realize its maximum effectiveness. This insight provides concrete suggestions for theory and policy development among the interventions described in this volume. More broadly, social scientists should identify the level at which their research is centered, and consider whether taking a more micro- or macrolevel perspective might offer additional insight about mechanisms or reveal additional distributional consequences.

Several contributions in this volume highlight the value of examining how policies influence the proximal environments in which children develop and can help to explain why policies may fall short of their intended goals. DeLuca and colleagues' rich description of the person–environment fit and proximal environments (e.g., friendship networks, parenting practices, engagement with schools) in housing mobility programs may help explain why some housing mobility programs are more successful, for some groups, than others are. The authors' insights also suggest concrete ways that future interventions might tailor services to support families' adaptation to new neighborhood environments and to ensure that institutions in receiving neighborhoods understand how to best support the new families.

Similarly, Nelson and Edin describe a child support system that is ineffective because the policy treats fathers as financial contributors only, ignoring the fact that many men want greater involvement and influence in their children's lives that goes beyond money. Concrete policy recommendations follow from this insight, providing institutionalized opportunities via policy and legal mechanisms for men to be more involved as coparents. The mismatch between the way that the government views fatherhood and the way participants view fatherhood suggests a broader lesson about the importance of understanding how participants experience a policy in their daily lives and how it affects their social relationships, for better or for worse. This insight might be applied fruitfully to tackling other unanswered policy questions in this volume, such as why social policies rarely have complete take-up, which forms of school spending benefit students, and which proximal environments might contribute to early-childhood education (ECE) interventions' potential fade out over time.

Other contributions in this volume encourage us to consider the macrolevel implications of policies and interventions designed to support individual families and children. For example, East and Page show how the rollout of social safety net programs—such as Head Start, Medicaid, and Food Stamps—has had intergenerational benefits that are rarely captured in traditional benefit–cost analyses. They also show that national policies can affect population-level fertility and mortality rates, thereby producing compositional changes for entire population cohorts. In a different vein, Jackson shows how school spending is not similarly effective across different states, and he argues that more intentional study of effect heterogeneity might help us understand how different states are influencing the learning environments of their schools. Considering the macrolevel implications of a particular policy or intervention provides information about societal costs and benefits and reveals whether such initiatives can really move the dial on persistent population-level inequalities in children's developmental settings and outcomes.

THE IMPORTANCE OF TIME

A key insight from human development is that developmental stages matter enormously for the efficacy of interventions. Is the intervention developmentally appropriate for the age of the participants? Is exposure to a context more consequential during certain developmental stages? Do effects of contexts accumulate over time, or are there particular thresholds of exposure? Several of the contributions in this volume take a developmentally informed approach, which yields fruitful insights about when and for whom certain interventions might be most effective. For example, DeLuca and colleagues show how friendship networks are formed more easily among younger youth moving to new neighborhoods, while adolescents have a harder time; this may partly explain why younger children appear to benefit more from housing mobility interventions than adolescents. Several chapters, such as those by Currie and Rossin-Slater and by East and Page, focus on interventions during the prenatal period—a period particularly sensitive to environmental stressors that is also responsive to positive interventions that improve economic and food security. Others, such as Watts and Raver and Mayer and colleagues, focus on learning environments in childcare centers and the home, respectively, during the early childhood period, which is also a developmental period that generates great long-run dividends to investment. Helpfully, Adam and colleagues remind us that, although certain developmental periods may be particularly consequential for long-run life outcomes, scholars have also identified a certain amount of plasticity in biological systems, meaning that adverse impacts need not be permanent. Social scientists studying inequality, and efforts to reduce it, would do well to bring a more developmentally informed perspective to their work, both to improve our scientific understanding of human development in context but also to inform when policy intervention will be most effective. At what ages, for example, are paternal involvement and investment most beneficial for children? When is school spending most consequential, and how does spending influence school environments differently across grade levels?

Considering time also means examining both short- and long-run outcomes. This volume makes clear that, for several policies and programs, there is evidence of substantial short-run impact but insufficient evidence as to whether benefits are sustained in the long run. Adam and colleagues call for longer run tracking of biological outcomes of stress-reducing interventions; Currie and Rossin-Slater call for research on the longer run outcomes of participation in WIC; Mayer and colleagues ask whether the effects of "behavioral nudge" interventions on parenting persist after the intervention ends. The volume contributors also show how the effects of policies and interventions may not appear in the short- or medium-term, which calls for persistent longitudinal examination. Watts and Raver make a case for the need for long-term follow-up of ECE programs, even when medium-term results may indicate fadeout; DeLuca and colleagues show how adaptation to new residential environments unfolds over time. The interventions described in this volume also fall along a continuum that ranges from focusing on short-run, modest interventions that help parents and children manage and respond to their existing environment to long-run interventions that aim to change the environment itself to be more equitable and supportive of healthy child development. At the far end of this extreme, East and Page show how the benefits of certain environmental shocks—either naturally occurring or socially induced—can produce intergenerational consequences that amplify the benefits (or harms) of policies targeted at one generation.

BLURRING THE LINE BETWEEN BASIC AND APPLIED RESEARCH

Bronfenbrenner rejected the traditional distinction between basic and applied research, arguing that the best way to understand something was to try to change it. This volume continues in Bronfenbrenner's tradition, breaking down traditional divisions between basic and applied science by blending theoretical principles and conceptual development with the evaluation of novel social interventions. In some cases, the contributors showed how interventions can be used to develop theory and generalizable evidence. Adam and colleagues, for example, showed how changing a person's environment yields new information about biological processes and functions, which in turn influence health and developmental outcomes. DeLuca and colleagues showed how a person–environment fit can moderate the effects of the residential environment on youth. For many of the policies covered in this volume, creative use of variation in policy implementation could help the social science community build a generalizable toolkit of knowledge that can guide future policymaking.

The analyses in this volume raise as many questions as they do answers. Why do mothers of young children drop out of the WIC program? What is the optimal design of the child support system? Is ECE intervention fade-out really a myth, and if so, what should we be measuring instead? If school spending matters in general, which types of school spending are most effective? As commentator Sean Reardon notes in Chapter 11, each of these questions would benefit from attending to the questions of basic science that underlie them. Focusing on the enduring social processes at the core of the questions posed in this volume will not only help to answer these specific questions but also provide a stronger evidence base for future policy development. This will offer policymakers and practitioners a deeper understanding of human behavior and social mechanisms and allow them to better anticipate potential unintended consequences or effect heterogeneity.

Collectively, these contributions reveal that the details of policies and programs matter, and that there is room for improvement. Housing mobility programs do not provide equally beneficial moves for all disadvantaged youth. WIC take-up is high during the prenatal period and infancy and helps equalize health disparities during those periods, but program participation and its benefits taper off in early childhood. Although most agree that high-quality ECE programs and K–12 school spending are crucial investments for equality of opportunity, much remains to be understood about which types of investments offer the greatest equalizing potential. Behavioral nudges appear to improve parental decision-making, but we know much less about how to deliver such interventions to be maximally effective and how much they can really reduce persistent structural inequalities. The contributions in this volume encourage us to think past simple questions about whether an intervention matters to more nuanced interrogations that ask in what way, for whom, and when such interventions matter. We note that cross-disciplinary insights and multiple methodological tools are particularly promising ways to push these investigations forward. We encourage social scientists to continue to bring together different disciplinary and methodological traditions to forge new, and richer, insights to support healthy development and upward mobility among children and their families.

REFERENCE

Bronfenbrenner, U. (1979). *The ecology of human development: Experiments by nature and design.* Cambridge, MA: Harvard University Press.

INDEX

ABOUT THE EDITORS

Laura Tach, PhD, is an associate professor of policy analysis and management at Cornell University in Ithaca, New York. She is also an affiliate of the Bronfenbrenner Center for Translational Research, the Center for the Study of Inequality, and the Cornell Population Center. Her research and teaching interests focus on poverty and social policy. Together with Rachel Dunifon, she codirects Cornell Project 2Gen, an initiative of the Bronfenbrenner Center for Translational Research that serves as a hub for research, policy, and practice that supports vulnerable caregivers and children together. Dr. Tach is the 2018 recipient of the William Julius Wilson Early Career Award from the Inequality, Poverty, Mobility Section of the American Sociological Association. Her work has appeared in peer-reviewed academic journals, such as the *American Journal of Sociology*, the *Journal of Policy Analysis and Management*, and *Demography*.

Rachel Dunifon, PhD, is interim dean of the College of Human Ecology and a professor in the Department of Policy Analysis and Management. She received a BA in psychology from Davidson College and a PhD in human development and social policy from Northwestern University. Prior to joining Cornell as a faculty member in 2001, she was the recipient of a National Institutes of Health (NIH)–funded postdoctoral fellowship at the University of Michigan. Dr. Dunifon's research focuses on child and family policy, examining the ways in which policies, programs, and family settings influence the development of less-advantaged children. As principal investigator, she has won numerous externally funded research grants, including from the NIH, the U.S. Department of Agriculture, and the William T. Grant Foundation.

Her work has been published in top peer-reviewed academic journals in developmental psychology, public policy, and family demography.

Douglas L. Miller, PhD, is a professor of policy analysis and management and economics at Cornell University. He is a microeconomist with research interests in social policy, especially policy that impacts demographically and economically vulnerable populations. His work also explores the relationship between the economic environment and health outcomes. Finally, he works to build and expand the econometric toolkit used to answer social science and public policy questions. Before joining the Department of Policy Analysis and Management at Cornell, Dr. Miller was a Robert Wood Johnson Foundation Health Policy Research Scholar Postdoc from 2000 to 2002 and then a faculty member in the Department of Economics at UC Davis from 2002 to 2016.